THE HOUSE

And The Art of its Design

THE HOUSE *and*

The Art of its Design

by

Robert Woods Kennedy

Progressive Architecture Library

Reinhold Publishing Corporation
New York ***U.S.A.***

Printed in U.S.A.

Library of Congress Catalog Card No. 53-9169

This book, personal though it may seem, literally could not have materialized were it not for the help of a great many people. Needless to say, even though I am indebted to those mentioned below for all sorts of suggestions and concrete ideas, they have undergone a sea of changes in the writing process, and I alone am responsible for their present inadequacies.

The time to write was largely made possible by a grant from the Guggenheim Foundation. It was further engineered by Professor Lawrence B. Anderson and Dean Pietro Belluschi, both of the Massachusetts Institute of Technology. It was still further aided and abetted by Mr. and Mrs. Paul Brooks. For space in which to write I am indebted to Mr. and Mrs. John L. Saltonstall, Jr. A large number of the ideas expressed grew from seed planted by Dean and Mrs. William Wilson Wurster of the University of California, by Dr. Herbert Harris of the Massachusetts Institute of Technology, by Professor and Mrs. John Gaus of Harvard University, and by Professor and Mrs. John C. B. Whiting of Harvard University. Certain clients, in particular Mr. and Mrs. John Hay, Mr. and Mrs. Henry Stokes, Mr. and Mrs. Rudolph Talbot, and Mr. and Mrs. Eugene Rust, have contributed many insights into the nature of an ideal process. I am indebted to Mrs. Judy Picket and Mrs. Joan Kennedy not only for typing, but for the best critiques—and to Mr. Richard Brown for an insight into how the best contractor plus client works. The Journal of the American Institute of Architects has been kind enough to allow the use of an article, "Form, Function, and Expression," which originally appeared there. And finally, the burden of reading and rereading, of shaping and reshaping the book has been as much my wife's as my own.

Table of Contents

ACKNOWLEDGMENTS v

CHAPTER I *Explanations*

The upper middle class house as distinct from all others.

Dwelling Units, Homes, and Houses 1
Modernism 16
"Practicality" 23
Architecture 27

CHAPTER II *Silhouettes*

The people who live in houses and what they want of them.

Housewives 35
Husbands 43
Babies 50
Children, One to Five 52
School Children 56
Teen Agers 61
Grandparents 65
Servants 69

CHAPTER III *Families*

People together form a family which in turn makes still other demands on the house.

Organization 75
Husband versus Wife 81
Parents versus Children 83
The Family versus Outsiders 89
Conflict 93
Privacy 95
Communication 100

CHAPTER IV *Livability*

How people's and families' demands get translated into a scheme for the house.

Activities 1
Zones 1
Duplications 1
Buffers 1
Bodies 1
Warmth 1
Quiet 1

CHAPTER V *Activities*

How what we do in houses should affect their plan, furniture, arrangement, and equipment.

Entering 1
Circulating 1
Living 1
Cooking 2
Eating 2
Bathing, Washing, and Excreting 2
Sleeping 2
Housekeeping 2

CHAPTER VI *Relations*

What kind of people are architects and clients, and how do they get along together?

Architects and Clients 2
The Professional Hierarchy 2
The Effects of Art 3
Clients, "Ideal" and Otherwise 3
The Shopping Client 3

CHAPTER VII *Process*

How the architect and client react to the crises of building.

Programming 3
Preliminary Sketches 34
Working Drawings 35
Supervision 36
The Weaning Period 36
Love, Hate, and Architecture 37

CHAPTER VIII *Style*

A dim view of both Modernism and Traditionalism, and a plea for a simple contemporaneousness.

Security and Innovation 377
Aims 386
The Main Stream 394
The Style Cosmos 406
The Fight 425

CHAPTER IX *Environment*

How the surroundings of a house should affect its style.

Creativeness versus Environment 437
The Ideal Neighborhood 441
Problems in Geriatrics 447
Stage Sets 452

CHAPTER X *Site*

How the site of the house should affect its plan and concept.

Cave versus Bower 457
Surface Modeling and Links 464
Views 474
Determinants 477

CHAPTER XI *Structure*

The structure of the house is like the human body and should be conceived as such.

The Status Quo 483
The Structural Problem 491
"Man Is the Measure of All Things" 496

CHAPTER XII *Expression*

The excitement of architecture is the result of analogies we make between buildings and ourselves.

The Appeal to the Intellect 503
The Appeal to the Emotions 508
Techniques 520
Self Expression 528

REFERENCES 535
SOURCES OF ILLUSTRATIONS 540
INDEX 543

CHAPTER I
Explanations

Dwelling Units, Homes, and Houses

. . . for our buildings, as a whole, are but a huge screen behind which are our people as a whole—even though specifically the buildings are individual images of those to whom, as a class, the public has delegated and entrusted its power to build.

Therefore, by this light, the critical study of architecture becomes not merely the direct study of an art—for that is but a minor phase of a great phenomenon—but, in extenso, *a study of the social conditions producing it, the study of a newly-shaping type of civilization. By this light the study of architecture becomes nautrally and logically a branch of social science, and we must bend our facilities to this bow if we would reach the mark.* —SULLIVAN

IT IS THE IMMEMORIAL CUSTOM to begin books such as this with a nod, or even a full dress obeisance to history. The author ties his subject in with the cave man and then brings it more or less rapidly up to date. As an architect, however, I cannot approve of cave men. They were, so to speak, in the ready-made house market. So, in an effort to avoid the cave and yet make a conventional bow, I shall start by paraphrasing Caesar.

> Housing is a whole divided into three parts, one of which is inhabited by the Home Builders, another by the Public Housers, and a third by a people called in their own tongue Designers—in the Latin, Architectus. All these are different one from another in language, institutions and laws. The Architects are separated from the Public Housers by the river Red Tape, from the Home Builders by the Taste and the Money. Of all these people the Home Builders are the most courageous, because they are farthest removed from the culture and civilization of the Province, and least often visited by merchants introducing the commodities that make for effeminacy . . .

Because housing is divided into three parts, it is always necessary to know with which part one is dealing. Who are these three groups of builders, and what are the differences in what they build? The Home Builders, as their name states, build "homes." The Public Housers, on the other hand, build "dwelling units," while the Architects build "houses." It must be remembered that people live in all three.

There are surely some differences between these groups of people, otherwise their dwellings would not have been given such different names. But the subject is a delicate one. According to our national myth, all men are created equal. Yet in practice no such equality exists. People seem to enjoy common characteristics by classes. Between classes there are distinct differences in opportunity, manners, income, taste, living patterns, height, education, etc.—in short in nearly every respect. Their dwellings are equally varied. The underprivileged classes get dwelling units. The white collar classes get homes. A third group, the one we are concerned with in this book, gets houses. The Home Builders, the Public Housers, and the Architects not only build different kinds of dwellings, they build them for distinctly different groups of people.

As in ancient Gaul, these three groups, at least as far as architecture is concerned, actually do differ as to language, institutions, and laws. Because we are here to be concerned with the architecture of houses, it is first necessary to decide which camp gives that art the most scope. Which social class, which kind of builder, which kind of dwelling is most prone to architectural expression?

The Dwelling Units which Public Housers build are government sponsored and subsidized. They are rented to a small number of people in the lower income groups, the "one third of a nation" who are incapable of providing new housing for themselves. The act which enables such housing to be built starts off in this guise:

"Section 2. The Congress hereby declares that the general welfare and security of the Nation and the health and living standards of its people require housing production and related

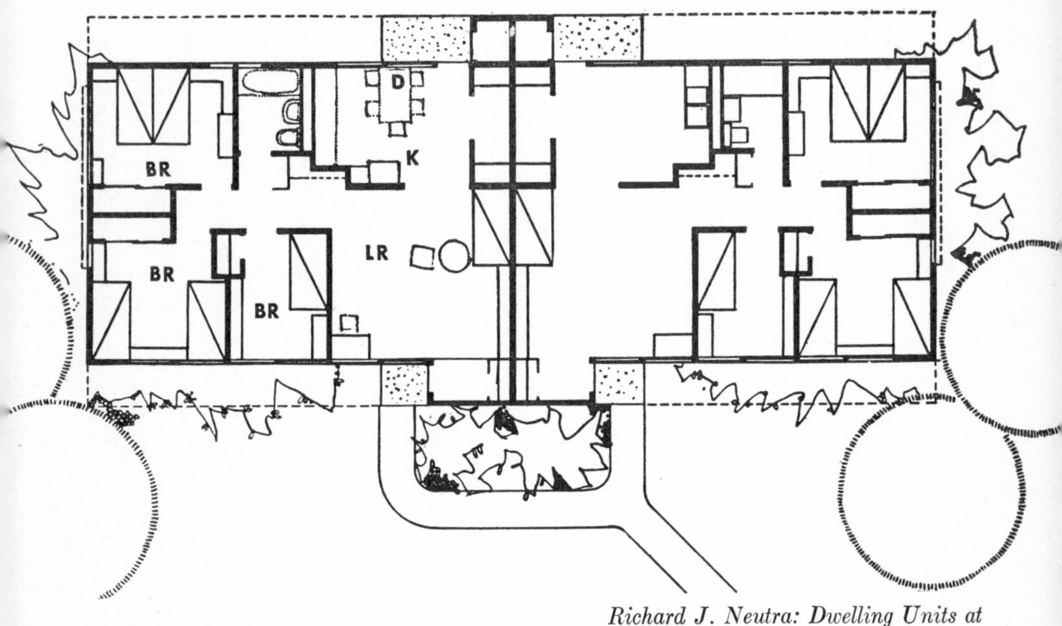

Richard J. Neutra: Dwelling Units at Channel Heights

> community development sufficient to remedy the serious housing shortage, the elimination of substandard and other inadequate housing through the clearance of slums and blighted areas, and the realization as soon as feasible of the goal of a decent home and a suitable living environment for every American family, thus contributing to the development and redevelopment of communities and to the advancement of the growth, wealth and security of the Nation."

But in actuality "every American family" is not meant seriously. The Act specifically states that

> ". . . (a) the public housing agency shall fix maximum income limits for the admission and for the continued occupancy of families in such housing. . . ."

Nor are its policies carried out in the fullest sense now possible.

The Act calls for

> "... (1) the production of housing of sound standards of design, construction, livability, and size for adequate family life; (2) the reduction of the costs of housing without sacrifice of such sound standards; (3) the use of new designs, materials, techniques, and methods in residential construction, the use of standardized dimensions and methods of assembly of home-building materials and equipment, and the increase of efficiency in residential construction and maintenance. ..."

The goal here suggested appears to be an open-minded and progressive attack on the design and construction of the dwelling unit. It is not achieved. The reason for the failure does not lie wholly in the technical difficulties involved. Behind this very real problem is a force which negates the whole idea of progressivism in housing at its source. This force is the conservatism of the people who administer the Act. The average middle class American does not understand and positively dislikes planning and innovation. Gadgets, yes; but the fundamental approach suggested by the Act, in that it would change the appearance of housing, cannot be accepted. It attacks one of our principal security symbols. For the typical administrator, *Home*, like *Mother*, is a mental contraption which must not be monkeyed with. Thus, while public housing projects always have an architect, he cannot be said to design his own job. The whole plan, the way of life of the families concerned, as it is affected by environment, is fixed in advance by regulation. These so-called "standards" are, in reality, a compilation of the desires and prejudices typical of dead center opinion within the middle class. It must be remembered, however, that public housing is in large part a reform movement. While it is administered by the conservative elements in the middle class, it is under constant attack by progressives, who are, as we shall see later, also of the middle class. The working class, the class which lives in public housing, have nothing to do with its design.

Homes, the product of the Home Builders, are more or less mass-produced for the middle class itself—designed, built, and

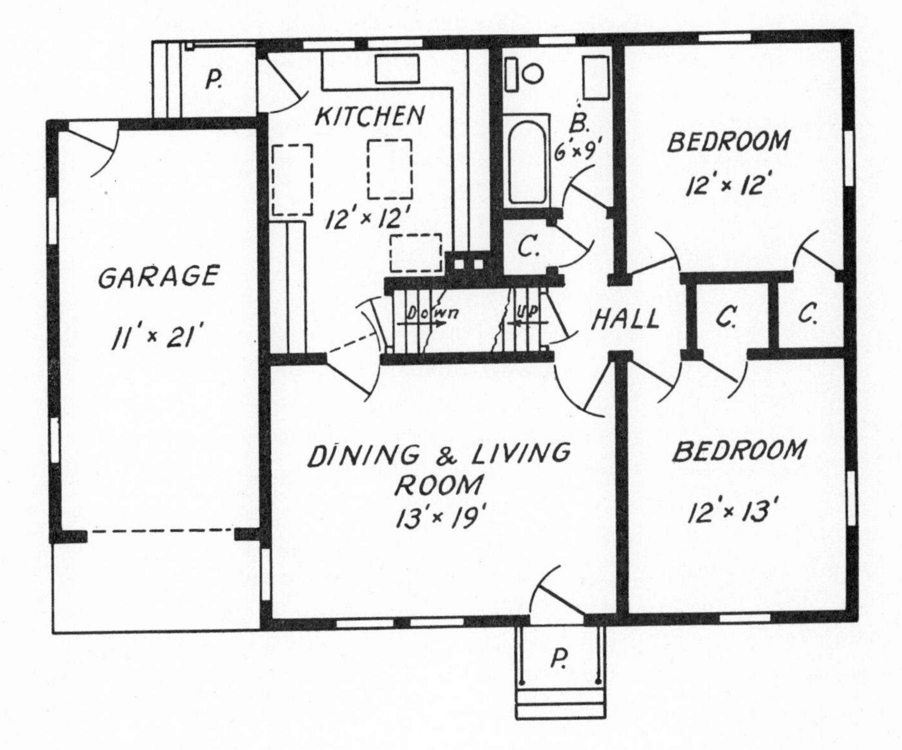

Architect unknown: "Plan of a small bungalow with an attached garage." From Planning Your Home for Better Living.

sold by speculative builders, usually with some government aid. The very word is a sales device. "We are selling you," it implies, "far more than a mere shelter." In this area progressives are aggressively excluded, the subsidy is less, and the administrators are free to create housing of the sort which they want. Thus we have the Federal Housing Administration. It is the fashion in progressive circles to excoriate the F. H. A. for its low standards. Its exclusion of architecture and architects, symbols of planning and progressivism, may have something to do with this. But it is also true, in the light of what it could achieve in terms of livability, that the conservative middle class is cutting its own throat.

F. H. A. housing, by means of a universally agreed upon euphemism, is known as "private." The private speculator expects and is expected to bleed housing for all it is worth. As in the early days of railroading, factory management, food, advertising, lumbering, and farming, so in homes: long term values are not considered worth worrying about. The worst speculators do not even build a sound house. They have not yet developed a sense of social responsibility. Sooner or later, as has happened in so many other fields, home builders may have their own kind of Pure Food and Drug Act rammed down their throats—but not until the situation has been seen in its true light, as a waste of natural resources and as a menace to the public's emotional health. It would be unfair to ascribe this entirely to "venal" or "selfish" or "greedy" speculators. Some of them may deserve all three epithets. Most of them are behaving in the only way they know, strictly according to the tenets of their class. The great majority of the middle class does not recognize architecture in any but conventional terms. The symbol "home" comes first. Architecture and even livability are qualities beyond their ken. They don't understand it, don't like it, and don't want it.

Progressives make periodic efforts to promote good home design. These are programmed as "Education and the Dissemination of Ideas" through publications, lectures, competitions, etc., just as all reform movements, be they New Art, Planned Parenthood, or Political Clean-up, are promoted. Such movements, Lincoln Steffens to the contrary notwithstanding, do produce results in the long term. But at present the home, like the dwelling unit, offers the architect little or no scope. The situation is such that it prevents him from using his creative faculties. It is fruitless to blame individuals or groups for this state of affairs. The problem is an economic and cultural one of titanic complexity. One can only mourn the fact that our society is not able to utilize its highest skills throughout its structure.

The third and last general category of dwellings—houses—are built by an income group that is able to afford them, without government aid, and through a private agent, the architect. They are built when, where, and how their individual owners choose, i.e. to individual specifications and according (at least theoretically) to individual tastes. There is no administrator or home builder between the designer and the family which is to live in the house. In the case of both dwelling units and homes, the builders do not know the people who will live in their products. The families concerned are statistical entities only. In the case of the house, the architect and the client are very intimately connected. The architect can find out a great deal about his client's needs simply by asking him. He can also persuade this private client (if any persuasion is in fact necessary) to go at his house building venture with a view to achieving fine architecture. No government regulations are in the way. And, because the relationship is between individuals, class patterns of behavior are not always and necessarily in the ascendant. Thus this third realm is, of the three, that one which offers the architect the greatest opportunity to use his creative faculties. And it is this third kind of housing—the new detached house for one family, privately financed and built—with which this book is to be concerned. Furthermore, the family with which it will deal, unlike the old time census Family Group, which could have been no more than some miserable bachelors holed up together, consists surely of a mother, father, one or more children, and may possibly include a grandparent or other elderly relation, as well as a servant either by the day or living in.

One might well object that, with the exception of help, such families are common to all classes. Indeed they are, but their patterns of behavior, and thus their houses, are very different. This hypothetical family is regarded neither by the building industry, by the public, nor by itself, as like other families. It is styled as upper class, or upper income group, or intellectual, or well off, or rich. Such phrases prove little more than that it is high on our socio-economic scale. Furthermore, while the majority of houses intended as creative architecture are commissioned by the upper income group, even this group builds an enormous number which are, to all intents and purposes, like the home builders' homes. The chief difference is that they are more expensive. How can one explain this divergence within the ranks of the upper income group?

The fact is that the "upper class" is not a single homogenous class at all, but a collection of quite separate classes, with very different attitudes and goals. Thus not only in order to answer our question, but also in order to attack the problem of the house, it is necessary to dissect this "upper class," and to discover, if possible, how each of its segments feels about its houses. And indeed the uses of socio-economic class distinctions are manifold, not only in life itself but in terms of architectural design. No architect can find out all about his client's needs. No client could express all his needs. In practice, a very short list of pecadillos is offered the architect as a program. He fills in the rest on the basis of his background knowledge of the client's class patterns of behavior.

In one of the pioneering studies of social class in America, W. Lloyd Warner and his collaborators discovered six distinct groupings in the Yankee City they examined. The houses used by these groups varied considerably. Mr. Warner describes the attitude towards house typical of the topmost, or upper-upper class, as follows:

> "Many of the houses themselves, as previously mentioned, may be said to possess lineages of their own. Those which do not, have less value, however old or beautiful they may be. A house with a distinguished lineage is concrete evidence of upper-class status. Although the spatial arrangements of the rooms and their specialization of function help to impress an elaborate ritual on the occupants, the spiritual presence of the ancestors, as experienced through the use of ancestral rooms and furniture,

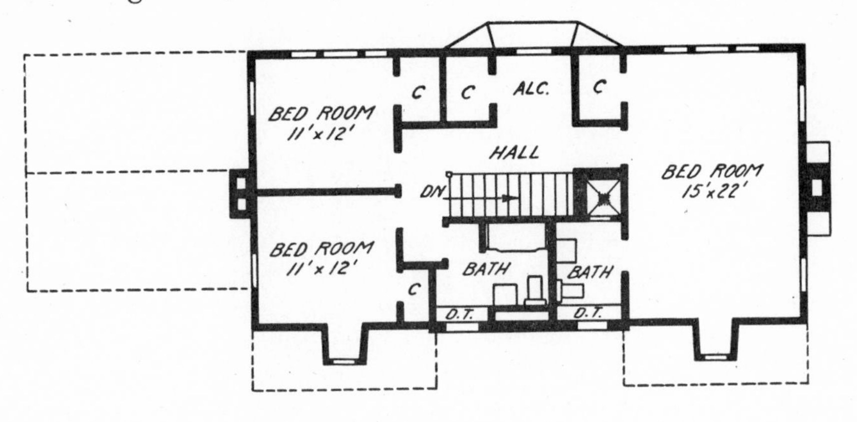

SECOND FLOOR PLAN

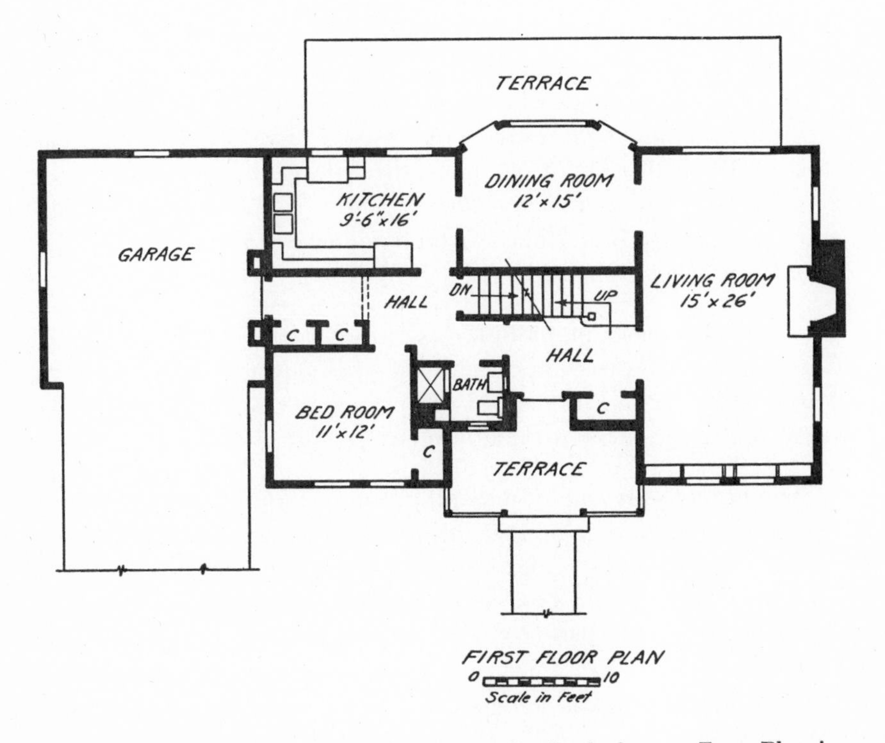

FIRST FLOOR PLAN

Roscoe D. Hemenway: L. R. Centro House, Portland, Oregon. From Planning Your Home for Better Living.

is more important in maintaining a disciplined continuity in the minds of the inhabitants."

To a person operating upon such values, building is more or less obnoxious. A new house cannot contribute in any way to the ancestor worship by which class status is maintained. When members of this group do build, they are apt to select a "traditional" model. The attempt is to achieve the same sort of house their parents lived in. Thus, because of its small numbers, and because of its nostalgia, the very topmost group is not of much interest to the architect. True, its members occasionally build a magnificent modern house, but such jobs are few and far between.

The next group down, the lower-upper class in Mr. Warner's nomenclature, is a mobile group, on its way to upper-upper status.

"The possession of "a house" is a prime requisite for social mobility; after several generations, the "new people" who live in these houses and who have adopted upper-class behavior will become members of old families and enter the upper-upper class. The value of an old house is so high that even an individual who is a member of an old family is open to criticism if he does not possess a house which is deemed a suitable setting for upper-class behavior.

A typical symptom of mobility is the over-elaboration of some aspect of the class to which the individual aspires to belong. Mr. Warner notes that it is typical of lower-upper behavior not only to buy old houses, but to make museums out of them:

"The Starrs were one of a small group of families who recently purchased Georgian houses in one of the more handsome sections on Hill Street. The large-square house is one of the old ones on Hill Street. Two well-known architects have declared it to be "one of the most beautiful surviving examples of Federal architecture." Several members of certain old families admitted that it was a beautiful home, but they said: 'She's made a museum out of it. It's too perfect. She spent thousands of dollars to remodel it and made it a perfect example of

Federal architecture. The trouble with her is that she imitates and always overdoes it.' Only a few feet of well-clipped grass separate the house from the sidewalk, but in the rear an expensive lawn, flanked by meticulously tended gardens, glistens in the sunlight. Some people feel that the gardens are overcared for, that the gardener has been too scrupulous, and that the house has been so frequently painted that it shines just a little too much."

Like the upper-uppers, lower-upper people seldom build. The necessity of the right symbol, for a house with a lineage, is more important than personal creativity or modernity. Because lower-uppers tend to exaggerate, and perhaps because they bring with them from the middle class a delight in comfort, they do remodel. But remodeling adds nothing to the main stream of architecture. The upper-uppers, in contrast, often seem to take a delight in drafts, chill, and plumbing so antique as to resemble booby traps. Thus, the upper class as a whole does not build. It is of little interest to the architect except as its housing serves as a model for emulation by the social classes below it.

In pursuing Mr. Warner so far, an interesting relationship has come to light. The shift from the inexact generally used term *upper class* to the sociologist's more exact categories leaves us without that "upper class" which at first promised to provide clients interested in creative architecture. We must descend the socio-economic scale again, in order to discover a group oriented towards building, rather than towards inheriting their houses. Mr. Warner describes a house in the next category down, for the upper-middle class, as follows:

"It is a house with all of the most modern plumbing and mechanical conveniences built into it. There is a stained-shingle exterior which does not have to be repainted or stained again. The trim around the windows is white with blue blinds. The walk to the front door from the sidewalk is concrete as are the front steps. This use of concrete is a departure from what is approved by members of the higher classes. The middle-class Frenches follow out the same social pattern as others of their status and mix the latest of modern improvements with the old or with reproductions of the old. The living room has polished hardwood floors and bright paper with green background on the walls. Mr. French is very proud of several pieces of old furniture, but his pride seems to consist in how much they are worth and how much he could sell them for. Most of the pieces are reproductions of antiques. The bellows hanging by the fireplace are new and an improvement on the old models. The lawn has small well-cut evergreen trees planted in front of the house and the small shrubs are carefully trimmed."

Here, obviously, is a class which sets great store by modernity —of a certain kind. The typical upper-middle class client wants a "modern" house, by which he means a new one, and the best in the way of plumbing, materials, and heating. In most cases these must not only *be* the best, they must very obviously *look* like the best. He is not above feeling the lavatory to see whether it is thick (porcelain) and therefore good stuff, or thin (enamelled iron) and therefore cheap stuff. Indeed, the bath room seems to be one of his greatest symbols. Tile and Carrara glass he must have. Carrara marble, which one might find in an occasional upper-upper bath room, is less desirable. It is not the latest or most patently expensive thing. Money and materials are directly equated. Natural materials are not worth while for themselves alone. By the same token, such imponderable values as expression, which cannot be directly equated with money, are thought worthless or, if they cost extra money to achieve, sheer foolishness. The architect is conceived of, by this group, as a technically trained business man. Specifications and contracts are his most important services. It is taken for granted that the client designs the house, and that the architect, under his direction, "draws the blueprints."

The upper-middle class house is a visible symbol of economic power. A symbol is like a word. One must know what it means, and that can only be done through memory. Thus the house, as symbol, must be in a known style with known connotations. If it is in a new style, one cannot readily tell how expressive it is, or what class lives in it. Considerable experience is necessary before it becomes generally known to be cheap or costly, upper, middle, or lower class. This fact tends to make the upper-middle class extremely conservative, particularly as regards style. The style must be an old one, with clear honorific overtones. The judgments as to what style is the most honorific varies by region, and changes every so often. In New England, for example, some twenty years ago, it was very stylish to be English. To live in an English house, whether one's name was Cabot or Wrobleski, was to partake more fully of the region's Anglo-Saxon culture. Nowadays, for the richer groups, it is Colonial or Cape Cod. English culture is no longer a la mode, while a sense of belongingness is best expressed by a native style. The esthetic uneasiness characteristic of the upper-middle class house is a result of this attempt to wed incompatible elements. An old style based on an extinct movement in our culture cannot be harmoniously integrated with our current concepts of what a house consists of.

The emphasis on modernity, the economic security, the pride in income, the instinct to buy and sell for profit, all conspire to make the upper-middle class in general great builders of houses. Their suburbs—monumental graveyards of old styles, uneasily wrapped around "modern conveniences"—stretch for miles around our cities. The old ones have become slums. The middle-aged ones are in social transition, while the new ones bristle with the latest "traditional."

The next group down in the socio-economic scale, the lower-middle class, gets us into the category of those who buy houses, rather than build them. Mr. Warner describes one such as follows:

"The Stanleys were proud of their home. They owned it outright, and the husband and wife had planted the flower garden. Mr. Stanley had painted the house and fences with two coats of white paint. He placed cast-off tires in appropriate places in the front yard and had given them a coating of white paint. After Mr. Stanley had spaded the ground inside the tires, his wife had planted petunias. Rows of hollyhocks grew beside the white fences. The smaller sons had collected flat stones and made a walk from the sidewalk to the door. Mr. Stanley dug a trench on each side of the neat rows so that they formed a glistening border to the path that his boys had fashioned."

Homes such as these are usually imitations of those of the upper-middle class. But eclecticism, the mixing of styles, is far more pronounced. And as with the upper-middle class, each period has its favorite style. To take New England again as an example, the Ranch House is the ruling taste of the moment. Lower-middle class subdivisions quite seriously restrict houses to "New England Ranch House type" under the heading of "preserving New England's historic character." Though they may have been designed by dining room table architects, they are seldom "architected" in the full sense of the word. They are speculatively built, or especially built with limited services. Numerically they represent the great volume of residential construction. But from the creative architect's point of view, they are undesirable.

Below this socio-economic level are two others, the upper and lower working classes. Because of their economic limitations, they are very seldom able to build. When they do, they are apt to do it themselves. More generally they inherit housing abandoned by the classes above them. And of course a certain number of them can, if they are eligible, live in dwelling units, always providing that there are any available, and that they are not too proud to "descend" into a public project, that last step in housing's pecking order. Thus of all classes in our social structure, the upper-middle would appear to be the only one rich enough, secure enough, and adventurous enough to build.

Upper-middle class houses such as that of the Frenches, described above, are not, from the creative architect's point of view, good jobs. They may pay, but because they are always compromises of some sort—i.e. between modernity and "tradition," between beauty and "practicality"—they are seldom successful in any respect. We can, for the time being only, define a good house, in the creative architect's sense, as being esthetically fresh and functionally practical, or, roughly, as modern. The foregoing catalogue of house types included none in this category. Yet large numbers are built. Who builds them?

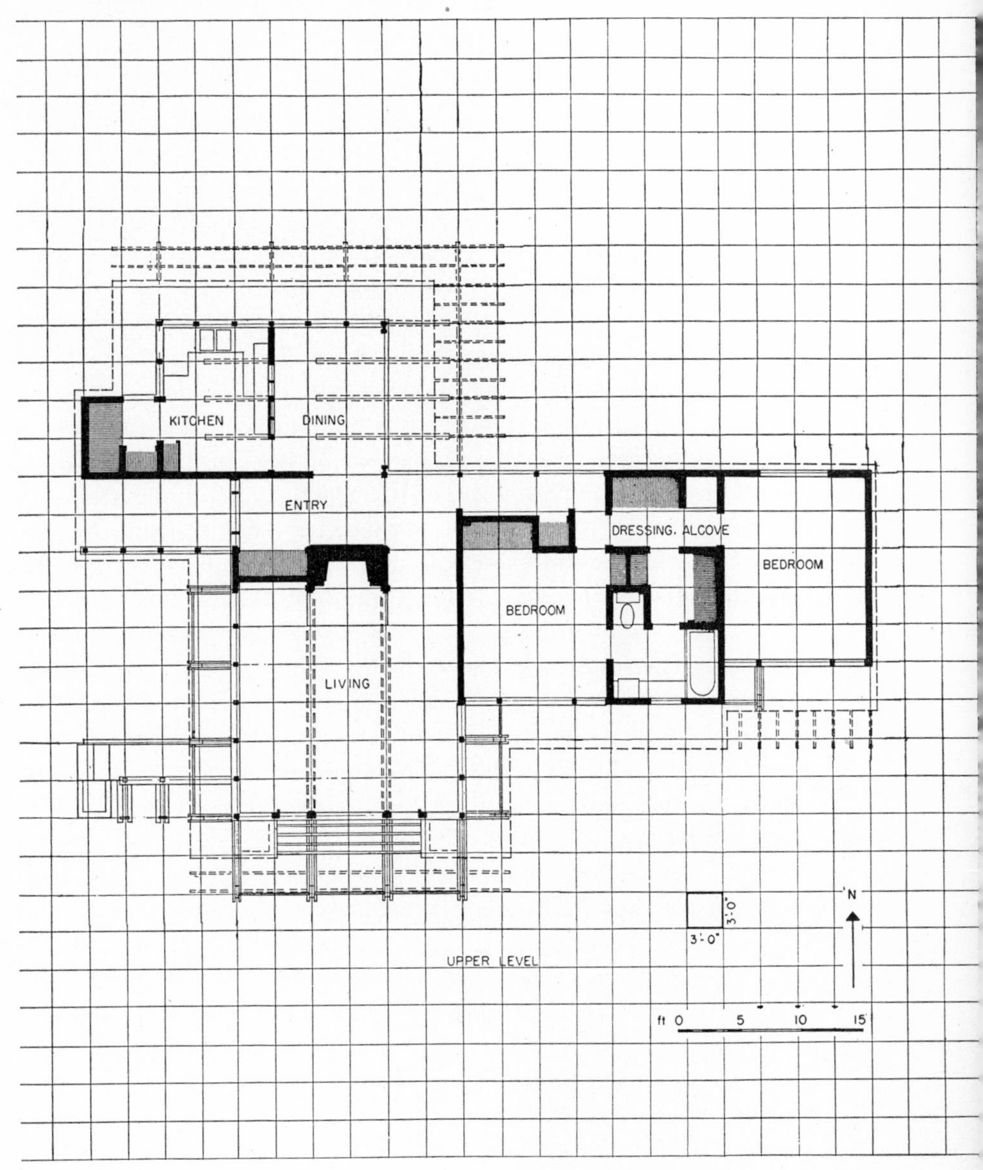

Harwell Hamilton Harris: House in California. Photographs are on pages 29 and 31.

Modernism

Because the upper-middle class is the only group which builds large numbers of houses, it is obvious that modernists must be upper-middle class. And this leads to a view of that group as split—as containing a large conservative sub-group, and a small innovating sub-group. The upper-middle class family in the innovating sub-group is responsible for most of the progress in architecture. It forces the expression of new patterns of living, and of new technical advantage. It is the fashion among architects to conceive of themselves as leaders in this respect. But an honest examination of their role would seem to place them in the category of a partner in a team composed of client and architect. Where fine architecture is the goal, the client is exactly as important to the result as is the architect. Thus, next to the question of clients or no clients, that of good clients must be the architect's principal problem. Without them he is impotent. What elements in the make-up of the middle class client makes him tend towards one or another sub-group?

Irving Rosow, in a study of the modern houses in and around Detroit, found that their owners' adjustment to life varied significantly as they built good or bad modern houses. He writes:

> "The consistency of a Modern house reveals an orientation toward realizing individually-defined interests, activities and living pattern goals. This is primarily an adjustment of intra-family roles and relationships. But the eclecticism of the Semi-Modern home, with its admixture of conventional space relationships and unconventional style, vitiates the aesthetic function and makes of it a form of conspicuous consumption in the Veblenian sense. The house is not construed as an opportunity to realize personally-defined living pattern goals and to adjust relationships within the family by exploiting house

space in new ways. These considerations are subordinated in favor of a superficially "different," "dramatic," or "striking" house. The house becomes clearly an instrument of the family's social role, status identification or an expression of social aspirations. The element of pretension and emulating "social leadership innovators" is an important motive. The contrasts of housing attitudes may be summed up as, "How can we live in the house?" as opposed to "What can the house do for us socially?"

"These attitude differences bespeak different social types—different *kinds* of people build Modern from those who build Semi-Modern houses. The two social types . . . show characteristic differences of Weltanschauung, goal orientation and aspirations, self-conceptions, spheres of interest and activity, occupational status, use of leisure time, . . . type of family organization and relationships. The Semi-Modern group . . . shows pronounced stereotypes with strong status drives or more individuation (ego expansion and personal differentiation) to achieve recognition. The Modern group . . . shows significantly less awareness of social conformity or assertion goals and thinks more in terms of personal needs and wants."

Rosow's Semi-Modern client can be seen as half way between a Modernist and a Traditionalist, but only in terms of the style of his house; that is to say superficially. The Semi-Modern client and the Traditionalist client, in terms of fundamental architecture, want exactly the same thing. They are the same kind of people. As a group, they pick and choose among the styles, which is to say that they are eclectic. The Modernists, in contrast, are highly selective. Their search for style takes place in one narrowly confined area, which we can define, for the moment, as that in which they can achieve the greatest personal creativeness and technical advantage. This leads to a view of the whole upper class, or wealthy, housing picture as in the form presented in the following chart. Because it is largely based on intuition, it cannot be called either accurate or conclusive. If it suggests profounder truths, or stimulates the design of better, more commodious pigeonholes, it will have served its whole purpose.

	Upper Upper	Lower Upper
Approx. % of Population.*	1.44%	1.56%
Build, buy or inherit.	Usually inherit, sometimes buy an old house with a lineage. Build infrequently.	Usually buy old house, (if possible with a lineage) to remodel. Build infrequently.
Use of architects.	Use architects of own class for "traditional" design, famous architects for innovating design.	Use architects of upper upper class.
Attitude toward design process.	Taken for granted.	Taken for granted.
Attitude toward architect's fee.	Usually accept going rate.	Usually accept going rate.
Attitude toward building process.	Left to architect.	Left to architect, but often many pains taken with detailed choices.
Attitude toward esthetic values.	Seen as essential and left to architect.	Seen as essential, but often carefully screened by client.
Attitude toward innovation.	Conservative with occasional experiments.	Conservative.
Influence of magazines.	Have little effect on values.	Extensively used as source material.

* The percentages used come from Warner and Lunt's "The Social Life of a Modern Community"

Modernism

Upper Middle		Lower Middle
Innovating Group	Conservative Group	28.12%
10.22%		
Build more frequently than other groups. Otherwise buy and remodel.	Build very frequently. Sometimes buy new speculative houses.	Usually buy speculative houses, build very infrequently.
Use architects of own class, and occasionally famous architects.	Use architects less frequently, sometimes design own house.	Very seldom use architects.
Ranges from very sensitive adjustment to being taken for granted.	Usually not understood. Sometimes disliked, with attempts to circumvent architect or do-it-oneselfism.	Usually no comprehension of process or knowledge of its goals.
Accept going rate. Consider it good investment.	Usually attempt to cut fee, feel they have not gotten money's worth.	Want partial service. "Just draw some blueprints."
Left to architect but with great client participation.	Much client questioning of materials, method and value received.	Architect usually excluded.
Seen as essential and involves much client participation.	Seldom seen as worth money. Often distrust architect.	Confused with conventionalism.
Most experimentation done by this group.	Conservative with occasional desire to be "modernistic."	Very conservative, dislike experimentation.
Extensively used as source material.	Use magazines as shopping guide. Often pick out specific house.	Use of "house hints" and "ideas" pages only.

	Upper Upper	Lower Upper
Approx. % of Population.	1.44%	1.56%
Husband education.	College.	College or graduate work.
Wife education.	Finishing School or College.	Finishing School or College.
Servants.	Usually more than one, living in.	Usually more than one, living in.
Use of help.	All household functions.	All household functions or, at a minimum, social functions.
Housekeeping standards.	Impeccable when done by servants, otherwise apt to be poor.	Impeccable.
Child care pattern.	Entirely by servants. Children banished from adult life, but lead parallel social life.	Same as upper upper where money permits.
Social focus.	Largely between individuals, or small groups, both sexes, men dominant.	Largely between individuals.
Social activities.	Largely "society," some civic.	Largely "society," some civic work.
Family Structure.	Authoritarian, little cross category contact, much contact with relations.	Less authoritarian, smaller "family group," otherwise as upper upper.
Motives for building.	None.	None.

Modernism

Upper Middle		Lower Middle
Innovating Group	Conservative Group	28.12%
10.22%		
Often graduate work.	High school or college.	High school or grammar school.
College.	High school or junior college.	High school.
Usually help of some kind, seldom living in.	Usually help of some kind sometimes living in.	Service very infrequent.
Household.	Household and child care.	Sitting with children.
Not emphasized.	Highly emphasized, usually impeccable.	Women's chief purpose in life.
Usually by parents cooperatively with servants' help. Children included in social life.	Usually by mother, with servants' help. Less inclusion in social life.	By mother.
Apt to be groups of both sexes large private participation.	Sometimes one group, apt to divide into subgroups of men and women.	Men and women apt to form separate groups.
Large amount of civic, professional, special interest groups.	Small amount of lodge, club, civic and clique.	Small amount of lodge, club and clique.
Equalitarian.	Authoritarian.	Authoritarian.
Better living facilities and self esteem.	"Gracious living" and social or psychic security.	None.

Saul Steinberg:

"Practicality"

Every book, no matter how slight, must have its villain. In this instance that character is the so-called "practical man." Pure practicality, mildly tempered by the "artistic" urge which often evidences itself in architects, is all too pervasive a quality to be easily evoked. Only a Tchekov can do it justice. He describes a "practical" architect as follows:

> "Look!" he said to my sister, pointing to the sky with the very umbrella with which he had just struck me. "Look at the sky! Even the smallest stars are worlds! How insignificant man is in comparison with the universe."
>
> And he said this in a tone that seemed to convey that he found it extremely flattering and pleasant to be so insignificant. What an untalented man he was! Unfortunately, he was the only architect in the town, and during the last fifteen or twenty years I could not remember one decent house being built. When he had to design a house, as a rule he would draw first the hall and the drawing room; as in olden days school girls could only begin to dance by the fireplace, so his artistic ideas could only evolve from the hall and the drawing room. To them he would add the dining room, nursery, study, connecting them with doors, so that in the end they were just so many passages, and each room had two or three doors too many. His houses were obscure, extremely confused, and limited. Every time, as though he felt something was missing, he had recourse to various additions, plastering them one on top of the other, and there would be various lobbies, and passages, and crooked staircases leading to the entresol, where it was only possible to stand in a stooping position, and where instead of a floor there would be a thin flight of stairs like a Russian bath, and the kitchen would always be under the house with a vaulted ceiling and a brick floor. The front of his houses always

had a hard, stubborn expression, with stiff, timid lines, low squat roofs, and fat pudding-like chimneys surmounted with black cowls and squeaking weathercocks. And somehow all the houses built by my father were like each other, and vaguely reminded me of his top hat, and the stiff obstinate back of his head. In the course of time the people of the town grew used to my father's lack of talent, which took root and became our style.

"My father introduced the style into my sister's life."

This brilliant description includes the practical architect's three salient characteristics. He is insensitive to people's needs. He lives in a "miracle" which divests him of responsibility. He designs by accretion, adding item to item without forethought, until the job is finished.

Pure and unadulterated expediency would be of no interest here were it not for the fact that, just as there is a little of the God in every man, so also there is a little of the pseudo-practical. The architect must ward off the tendency in himself, and in his best clients. But the problem is not only of the inner conflict variety. The house designer is responsible for a large segment of our man-made environment, and, by extension, for many of the changes in nature required by the house. Most houses are not designed, they are accumulated. Thus architects and practical men are, in the first instance, in fundamental competition.

The architect, part artist, part technician, part business man, takes, at his highest development, a personal responsibility, a dedicated attitude towards environment. The practical man, guided neither by professional ethics nor interest in essence, takes on no such responsibility. On the one hand the house, or whatever part of the environment is to be created, is conceived of as having something of the creator's personality built into it. This is the forerunner of accountability. On the other, the object created is conceived of as having no connection with the creator. Its use only is considered. Its relationship to its surroundings as a whole is ignored.

"Use" is very broadly defined by the architect as including all the senses, the ethical and the esthetic sensibilities. Use is defined by the practical man almost exclusively in terms of money. The architect's definition makes it necessary for him to spend money for the delight of the soul, an entirely intangible value. The practical man's makes it necessary to spend no money for anything which will not surely make money.

This limited and limiting approach is an essential element of our culture—so ingrained as to be thought of as typically "American." Actually, it is a distortion and debasement of pragmatism, the doctrine ". . . that the meaning of conceptions is to be sought in their practical bearings, that the function of thought is as a guide to action, and that truth is preeminently to be tested by the practical consequences of belief" (Webster). Architecture is an intensely pragmatic art, and architects, of all people, must be pragmatic thinkers.

A *truly* practical environment is obviously a healthy one, a productive one, an energy-producing one, and a beautiful one. The truth of the fact that by and large those environments which are considered most beautiful endure longest, and thus make most money, hardly needs argument. This is the definition of environment the architect has in his mind's eye.

Over and against this, the pseudo-practical man, thinking only of immediate use and profit, stores explosives in the Parthenon, pollutes rivers, denudes forests, breaks the plains, etc. He is unable to see the end results of his present actions. He is without time sense. The principal quality of the good architect is to be able to think around his problem, to see it related to past and future, as well as to the present. The common or garden American practicality is in essence only opportunism, "a taking advantage . . . of opportunities or circumstances with little regard for principles or ultimate consequences."

The history of our physical environment is one of constant war between the opportunist and the pragmatist, between the pseudo-practical and the dreamer. The dreamer usually wins, but from a rear guard position as it were, and only after expediency has ravaged some resource almost beyond repair. Housing is no exception. The majority of all houses now being built are more or less obsolete in terms of livability, and they are more or less destructive in terms of environment.

The hostility of the practical man towards the architect is by and large motivated by the same drives which make him dislike government. But the architect has no big stick. Thus, rather than demanding taxes to be used for conservationist purposes, he must wheedle them, on the sly. As most clients are to some small extent pseudo-practical people, the architect often goes about the world in disguise. He must escape detection as belonging in the camp of his clients' enemies. In most architectural circles, the words *art*, or *esthetics* are shunned as obscenities. They give the game away. New euphemisms, expressions "acceptable to the average client" are always in great demand. Indeed an inexhaustible supply is necessary, for as soon as their true meaning is discovered, they must of course be instantly abandoned. The architect who can describe, explain, and defend a design without once mentioning such words as taste, art, appropriateness, or future value, is considered a near genius by his peers, and seldom has any trouble with his clients. At least not until they catch up with him. Many of the explosions of temperament which occur in building are directly traceable to the client's discovery that such values entered into its design. He feels, very justifiably indeed, that he has been deceived. The architect is giving him not the opportunistic house he thought he was getting, but a pragmatically conceived design for living.

Most good things seem to come as a result of taking the long way around. Tchekov's architect's principal failure, in terms of technique, was that he approached his problem too directly. The way to fine architecture, through pragmatic process to expressive end, is complex, apparently irrational, laborious, and terrifically exciting. How explain these contradictions? There is no possible answer, because in actuality the process of design is neither contradictory nor mysterious. It has only been made to seem so, in offensive defense of expediency. Good design is full, in the same sense that a good life is full. Every man knows, in his deepest soul, that there is joy in labor, ugliness in beauty, tragedy in humor, irrationality in practicality, hate in love, and so on through every human enterprise. Houses are only extensions of people—they are nothing in themselves—and as such are most satisfactory when they reflect the whole man.

Architecture

In the pages which follow it is my intention to examine the architecture, architects, and clients of the upper-middle class in the innovating sub-group in some detail. In the meantime a dry-run at all three might be useful. The purpose of the architect-client partnership, a single family house, is by and large a specialized building for the production, care, and education of children. As such it must not only provide for those needs common to all human beings. It must also particularly adapt itself to the special requirements of its functional purpose. The problem it poses the designer is not at all like that of the apartment for childless couples, or of houses for other combinations of adults. The addition of the process *child care* to the basic business of *living* materially affects its physical requirements. The family relationship involves a host of specialized equipment, complex room relationships and functions; in addition it involves a characteristic emotional atmosphere which should be taken into account in planning. The architect is faced with a unique problem, just as he is in a school, or in a courthouse. People want, of course, certain basic things from all buildings—such as shelter, heat, light and safety. A building gets its special character from the activities it houses. The single family house has four peculiar functions. It must serve

1. for living, sleeping, eating, excreting, etc.,
2. for the care and education of children,
3. for individuals subject to group pressure,
4. as symbol, background, expression, and joy.

If the first three of the four categories are well taken care of, and there is never any reason for them not to be, then the last is by far the most potent. The themes of living are love, sociability, privacy, self expression, comfort, belongingness, and the like. They will suffuse a good house, i.e. a house willing to be suffused, with meaning. The house is no more than a receptacle to receive them. Houses are only really important to people who do not know how to live, or when the house prevents them from living. An important house is a bad house. You can tell an important house easily because it is *all* something or other: all Colonial, all glass, all open, all closed, all wood, all in the latest style, or all American. Such houses, because they are insistent and stuck up, prevent us from properly exercising our emotions.

A good house has been warped, pushed, moulded, compromised, and recompromised by its architect, client, site, climate, the laws it is built under, the amount of money available, and by the customs, traditions, and history of its location. If it is one hundred and twenty years old, and has wings in the Greek Revival and International styles it may be, like an old cheese, just about ripe. If it has unexpected places in it, if the truths of its construction and form are occasionally evident, if it will bow out of one's consciousness when not wanted, remind one of China, Southern France, or rural England on occasion, refuse to admit it ever has received the finishing touch, make people seem more beautiful, wise, or charming than ever before, if it will do these and a few other things, as well as treat you right physically, then it is a really good house.

The client's role in the creation of such a house is positive, not negative. He is by no means all on the receiving end. He must be able to afford it. He must be personally secure enough to innovate. He must see innovation, rather than conservatism, as the foundation of security. He must be capable of thinking out his living problems, and intensely desirous of doing so. Because the ultimate goal of fine architecture—and that is what we are here concerned with—is the *expression* of functions, emotions, and techniques, the client must be sensitive to and desirous of fostering a series of transcendental, or "impractical," or imponderable values. He must be capable of team work, that is he must not be of the "I'll do it myself" school of thought. Finally, his most important contribution to a good result is the definition of func-

Harwell Hamilton Harris: House in California. The photograph on the next page is an interior of the same house. The plan appears on page 15.

tion in terms which are essentially noble, and human, and beautiful. This is a large order.

The architect's role is no less demanding. The first element he brings to the team is perhaps the ability to manipulate techniques to his client's advantage. The second is artistry. Artistry and good design are by no means synonymous. "Good Design" is all too often "Important Design."

There seem to be two general varieties of important designers. One kind is tremendously concerned with structure. In his own group he is known as "practical" and "sound." By other groups he may be called a "poor designer." The second kind of bad architect is apt to be unconcerned with structure, though he may talk about and try rather radical ideas at times. He is very much concerned, on the other hand, with visual order. He works out and organizes his buildings, as far as looks go, with the greatest of care. In his own group he is known as "a good designer," and by others as "unsound" or "stimulating." Both kinds of architects are alike in that they pay very little attention to the human beings' needs, though both would ardently deny it. The first thinks of these needs as a lack of leaks, the second as a lack of disorderliness. Both are partially right.

An outstanding characteristic of the two sorts of important designers is the extreme emphasis they place on rules. The ability to follow rules is unquestionably, and in large measure, absolutely essential. But the ability to rationalize is also of great value. Such are the complexities of architecture that no matter how exhaustively the individual relationships involved are thought out—that between people and views, for example—there always remain uneasy areas where it is essential to rationalize away those "indigestible portions which the leopards reject." (T. S. Eliot) Why should the architect need utter consistency any more than the leopards need utter consumption?

Fine architecture cannot be achieved solely with objective means. Accurate thinking, infinite pains, a wonderful site, lots of money, a ready-made formula, and similar aids are not in themselves sufficient. Such qualities and facilities will take one a long way, but not all the way. A good house must also represent a compromise with the unconscious, or in strictly Shakesperian

lower middle class-ese, with "the stuff that dreams are made on." The good architect must be passionately concerned with dreams, with bringing them to the surface, and with interpreting and using them once he has them there. He must also, of course, have the same interest in construction and design which important designers have. But the element which makes fine architecture, the one which he derives in part from his dreams, is Louis Sullivan's "sweet, abundant and gracious gift of expression." Expression is a transcendental value. It is hidden from many people. To others it is sometimes understood, sometimes not, like a word on the periphery of vocabulary. For still others it is the most important value there is, in any change.

There are plenty of books, good ones, about structure and design, and of course there are Sullivan, Ruskin, Read, *et al.* on expression—and these are all very good too. As far as I know, there is nothing that describes the urgency of the architect's desire to fuse form and function expressively. The interplay of the three is a vastly complicated subject which must be dealt with by each creative architect in his own way. Ruskin believed, or so it would seem, that expression is like the kind of dog which can be picked up, tickled, felt, played with, smelled and, so to speak, discovered. Sullivan on the other hand felt that it is the kind of dog that one must creep up on from behind, with great stealth and self-effacement, only to find, just as it seems to be within reach, that it has escaped. The latter sort of approach, though disheartening, seems to promise an adventurous chase, and will be used here.

The expressive content of architecture is affected in some way by every technique, drawing, writing, and person involved in its accomplishment. The search for beauty begins with the class-conditioned goals of clients; involves their social orientation, the family, their bodies, the living activities; the architect-client relationship, not to mention the architect's and his client's personal pecadillos; the building process, style, environment, site, structure; and finally expression itself. In the present instance, only the last chapter will deal directly with that dog nicknamed "Stuff." And it will be little more than flash impressions of his tail, as he bounds out of reach and sight.

Architecture

In the meantime, Lewis Mumford has, perhaps, already proffered as good a working hypothesis for design as it is possible to express. He says:

> "Good design means going back to fundamentals: a child at work in a stable and reassuring world: a pair of lovers at play in a room where the scent of lilacs may creep through the window, or the shrill piping of crickets be heard in the garden below."

Berman: The Lovers

Cocteau: La Comtesse de Noailles.

CHAPTER II

Silhouettes

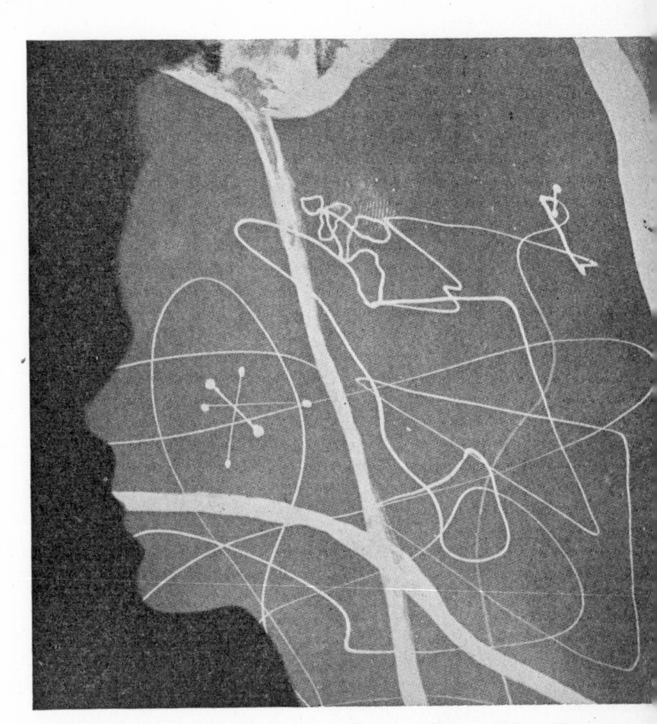

Gyorgy Kepes: Mrs. Kepes

Housewives

HOUSEWORK, COOKING, AND CHILD CARE are the primary responsibilities of women. But houses are designed by men, who have very little to do with the work which goes on in them. That is why, perhaps, woman's essential problems are so often ignored. Furthermore,. the lady client sitting across the desk from her gentleman architect, bedecked in the symbols of her class—her accent, clothes, and manners—obscures the basic female who will have to cope with the house he plans. One of his essential functions is to discover and reflect accurately her personal tastes. But this is of no utility unless to begin with he understands her fundamental problems. Taste is like frosting. Before that comes a cake. What is the housewife's cake really like?

This question concerns the architect in two related ways. First, unless he understands his client's basic position, he will be unable to design a satisfactory house from her point of view. Second, unless his client understands the design process, the house will not be satisfactory from his point of view. Every architect recognizes that clients come variously equipped. Some can take a constructive part in the process of design. Others behave in an almost systematically destructive way. One of the first requisites for positive behavior has to do with the housewife's primary relationship with her husband.

> "Kirkpatrick has posited three different roles of the married woman in the family group: that of wife-and-mother, that of companion, and that of partner."

Women in the first two categories are in a position of inequality with men. They may be subservient or dominant, but are usually the former. Their duties are considered menial, and chiefly ones of support. This is a view rooted in the past, when women were treated as slaves. But if they suffered less social equality, they also enjoyed greater contact with the world of production, if they did not do nearly all of the producing themselves. Today they can play only a spasmodic role outside the house. Wives were divorced from business when the work shop was removed from the house to office and specialized industrial buildings. Lewis Mumford remarks that

> "As a result of the household's becoming exclusively a consumer's organization, the housewife lost her touch with the affairs of the outside world; she became either a specialist in domesticity or a specialist in sex, something of a drudge, something of a courtesan, more often perhaps a little of both. Therewith the "private house" comes into existence; private from business. And every part came increasingly to share this privacy."

The prevailing attitude of the last century, that upper class women could find no respectable place in the world outside the home, has now been abandoned. Indeed, one hears that the pendulum has swung too far towards careers. The average upper middle class housewife nowadays has a college education, and experience as a secretary, teacher, buyer, or even in a profession. But during the long period when she is having and rearing children, she has a full-time domestic job on her hands, unless she has help. Even with servants the tendency is to feel that the mother's constant presence is desirable, if not essential. The organization of our society pretty much limits her to three essentially private activities—sex, housework, and child care. The housewife immured in this privacy, cut off from the discipline and excitement of the man's world she has glimpsed in school and before marriage, usually cannot play a creative role in her house planning unless she has the compensatory benefits of equal partnership with her husband. The authoritarian relationship is basically non-creative. It is antipathetic to the deep desire to *adjust*, which is essential to the proper planning of the house. Unless both husband and wife see sex, housework, and child care as dynamic, important, and creative enterprises on which the health and happiness of the family depend, the house can only be regarded as a sort of garage, as a mere shelter for activities. But even when the family functions are seen in this creative light, the housewife's role is still fraught with difficulties.

For example, housework has traditionally been performed by servants, at least for this socio-economic group, and is still apt to be considered by both men and woman as menial. Women may also have taken over some of men's particular dislike of it as a result of their education and business training. For many women it is a hateful and unrewarding task. Like men they wish to produce more durable things, think more noble thoughts, than is possible in the hectic round of child care and housework. It might be less difficult to resolve this conflict were it not for the fact that our tradition exalts neatness, cleanliness, and visible order in household furnishings. A well-kept house is the surest, most visible, most important symbol of socio-economic status. It is difficult to outgrow one's parents' dictum that anything but perfect housekeeping is "low class," in spite of the obvious fact that these same standards were founded on relatively cheap service. Veblen writing in 1899 excellently describes the two factors involved:

> "... the vicarious leisure performed by housewives and menials, under the head of household cares, may frequently develop into drudgery, especially where the competition for reputability is close and strenuous. This is frequently the case in modern life. Where this happens, the domestic service which comprises the duties of this servant class might aptly be designated as wasted effort, rather than as vicarious leisure. But the latter term has the advantage of indicating the line of derivation of these domestic offices, as well as of neatly suggesting the substantial economic ground of their utility; for these occupations are chiefly useful as a method of imputing pecuniary reputability to the master or to the household on the ground that a given amount of time and effort is conspicuously wasted in that behalf."

Though there has been a lessening of the value we place on neatness, the fact remains that a degree of it is still necessary to every family's self respect. The symbolic value of good maintenance has simply shifted from the husband, as he slowly relinquishes his masterful role, to the family, as it evolves towards a democratic social unit. Veblen notes this shift as follows:

> "The largest manifestation of vicarious leisure in modern life is made up of what are called domestic duties. These duties are fast becoming a species of services performed, not so much for the individual behoof of the head of the household as for the reputability of the household taken as a corporate unit—a group of which the housewife is a member on a footing of ostensible equality."

Today we find the situation where the wife is literally sacrificed at the altar of the Joneses barbarous and inhumane. Our desire is to free women of as much menial labor as possible, even at the expense of housekeeping standards. Their looks, their intellectual development, their emotional balance, are seen as more

Picasso: Women by the Sea

important than a spotless house. But as if to counteract this trend, our greater emphasis on child care uses up the time formerly applied to housework. Thus the housewife is caught in the multihorned dilemma of desiring high standards of housekeeping, of not being able to accomplish them, of working as hard, nevertheless, as her mother, and of not being able to lead that outside life she so ardently desires. This is the housewife's most basic problem.

As if this were not enough, woman's social role is sometimes fraught with further and more delicate complications. She must also serve as symbol of her husband's socio-economic status, or even worse, must pretend to a status greater than is actually the case. A man is thought the better of as his wife is more beautiful or attractive sexually, and as she does less useful work. Her body, her sex attitudes, her clothes, accessories, hair—in short, every iota of her physical and social make-up are involved in this symbolization. Ideally, she should be ravishingly beautiful, very sexy, and do no useful work at all, spending her entire time making herself attractive, and in social or artistic affairs. Nowhere is this requirement more fully, if euphemistically expressed than in the women's magazines. Bernard de Voto parodies their currant image as

> "O bright Anadyomene! Foam-born or at least foam upborn in a verbena bubble bath, she is thin-faced as Botticelli's Venus was. We do not know about her hair, whether it be the same dull-red gold and long enough to reach her knees if modesty would free it to, because she has wrapped a towel around it. No, not a towel, this is a turban; she will wear it all day and her hair is soaked in olive oil; tomorrow, docilely yielding to a whim manufactured for her, she will change the part in it. Beside her on a stool are a half-emptied cocktail glass and a portable phonograph. Her lips are parted—perhaps they are moving too—and she is reading a book. It is Maurois' Portrait of a Genius. The phonograph is playing Saint-Saens' Sonata in D Minor. The genius of Maurois' title is Proust, and with Proust one takes Saint-Saens, as with the blanquette of veal for a family dinner one takes an unpretentious Beaujolais.
>
> So Vogue lets us see her. . . ."

No matter how laughable these serialized text books on how to live above one's status are, the fact remains that they fill an overwhelming and compulsive need. Our general desire is for women to consume beautifully. In the under-serviced household of our era, involving some sixty hours of housework and child care per week, it is impossible to live up to this picture. Yet men, and by extension women too, feel strongly that wives should symbolize their husbands' ability to provide both the things to be consumed, and the time in which to consume them.

The reputation of the wife suffers through lack of proper symbolism as well as that of the husband. Her social position is strengthened as she is married to a richer, or more predatory, or more talented, or more learned husband. And, at least in the two latter categories, as she marries a more complex man, her need for time in which to keep up with her husband and her milieu in terms of feeling, or information, becomes more acute. The tendency of our society is to demand of women good housework *and* intellectual equality. The wife must be desirable on both counts if she is to keep her sex life and self respect intact. To fail in only one of these areas may be to lose her economic security. Hemingway's hero, Colonel Cantwell, expresses our current sense of revolt from the beautiful but dumb:

> "With us, if a girl is really beautiful, she comes from Texas and maybe, with luck, she can tell you what month it is. They can all count good though.
>
> "They teach them how to count, and keep their legs together, and how to put their hair up in pin curls. Sometime, . . . for your sins, . . . you ought to have to sleep in a bed with a girl who has put her hair up in pin curls to be beautiful tomorrow. Not tonight. They'd never be beautiful tonight. For tomorrow, when we make the competition."

It is this increasing desire for sexual-intellectual-physical harmony which makes the charm and dress magazine formulas, those mandatory and manufactured whims, so ridiculous.

Until recently the housewife symbolized her subservient position vis-a-vis men by means of manners. Veblen notes that

> ". . . it is this aptitude and acquired skill in the formal manifestation of the servile relation that constitutes . . . one of the chief ornaments of the well-bred housewife."

Nowadays specialized manners are confined to the upper upper class. Rather than adopting this device, the upper middle class seems to be growing away from it. The housewife's actual role is evolving from that of the straw boss to that of equal partner in a team. This present stage in its evolution is often a difficult one. Most men have not yet entirely relinquished their assumption of supremacy. Nor have they fully accepted their new responsibilities. The concepts of the family as a cooperative, of children as personalities, are new and therefore take time to assimilate. Men's domestication is doubly difficult because they are immune to childbearing and, perhaps, partially immune to the full consequences of romantic love.

The sex characteristics which determine women's social role also harass her in other ways. The daily, weekly, and monthly cycles never allow her to forget that she cannot perform those social functions which her education and the sense of the times seem to promise. The housewife wears the contraceptives, not the husband. The housewife does the laundry, not the husband. More fundamental still, the menstrual period reappears like clockwork. Many women exhibit marked emotional disturbance before or during it, and are also physically weakened for a time. Pregnancy and the post-natal period also find them physically less able to work. The demands of children, particularly when young, are nervously exhausting, harrying, and very nearly continuous around the clock. Yet our ideal is that the wife must be calm, loving, and understanding of her children and husband under all circumstances. She must maintain this subjective-objective balance through loss of sleep, and of blood, in the constant crises of childrearing, during pregnancy, and post-natal weakness, and at the same time she must keep a good house. She must also maintain her relationship with her husband as it evolves and is affected by age and experience. And always, she must contrive to look as ornamental as it is possible for her to be. How to mitigate these problems of the upper middle class housewife with architectural means is the first fundamental question. In the most general and inclusive way, her needs might be listed (in no order because they are all equally important) as follows:

A sense of the cooperativeness of the family.

The least possible necessity for being segregated because of having to perform a "service" function.

Proper symbols of socio-economic class, in plan, appearance, furniture arrangement, and color.

Maximum ease of housework.

An effective and glamorous background for her as a sexual being, commensurate with the amount of energy she expends on clothes, make-up, and society.

Enough floor area, properly zoned, to foster full emotional and cultural development in her children.

An atmosphere and appearance which she can use creatively.

James Thurber: House and Woman.
Reproduced by permission. Copyright 1935, The New Yorker, Inc.

Husbands

The husband's social role is perhaps no less complicated than that of his wife, but since most of it is played in the outside world, his demands on his house are apt to be less complex than hers. The actual amount of time men spend at home varies too much to warrant any but the haziest generalizations. Certainly they do far less housework than their wives. The father's daily contact with the children is apt to be limited to a romp, or a social half hour before dinner or their bedtime, and to occasional night changing and comforting. The story of the suburban child who asked its mother "Who is that nice man who comes and stays with us on weekends?" is sharp commentary on the amount of time some upper middle class fathers spend at home. The husband's housekeeping activities are apt to be even less extensive. He may pick up his clothes, and infrequently help with the dishes. Then again, he may do neither. He is very apt to carve the meat, mow the lawn, light the fires, stoke the furnace, make alcoholic drinks, fix things, and either make himself, or have made, repairs and replacements to the house. There is so much flexibility in the amount of work men may elect to do that the architect, for want of a general pattern, must discover the facts in each individual case. Lewis Mumford, in commenting on the change in woman's status when the work shop became divorced from the house, did not mention the equally significant change which took place as a result of the same move—the divorce of the husband from the home.

The productive hours of man's day, with the exception of a few artists and professionals, are spent outside the house. The husband's pattern is like the sun's, one of diurnal foray and retreat. Indeed, he is sometimes seen by the children as a resplendant figure, bathed in the mystery of the outer world, who departs as the sun rises and returns as it sets. Behind him he leaves the symbols of his status. The armchair at the head of the table, all other chairs being armless, is beginning to disappear. But the belongings which are sacredly his, the guns, fishing tackle, books, shaving things, or perhaps his easy chair, remain to remind the family of his absence. When he returns he is tired, and insists on his paper, or his nap, or chat, or drink, or his play with the children, or whatever else he uses as a transitional activity between the day and the evening. Because he does use the home to rest up in, he is considered lazy, indolent, slightly tyrannical, and perhaps a little weak. "The Berrys," a comic strip of lower middle-class life, pictures him thus, frantically rushing to work in the morning, trying desperately to relax in the afternoon, avoiding small chores, resisting his boss, harried by his wife, very conscious and somewhat ashamed of his power as meal ticket, but withal to be depended upon in a pinch. The upper-middle class family is not immune from visions of its lord and master in this same light.

Carl Grubert: The Berrys.

Husbands

Coming home as he does, after his "hard day at the office," tired, and often somewhat disappointed with the world, he is very apt to find his wife equally tired and disgusted with housework and child care. And today, he is no longer allowed to grouse in his study as he was in the past. Gesell and Ilg note that:

> "A new era is opening for fathers. The status of children is changing; and the role of father in the home is coordinately changing. Not long ago he was truly a monarch. His word was law, and the law was stern. He held himself apart from the plain everyday affairs of his children, reserving his powers for higher occasions of discipline and admonition. He did not unbend. Even during the long prenatal period he maintained a fitting detachment.
>
> "All this is now changing under the irrepressible tide of cultural forces. Fathers are actively sharing in the numerous everyday tasks that go with the rearing of children. Participation rather than detachment is the trend. The careful mutual planning which now characterizes pregnancy and maternity hygiene marks a new advance in our ways of living. With the aid of the famous Broadway success *Life With Father* we wave a gay goodbye to the paterfamilias of the good old days.
>
> "The modern father is now in the process of finding his new role. He has already discovered that he is not satisfied by emergency help with night feedings and laundry, nor by sketchy contacts with his children at evenings or on a Saturday afternoon."

What will this mean in terms of house design? American men's impatience with inefficiency, together with an exact appreciation of the problems of child care, is likely to revolutionize not only the plans of houses, but the ridiculous bathinettes, pails, and "toidy seats" now foisted on long-suffering and uninventive women. As the father gradually consolidates his role as a working member of the family, our living patterns will undoubtedly change in many ways. Demands on the house in terms of privacy will certainly increase. More area and equipment may be required in order to allow children to parallel some of his activities. In particular, sharper and more complete divisions of functions may be necessary in order that certain of men's activities which are incompatible with children's can go on without conflict. If men work at home they must have a house which provides the requisite conditions.

While men may not yet see the house as a work place as far as they themselves are concerned, they do accept it, in a total sense, as their responsibility. In their role as head of the family, they are concerned with its defense against want, the elements, other men, etc. It is a sort of cocoon wrapped around their family for its protection. One of the frequent desires is that its design should express this relationship. Because men usually earn or control the money which carries the house, they are intensely concerned with the relationship between its cost and their total income. By and large, however, this does not mean they are more saving of money than women. It is indicative of men's relation to the family that where extra money is needed to symbolize socio-economic status, they are apt to be more willing to spend it than are women, who usually take a more practical view. The house is the most visible symbol of a man's ability to earn. His financial prowess is measured by its location, size, design, and appointments. The fact that men are interested at all in kitchen equipment and the like is perhaps because it is essential to the social image they desire their wives to live up to.

Veblen notes that

> "It is by no means an uncommon spectacle to find a man applying himself to work with the utmost assiduity, in order

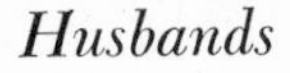

Saul Steinberg:

that his wife may in due form render for him that degree of vicarious leisure which the common sense of the time demands."

Men feel in most need of the symbolic support of proper design when they entertain. They are acutely conscious of the symbolism of entrance and living room. Entertaining is often a function of business or professional relations in general, and as such is seen as an extremely important matter. To indicate to a competitor that one's ability to earn is less than his is embarrassing to say the least. To make a favorable economic impression on a potential customer or client is often absolutely necessary to business or professional success. It may also be true that because of their greater experience with the world, men are by and large more understanding of the architect's problems than are women. They are sometimes willing to weigh such imponderables as expression and symbolism with the more practical aspects of building. Even when this is the case, however, it is a very rare person who will admit that he is dealing in symbols. Such judgments are seen as "not using cheap materials," or as "comfortable," or as, disarmingly, nostalgia for things past. Proposed variations from the norm are usually checked against inner references, or sometimes with the "little circle", and in the latter case, of course, are inevitably found wanting. The herd instinct is conservative. It would be a mistake to ascribe this kind of reaction to men only. Nevertheless it is more typical of men than of women. The architect who wishes to deviate must usually first persuade the husband that no loss of social prestige is involved.

In the most general sense, most of men's problems revolve around these symbolic themes. And as the wife is a symbol in herself, the keeper of most of the other symbols, and the one principally responsible for the emotional balance of his household, his problem revolves around her, rather than around his house. Lynn White, Jr. has noted:

> "The considerable, and apparently increasing, majority of college women will, and should, devote the first two or three decades after graduation to building and maintaining homes and families. This is a more arduous job than most men dream. Of the technical skills needed I shall speak presently. But a firm liberal education is of great help to a married woman. Her task is only partially to manage a house and keep the babies' noses blown. It is also to foster the intellectual and emotional life of her family and community, while avoiding the pitfall of being just an uplifter. To this end she must have and develop, and continue to cultivate as an integral part of her being, interests and enthusiasms which will infect her children, her neighbors and even her husband. An education, no matter how obviously useful and plausible, which fails to give

*Covarrubias: Leyak, (from a Balinese manuscript).**

a young woman capacity for this is inadequate. Cardinal Tisserant is reported to have said that 'women should be educated so that they can argue with their husbands.' While from such a source the remark may seem a sign of vicarious courage, many a happily married man will bear testimony that he would be less a man save for his wife's arguments, both spoken and unspoken."

Aside from such obvious needs as reasonable total carrying charges, appropriate symbols of class, adequate provision for maintenance of building and grounds, the husband's most vital requirement of the house is, perhaps, an arrangement which does most to facilitate communication with his wife.

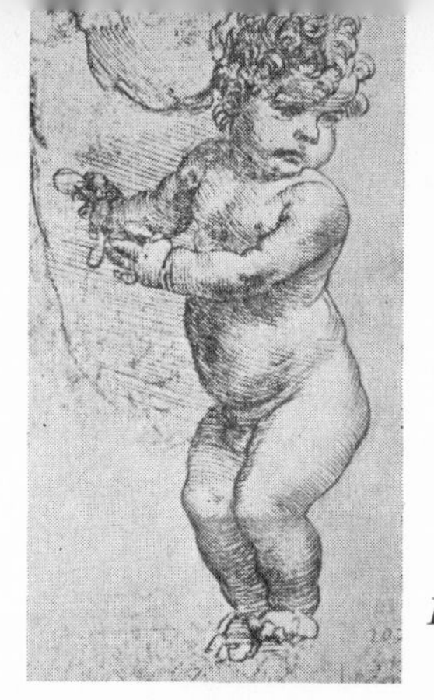

Leonardo da Vi[illegible]

Babies

The advent of the first child makes drastic changes in the living patterns of its parents. They are either tied down, or must carry their baby about with them, with all that entails in fuss and equipment, or they must depend heavily on others for help. It makes equally drastic changes in the way rooms are used, and thus in their proper area, arrangement and furnishings. Ideally, babies should have rooms of their own from the beginning. The American Public Health Association notes:

> "A child in the parents' bedroom inhibits full use of the room by adults and the child's sleep is apt to be disturbed. Child psychologists are agreed that, ideally, no child should ever share the parents' room, and certainly not after six months of age."

At birth, children sleep most of the time. More accurately, they have seven to eight sleep periods in a twenty-four hour stretch. They must be cared for immediately on each awakening. They are fed seven to eight times a day, which decreases to four or six feedings at four weeks, have three or four bowel movements a day as well as wet diapers when they awake. Their care and feeding is thus an around-the-clock activity. It is not hard work, but tiring because the mother's sleep is constantly interrupted. This is the period of the sleepy mother. As time goes on, the number of times a child must be fed and changed per day decreases slowly but steadily. At four months, he sleeps from six to six, has about three naps, feedings, and bowel movements a day and, as always, one bath. For the parents this is the easiest period they are to know. It is also the beginning of demands on the house. Babies nap best in a carriage, out of doors, in a sunny and protected place where, later, the playpen can be put up.

At seven months the child can sit up, and be fed with a cup and spoon in a high chair in the kitchen. Anything within his reach, which is often remarkably long, is no longer safe. At ten months he still goes to bed about six p.m. and wakes between five and seven. He sits up, has three meals, only one or two movements a day but numerous wettings. He is just beginning to be able to crawl about, and cannot be left alone on a bed, chair, or bathinette for one second unless he is strapped on.

Sometime between ten months and one year children begin to crawl in earnest. While they are more fun, they now need almost constant watching. One year marks the end of the easy to care for, supine, and undemanding baby. At this age he likes to cruise around the house on hands and knees, stand up holding on to chairs, knees, or tables, and as a result nothing lower than three feet is safe from him. The one-year-old's day is roughly as follows:

6 to 8 a.m.	Wakes, plays by himself 15–20 min., change diapers, clothes. Back to crib.
8:30	Breakfast, toileted, back in crib.
10:00	Changed, put outdoors in play pen.
10:45	Bath.
11:00	Nap.
1:00	Wakes, change diapers, clothes—cracker, high chair in kitchen.
2:00 p.m.	Ride in carriage, change.
3:00	Social hour with mother or others, change.
5:30	Supper.
6:00	To bed.
6:00 to 8	Falls asleep.

What this chart does not do is indicate the crisis nature of the period so blithely called "six to eight—falls asleep." As anyone who has struggled with a baby (and his own temper) through the cocktail, dinner, and clearing up hours knows, these are the times when child care really hurts.

In the most general way, the needs of this age are: bedroom near parents; sunny, quiet outdoor place protected from wind; space in kitchen, bathroom, and hall for the necessary equipment.

Dorothea Fox: Illustration from Dr. Benjamin Spock's "The Pocket Book of Baby and Child Care."

Children One to Five

At a year and three months, children begin to walk, and as time goes on, run around as continuously as possible. It is the age when gates appear at stairs and between rooms, wastebaskets are always overturned, and when the play pen disappears, since it is no longer acceptable. The fifteen monther will stay in his room for an hour, at most, in the morning. As the day wears on, his span of contentment at any one thing, in any one place, gets less and less. He is difficult to dress because he squirms unmercifully. He is difficult to put to bed because he calls his mother back many times. He is difficult to feed because he no longer simply spills his food, he throws it. He is difficult to toilet because he resists the pot, though a potty chair in the bathroom may help. He wakes at night, and must be comforted or changed. He cannot be trusted alone in any room but his own, and there only if it has been carefully and systematically arranged for him. He is a book tearer, wall paper picker, drawer and wastebasket tipper, furniture mover, climber, and self undresser. Nothing is really safe from him, and he is safe from nothing dangerous. As if to compensate, his charm is tremendous. He speaks a few words, enjoys company, dances to music in a delightful way, helps to dress and undress himself. His favorite room other than his own is the kitchen. Its potentialities and equipment hold all he desires.

At two the average child starts a trend in behavior which reaches a low point, as far as the parents are concerned, at two and one half, but turns into angelic behavior at three. He becomes limp and rubbery when being dressed, and runs away when you reach for him. He will not give up toys; he is in the snatch and grab stage. He begins at this time a habit to last for years, that of long soliloquies, particularly in the bath tub which he loves and is hard to get out of. These monologues are endless, loud, and dramatic. He demands long, drawn out and time consuming going to bed rituals, stories, endless adjustments, endless trips to the toilet, and endless last words. He begins to want to be left strictly alone on the toilet, but must be helped on and off, and wiped. While he still has bowel and bladder accidents in his pants, they begin to decrease. He can very effectively wreck a room he is left alone in because he now has the idea of using tools. He is apt to have difficulty with his parents together, or with parent and maid, demanding loudly that one or the other leave his sight. Gesell and Ilg call it the age of immoderation, of rampant conservatism and ritualism, or of wildness and destructiveness. But, as if again to compensate, he can be companionable and fascinating at times. He likes to help, particularly in the kitchen and at household repairs, though this "help" is apt to be a considerable nuisance. He passes plates of food, hammers nails, feeds himself at least half the time, goes to and enjoys nursery school. This last activity, from 9 to 12 on most weekdays, is an invaluable relief from his tyranny. This period sees the end of the baby carriage. He has now outgrown it. But that is usually replaced by a stroller, if walks are not to be too long and circumscribed. His day, condensed from Gesell and Ilg is about as follows:

5:00 to 9:00 a.m.	wakes
usually 8–8:30	toilet
	breakfast in bath robe, or dress, breakfast and nursery school.
9:30	play alone in room
10:30	toilet, dress, play outdoors
11:30	undress, toilet
12:00	lunch, feeds self, toilet
12:30	starts nap
1:00	put to sleep
2:00	wakes, toilet

3:00	walk, visit, or play in yard
5:00	supper, must be helped
5:45	play with father
7:00	bath
7:30	going to bed ritual
8:30	finally asleep
10:00 to 12:00	picked up to toilet

The two years between three and five start by the child's being willing and very ready to conform, and end in a lively, assertive, and boastful mood. They are delightful years. Waking up, while it may again be early, is apt not to start the day for the parents. The child will put his bathrobe on by himself and play alone for a while. He likes to visit his parents in their bed, and romp with his father before he gets up, or watch him shave. If left alone he can feed himself. While he may no longer sleep during his nap, he will play by himself, and only come out at the appointed hour. Going to bed loses its ritualistic character, and the child may even ask to go to bed of his own accord, though when the parents are going out he may create scenes, or cry until they come back, or until he falls asleep. At four, he wakes himself

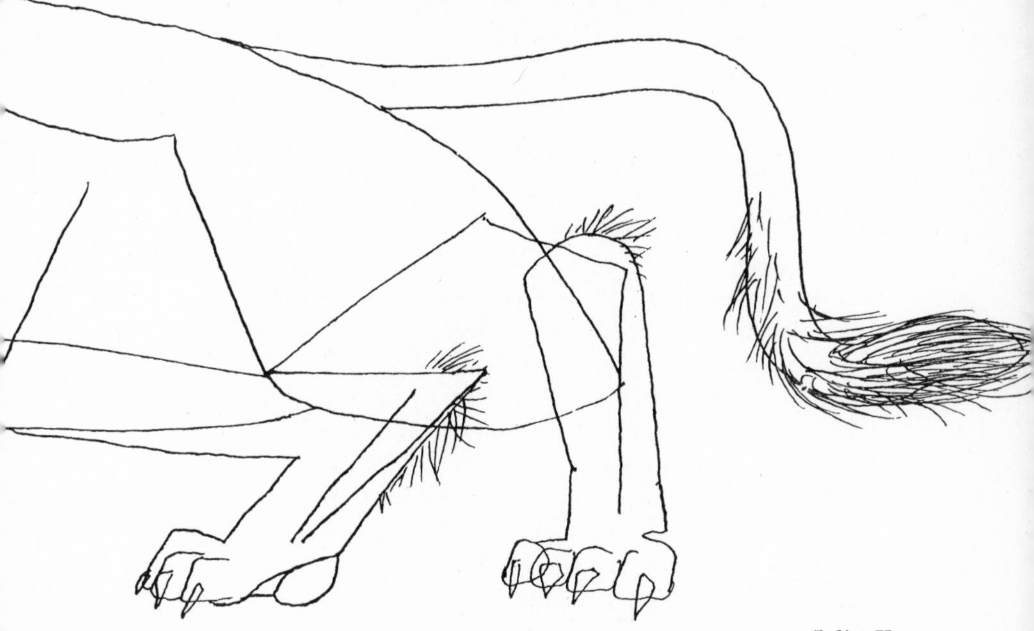

Juliet Kepes.

to go to the toilet, but as he dreams about wolves, he must sometimes be visited in the night to be comforted and reassured. Above all this age is imaginative. The principal and most symbolic places in the house, the fireplace, the kitchen sink, the landing in the stairs—have from the very beginning strong attractions for most children. They will always help make a fire, and often insist on herding the family around it as if a colored picture were to be taken for an advertisement for home life. They make "offices" and "forts" on the landings of stairs, avoid bears by stepping over the lines on the front walk, foxes by arranging the curtains in a certain way, and experiment with caves under the kitchen sink. They are animists from way back. A. A. Milne's poetry for children is a dictionary of these areas of sympathetic magic. What makes a house more or less subject to the spell cast by children is impossible to formalize. Alvar Aalto, the great Finnish architect, perhaps came closest to it when he said to a student showing him plans for a nursery school, "This is all right as far as it goes, but where does the lion live?" Wherever he lurks in the house, and however nice he has been, the school age child throws him out, once and for all.

School Children

This period roughly from five or six to eleven or twelve, carries the child from babyhood (for they are still in that stage at five) to teen-agism. It spans a tremendous change, not only in the child, but also in the parent-child and house-child relationship. Children enter it more or less totally dependent on their parents' supervision, help, and direction. They also accept these same parents as all-seeing, and all-knowing. At its close they have largely transferred their loyalty to the gang, and can bring extraordinarily accurate insights to bear on the social relations and personalities of the various members of their family. The intellectual climate of the age is one of squalls. The children begin to size up and be critical of their parents as people. As their talents begin to be revealed, mechanical, artistic, social, etc., the parents in turn may feel critical or disappointed. It is a period of dawning objectivity. This quality can infuse the mother-father relationship as well, and thus affect the whole family. Husband and wife have been through romantic love, the adjustments of early marriage, the excitement of child making, the charming and somehow creative period of little children, and are apt to come face to face with each other without intervening layers of romanticism, hope, and unrealized potentials. Objectivity can produce stark moments. During this period the family must realign itself several times. Such adjustments are perhaps made easier by the fact that the school age child forces certain changes of his own accord and, perhaps as a result, makes it easier for the father and mother to change and reconsolidate their own relationship.

While the amount of sheer work which must be spent on the care and training of children steadily decreases, it is still, for this new period, an important segment of the housewife's total working hours. This is the heyday of children's communicable diseases. Chicken pox, measles, scarlet fever, mumps, and the like, follow each other with monotonous regularity through the fifth, sixth, and seventh years, not to mention colds and other such minor ailments, plus a succession of accidents. At eight, children are physically daring, always on the go, running, climbing trees, beginning organized sports, and riding bicycles, yet they have by no means reached maturity either of muscular coordination or judgment. Deaths from falls, drowning, and automobile accidents reach a peak. Outdoor play space, flat, and suitable for a variety of functions, is vitally needed. Children of this age need and really use it, in a concentrated and fairly well organized manner. The constant watchfulness which characterizes the period immediately preceding is no longer necessary, or possible or, indeed, suitable. But as they are still learning the social game, they inevitably get into trouble which may sometimes be ameliorated by quick adult action.

The period seven to eight seems to be the break point as far as dressing and putting to bed are concerned. The seven-year old still needs help and a small amount of comfort. The eight-year old can do it himself. The long, drawn out and boring rituals of an earlier age have disappeared. Six is nearly the end of night toileting, though bad dreams still occur and sometimes need to be dealt with. Losing clothes and extreme messiness, alternating with fits and starts of neatness which come under the heading of turning over a new leaf, are characteristic. As this is human and compulsive, ample provision for the storage of toys and belongings is no solution in itself. But the simpler this storage is, the more apt it is to be used. Bins and hooks rather than drawers, trays, or poles with hangers, are the easiest and most direct way to achieve a purposeful and usable mess.

Manners, in particular and in general, are the most obvious themes of the school age period. Both the parents and the children are apt to be fascinated by the subject. The children's first interest lies chiefly in the modes of getting on with their friends. They are totally uninterested in table manners, which usually range from bad to atrocious. But at the age of nine they improve rapidly, and may even become so polished they put their family to shame. Gesell and Ilg go so far as to recommend that the six-year old be given a tray beside his omnipresent radio, at least for his evening meal. This perhaps is a sensible suggestion in that it relieves both camps of irritation—the one of chaos, the other of nagging. For those who were, in their childhood, sent to the bathtub to finish their dinner, it seems almost too humane. This group of school age behavior problems is chiefly significant for the parents. But if it is well handled by the adults, and if the house is designed to make adult responsibilities easy, the children may avoid a lot of unnecessary bad temper and nagging.

At the same time the children are exerting new pressures of their own on house and family. Most of these have to do with space, privacy, and noise. The child of two to five has been satisfied, as far as cultural noise is concerned, with a phonograph and a small collection of his own records. At five or six he quite suddenly develops an overwhelming and completely absorbing interest in the radio, or the television screen. At six or seven he may only want to look and listen endlessly. He becomes glued to his set, and behaves as if he were in a trance. Children's hours, Westerns, detectives, soap operas, news, are all grist to his mill. He is introduced to western culture through the back-house door, but maybe this is appropriate to our growth process—one of slow emergence from and then return to a primitive state. This first flush of absorption wears off in time, and is replaced by a ritualistic observance of a few programs which proceed to permeate his whole life. The Lone Ranger, or whoever his dream merchant may be, fills the house with frontier talk and allusions, the sound of gunfire on the western plains (strictly as produced by a sound effects man), war whoops, elaborate stage coaches made of chairs and blankets, and similar props.

At this point comic books enter the picture, replacing as a text the indiscriminate radio listening. As they take at most a half hour to read, they come in force and involve much traffic in money and swaps, with all the attendant business of telephoning, business conferences, and sharp practices. The indiscriminate phase of the comics also wears off, to be replaced with children's classics. The nine-year old likes to read in bed, though the younger ones become completely absorbed in their books anywhere. In this phase they really need the kind of bed-table an adult requires, with space for radio, reading light, books, and personal possessions. They also need certain other furniture and storage space. As they become more and more fully aware of the breadth and depth of our culture, they strike out into some particular phase of it—religion, music lessons, collections of leaves and stamps, model airplane making, electric trains, mechano sets, and so forth. Indeed, they may all be tried and abandoned, or tried and then re-tried, thus compounding the need for storage space, area, and noise control. The same proliferation occurs outdoors, and space must be found for the proper storage and preservation of a host of sports equipment—balls, bats, bows and arrows, bicycles, skis, and the like.

These years are extraordinarily active, characterized by great boisterousness and constant running around, falling, sliding and foot dragging. All of this cannot be confined to outdoors. Most boys like to rough-house with their fathers. Some would even make it a nightly ritual. As it loses its charm, they take to tumbling on a mattress, or just plain horsing around. Some place where they can let off high pressure steam without irritating adults, hurting themselves, or breaking things is tremendously useful. Five- and six-year olds like to paint, and have a natural genius for it. Some children continue to paint pictures, others take to painting scenery, models, and the various other things they make. They not only need but demand supervision at such

Dorothea Fox: Illustration from Dr. Benjamin Spock's "The Pocket Book of Baby and Child Care."

tasks. Gesell characterizes the eight-year old as under foot, and indeed he is always pestering for glue, paper, paint, wire, wood, tools, etc., let alone for help and instructions. If his activities and the necessary equipment can be localized near the kitchen, from which most supervision emanates, a great deal of fuss can be avoided. In a plan of this sort, the father's own tools and work place must be in the same location, but preferably locked, not only to save the transfer or duplication of materials and tools, but because he is inevitably involved in most of the more mechanical aspects of construction. Housewives, and especially maids, whether by nature or in sheer self-defense, are usually inept at anything involving more complicated tools than a high-heeled slipper, a bobby pin, and a nail file. A large part of some fathers' enjoyment of home life arises from these joint projects. As they get more complicated, and as the child's standards of performance get higher, they can involve a lot of effort, pride, and joy.

Children in this age group are not always boisterous, noisy, active, or listening to the radio. In fact, as it progresses, they have more and more need for privacy and passive recreation. They will play cards, chess, dominoes, and a variety of other games of concentration with great earnestness and even passion. To lose quietly is an important and difficult lesson to learn. They will converse after a fashion, and listen avidly to adults' conversation. At nine they begin to want the family to act properly, with manners, decorum, and style, and according to the Joneses. Sex characteristics emerge at ten, and with them the beginning of secrets, and the absolute necessity for privacy.

Homework also starts in these years, and involves a new adjustment, not only for the child, but for the family. Its value is perhaps as much in the discipline enforced, as in the preparation achieved. Where it is to be done is best decided in each individual case. But certainly most children respond with delight to a desk in their room, particularly if it is fitted with drawers, book shelves, pen, ink, etc. Such accessories lend it adult and thus honorific overtones, and as a result make homework far less onerous. In the teens, it is an essential adjunct to every child's room.

Teen Agers

The adolescent exhibits certain typical drives which put new demands on the house. The principal emphasis of the age is on social learning. This may start with a tendency to pick out, as an object of love or admiration, some one older person of the same or opposite sex. But from the age of fourteen to sixteen for girls, and from fourteen and a half to seventeen for boys, the pattern becomes one of attraction towards and companionship with members of the opposite sex. As Dr. Kinsey has indicated this is a highly sexed age. Yet our culture, particularly that part of it represented by the intellectual middle class, puts the most stringent taboos on sex. Lewis Mumford has remarked that

> ". . . as children draw on toward maturity, they need, no less than their parents, inviolate apartments in which their hot discussions, their high confidences, their first essays in courtship, may take place. For lack of such space in American homes, a whole generation of girls and boys has grown up, cramped in the vulgar promiscuities of the automobile, from which they are too often graduated proudly into the no less shabby intimacies of the roadhouse or the overnight cabin: carrying into their erotic life the taint of something that is harried, esthetically embarrassing and emotionally disintegrating."

In a period when the chief emphasis is on the acquisition of social skills, to be forced to learn in such circumstances *is* disintegrating. The manners and attitudes which the teenager so desires to acquire are, furthermore, exactly those of the adult. The California Growth Study indicated that after having gone through several periods in which different values were placed on various social skills and types of adjustment, boys ended up by asking tidiness, social ease, and "poise" of their contemporaries, while girls admired the well-groomed, sophisticated girl, attractive to the "right" boys.

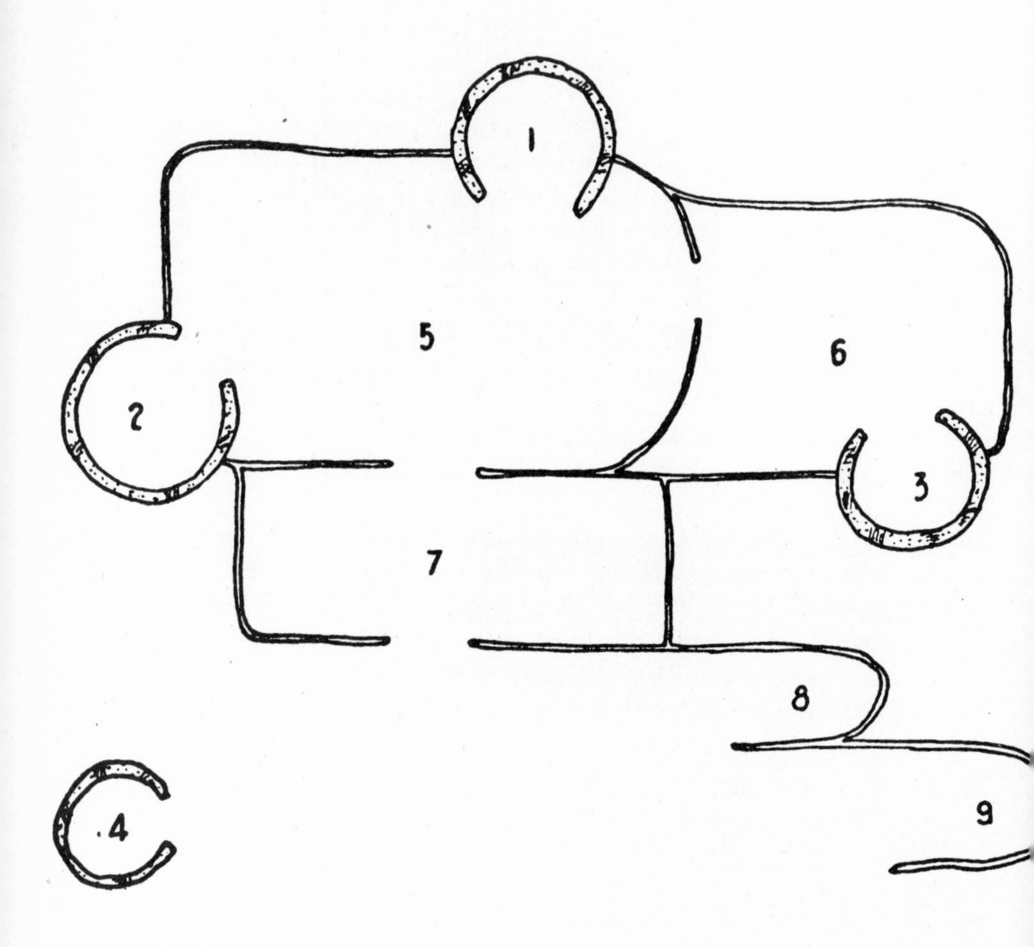

Plan, Yungur Compound, Africa. After Meek. 1. Kitchen hut; 2. Sleeping hut—man and wife; 3. Sleeping hut—affianced daughter; 4. Sleeping hut—young male children; 5. Roofed sitting room; 6. Roofed room private to daughter and fiance; 7. Roofed sitting room and store; 8. Unroofed pot storage; 9. Unroofed beer making yard. The disposition of functions, circulation, and degree of privacy allotted the living activities all run counter to our western sense of how such things should be arranged. Nevertheless this scheme would seem to contain some remarkably humane notions.

Teen Agers

Teen-agers suffer acutely from adult ridicule of their awkwardness. Clumsiness,—the breaking of bric-a-brac—is in fact one of their chief problems. They have no greater wish to wreak havoc than their parents, cannot help it, and thus feel doubly guilty and disturbed. Fleming remarks that:

> "This sense of inferiority may be increased by comments on the disproportionate over-development of feet or hands which results in clumsiness and awkwardness which are socially annoying—especially in the small over-crowded houses to which many adolescents are required to adapt their changing bodily dimensions."

This would seem to indicate that space and lots of it, and a certain solidity and massiveness of furniture and even walls is an important requisite. With this concern over manners goes an even deeper one with appearance. The period, tragically, is apt to be accompanied by pimples and rashes of glandular origin, which are embarrassing in the extreme. Even when the adolescent is mercifully spared this particular cross, appearance in general, plain good looks, big enough breasts, broad enough shoulders and the like, are still in the balance. It is the time when both boys and girls begin to experiment with cosmetics, the boys being held by the taboos of our culture pretty much to hair tonic and shaving lotion, or to manly perfumes.

Adolescent anger, so often remarked on, is usually caused by a social slight, or what appears to be a slight. The adolescent is desperately desirous of being accepted by his peers, and by his parents, as an adult. To be thwarted in this desire is the most difficult cross he must bear. By the same token, unfamiliar social occasions are apt to be terrifying. The tongue-tied adolescent, so often thought to be merely boorish, is more apt to be undergoing a paroxysm which would exhaust an older man. The elaborate plans and excuses made to avoid a dance or party are symptoms of the same phenomenon. So is extreme aggressiveness. Quick alternations of hope and despair are typical of all ages in the face of unknown and terrifying situations. When hounded by such emotions, adolescents need opportunity to watch one another from relative privacy and, when the plunge is finally made, to accomplish it unobtrusively. Fleming notes that the critical attitude taken by adults brings a correspondingly increased fear of being ridiculous.

> "For these reasons it seems important that adolescents should have a place of their own in which their tentative approaches to participation can be made without undue publicity or distress."

Another set of adolescent difficulties are superficially somewhat contradictory. Teenagers need and ardently desire independence, and at the same time feel an equal need for companionship with their parents. These two desires, however, seem less at variance when they are recognized as the prerequisites of adult status. The adolescent desires to get out and explore the world, and only creates scenes when he is prevented from doing so. Parents who place obstacles in his way, because they feel this desire indicates an emotional withdrawal, retard their children's development. New experience is as much a basic need of the age as security. Both can only be achieved if the adolescent is recognized and responded to on his real level of development. Fleming lists the teen-ager's needs as: acceptance by the group, tenderness, admiration, appreciation, the opportunity to learn new things, understanding, and some regular and genuine responsibility in the home. Most of these needs are supplied operationally, that is, as a function of the personalities in the family. But the ability to give and receive them generously is certainly affected by the house. The teen-ager's basic needs in this latter respect are perhaps as follows:

A room of his own, where he can retreat from the world.

An arrangement which will allow him to entertain boisterously, noisily, and destructively in privacy, and without impinging on the privacy of others. The ability to drift, unobtrusively, into the kitchen, or even into the basement in order to catch his social breath, seems to be a secondary aspect of this need.

Artist unknown: Roman Matron, Empire Period.

Grandparents

The very characteristic which makes upper middle class parents the architect's best clients is the one which makes their relationship with the aged so difficult. If class patterns of parent-child relationships can be characterized, the way of this group would probably be that of parent rejection. It tends to discard the patterns of the generation which trained it in favor of new ways which it conceives of as better suited to the new times in which it must operate. As a result the parents' ideas are often seen as old fashioned and impractical, in fact, tiresomely so. Thoreau says of them:

> "What old people say you cannot do you try and find that you can. Old deeds for old people, and new deeds for new. Old people did not know enough once, perchance, to fetch fuel to keep the fire a-going; new people put a little dry wood under a pot, and are whirled round the globe with the speed of birds, in a way to kill old people, as the phrase is. Age is no better, hardly so well, qualified for an instructor as youth,

for it has not profited so much as it has lost. One may almost doubt if the wisest man has learned anything of absolute value by living. Practically, the old have no very important advice to give the young, their own experience has been so partial, and their lives have been such miserable failures, for private reasons, as they must believe; and it may be that they have some faith left which belies that experience, and they are only less young than they were."

Both groups of course insist on the rightness of their own approach to life. The two ways often seem irreconcilable. Consequently relations between generations are seldom completely happy or open. Both refrain from a full accounting of their thoughts in order not to hurt the other. Their friendship tends to take on the reserve and the caution of Republicans and Democrats in an election year. It is for this reason that the upper middle class does not, in general, believe that the three generations should live together. When one of the parent's parents comes to live with the family, a difficult atmosphere is created. The middle generation is often still in revolt, still exploring new attitudes towards life. The youngest, so far away in time, are apt to look on their grandparents as relics from an antediluvian period. Even in the most successful joint ventures, tension between generations lurks in the background.

Where the grandparents are hale of body and mind, their demands on the house, and their problems vis-a-vis the family may not be of great moment architecturally. But as they are more immured in the patterns and attitudes of their generation, less competent physically, or less healthy, their problems multiply. They join the family as aware of the general distrust of the relationship as are their children, and are thus usually disturbed by a sense of guilt—of imposing on others. Their efforts to overcome this feeling by means of financial or physical help often turn out badly. Their outdated ways of doing things may cause more trouble than if they had done nothing at all. It sometimes happens that the most help they can offer is to do as many things for themselves as they can, and in general play the least possible role in the family. This may be physically or psychologically impossible, or it may be exactly what is wanted. The aged besides being physically weak often turn their minds and energies away from the future, which so occupies the young, to become involved in an endless review of their past. This process, perhaps a preparation for death, is at its best a terribly human attempt to rationalize the meaning of life. It is not entirely a mental process. Marcel Proust, so it is said, long after he had retired to his cork-lined room, went out on occasion to ask some friend of his youth to exhume an old hat or dress from her attic. So the aged often depend heavily on the mementos of their active years. Their rooms are often veritable collections of memorabilia. At the same time they are also apt to desire a degree of comfort or even of luxury. This is due not only to the fact that they have usually closed up establishments of their own from which they have kept the best bric-a-brac, but also to the fact that comfort and luxury are real necessities for the aged. They have done their work, raised their children, suffered their troubles, and feel that their old bones deserve the soft places. The rites of comfort become ritualistic. Dressing, bathing, tidying, and those minor chores, which in the prime of life take so little time, now consume numberless hours, and are performed in meaningful and reminiscent ways.

As the process of living today and reliving yesterday becomes more complex and time-consuming, the need for company is apt to become less important. The aged can take or leave most of the amusements so important to the young, and are often content to leave them. Strong notes that

> "Older men also prefer, more than younger men do, those amusements pursued largely alone in contrast to ones involving others."

And, while he found that most likes and dislikes occur less frequently as men advance in age, certain others occur more often. The likes which showed the most significant increases with age were: raising flowers and vegetables (18%); decorating a room with flowers (6%); teaching adults (6%); making a speech (6%); adjusting difficulties of others (7%); being left to oneself (9%);

methodical work (16%); continuing same work until finished (11%); contributing to charities (27%); conservative people (8%); cautious people (11%); cripples (10%); methodical people (24%); independents in politics (18%). The likes which showed significant decreases were: arguments (–13%); organizing a play (–14%); calling friends by nicknames (–22%); being called by a nickname (–25%); continuously changing activities (–17%); and so forth. Dr. Strong's list characterizes the older man as tending towards dignity, and habit, and as intensely desirous of helping both his friends and people at large, as long as he does not have to have too much contact with them.

When the elderly live with their children and children's children, their need of amusement is often automatically taken care of by the family itself. No matter how far it may have progressed away from the patterns of the grandparents' generation, no matter how outlandish and newfangled its organization and customs may appear, it is the most vital, visible, and potent symbol of the elders' own creative period. Despite the fact they may fail to understand, or may be bewildered by their offspring, they are still proud of the achievement their children and grandchildren represent. It is indeed pardonable that they say, literally, "We created this," and it is touching when they manage to feel pride in the hydra-headed monster of their creation. It is their dearest wish that the family live up, somehow, to their image of what they wished it might have been. On visiting days when they are entertaining guests of their own age, the kind and understanding family dresses for the occasion, arranges itself and its house for the ritual, suppresses its vitality, and acts out a play for which the grandparents are eternally grateful.

The needs of the aged might be summarized as follows:

A sense of being useful.
The ability to retire, both physically and emotionally from the hurly-burly of the family.
A modicum of luxury and comfort.
The possibility of entertaining friends of their own generation in their own way.
Provision for safety and convenience commensurate with their failing physical abilities.

Servants

"Meantime Charley entered as Mrs. Tennant yawned. She said to him, 'Oh yes I rang didn't I, Arthur,' she said, and he was called by that name as every footman from the first had been called, whose name had really been Arthur, all the Toms, Harrys, Percys, Victors one after the other, all called Arthur. 'Have you seen a gardening glove of mine? One of a pair I brought back from London?'

" 'No Madam.'

" 'Ask if any of the other servants have come across it will you? Such a nuisance.'

" 'Yes Madam.'

" 'And, oh tell me, how is Eldon?'

" 'Much about the same I believe Madam.'

" 'Dear, dear. Yes thank you Arthur. That will be all. Listen though. I expect Doctor Connoly will be here directly.'

"He went out, shutting the mahogany door without a sound. After twenty trained paces he closed a green baize door behind him. As it clicked he called out, 'Now me lad she wants that glove and don't forget.' "*

Until recently, at least in the coastal cities, a servant whose parents were born in this country was a rarity. The kitchen, in atmosphere, was more often than not as far from the rest of the house as the other side of the world. It was the domain of Kasha, the tea drinking Irish Catholic cook, of Joe the Japanese butler, of "Charlsie Dear," the negro ex-slave and man of all work, or of Marie the French Canadian maid. Their pet names, given them by the children, were as much a reflection of the fascination they held as representatives from a different culture, land, and class, as they were of personal endearment. And this sense of domain often transcended mere atmosphere. The very appoint-

*From "Loving", by Henry Green, The Viking Press, 1949.

ments of the kitchen, its furniture, equipment, and arrangement were sometimes compromised so that they might recall the pattern of a distant country. With the end of mass migration the constant supply of foreign servants has ceased. And due in part to the tendency of our culture to take on middle class manners, trained servants, that is, a group who know how to express the servile relation in traditional European form, are disappearing. The servant of the future seems destined to be a self-important specialized helper rather than the self-effacing general drudge, or highly trained decorative adjunct of the past.

Several factors are operating to change and equalize the family-servant relationship. But the extent of its evolution is often, and mistakenly, overestimated. The servant is still unrelated to the family, still paid to perform certain services, still of a lower socio-economic status, still less well educated, still looked on as a utility with certain advantages and liabilities. Nevertheless there have been sufficient changes in the family's attitude towards servants, and their's towards the family to make the plans of most old houses obsolete. The change from a foreign to a domestic background is the most potent reason for this. The American Dream, with its insistence on the idea of equality between people, cannot help but force its forms on everyone. Servility, once an asset in a servant from the master's point of view, is now repugnant to both. The servant's "rights" now not only exist in the abstract, they can be enforced. They must be recognized physically and operationally. They are also reflected in social relations within the family. The maid is a human being who was born equal to her mistress even if she has not maintained equal status with her since the instant of birth. The basic unreality of this point of view, where each party is pretending to a relationship they are both apt to realize is false, creates a difficult situation. As a result, native working class people would rather not be servants. This trend is implemented by the fact that there are better paying and less arduous jobs outside the house, and by the fact that upper middle class families are increasingly unable to afford traditional service, even when it is available. Furthermore, the false social situation, the reduction in privacy involved, the fact that they often wish to isolate their children from certain working class religious and cultural phenomena, all conspire to make constant service less desirable.

An inevitable result is specialization. It is advantageous for the servant, who becomes a minor sort of expert, and thus achieves greater freedom. The housewife gains in privacy, and is absolved of paternal responsibility, as their relationship becomes more businesslike. She may hire and fire, and is not bound to provide pensions. The relationship becomes typical of business, where social irresponsibility and personal autonomy are the order of the day. The extension of Social Security to domestic help reflects this new situation. The maid of all work, or the cook, or the laundress have more or less disappeared in favor of such categories as the cleaning woman, the baby sitter, the mother's helper and the like, all of whom will perform only certain fixed tasks. The way the individual family uses its service hours varies tremendously. A few examples might serve to point up the choices.

1. A maid who "lives in" and whose duties are cooking and house cleaning, but often not making beds or tidying up, or laundry, or any but occasional child care.
2. A cleaning woman who comes in to wash floors, windows, sweep, mop and perhaps iron.
3. A baby sitter who comes while both parents are out, but who will do no dish washing or other useful work.
4. A mother's helper who will come in for certain limited hours to look after children and feed them, but who will do no work such as cleaning or cooking the parents' dinner.
5. A maid who comes in to do light cleaning, bed making, ironing, etc. while the housewife cares for the children.
6. A maid who comes in to clean up after, and/or serve at a dinner party in order to allow the housewife to participate fully with her guests.

As these possibilities are all so dependent on income, living pattern, background, and mobility, no generalization in terms of architecture would seem to be worthwhile. But three general areas for question do emerge, each of which will be considered in detail later. The first of these has to do with the cases in which the housewife performs certain functions at certain times, while a servant performs them at others, and where the privacy arrangements must be altered for each situation. For example, some women treat a maid as a more or less equal partner during the day and desire a plan which facilitates joint work. But at night, particularly if guests are present, they may wish complete separation of dining and cooking areas, and a general air of formality accompanied by "service" in the traditional sense. Compromises of this sort range, architecturally speaking, from a plan which is basically for day, the night time need for formality being satisfied by an essentially symbolic adjustment, to a plan which is flexible enough to satisfy both requirements completely.

The second and third areas are similar in that they have to do with the servant's sense of domain, and the family's sense of privacy. They involve the question of what is needed in both respects, by the servant who lives in, and by the servant who comes in. The facilities provided in the two cases are very different. The social attitude they represent however must be identical if both camps are to be comfortable. Provision must be made for every living function involved in the specific operation, commensurate with the trend toward a businesslike relationship, the eight-hour day, and the feeling that the servant, particularly as regards child care, has a significant responsibility. But at the same time, excessive building costs have resulted in a trend towards scandalously cramped maids' and couples' rooms, with little or no space for them elsewhere. If for no other reason, it seems unrealistic not to provide servants with the best possible working conditions, since it is becoming increasingly difficult to get them at all. Not only will they move on unless treated well by their physical environment, as well as by the people concerned, but they may be so harried by the house as to create tensions throughout the family.

The servant's principal needs might be summarized as follows:

A sense of domain,
Adequate provision for all the living functions to be performed in the house,
Well planned work sequences,
A plan which recognizes the owners' privacy attitudes, so that embarrassment and irritation for both parties are avoided.

Alan Dunn: "Come here a minute, Anna—I want to show you how to make the dining room—"

George Cruikshank: "My wife is a superior spirit."

The drawing on the facing page is of a relief by J. Della Quercia, Church of S. Petronio, Bologna.

CHAPTER III

Families

Organization

THESE THUMBNAIL SKETCHES of wives, husbands, children by various age groups, grandparents, and servants, describe the members of a household. But they in no wise describe a family. As the family, rather than the individual client, is the unit the house is designed to serve, a closer definition of some sort is essential. Cavan has described it as follows:

> "The American family is a group composed of parents and children, bound together by common needs, a feeling of loyalty and affection, and the belief that incorporation in the family provides a good way to live; adults enter family life by way of a publicly recorded wedding ceremony after a free choice of mates from the same racial and cultural background; only one spouse may be had at a time, but divorce provides release under certain conditions; the family is organized around the father as the head of the family; children enter the family through birth (or adoption) following the legal marriage, and the family provides for their care and education; the family is the accepted outlet for affection and sexual relations and fulfills many other functions for all members of the family; the family is a public institution, controlled by laws."

This definition leaves much to be desired, and so would any other of finite length. Architecturally speaking, the important facts are, perhaps, that men impregnate women, that human children are helpless for many years and must be nurtured by their parents, that children need other children to play with if they are to develop normally, that grandparents, like babies, are often helpless and must depend on their children for physical help, that the creation of children is as important a need of the parents as the parents are of the children, and so on and so forth. Ideally, the family is a "Strength *and* Joy through Mutual Cooperation Association."

The practical nature of these reciprocities still does not fully explain why families cohere. Ogburn, in one attack on the problem, postulates seven bonds of family union. Chapin describes their uses as follows:

> "Those functions of the family involved in shaping the personalities of the children depend upon the affectional, recreational and protective bonds, whereas the function of passing on the social heritage is perhaps more closely connected with the economic, religious, educational and status bonds. Obviously the kinship family group develops the former, while the household contributes to the latter."

The house plays a part in each of these categories, with the possible exception of the religious:

Affectional	in reducing tensions due to overwork, lack of privacy, and inadequacy of status symbolism.
Recreational	through the provision of proper area, facilities, and status symbols.
Protective	against climate, other human beings, social exposure, and the like.
Economic	through proper adjustment of capital costs, operating costs, family spending patterns, and income.
Religious	no obvious connection.
Educational	through proper provisions for study and as a repository for the tools of acculturation.
Status	as accurate reflection of the family's image of the class standards with which it is identified.

The strength of these bonds, and the social import of the family as a whole depend in part on the family's organization. Rosow discovered that the good houses in his sample had been built by equalitarian families, while the poor ones had generally been built by the authoritarian variety. He notes:

> "Modern clients showed a stronger pre-disposition to equal planning roles for the adult family members, while the Semi-Modern tendency showed the main influence to reside in one of the spouses. A conscious recognition of the needs of the children in the family was more conspicuous in the Modern group than among Semi-Modern clients."

The living patterns of the two kinds of family vary in architecturally significant ways. Each day's activities are different, and the way in which they are performed varies. Chapin describes them as follows:

> "The differences between the two family patterns are striking. Parents in the Xa (Equalitarian) type are more than three times as active in other groups as parents in the Ya (Authoritarian) type, and the children are over 16 per cent more active than the Ya children. There are over four times as many meetings in the homes of the Xa type as of the Ya type. The schooling of the Xa parents is far superior to that of the Ya parents. Family size, both in the parental generation and in the present generation, is smaller in the Xa type than in the Ya type. Clearly those traits that are commonly regarded as of social value are more largely possessed by the family with equalitarian pattern of organization than by the family with the authoritatian pattern of organization."

As the authoritarian family presents the architect with a problem which usually cannot be successfully resolved, there is little point in pursuing it here.

Basic family living patterns revolve around the daily chores. The outstanding requirement for their performance is the ability to give and take directions, to understand one's own and others' roles, and to compensate for others' basic or momentary inabilities. Ideally, each of the family's members should be communicative, cooperative, and understanding.

These qualities apply not only to individuals, but also to sub-groups within the family. The separate parts of the family are, obviously, people. These "parts" have been examined above as actors playing certain roles based on their age, experience, and sex. One cannot play a role alone. It must be played out with and for other people. Thus, implicit to the role "father" is that of "mother," to the role "children" that of "parents," and so on. Indeed, the parts, like magnets, automatically click together into sub-assemblies. These sub-groups, or "cultural categories" as Professor John Whiting of Harvard has called them, even after they are combined to form the whole family, continue to act independently. Each unit is held together by approximately equal age and experience.

The sub-groups not only cohere. They are seen by the other individuals of the family as units with their own levels of communication. We use different words to describe the members of the family depending on whether we are looking at them as individuals, in a role, in a sub-group, or as between sub-groups. A father is, in various guises, Mr. John Doe, John, husband, father, spouse, and parent. His responsibilities in each of these roles are slightly different. One does not communicate with one's spouse in exactly the same way as with one's children or grandparents. Thus the number of channels of communication in the family can serve here as a rough indication of the complexity of the group. The sub-groups can be visualized diagrammatically as follows:

INDIVIDUALS					CHANNELS		SUB GROUPS
Husband Wife	= =	Father Mother	♂ ♀	=	2	=	Parents
		Boy Girl	♂ ♀	=	2	=	Children
		Boy Boy Girl	♂ ♂ ♀	=	6	=	Children
		Servant	⚥	=	0	=	Servant

Organization

The diagrams indicate that a single individual has no channels of communication, while a group of three have three times as many as two, which would appear to be a rough approximation of reality. When putting these sub-groups together to form a whole family, again for architectural purposes, the give and take between cultural categories is more important than that between individuals. A great deal of intra-family life is just that, for example, the children giving a play for the adults, or the adults as a group feeding the children. The sub-groups, put together and connected with two-way communication channels, then look like this.

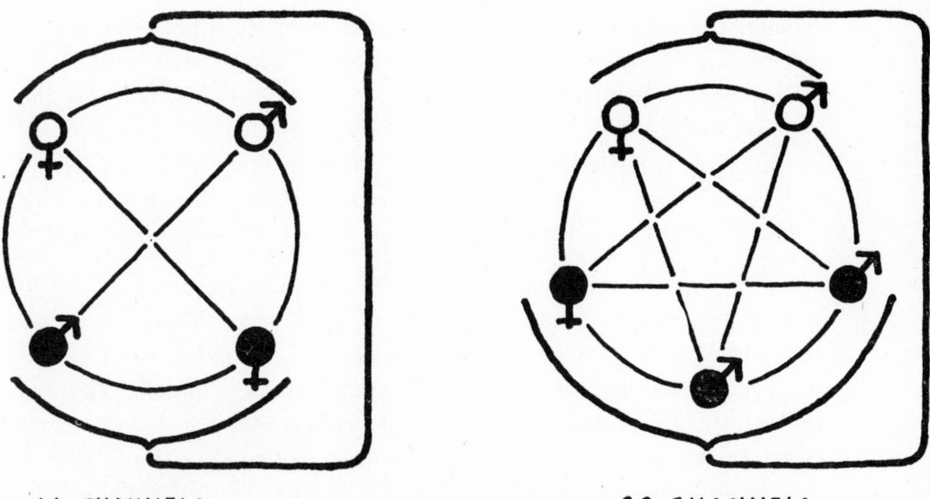

The complexity of a house plan, both as to the number of zones it contains, and as to the interior arrangements within zones, is directly related to the structure of the family seen in this light. Some families maintain a remarkably simple organization, particularly those with only three members. The dangers of single children are much touted. But the difficulties which beset the resulting triangular family are not, as yet, well documented. Such families labor under subtle disadvantages which the house can do little to affect. In contrast, the very complex family can profit enormously from proper planning. Consider for example a house for Thomas Mann's Cornelius family, which he describes as follows:

> "The Big Ones called their parents the 'Ancients'—not behind their backs, but in all affection and as a mode of address, though Cornelius was only forty-seven and his wife eight years younger. They would address father or mother as 'Beloved Ancient!' or 'Faithful Ancient!' The professor's parents, who led the lives of permanently astounded and intimidated old people, were called the 'Arch-ancients.' As to the Little Ones, Lore and Biter, who are in the upper nursery with 'Blue Anna' —so called from the colour of her cheeks—these were accustomed to address him as their mother addressed him—that is, by his Christian name, Abel. There was something indescribably droll in the rather extravagant and ingratiating manner and tone they assumed when they called or addressed him thus, especially in the sweet-chiming voice of five-year-old Eleonore, who looked exactly like Frau Cornelius in her childhood pictures, and whom the professor loved above everything."

Here certainly, where the needs of five quite distinct cultural categories are at issue, the architect has a wealth of material with which to deal. It would be strange indeed if his plan did not materially affect the family's every living pattern. As one goes from relationships between sub-groups, to relationships within sub-groups, to relationships between individuals, the house becomes progressively less important. There remain the relationships between individuals and the family as a whole. Some of these, such as the father's function of making the money, may affect the size of the house, but do not affect its plan. Others, like the wife's housekeeping activities may not affect its size, but do affect its plan. By-and-large relationships between individuals in the same category affect rooms, while relationships between cultural categories affect the plan as a whole. Its basic organization depends on how these sub-groups cooperate and conflict. Certain specific intra- and inter-category relationships have been singled out below for closer examination.

Husband versus Wife

The primary sub-assembly within the family is, of course, husband and wife. We are used to conceiving of them as a unit opposite in sex, linked by love, marriage, the same interest in family, and thus belonging together. But the fact remains that no two people can, in the last analysis, create a unit. They are inevitably two separate individuals with very different functions and needs. To provide a "master bedroom," to use the horrible locution generally adopted, conceiving this to be their only need, is perhaps to jeopardize that unity it is designed to foster. Certainly husband and wife need a jointly owned and private space for the enjoyment of their most intimate moments. But their working relationship must develop around the clock and everywhere in the house. They must be able to communicate at all times.

Because the husband is away so much of the time, the hours available for being with his wife are roughly at meals, in the late afternoon, and in the evening. Meals are no problem in that husband and wife are face to face in any case. Late afternoon however is apt to find the husband tired, and his wife harried by her round of housework and child care. The children's tempo increases just before bedtime. Because they are tired too, they are usually obstreperous. This is also the period when they must be fed, bathed, put to bed, and when their personal disappointments and difficulties are most apt to explode into active despair. It is the most hectic part of the day.

Communication between husband and wife, in such circumstances, must of course take place wherever she is working. Because the kitchen is the hub of the most social of these activities, it is the place most in need of space, comfort, and the congenial atmosphere which makes for group communication. If the husband is to help his wife, enjoy his children, and if they are to swap the stories of the day, there must be a place in the kitchen for that husband. Many wives hate to be immured there while the family and guests carry on somewhere else, out of earshot and out of touch. It is not uncommon nowadays to see kitchens in close association with the living furniture group, for the express purpose of breaking down this barrier. Where the demands on the living room are too complex to allow such close association, the kitchen must become bigger, and be expressly designed to hold guests and members of the family in comfort, whether or not they happen to be working. The parents may drink a cocktail there while the children eat and the wife cooks dinner. Some of the guests may even congregate in the kitchen while the finishing touches are put on a meal. A kitchen which is conceived of only as a work place makes such moments uncomfortable. Where it is designed for enjoyment as well as work, they become infinitely more pleasant. They are welcomed as appropriate, and this new place in which to enjoy family and friends adds to the variety of atmospheres the house affords.

The evening brings up what would appear to be a most simple-minded aspect of husband-wife relationships. But it is one which, nevertheless, seems to be remarkably often neglected. If the parents are to be able to be together, they must have in some one room the exact comforts or facilities each requires for the evening's occupation. Of course in some cases this is not possible. But in many others, a poor plan and inadequate furniture literally keep people apart who would gain much by being together.

A further requirement for husband-wife communication is the emotional ease which for many people can only come from a balanced diet of privacy and sociality. Wives suffer more in this regard than do their husbands, who often have private offices or studies. The mother of young children is subject to more continuous pressure from the family as a whole than any other of its members, and thus has a greater need for withdrawal. One of her most common difficulties is that the average house provides no specific place she can call her own.

Parents versus Children

Even such a cursory view of husbands and wives as this inevitably slops over into their problems as parents. Perhaps the most striking evolution we have experienced in the last few years is in our attitude towards children. Most of our parents were brought up on the theory that children should be seen but not heard, with all this implies in the way of segregation. In our own time, the children of some families are allowed to usurp the whole house.

Houses can do a great deal either to aggravate or ameliorate the inevitable difficulties of child care. It is unfortunate that they are, by and large, planned without children in mind. This is usually rationalized, and to a certain extent justifiably, by the fact that children do grow up. One occasionally runs across the absurd situation of a plan especially gauged to the problems of a two-year old, or some other specific and very temporary age and behavior pattern. To ignore the problem completely is equally absurd. Ten to eleven years are required to get four children about two years apart through their first four years. Twenty-three years are required before they are ready for college. This is long enough to make provisions for children worth their weight in gold. There is no reason, furthermore, why they need interfere with the stable patterns of adult living. Lewis Mumford has commented on the problem as follows:

> "For one thing, the child is no less entitled to space, room for play and movement, a place for quiet retreat and study, other than his bed. No housing standard is adequate that provides only cubicles or dressing rooms for the child, or forces him into the constant company of adults. The dwelling must be so arranged, so spaced, that the routine of physical care and the overseeing of activities shall demand the least wasteful sacrifice on the part of the mother: architects, even the best of them still have much to learn in the proper arrangement of kitchen, living room, playroom, and garden."

The behavior patterns of children of various ages are reasonably uniform. Their personalities may be distinct and unique, but they are apt to act like other children of their age. Their needs and requirements, insofar as the house is concerned, are dependent on three factors. First, unlike adults, who have presumably been indoctrinated with our culture, children have everything to learn. The house is therefore a part of their training, while for an adult it is an expression of established attitudes. Second, child training is largely an adult responsibility, and thus for the adults' sake as well as that of the children, should be facilitated in every possible way. And third, children's own needs at various stages are entirely compulsive, cannot be altered except at great cost to both parent and child, and thus should be provided for in terms of space and zoning. Both camps remain more even tempered if they can work out their own lives unmolested.

The principal items of equipment required during a child's first year fall into seven categories. Babies need, of course, a bed, and bed things, sheets, blankets, etc. They need diapers and a three-gallon diaper pail to keep them in, once used. They need clothes. They need a variety of nursing and food sterilizing equipment and a high chair or chair-table. They need bath equipment including a bathinette, various oils, powders, and scales. They need a carriage and a play pen. Finally, they need and will get a mass of toys. A baby's bath, diapers, oils, powders, etc. scales and clothes can be kept in any room. But as this whole group of equipment revolves around water, it is convenient to have a lavatory in the room. Perhaps an even more convenient arrange-

Dorothea Fox: Illustrations from D. Benjamin Spock's "The Pocket Boo of Baby and Child Care." The pi tures on the next three pages com from the same source.

ment is to keep this whole group of things in a bathroom. If this is to be done, the bathroom must be large enough to hold, as well as its fixtures, a bathinette next to the lavatory, and a bureau. The pail can go under the former, while the scales can go on a shelf over the latter. One advantage of this scheme is that movements can be dumped directly from a diaper into a water closet and the diaper thrown right into the pail without leaving the room or putting it down temporarily. A bathroom with extra space in it will continue to be useful throughout a long period. Because children very soon begin to grab everything in sight, bottles of oil, thermometers, powder, pins, and the like, should be put on shelves well above the level of the bathinette or counter on which they are changed and dressed.

Food preparation equipment and a high chair or chair-table combination are perhaps best kept in the kitchen, in that the baby's eating patterns change rapidly in the first eight or ten months, and stabilize from there onwards for several years. Space for children's tables, chairs, and for a play pen is really an almost essential part of a kitchen. Play pens use an area of about 5 feet by 5 feet and fold up into an area of 3 feet 6 inches by 6 inches. Folding them is a tiresome process, and cannot be done with any safety while holding a baby. Ideally there should be enough room to leave them open and ready to use at all times. Play pens are also used in the living room, and indeed, except by upper class families, wherever people congregate in the house. If doorways are wide enough to allow it to be rolled around inside and pushed outdoors without having to fold it up, much fuss can be avoided.

Dr. Spock says:

"It is not wise to let a baby be crawling or a small child be walking around the kitchen during the cooking or serving of meals. There is danger from spattering grease, from the child's pulling a pot off the stove. This is the best time for the play pen or a pen made by laying chairs on their sides, or for him to be in his own chair. His chair or pen should be well away from the stove. A baby can reach a surprising distance when he tries."

This is all very well if there is enough room in the kitchen to accomplish it. But in most current kitchens it is an impossibility. The "efficient," "streamlined" kitchen is unworkable for the family with young children. The factors which go to make up a good kitchen for growing families, other than those mentioned by Dr. Spock, have to do with space to play and eat. Women spend a larger part of their time in the kitchen now than when laundry equipment was elsewhere. Children need their mother's companionship and supervision during most of these hours. The kitchen should be arranged so that children can play in a section of it, in clear view, out from under foot, and separated by a gate to keep them there. This arrangement can be worked out alternately using the dining room as the play space. It can also be elaborated until the dining room becomes in reality a dining-play space with toy storage and movable partitions to change its character back and forth.

It is much easier and less hazardous to feed children in the kitchen than in the dining room, away from supervision. Many families feed them before the parents sit down. This scheme gets the children off to bed or to homework earlier and gives the parents uninterrupted time together. It does not work well, however, unless there is a reasonably adequate, safe, and easily cleaned dining arrangement for children, in good relation to the work surfaces and circulation.

For the first several years of the children's lives it is convenient to be able to supervise their outdoor activities from the kitchen. It is even more of a luxury to be able to communicate with them, let them in and out, etc. from a nearby door. Furthermore, children of their own accord are apt to wish to check with their mothers at frequent intervals. A toilet at the back door, and ample, warm space to hang up wet playsuits, mittens, caps, and toys, is invaluable. Many adults prefer to enter here from outside work such as gardening, car washing, repairs, or building maintenance. A clothes drying space and toilet is thus useful permanently, for them as well as for servants and children.

Children must also be introduced to our culture and manners. They must develop attitudes toward people, society at large, music, the graphic arts, morals, etc., in short to the whole of civilized life. Where this takes place in a room which is designed for, and operationally dedicated to the process, they are apt to adapt themselves without being aware of the fact. However, children's span of attention is relatively short, and they positively must be allowed to let off steam. They need a place in the house

where they can do this without disturbing others. This need for the occasional separation of age groups becomes most important and most difficult during the time children are in their teens. Not only are teen-age parties repulsive to adults, adults can spoil them for the teen-agers. To quarantine the teen-ager is, however, equally destructive. There is no simple answer to this problem. The converted basement, the fixed-up attic, are seldom adequate substitutes for the honorific adult atmosphere of the family living quarters, or for a physically and symbolicly adequate entertainment place of their own. Where, as in Thomas Mann's Cornelius family, there is a very great age spread between sets of children, the elderly teen-agers are actually in a third generation. And while they may take over some of the parents' duties and prerequisites, they still need a sense of their own domain.

Particularly in large families another kind of break-down sometimes occurs, which cuts across these sub-groups of people quite arbitrarily, that is, between the well and the sick. One of the periodic crises every family must contend with is more or less mass illness. If the wife is sick, and there are no servants, they must either be obtained, or the father must substitute for her. If the husband or children are sick, the housewife's chores are multiplied. The old saw that disaster breeds disaster may not be true, but in any case it is those fortuitous occasions when disasters come together that are remembered. The most hectic moments of family life, when the children and husband are sick, are also the moments when the wife has female troubles, the furnace breaks down, and a snow storm interrupts all public utilities. The extra work load for the well, and for the sick the sense of being a burden, are states neither party enjoy. When the inevitable happens, and the family is in for a siege of chicken pox, the housewife's trial begins. She must serve meals in bed as well as at table, and devote enough time to the patients to keep them from exploding with boredom or melting with self pity—separately and simultaneously. This is when close bedroom-kitchen arrangements are invaluable. They not only shorten the endless trips. They may eliminate many entirely, in that for children, verbal reassurance is often the requirement, rather than physical presence or help.

The Family versus Outsiders

The parents and the children are, in the upper middle class view, the family. The addition of such new cultural categories as guests, or servants, or grandparents creates a situation where parents and children as a block are contrasted with the "outlander." When a grandparent comes to live with the family, demands on the house in terms of privacy, passive recreation, work patterns, and the like are apt to increase incalculably. It becomes a three-part, or, if servants are living in, a four-part organism. Each of the four sets of interests and behavior patterns must somehow be resolved. The situation might be pictured as follows.

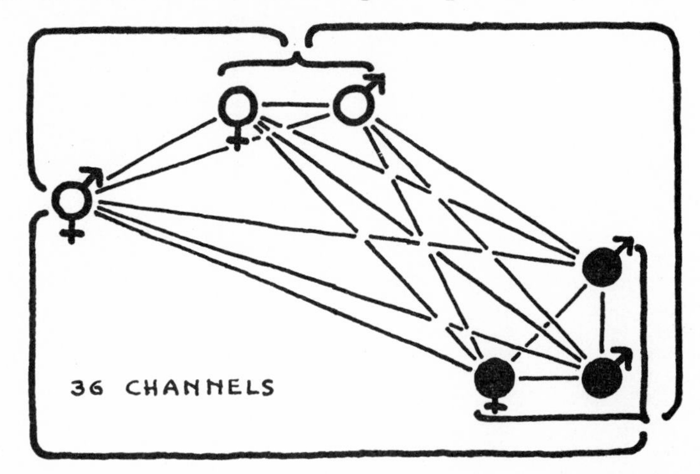

As the number of relationships increase, so do the possibilities for conflict. Through interference with the new patterns of the new family, grandparents can cause friction not only between themselves and the children, parents, and servants, but indirectly create tensions between the children and their parents. This can be to a certain extent ameliorated by separation.

The grandparents' apartment itself, for ideally it should be that rather than a room, must usually meet three characteristic demands. First, it must be comfortable. One of the principal symbols of luxury is a soft and good-looking floor covering. Another is one's own possessions, for they breed a sense of continuity and security. Second, it should be as private and as fit

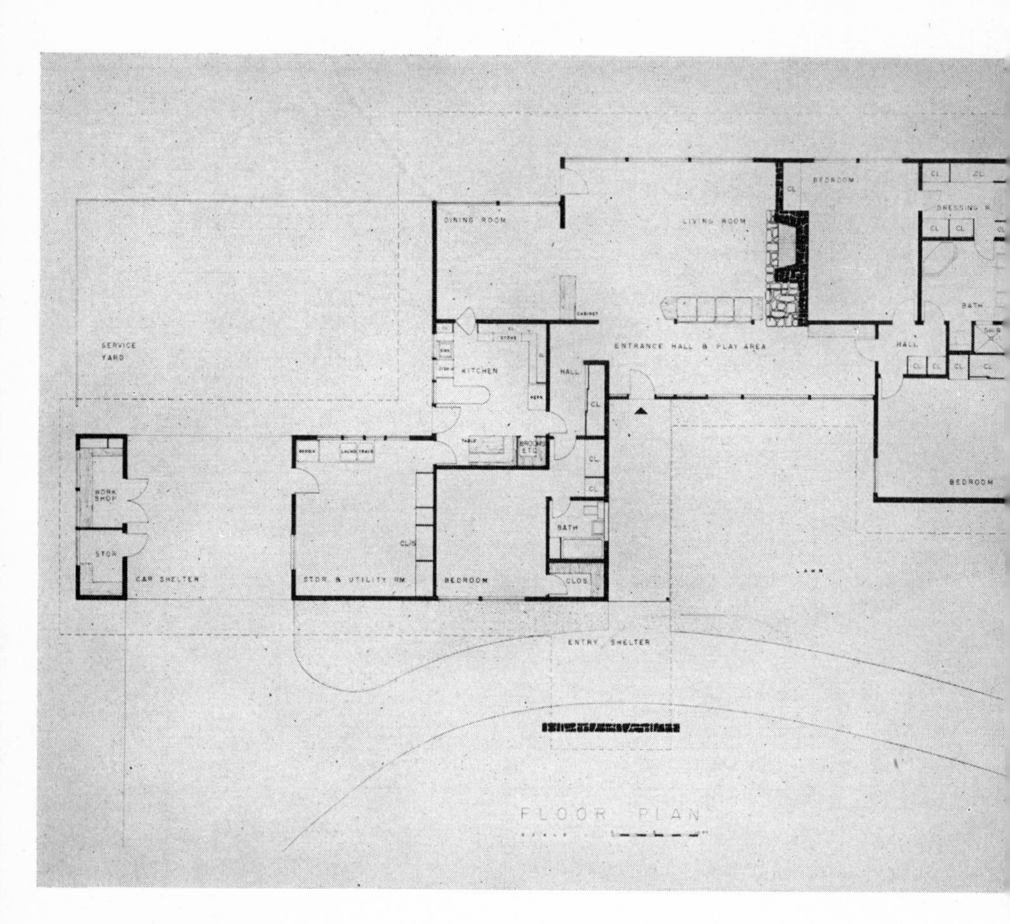

Pietro Belluschi: Charles Wilson House, Oregon. The bed room next to the kitchen, with its own bath, closet, coat closet and private entrance circulation seems an ideal arrangement for the elderly relation. In this case, the living room with its contiguous entrance hall, play area and circulation to bed rooms is conceived of as a sort of club room, where the various generations come together. The photograph opposite shows a view toward the parents' bed rooms.

for entertaining as can be. Third, it must be easy to get around in. Seventy-eight per cent of fatalities from accidents to people of sixty-five and over are caused by falls. Thresholds, scatter rugs, steps, furniture, and cranky circulation patterns are all potential death traps. The trip to the bathroom should be free of steps, changes of flooring material, thresholds, and similar hazards. The probability that the aged will be ill a large part of the time makes it desirable that their rooms be near the kitchen. Nearness to the children's rooms is also convenient. One of the most useful functions a grandparent can perform is that of baby sitter. A ground floor room, one riser above grade, with its own bath, carpeted throughout, near the kitchen, with a sitting room character, is what most grandparents would most like.

The addition of a servant has a more drastic effect on the family, in many respects, than does the addition of a grandparent. Unlike the grandparent who is related by birth and belongs to the same socio-economic group, the servant is likely to be totally different. Thus both the servant's and the family's need for privacy is more acute than in the case of a grandparent.

As it is not always thought proper for the servant to use the same facilities as the family for eating, entering, bathing, washing, excreting, drinking, entertaining and recreation, and as they must have their own private areas for the rest of the living functions, many spaces must be duplicated. The exact division depends on

the individual client's choice. The needs of the servant (or specialized servants) who come in by the day are minimal, but still cannot be entirely ignored, as is so frequently the case, without causing embarrassment. They need a place for indoor and outdoor clothes, a place to change in privacy, a toilet located in such a way as to give the family appropriate privacy, a place to eat, and a place to rest. The servants' requirements for entering, clothes storage, toilet, and dining space parallel those of children throughout the school age. Dressing space, of minimum size, can be provided by simply enlarging the toilet and by adding indoor clothes storage space on the inside. On a minimum level, rest space can be provided by a comfortable chair in the kitchen which, again, parallels the husband's kitchen requirements.

Where a single servant or couple lives in, a greater range of functions must be provided for. The servants should be able to come and go without a sense of being supervised and without disturbing the family. Their room is their principal living place. As they may also listen for the children when parents are out, it should be near the children's rooms. Space for them to entertain in the kitchen, with a character somewhat more friendly than is now usually provided, also seems desirable. Again, it parallels the family's own needs. Where servants' duties are as much child care as housework, the kitchen requires those same plan and safety features necessary to fit it for child care in any single family house. The servant's problems vis-a-vis children are, in most operational respects, exactly the same as those of the mother.

An understanding of these relationships within and between sub-groups helps to broach the livability problem. But it does not reduce it to practically usable terms. It points up the need for children's rooms near the kitchen; for large and commodious bathrooms containing far more functions than are now acknowledged; for certain types of living facilities in the kitchen; and for fuller entrance services at the back door, such as coat closets, clothes driers, and toilets. The mere existence of proper space, furniture, and equipment, however, does not guarantee livability. Other factors enter in. These relationships all hinge about three necessities of family life; to wit, conflict, privacy, and communication.

Signorelli.

Conflict

Areas of conflict are as vital and constructive a part of home life as are areas of cooperation. Friction is essential to the growth process. Too little is perhaps as harmful as too much. This is particularly true of children, who as they grow come to question not only their parents' decisions, but also their manners, their brains, and finally their degree of correlation with the evolving culture. The process is like a second weaning, necessary to the child in order that he may, in his turn, grow up. This second weaning cannot be visualized as following a smooth curve. Children draw far away from and then very near their parents and other members of the family. Their tendency is to accept and reject others in alternating cycles. The educational value of the process is, perhaps, to go too far in one direction or the other. The peace and quiet of the middle ground is appreciated far more fully after an experience with the extremes.

The rejection-acceptance cycle is only one reason for an individual's need of a certain amount of privacy and of a certain amount of companionship. Privacy and sympathetic personal contact are regenerative, and help consolidate our knowledge.

One must withdraw from violent group activity in order to assess and understand it. One must be able to identify oneself with the group and its cultural manifestations in order to accept it. Unless these needs are understood and provided for, the opportunity to assess, reconsider, consolidate, forgive, understand, in short to grow emotionally and mentally, is made materially more difficult. In addition, the family is a great modifier of the individual's demands. For example, a bachelor living in a single room and eating in restaurants has very different needs, as far as privacy is concerned, from the father of a young family. The bachelor may get too much privacy and be forced to seek companionship, sex, and the like outside his home. He may also be conditioned by his lonely life to demand a great deal of quiet. The father on the other hand may have a higher tolerance for noise, but because he can get little privacy in the normal course of events, may have to seek that state as consciously as the bachelor avoids it. Our needs and tolerances are conditioned by our relationship to the social unit to which we belong.

The single family house problem is, in part, that of balancing the requirements for group living with the peculiar requirements of individuals as they are affected by the group. According to current theories, all members of the family need places of their own in which to relate social experience to themselves, or in which to regain a sense of their own individualities free of outside pressures. Communication is not only part of this particular equation, it is the very essence of social organization. The family lives in a sea of talk. Its nature varies from a curt command to the kitchen to an hour-long analysis of a Beethoven quartet. And it does not stop with talk. The messages imparted by the style of the house, by the furniture arrangement, by the colors used, are as understandable a means of communication as words.

Privacy and communication are in reality different degrees of the same thing—sociality. One is alone on a desert. One sails the Atlantic alone, not in private. It is impossible to be truly alone in the single family house. One can however approximate the sensation, but only if the house is, in terms of both form and technique, excellently designed. What are the prerequisites of privacy and communication?

Ingres.

Privacy

The state of being private cannot be disassociated from an activity. We conceive of the various things we do in houses as in a scale—from most private to least private.

Some require complete withdrawal from the group, others none. The things the family does as a whole are also in such a scale. Some are private to the family, others are performed for the express purpose of bringing outsiders in. While it is possible to classify the living functions in terms of privacy in a general way, a specific and universally applicable pigeonholing is not possible. Our conception of what is private is in a constant state of flux. For example, not so long ago, a woman's ankles were the only part of her "limbs" which she could expose to public notice. More recently, the Bikini bathing suit exposed her entire "leg." Similar changes take place in other areas. The radio, for example, is now tolerated as a companion of study, particularly by children. And in a subtler form the telephone allows even more drastic invasions of privacy.

As the general cultural conception of privacy shifts, some individuals anticipate the swing while others exhibit cultural lag. In a three-generation household the old folks may always appear swathed from top to toe, their hands and faces being the only exposed areas, while the youngest folks may wander around naked. Such variations occur in every area. For example some married couples, or whole families may consider no bathroom function private from each other. Others may consider them all private. Still others may include the excretory functions, but not bathing. However, no matter what a family does within its own privacy, when it is exposed to the general view, that is when it has guests, it must adopt the most stringent "decency" in order to avoid embarrassment. The guests may happen to have an entirely different view of propriety from the family's own. The only sure way to keep one's self respect is to be conservative. As we are going from a more private to a less private view of life, the more private way is the conservative way.

The tendency of recent years among avant guard planners has been to make fewer and fewer provisions for conventional privacy. For example, Le Corbusier's own bedroom contains lavatory, tub, and bidet in the volume of the room, visually uncompartmented. The open plan very often allows a complete view of the living, dining, kitchen area and sometimes even into the bedroom circulation from as near the public domain as the front door. An even more curious phenomenon, particularly to Europeans, is the American habit of leaving windows uncovered at night, allowing every passerby a view of the interior and of the life going on in it. The question is then, where does too little privacy begin to have bad effects on the individual and on the family's self esteem as a whole? In the most general terms this might be answered as follows: When the individual is not able to withdraw without undue manipulation of architectural gadgetry; without apology; and when, in emergency conditions, the family cannot operate the house according to the most conventional patterns of its time and class.

There are several degrees of privacy, each with its own special characteristics. Utter privacy may be defined as freedom from being seen or heard by others, and freedom from seeing or hearing

Le Corbusier.

others. This is impossible to achieve in the fullest sense. Our urban culture and the inadequacy of current building techniques do not allow its realization. In any case, an approximation of utter privacy is usually considered sufficient. We accept as a reasonable degree of withdrawal not to be seen, not to hear more than a general level of background noise, and not to be heard. We cannot, unfortunately, shut our ears, whereas we can shut or turn away our eyes. This kind of privacy is demanded for very few activities. We would like it only for concentrated work, excreting, and for rest and emotional regeneration. These are the functions usually performed alone. The same specifications, however, apply to sleeping in double beds, and to love making.

The next most private activities are probably bathing and dressing. Most people would agree that freedom from being seen is a sufficient degree of privacy for them, though in individual cases not to be heard or to hear might be considered desirable. Because dressing and bathing are thought of in our culture as private, they have taken on secondary qualities. They can be more significant than merely getting one's self clean and covered. Dressing and going to the bathroom are golden moments to be alone, to enjoy one's own thoughts, to review the day just passed. or plan the hours to come. The quality of one's inner state of mind while performing one of them is tremendously affected by what comes next. To dress for work in the bright morning is very different from dressing for a party in the gathering dusk. To consider such occasions as "service" is to under-rate them. They may be the most vitalizing moments of the day, and are greatly enhanced if the rooms where they take place are conceived of in terms of living in depth as well as in terms of functions. The hygienic bathroom, the monastic bedroom, are as lopsided as a three-legged horse.

Such is the value of these moments that many families, particularly in the two upper socio-economic groups, ritualize them. Between the end of the working day and cocktails, the adults bathe, change, and perhaps rest. This group movement towards the bedrooms and baths is a delightful comma in the day. It creates an atmosphere of peace and unity, besides making the coming together again to eat and drink far more exciting. The social and regenerative value of private functions shared can be very great if they are well planned for in terms of house. To dress and bathe with someone else, to share a joint privacy from the family and its guests, is to have, also, the opportunity to share one's thoughts. Such occasions have a unique quality. They are transitional, short, and intimate. They may be between parent and child, spouse and spouse, guest and host, or guest and guest. Each one is different, depending on who is involved.

For these semi-private functions, the lines are drawn, with the exception of children and married couples, between the sexes. Where the sex of the people concerned is less important, privacy becomes akin to being inconspicuous. One does not wish the acts of going to the toilet, emptying the garbage, putting out the wash, and the like advertised. On the other hand, they need not be utterly private. A toilet door into the living room, or a laundry pole in the front yard are unthinkable. But to be discovered going to a toilet, or hanging the wash, by a member of the family or by a close friend is not embarrassing—provided it is in the conventionally accepted place.

The family as a whole also makes demands on the house in terms of privacy. For example the act of eating seems to be felt as putting it at a disadvantage socially, provided the guest arrives during or just before the meal. Privacy from guests is one of the greatest variables. It is not uncommon, particularly on the West

Coast, for houses to have quite separate guest quarters, more remote than those of the servants. In other instances, the guest room is located next to, and may even share a bath with the master bedroom. The more isolated the family, the fewer modifications in their customary living patterns need be made. And it is essentially the family which needs this isolation, not the guest. He is a manifestation of the outside world from which the family is private. Warner notes of the upper upper class house:

> ". . . the two rooms in which the family spends most time as a group are without question the living and dining rooms. Frequently the living room is divided into two rooms, the smaller and more intimate being set aside for family use, and the other, a parlor, used for the entertainment of guests. If outsiders are invited to such a function as tea, for instance, the larger living room is used; but if the guests include only more intimate friends, they are received in the family living room. The larger living room is seldom used by the family alone."

From the architect's point of view these distinctions are of the essence, in that the location, character, size, orientation, etc., of rooms, if they are to be satisfactory, must grow out of their place in the social-to-private use scheme.

As living patterns become more complex and as the amount of money available becomes greater, the initial processing of the guest becomes slower and more complex. There are worlds of difference between the lower middle class front door directly into the living room, and the porch, vestibule, entry, and separate coatroom with toilet typical of the two upper groups. In the former, the guest is plunged directly into the family, more or less regardless of what is going on. In the latter the house provides for a slow transition between the outdoors and the occasion, as well as the opportunity to fix one's self up. Exactly how long and how formal this transitional period should be depends mostly on class, but also, of course, on the individual family's needs. The more it entertains, the more important it is, the more besieged it is, the greater its need to express social distance by means of lengthy entrance paths, both indoors and out.

Communication

The need for privacy of various sorts continues far into the realm of sociability just as sociability begins far back in what we consider, offhand, to be private zones. There is no sharp line of demarcation. The kind of privacy we need for most types of communication, we call "quiet." This actually means freedom from distracting noises, i.e., those far above the general level, and freedom from constant interruption. A steady background of noise without undue peaks or lows, and an occasional interruption of a sort which does not break the thread of whatever activity is going on, are acceptable, or sometimes even enjoyable. Because communication is a social phenomenon it can, to a certain extent, be in the swing of things. But our tolerance of interruption is still very limited. Where, for example, conversation is the goal, there should be no necessity to move, nor should there be too much noise. As it becomes a more important activity, the place where it occurs must be freer of interruption. Where it is regarded, as in some academic circles, as an art demanding all of ones attention, mental agility, and knowledge, its surroundings are apt to become as private to the group concerned as a bathroom is to the individual. Where conversation is regarded as give and take on various levels and with much variety, i.e., as a sequence of subjects treated in a sequence of ways, intimate talks, flirtation, general conversation, and talk between groups following each other closely, a minor number of interruptions may actually be desirable. They provide new situations or foci; new ways to approach the opposite sex, or the subject in hand. The kind of conversation favored by a family inevitably reflects itself in their living room.

The various other kinds of communication, that is between wife and maid, grandparent and grandchild, father and son, etc., all make slightly different demands on the house. The rough and tumble of father and son romping together is very different from the more fragile atmosphere of a grandparent and grandchild. In the former, the child must be protected, in the latter the grandparent. Both kinds may come under the ostensible heading of pure pleasure. But they also usually involve steps in the training

Carl Koch and Robert Woods Kennedy: House in Belmont, Massachusetts. The dining area is part of the living room. The kitchen opens out of this space widely. The doors are to a porch.

The coat closet is seen to the left of the himney. The front door and stairs lown to other rooms are hidden beiind it. The window wall, seen below, is directly behind the sofa.

This floor is conceived of as a single space, in which the living activities have been loosely distributed. The advantage of the scheme is that the area and volume seem greater than they actually are. The disadvantage is in loss of privacy. The selection of a semicircular sofa reflects, perhaps, the need for a sense of being protected from the hurly-burly of surrounding activities. *The plan is shown on page 115.*

of the child. As the parents' standards are higher, as the children are to be introduced into a more and more complex and demanding culture, so the need for a significant environment increases. One does not of course sit down and discuss philogyny with a two-year old. But one does, even at that age, begin introducing him to the social attitudes essential to him if he is later to discuss such things.

Contacts between three generations are apt to engender a curious sense of depth. They involve man in his savage, productive, and contemplative states. They give us in microcosm a sense of our life cycle. This same sense of living in depth can be increased by rooms and houses. It is perhaps largely a function of furniture, and of such things as books and records and pictures. But architecture also plays its part. It both informs, and is informed by the occasions it is designed to serve. It increases the meaning of the actual objects which contain our cultural heritage. Thus a room consciously archeological is of no value per se, while one which enfolds its books, pictures, and music in terms of storage, acoustics, lighting, and seating, automatically dramatizes their uses. One confusion which still leads to eclecticism is that between communication and decoration. A contemporary room, designed for communication on several levels, itself communicates. Old rooms, when they were, in terms of their own time, equally objectively designed, become richer as they build up more known associations. The room designed to look like something from the past implies that its owners wish they could communicate, and indicates their inability to do so. They are all dressed up with nowhere to go.

This formalized kind of communication with others and with our cultural heritage is of course as old as civilization. Its special requirements have not changed too greatly in recent years. The phonograph and radio are the latest equipment to be added, and like all new things, have taken a long time to assimilate. Indeed, there are still few houses where even a minor attempt is made to provide accurately for them. But by and large the problem holds no new elements. Nor does the age-old question of how to translate these various requirements of the family as a whole into architecture.

Frank Lloyd Wright: Living Room, Taliesen East. Spring Green, Wisconsin.

Jack Delano: Fragment from Interior of a Rural House, Virginia.

CHAPTER IV
Livability

Activities

A HOUSE IS, FIRST AND FOREMOST, AN ATTEMPT to influence benignly its tenants' living patterns. It can foster or inhibit relationships within and between subgroups. Its power to do this lies in the fact that its plan has a great affect on the amount of privacy the family can attain, and on the ease with which its various members can get together. Inadequate provisions for privacy and communication lead to conflict. Adequate provisions foster cooperation. The fundamental scheme of the house grows out of such considerations as these. A good plan reflects a family's social organization. A poor plan usually reflects a building's organization, in terms of structure, or style. As structure and style have but secondary relevance to family life, they are inadequate criteria for design.

Livability is not a constant. People are flexible, and adapt to inadequate houses with apparent ease. The family troubles resulting from poor houses are so bound up with other factors that the full role the house plays in them cannot be accurately determined. Variations within the norm of what is considered livable are so great as to make generalizations very difficult. Nevertheless some insight into livability may be gained by considering it first in terms of obsolescence.

We think of the things a family does as more or less constant. Yet their complexion, and thus the way they are reflected in architecture, is constantly changing. Obsolescence in houses occurs faster in terms of livability than it does in terms of structure. New equipment, furthermore, does not modernize a house. It is more apt to impose on itself, and on the house, problems neither can adequately solve. Each generation makes its own demands on arrangement, equipment, and structure, depending on its own peculiar concepts of family organization. Mumford notes that:

"Today, even the finest urban dwellings of the last century are, for the greater part, obsolete. They were conceived in terms of a limited and now outworn mode of living; few of them, even by drastic renovation, can encompass our modern demands. As mere shelters they are sometimes sufficient; but as a frame for living, they are absurd. All our new needs—our desire to avoid unnecessary menial labor, our more conscientious and efficient child care, our recognition of play as an essential part of life from childhood onward, our acceptance of the need for quiet and privacy—all these create a demand for a different type of dwelling and a different communal form."

We are used to thinking of houses as antique objects; as collections of rooms with certain names. We have long since forgotten how these same old rooms were lived in. For example, the impossible arrangements of the early New England houses can only be explained by the living patterns of the time. Woodward notes that:

"All the rooms of the new Walling home were small; indeed they were tiny as compared to the rooms in modern dwellings. The five bedrooms on the second floor were mere cubbyholes. This was not looked upon as a defect, for in those days people used bedrooms only for sleeping.

"There were no bathrooms in the house, but they were not missed, for no one in that era ever took a bath. The fanciful medical lore of the seventeenth century ascribed many human ailments to contact with water. Consequently, washing with water was limited to the hands and face. As was mentioned before, this prejudice extended to the drinking of water, and people in general avoided water as a beverage. On hot summer days even the farm hands, perspiring at their work in the fields, drank cider instead of water. Babies were given beer and cider as soon as they were old enough to toddle."

Activities

What makes a good house can only be discovered through a continuing examination of current living functions. If the preceding descriptions are correct, the everyday family activities are related in this fashion:

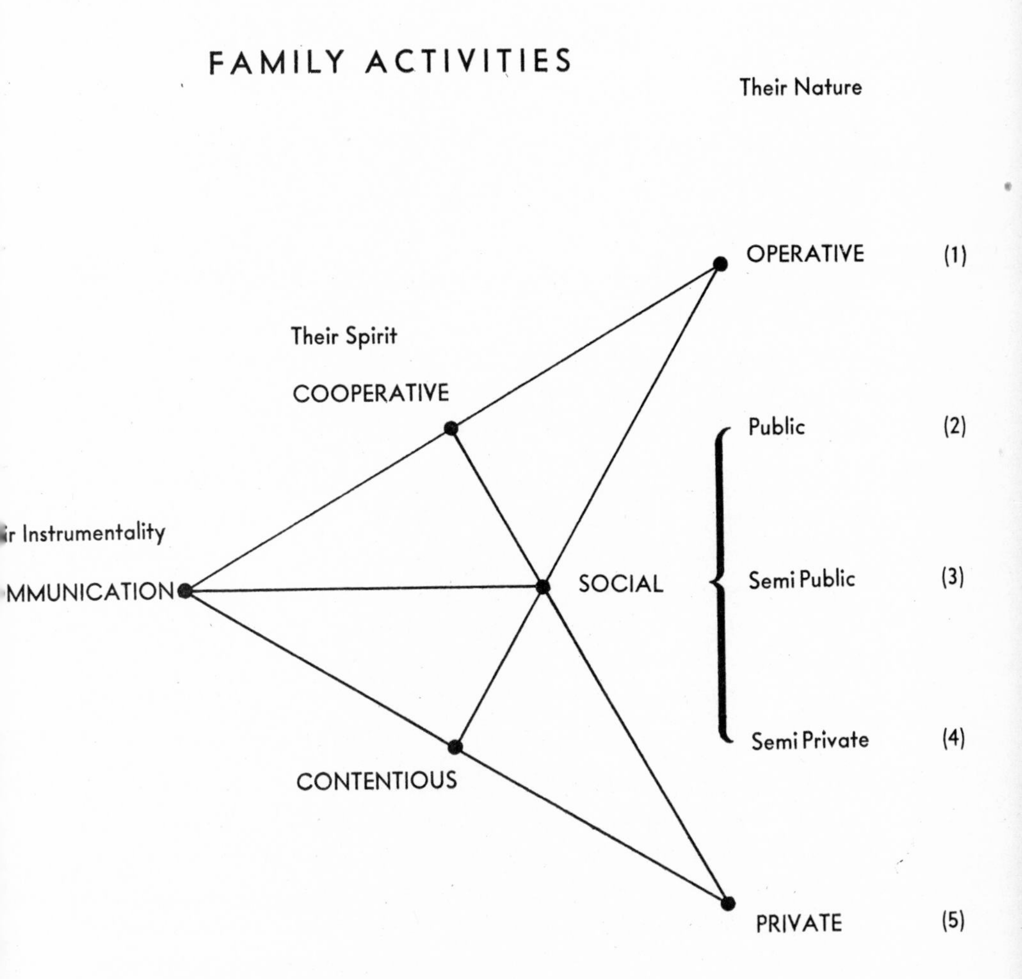

All five types of activities can take place at once. Some or all of them may be duplicated by any number of individuals, and by anywhere from two to six groups. This might best be visualized by means of an example. Imagine that the hour is eight p.m.

The maid is having a crony in to drink tea and discuss the old country. The parents are having a couple in to drink whiskey and to discuss life and its hidden meanings. The older children are having some friends in to drink coke, play the phonograph, and discuss school, the opposite sex, and parents, with much incidental horseplay and breakage. The little children have gone to bed, but are not yet asleep, and are loudly demanding water. Grandma has also gone to bed, for a quiet session with her book and a cup of Bovril. Unless all five of these groups are reasonably well separated they are bound to get in each other's hair.

In the average house such a situation must be taken care of operationally. But it is very subject to amelioration by means of architecture. Thus, strictly in terms of the family's activities, the livability question is:

Which activities are compatible, and can therefore be grouped together within the same envelope, and, which are incompatible and must therefore be separated? A complete answer involves four steps:

1. Classification of living activities.
2. Grouping of similar activities.
3. Provision of duplicate facilities for those activities which, because performed by individuals or sub-groups rather than the family as a whole, may both compete and overlap in time.
4. Provision of adequate barriers between incompatible groups of activities.

The classification of living activities is easier said than done. Personal judgments inevitably enter into any evaluation system one attempts to set up. Families can, in conventionally unconventional ways, deviate quite widely from any norm, even within the relatively limited framework of this country, time, class, and place. Thus only the architect and his client can set up an accurate system of classification for each case. Theoretically the client is able to state categorically into which pigeon hole any one function should be placed. In practice, however, certainty in such realms is by no means universal. The classificatory device used here is perhaps best expressed as follows:

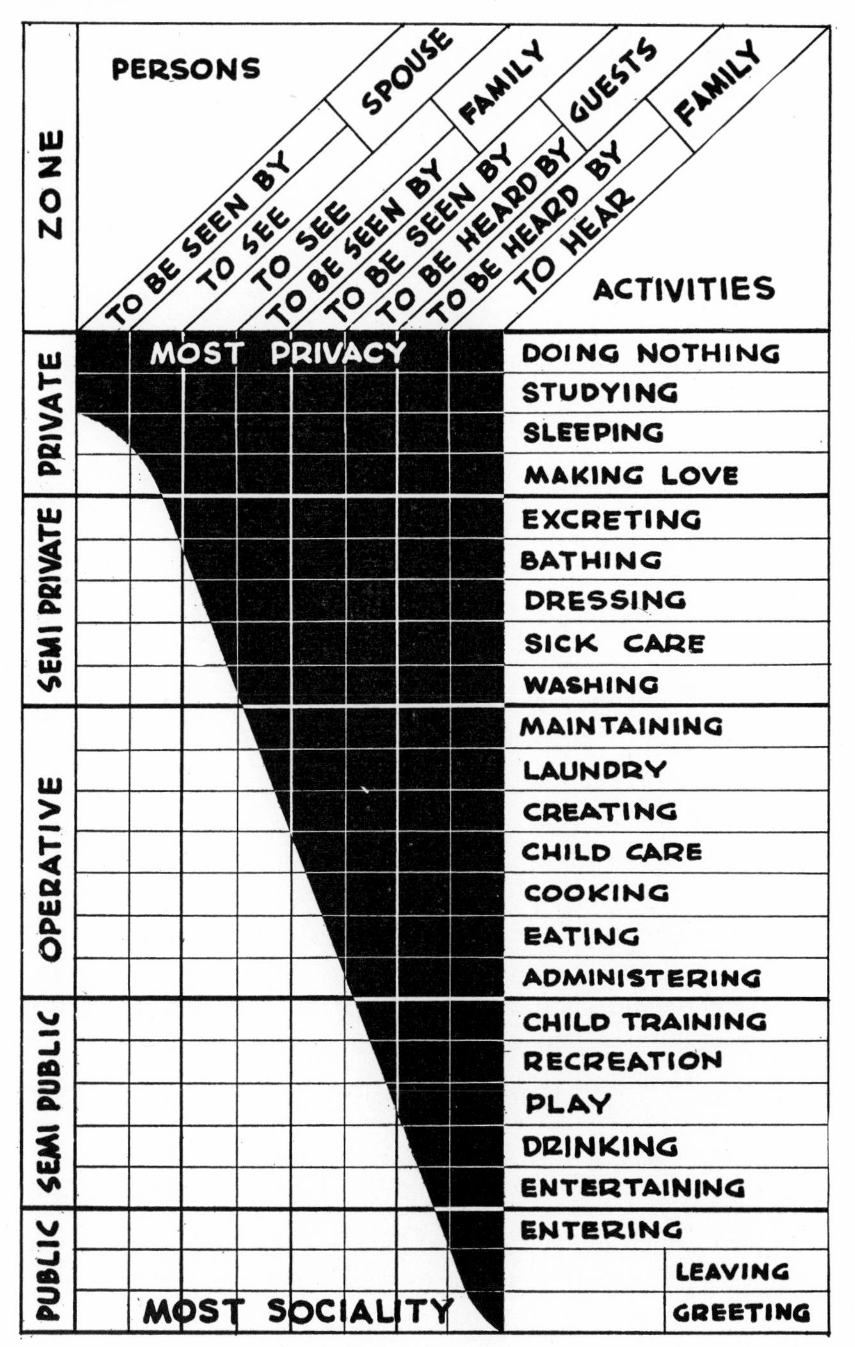
PERSONS
ZONE
SPOUSE
FAMILY
GUESTS
FAMILY
TO BE SEEN BY
TO SEE
TO SEE
TO BE SEEN BY
TO BE SEEN BY
TO BE HEARD BY
TO BE HEARD BY
TO HEAR
ACTIVITIES
PRIVATE
SEMI PRIVATE
OPERATIVE
SEMI PUBLIC
PUBLIC
MOST PRIVACY
MOST SOCIALITY
DOING NOTHING
STUDYING
SLEEPING
MAKING LOVE
EXCRETING
BATHING
DRESSING
SICK CARE
WASHING
MAINTAINING
LAUNDRY
CREATING
CHILD CARE
COOKING
EATING
ADMINISTERING
CHILD TRAINING
RECREATION
PLAY
DRINKING
ENTERTAINING
ENTERING
LEAVING
GREETING

The chart organizes the twenty-two functions selected in an order from top to bottom of from greater to less privacy, and from bottom to top, of from greater to less sociability. Each heading must be conceived of as a sort of portmanteau, carrying in its maw a host of minor functions. These are not worth considering in terms of the privacy—sociality spectrum, and can thus be suggested in a simple list, as follows:

PRIVATE

Doing nothing (relaxing, circulating, chatting, outdoor sitting).

Studying (homework, collecting, writing, reading, business matters).

Sleeping (reading, radio, naps, sickness, outdoor sleeping).

Making Love

SEMI-PRIVATE

Excreting (urinating, defecating).

Bathing (shower, tub, outdoor shower, sun bathing).

Dressing (undressing, storing clothes, shoe polishing).

Sick Care (caring, feeding, entertaining).

Washing (hands, face, hair, toothbrushing, make-up, shaving, lingerie).

OPERATIVE

Maintaining (washing floors, windows, woodwork, vacuuming, dusting, repairs, emptying trash, lawn mowing, sweeping walks, car washing, seasonal changes and storage).

Laundry (collecting, washing, drying, ironing, storing, mending).

Creating (sewing, music, painting, gardening, hobbies, writing, making things).

Child Care (feeding, toileting, bathing, dressing and undressing, getting up and putting to bed, comforting, putting outdoors).

Activities

Cooking (ordering, receiving, storing, mixing, cooking, table setting, clearing and washing up, cleaning, canning, freezing, outdoor cooking).

Eating (breakfast, lunch, dinner, snacks, small children's meals, baby bottles, feeding pets, outdoors and in).

Administering (accounts, telephoning, menu planning, replacements).

SEMI-PUBLIC

Child Training (supervision, play, outdoor play, educating).

Recreation (cards, quiet games (as chess), etc., reading, storytelling, scrapbooks, croquet, outdoor sitting).

Play (dancing, charades, plays, noisy games, romping with children, tennis, badminton, etc.).

Drinking (tea, coffee, cocktails, cold drinks in summer, soft drinks for children, outdoors and in).

Entertaining (conversation, radio-phonograph, live music, meetings, movies, eating and drinking, outdoors and in).

PUBLIC

Entering (leaving, taking off and putting on clothes and rubbers, storing toys, sports equipment, cars, or purchases, primping and neating up).

In a general way, the groups of functions adjacent in the chart and list should be, in fact, adjacent. In some cases this contradicts what we know to be common practice. Such cases arise from the way functions are assigned to rooms. For example, sick care has been placed in the semi-private zone. In terms of space this locates it next to the operative zone. On the other hand, the sick are confined to a bed which, because it is primarily used for sleeping, rest, and lovemaking, is in the private zone. Where the private and semi-private functions are grouped together and occur in one room no contradiction exists.

The chart, translated into a proximity and circulation diagram, appears as follows:

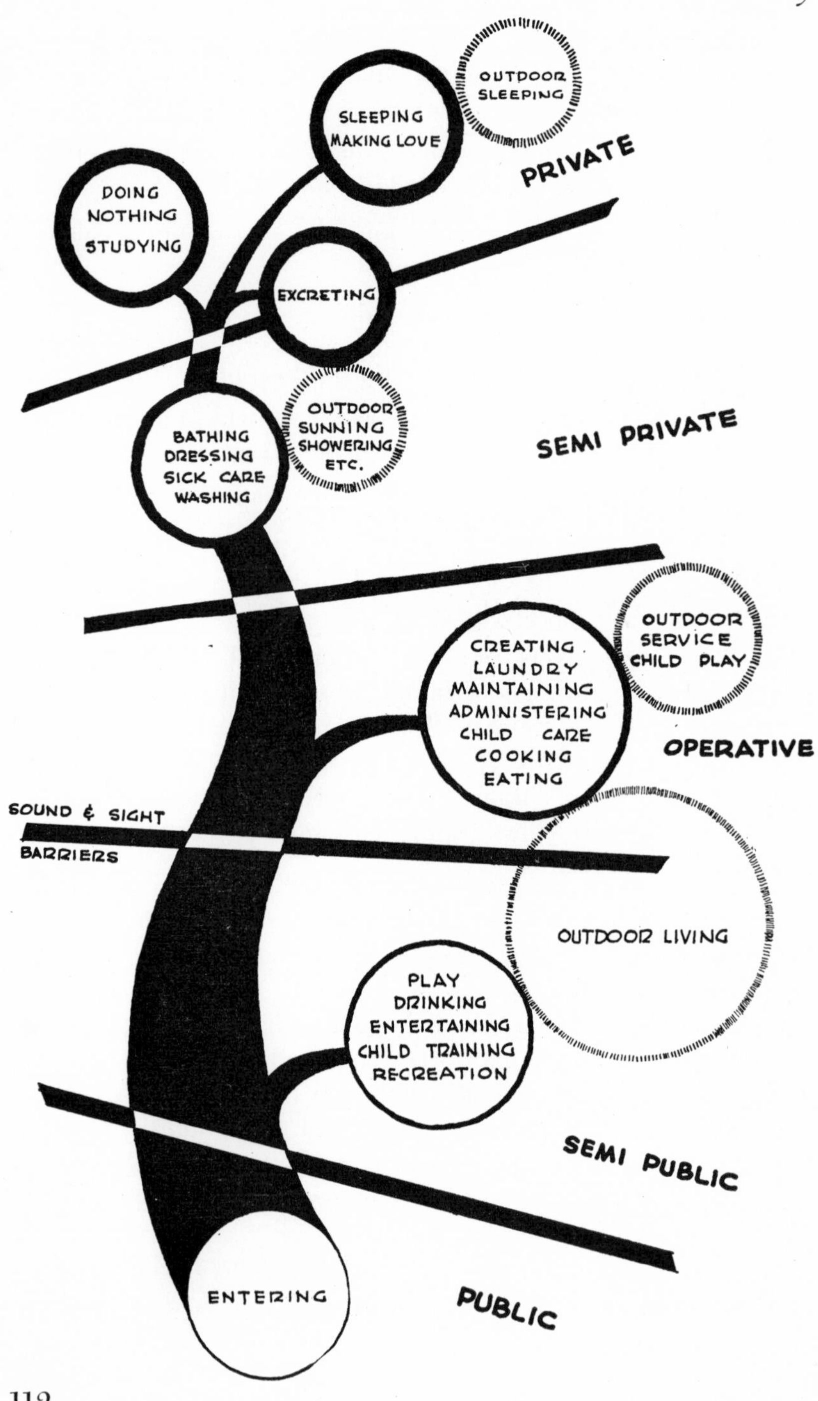
OUTDOOR SLEEPING
SLEEPING MAKING LOVE
PRIVATE
DOING NOTHING STUDYING
EXCRETING
OUTDOOR SUNNING SHOWERING ETC.
BATHING DRESSING SICK CARE WASHING
SEMI PRIVATE
OUTDOOR SERVICE CHILD PLAY
CREATING LAUNDRY MAINTAINING ADMINISTERING CHILD CARE COOKING EATING
OPERATIVE
SOUND & SIGHT
BARRIERS
OUTDOOR LIVING
PLAY DRINKING ENTERTAINING CHILD TRAINING RECREATION
SEMI PUBLIC
ENTERING
PUBLIC

Activities

The narrowing margin of acceptance of the guest is expressed by a narrowing circulation for him. The increasing desire for privacy, as one enters deeper and deeper into the family's activities, appears as a succession of barriers against sight and sound. In terms of privacy, the front door at one end, and the study, water closet, and connubial chamber at the other, are three worlds apart, separated by four distinct barriers. Each group of activities constitutes a little world of its own, cohesive and very distinct in atmosphere and character.

These five worlds spill over into the out-of-doors. Outdoor living presents exactly the same problems as its counterpart indoors. The sameness of the two, the need for total intimacy between them is of the essence. Garrett Eckbo notes the following:

> "When one buys a lot one buys a cube of air space to live in, the bottom side or floor of which is the earth of the lot. It is a mistake to follow the standard practice of designing the house as a box of living space, placing it more or less appropriately *on* the lot, and then landscaping it (adding beautification, or exterior decoration). It is more sensible, and productive of better results for the residents, to plan the use of the entire lot at once, as a coordinated series of rationally connected and related indoor and outdoor rooms. This is the only way to avoid the waste and inconvenience of the majority of our homes—useless side-yard and driveway space, front yards larger than necessary, rear garden accessible only through kitchen and laundry porch, clothes-lines and garbage cans cluttering up the backyard and too far from kitchen and laundry, no place for kids to play without damaging the garden, etc. An optimum solution of the home-planning problem must accept the basic premise that the four general units enumerated above are really indoor-outdoor units, because they all require complementing or supplementing by outdoor elements. . . ."

The essential fact is that nearly all, if not all of the functions performed indoors are also performed out-of-doors, including sun bathing and gardening.

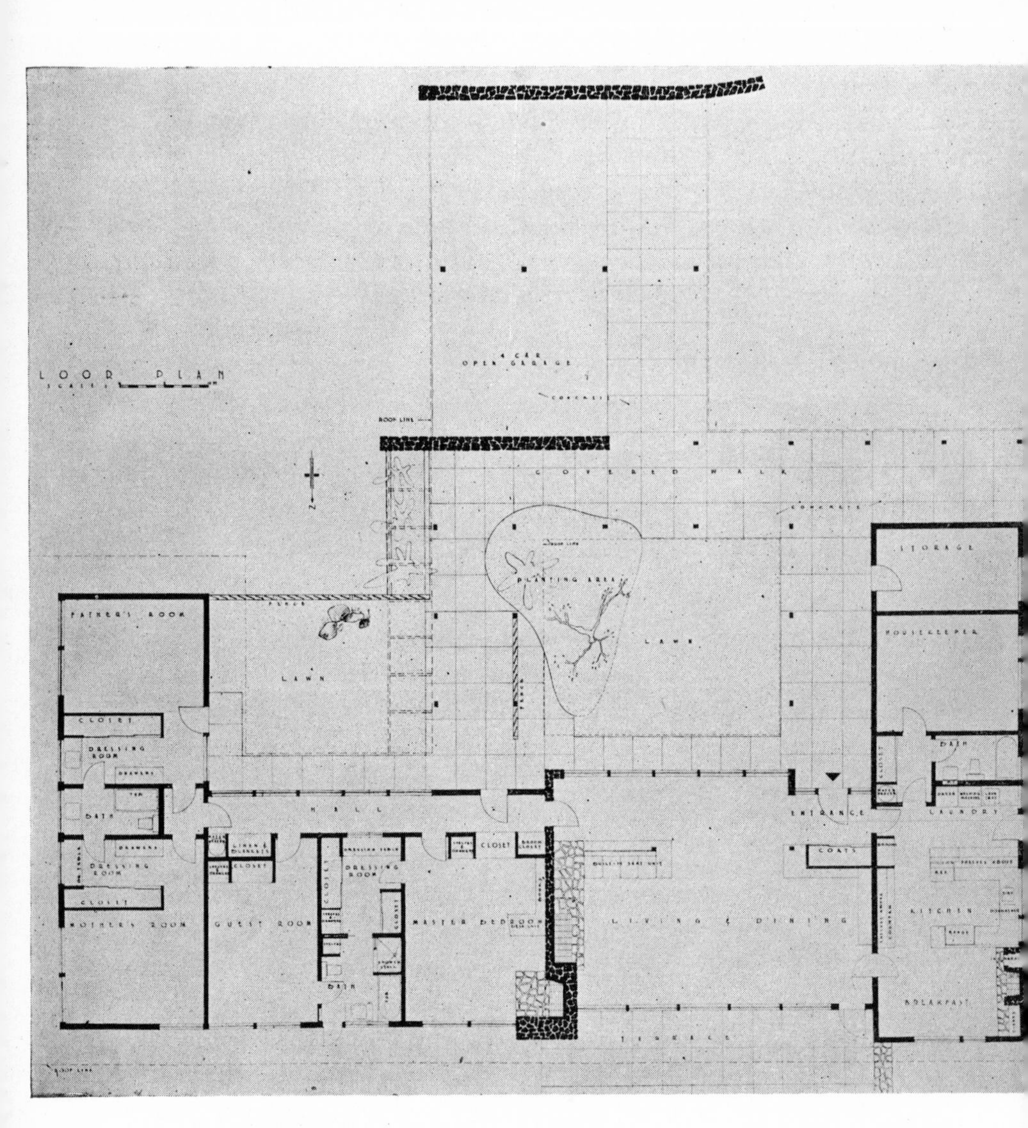

Pietro Belluschi: A house divided into four very clear cut zones. Reading from left to right, for the grandparents—for owners and guests, for living, dining; terrace, entrance, and circulation—and for service, housekeeper, and storage.

The plans opposite are for the house pictured on page 101. The kitchen is absorbed into the living, dining, entrance, staircase, porch zone. The studio with its workroom eblow constitutes a second two story zone. The bedrooms and bath are a third. Below all this is the heater room, storage room, and logia, on the rear ground level.

Zones

The classificatory device used above automatically groups the living activities. This was the second step suggested as necessary in order to answer the livability problem. Once the activities are grouped it is possible to approach very much closer to architecture, for these clusters of functions can now be translated into physically distinct zones. There are three reasons for zoning. Technically it is easier, and cheaper, to maintain a desired loudness level if the surroundings are also at more or less the same level. Secondly the larger and more complex the area or areas dedicated to one purpose, the greater their emotional impact, the more pleasant they are, and the more likely they are to be used as intended. The third reason has to do with sight, which because of our atti-

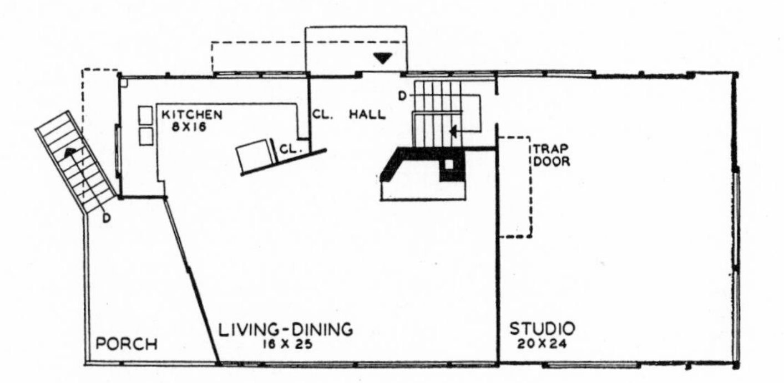

UPPER FLOOR

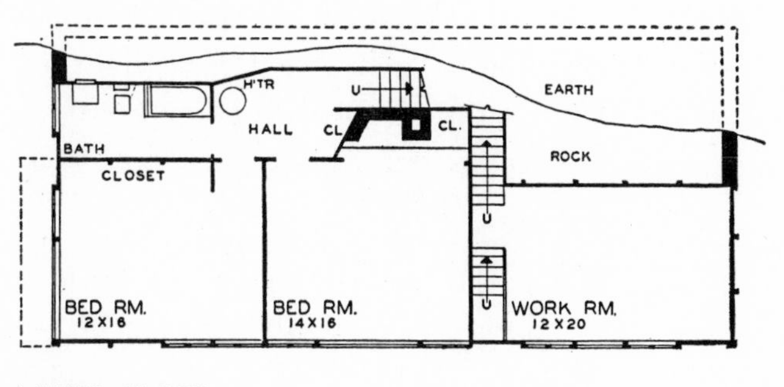

LOWER FLOOR

tudes toward sex, and because of our class structure, is the most important aspect of communication. To see and be seen in socially unacceptable circumstances is least embarrassing when it occurs in the properly connected physical space, most when it occurs in a space considered functionally inappropriate. The content of house zones must be decided on such considerations as these.

There is no word or locution in common use to express the development of a scheme from human relationships. Gross room relationships have been described in architectural jargon in terms of two words, circulation and zoning. Both have been worked to death. It might be revealing, momentarily, to use others more descriptive of the states of mind involved. Circulation means, in human terms, *going*, and zoning may be said to mean *being*. In the past the emphasis given circulation and zoning has been in inverse ratio to their respective importance. *Going* places has been considered pre-eminent, and indeed poor circulation patterns and ugly circulation pieces are hallmarks of bad architecture. *Being*, has been more or less completely ignored. Beginning architectural students, for example, never apply zoning principles to their first houses at all. Their difficulties involve circulation, not only in corridors, but also in rooms. The reason for this is undoubtedly that circulation is obvious, while the zoning off of functions can exist without being at all self-evident. To going and being one must add *doing*. The three together constitute the human states with which the architect is actually dealing. These states are so intermingled with minutiae of all sorts that they must be explored in relation to each function. In the interim the sensations *being* and *doing* can be approached, based on the classification above, through descriptions of the various zones.

PUBLIC ZONE

Privacy	The most public part of the house. It is the buffer between the world and the family, and thus needs more privacy from the rest of the house than it does from the world.

Communication	One of the two most expressive places in the house, in that the visitor gets, and makes, his first impression here.
Significance	Very great socially, because it is the symbol of home to the family—the place which witnesses its most frequent and important comings and goings.
Noise	Entering and leaving is unavoidably noisy at best, and sometimes requires noise as a part of the social occasion. This is least disturbing to the operative zone, next least to social, next least to semi-private, and most to the private zone. Family entering late is a prime cause for disturbed sleep.
Sight	Guests should be able to see the entrance clearly in order to find it, but once in, should not be able to see into any part of the house not primarily reserved to them.
Activities	Entering, leaving, maintenance, storing, greeting, clothes changing, bill signing, etc.
Spaces	Walk, driveway, front garden, porch, entry, entrance hall, storm vestibule, closets, store rooms, garage, etc. etc.
Location	Ideally this zone should be indirectly connected with the social, operative, and semi-private zones. Its least requirement is to be connected with the social zone.
Use Frequency	Sporadic, early morning, noon, late afternoon, early evening and late evening probably predominating.

SOCIAL ZONE

Privacy	The second most public part of the house where the family gathers by itself and where it is, as a unit, private from the world. The fact that it is where the world is entertained, or met, does not reduce its demand on group privacy.
Communication	Where most formal and intensive communication takes place, and must therefore be conceived with this in mind.
Significance	With the entrance the most significant spot socially in that as a symbol of the family—its earning power, status, etc.—it places them in the visitor's scale of values.
Noise	The amount of noise produced in it, because its functions range from very noisy to very quiet, varies greatly. Noises made by a dancing party for example, must be isolated from the private and semi-private zones. Parties often overlap the sleeping hours of various members of the family and, if noise can be transmitted, cause conflicts.
Sight	Needs isolation from immediate public view.
Smell	As family cooking odors should not impinge on this zone, proper isolation and ventilation for the operative zone is required to protect it.
Activities	Parties, entertaining, quiet games such as cards, dances, teas, cocktails, coffee, romantic cooking over a fireplace, telephoning, reading, conversation, plays and charades, live music, radio-phonograph,

	recorder, meetings, child training in manners and attitudes, maintenance, etc.
Spaces	Garden, terrace, pergola, porch, platform, screened porch, living room, library, parlor, reception room, flower window, etc.
Use Frequency	Noon, late afternoon and evening probably predominant.
Location	Between public and operative zones.

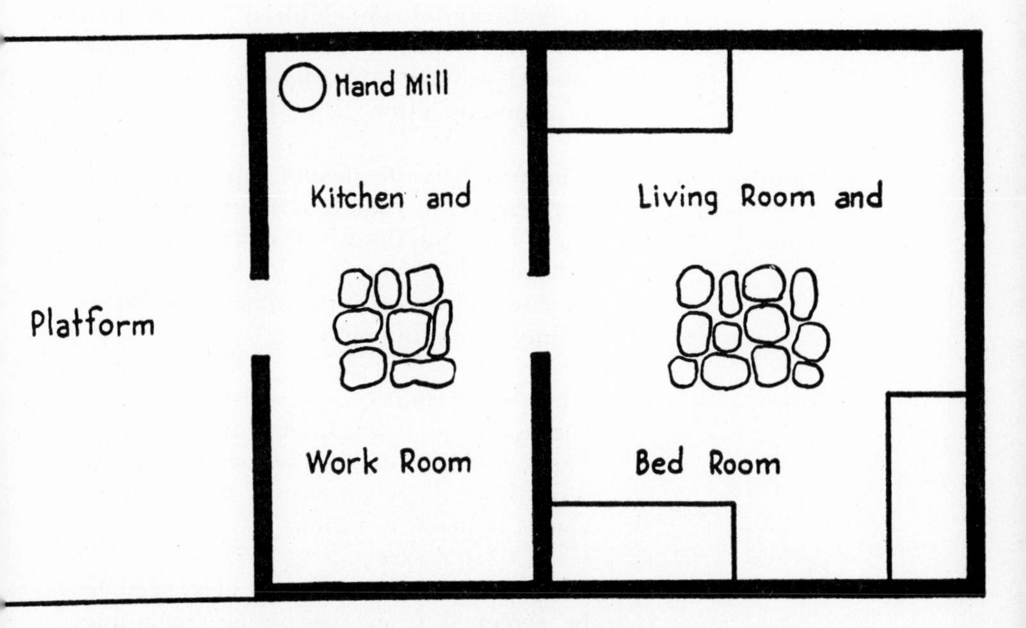

Lacustrine house, plan conjectural: This embodies a sort of zoning which in our society is frowned upon in theory, but often used in practice. Outdoor living and entrance are combined. One then passes through the operative zone, in order to get to the most private zone. This makes good sense in terms of privacy. But it makes the display of our sort of good housekeeping, and of our sort of manners, rather difficult. We therefore usually prefer to reverse the order of zones.

OPERATIVE ZONE

Privacy	This is semi-private from guests, who may enter it with increasing ease as they become better acquainted with the family. By the same token it is more private than the social zone. This is the servants' (when they exist) domain, and must be planned for their privacy.
Communication	Not too important to guests, but more important to the family than the social zone. The give and take required by the working functions of the family take place here, and also communication between parents and little children, family and servants, husband and wife. It requires special provision for these various types of communication.
Significance	The social significance of this zone is not very great, in that it is more or less reserved for the family. Its functional significance, however, is great, both in terms of ease of operation and ease of intra-family communication.
Noise	This is necessarily the noisiest part of the house on a day-to-day, hour-to-hour basis, and the noises produced here are objectionable when heard from other zones. It needs isolation.
Sight	The activities which go on here need to be screened from the public, including those which spill over into the outdoors.
Smell	Most smells are produced here by cooking and washing, and must be vented out directly in order not to disturb the rest of the house.

Zones

Activities	Washing clothes, (collecting, washing, drying, ironing, storing); cooking (ordering, receiving, storing, mixing, cooking, table setting, clearing, washing up, cleaning, canning, freezing); eating, (breakfast, lunch, dinner, snacks, children's meals, baby bottles, feeding pets); child care (feeding, toileting, bathing, clothes changing); child play and supervision, all of the servants' living functions, sewing, mending, maintenance, gardening, etc.
Spaces	Laundry, laundry yard, garbage and waste disposal area, toilet, servants' closet, children's coat closet and clothes drying space, toy and material storage, general storage space, sewing room, kitchen, shop, breakfast room, dining room, all purpose room, servants' dining room, rear entry, kitchen living space, kitchen garden, garden tool storage, garage, greenhouse, cold frame.
Location	Close to parts of social zone for easy service, such as tea and cocktails, etc. and to living garden and service yard. Direct connection with semi-private zone for ease of child care and care of the sick. Closely connected with servants' own living zone, but this should be planned as privately as the equivalent space for the family. Should be widely separated from studies, libraries, and rooms used for intensive and completely private activities.
Use Frequency	All morning, noon, late afternoon to early evening, and late evening probably predominant.

SEMI-PRIVATE ZONE

Privacy	This is well into the most private areas, not only of the family as a whole, but of cultural categories.
Communication	Intimate communication between small numbers of people with some exceptions when parents' bedroom is used for entertaining, when people are sick, or when teenagers use its facilities to entertain.
Significance	This zone is fairly well charged with significance on an individual and subjective level, due to the fact that its spaces are considered as the personal property of others, that its divisions emphasize sex differentiation, and that depending on the circumstances, it can offer embarrassing surprises, delightful moments alone, or moments of significant human interchange.
Noise	Noise by itself would not seem to be much of a problem, unless the spaces are inextricably mixed up with the private zone and thus cannot be differentiated by function.
Sight	The ability to shut off those of the opposite sex, of another group, etc., is highly important. Even though the family does not, when alone, observe such distinctions, they probably must when guests are present, and thus need the ability to achieve visual privacy.
Activities	Dressing, undressing, storing, maintennance, washing, bathing, writing, child play (probably solitary), and care of the sick.

Spaces	Bedrooms, bathrooms, toilets, compartmented baths, dressing rooms, storage rooms, laundries, sitting rooms, sun traps, outdoor showers.
Location	Close connection with the private and operative zones, and with outdoor sun bathing, etc.
Use Frequency	Early morning, late afternoon, early evening and late evening probably predominant, but can be used more frequently depending on living patterns.

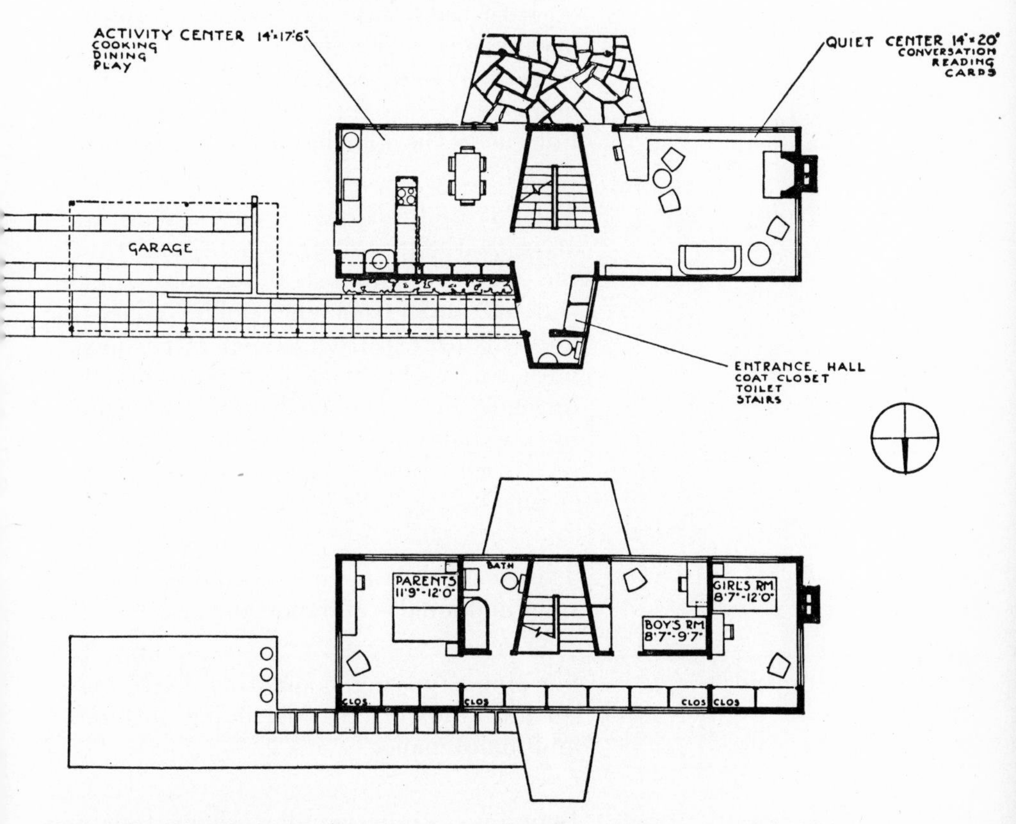

Robert Woods Kennedy: Zoning with the needs of young children in mind—after Mrs. Fields' The Human House.

PRIVATE ZONE

Privacy	The functions lumped together here would seem to demand the most complete possible privacy, operational as well as physical.
Communication	Minimal, though when its functions are shared with others in the same space communication will enter into design.
Significance	The zone's significance is almost totally limited to the individual. It has little to do with the family as a whole except as discipline is exacted for the sake of others' privacy. The less good the house, the more irritating the discipline becomes. For guests the zone has little significance.
Noise	The private functions cannot be heard by others without embarrassment, and thus the spaces should not allow noises out. Outside noise from the public zone is most disturbing, from the operative next most, and within itself least. Noise made by children or the aged should be heard by the parents or a servant, either directly with doors open, or by electrical means.
Sight	The ability to be completely out of others' sight and mind is of importance.
Activities	Sleeping, studying, copulating, excreting, certain kinds of creating, doing nothing, and maintenance.
Spaces	Bedrooms, studies, studios, shops, toilets, bathrooms, compartmented baths, sleeping porches.

Zones

Location	In close juxtaposition with the semi-private zone, as preparation for study or sleeping takes place there. Some should be near the kitchen, such as children's rooms, rooms for the aged, and servants' rooms. Studies, studios, and the like can be as widely separated as possible provided they have their own toilets. Parents' and children's bedrooms in the early years need close juxtaposition, in later years need more privacy from each other.
Use Frequency	Studies in mornings or afternoons, occasionally evenings, bedrooms at night, occasionally mornings.

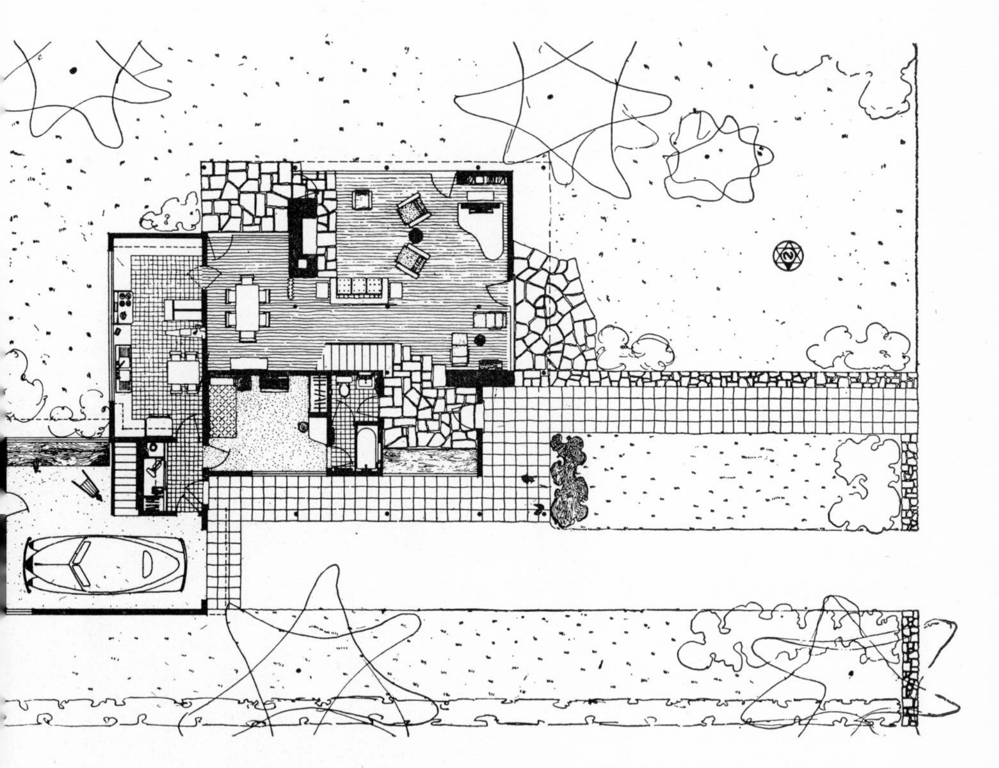

Robert Woods Kennedy: Typical upper middle class requirements, except that the maid's bath does not usually double as front hall toilet.

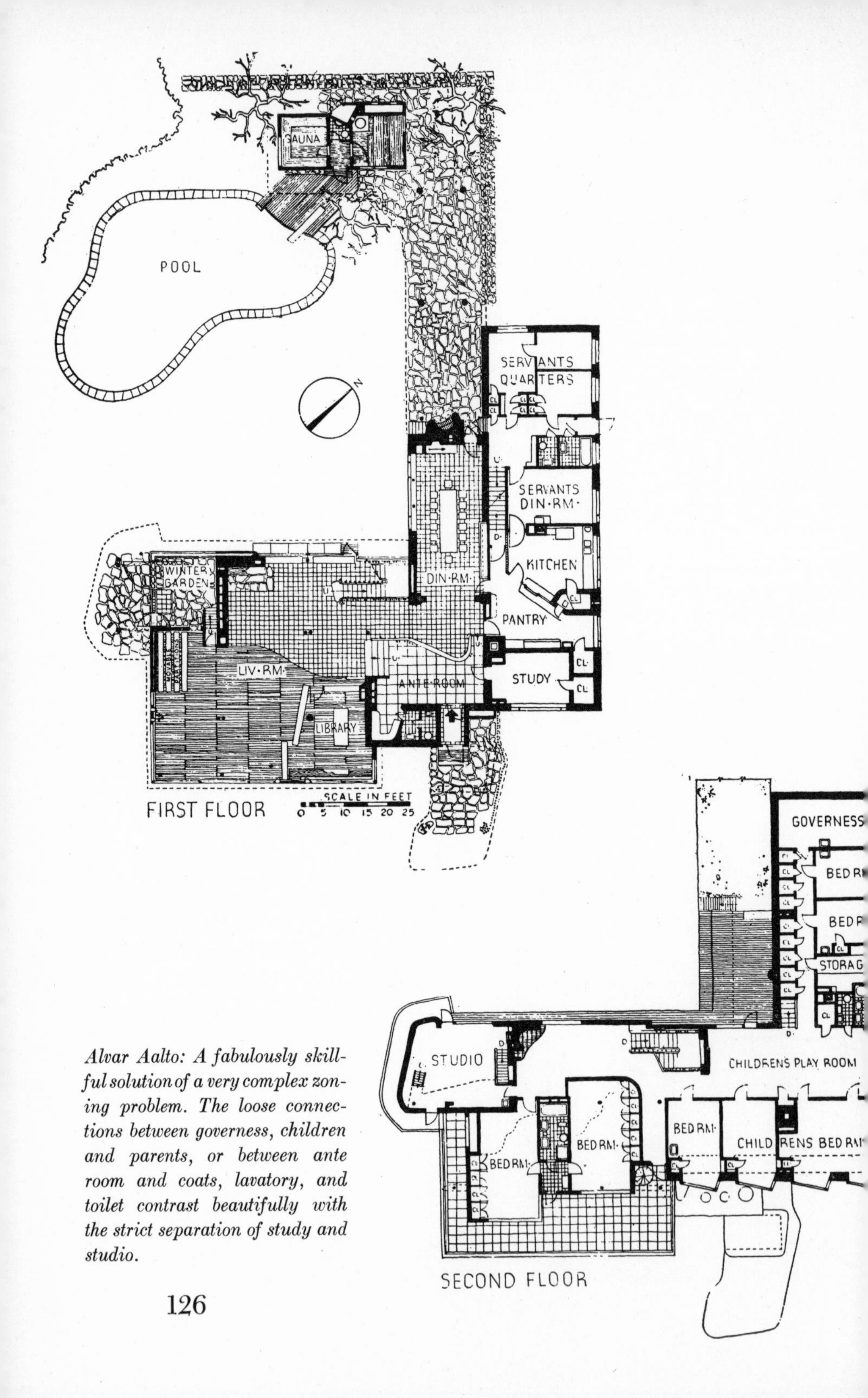

Alvar Aalto: A fabulously skillful solution of a very complex zoning problem. The loose connections between governess, children and parents, or between ante room and coats, lavatory, and toilet contrast beautifully with the strict separation of study and studio.

Zones

Because so many of the living activities can overlap from zone to zone, no one set of clusters may be laid down as universally applicable. Depending on personal preference, the amount of money available, and the number of people in the family, one can divide houses into any number of zones, from two up. The following are a few of the possible variations:

Two Zone	Private	Bedrooms, bath
	Group	All other functions
Three Zone	Private	Bedrooms and baths
	Operative	Cooking, dining, etc.
	Passive	Living, study, etc.
Four Zone	Private	Bedrooms, baths
	Operative	Cooking, dining, play, etc.
	Buffer	Halls, storage, garage, etc.
	Passive	Living room, study, library
Five Zone	Private	Family bedrooms, baths, etc.
	Private	Servants' bedrooms, baths, etc.
	Active	Playrooms, nurseries, etc.
	Operative	Kitchen, pantry, etc.
	Passive	Dining, living, study, etc.

Zoning, when it is applied to the family of somewhat limited means and without full time service, inevitably suggests the four zone house. In one of the most interesting arguments for the differentiation of a family's activities, Mrs. Field makes this suggestion:

"Instead of trying to provide separate quarters for the various members of the family when their needs conflict (i.e., father's den, mother's sewing room, children's playroom), with a common meeting place in the living room for group meetings; instead of trying to schedule its use as a playroom from four to five, and a study from five to six, plan for a permanent space in which quiet will *always* be found, a permanent space in which one is always allowed to romp, a permanent settled space in which each family member can find privacy."

Frank Lloyd Wright used her ideas in his "Two Zone" houses which he describes as follows:

"The letter from housewife Field is directly responsible for the germ plan of the two-zone house. New facilities make it desirable to lay aside the provincial squeamishness that made the American parlor and designedly make a beautiful circumstance to take the place of the kind of kitchen that should now go where the parlor went sometime ago. With modern kitchen appurtenances what used to be the kitchen can now become a high spacious work studio opening level with the garden. Therefore the zone of activity may be a natural get-together space in which to live while at work."

"The Car-port has been 'entered' as integral feature of the dwelling convenient and not the gaping hole it usually is as built in now. The features that distinguish the Two-Zone House from the Norm of the early One-Zone House given out from the same source about 1901 is the utilities concentration called the utilities stack, the development of the kitchen into the real living room completely furnished as part of the whole and the segregation of space called the study. A third zone—call it the slumber zone—is introduced as mezzanine with balcony opening into the living room or 'Work Room.' "

"The servant has no domicile in a house of this type. The whole idea of 'servant' would vulgarize the kind of life suited to the house. Outside help coming in at stated times—being more professional and should be all the labor the modern housewife would need with her modern labor saving devices and a proper regard for bringing up the young to accept normal responsibilities in the household."

Mr. Wright's house actually contains six zones. But however one counts the separate zones, houses which do not recognize the similarities and differences of the living activities are bound to cause undue friction. Furthermore, the different groups of functions must be given great distinction both in terms of character and separation, if the rooms which house them are to develop their optimum usefulness.

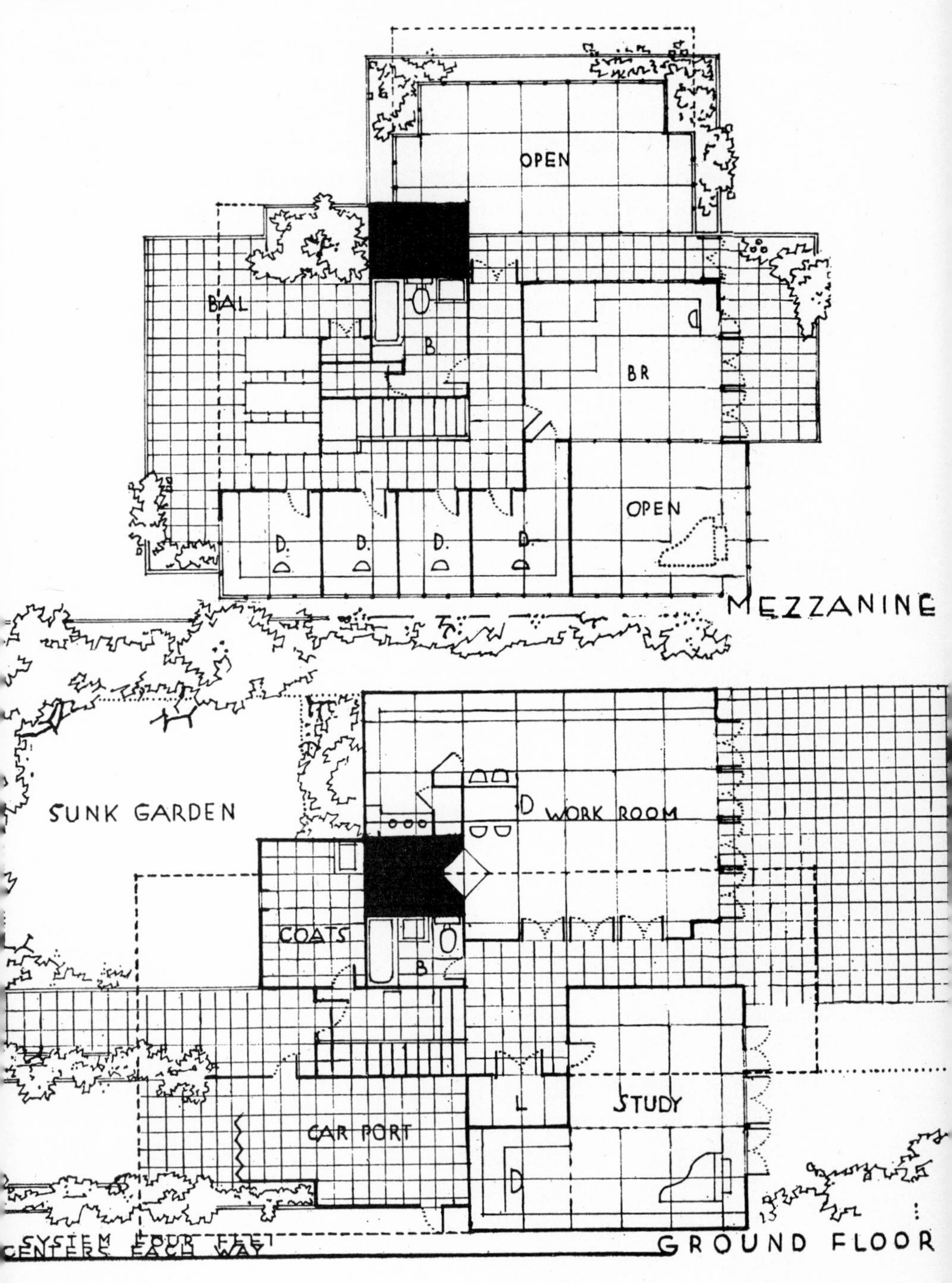
OPEN
BAL
B.
BR
OPEN
D.
D.
D.
D.
MEZZANINE
SUNK GARDEN
D
WORK ROOM
COATS
B
L
STUDY
CAR PORT
D
SYSTEM FOUR FEET
CENTERS EACH WAY
GROUND FLOOR

Duplications

The need to duplicate many of the living activities would seem at first glance to be so obvious as to require no comment. And indeed it need not be explored to any great extent. The client's program is apt to be primarily concerned with those things he wants two or more of, such as bedrooms and baths. Thus the architect more or less automatically finds out how many rooms are wanted. On the other hand so many houses fail in terms of livability, because duplicate spaces are not provided for certain living activities, that the whole subject must contain pitfalls which do not readily meet the eye. The deepest of these is, perhaps, the tendency to confuse living activities and rooms. They are not at all synonymous. When they are confused, the living activities are apt to suffer. For example, to provide an elegant front hall, conceiving this as taking care of entering and leaving in general, is to miss the boat entirely. Thus the primary distinctions are between living activities, the space, furniture, and equipment they require, the rooms by means of which they are separated or joined, and the zones by which incompatible clusters of activities are differentiated.

The important service the architect performs is to take care of every activity somewhere—somehow. This does not imply any specific number of rooms or zones. The specified activities can all be performed in one space. Or they can be dispersed over any number of spaces. Their exact deployment depends on such variables as the grandmother's health, the building budget, what functions the servant performs and whether she lives in or out, personal living patterns, and the like. The possibilities are infinite. Surely this is one reason why architecture is so rewarding as an occupation. There are always new worlds to conquer.

The peculiar interplay of functions, equipment, spaces, and zones suggests another aspect of architecture. Variety, freshness, innovation, and progress in livability stem largely from new combinations of these four factors. The living activities themselves and those similarities between them which allow them to be zoned, have been considered above. The development of the rooms themselves is dependent on the following:

1. The activity or group of activities to be performed.
2. The number of people concerned.
3. Their peculiar requirements by cultural category.
4. The spaces, furniture, and equipment called for by 1, 2, and 3 above.

The collection of the data required by these steps is programming. Its use is design. This suggests that, fundamentally, the architect must conceive of each room as an undetermined amount of floor space, which he arranges according to the criteria stated in the program. During the process he discovers its limits. He then encloses it, on these limit lines, with structure. We are here so close to the core of the design process that to continue it would be necessary to take up pencil, triangle, and T square. There is, however, a prior step. In order to design with any celerity it is necessary to build up a frame of reference, to develop attitudes towards a series of typical problems, *in advance*. They cannot be fully explored at the drafting board. The next chapter will, for a series of selected clusters of functions, explore some of these kinds of problems. In order to do this some point of view as to the duplication of activities must be developed. The family is so constituted that it almost invariably needs more than one of several kinds of things.

The fact that the same activity is performed in two places does not imply that two rooms are required. For example, a back door can enter directly into a kitchen, without a back hall. In such case, extra space may be required. But then again it may be dual use space, and not all at apparent as needed for the functions entering and leaving. Thus, in what follows, an increase in floor area or volume for the duplicated activity is not always implied, even though it is usually necessary. The reasons for duplication are primarily as follows:

1. The activity is conceived of as private (as excretion).
2. Frequency of use makes a duplicate desirable, as bath rooms.
3. In order to separate cultural categories for reasons of social distinction (as maids), or of behavior (as children).
4. In order to enjoy a greater sense of luxury.

Again, we are dealing here with an infinite number of possibilities. It would be quite fruitless to attempt to list them. In practice, however, a limited number of duplications are usually highly desirable in terms of livability.

Maintaining	Duplicated spaces usually depend on the scheme of the house, as secondary cleaning closets on the second floor, or secondary entering storage in the garage, etc. etc.
Creating	In certain instances work shops, die sinks, studios, and the like need duplication for functional reasons.
Child Care	Duplication of toileting, bathing, and dressing facilities within, or as an extra bathroom; extra toilet near the back door, extra clothes hanging and drying space near the back door, extra storage areas at all entrances, extra space and equipment outdoors etc.
Studying	By and large everyone needs furniture for study. Many housewives urgently desire a study cubicle of their own. The husbands need depends on living pattern.
Sleeping	Cultural categories must be separated, while separate bedrooms, except for married couples, seem increasingly essential.
Excreting Washing Bathing	Duplicates for servants usually seem essential, though this may be combined with a general use toilet, more particularly for children, at the back door. Duplication for cultural categories is often regarded as desirable. And of course, at the extreme, every bedroom has its bath.
Dressing	Usually duplicated for every person but not for parents.

Cooking	Freezing, storage, and wash up space and equipment can all be duplicated to advantage under certain circumstances.
Eating	Duplications for breakfast, maids, children, formal dining, outdoor dining, etc.
Administering	Usually done with the same things as studying, but sometimes duplicated in the kitchen.
Child Training	Extra chairs in living spaces, special closets with low hooks, places designed for children to put their own things away in, etc.
Recreation	Storage space in functionally connected space for all family members. For maid, grandparents, etc. in their apartments. For parents in their bedroom, particularly where the living room is also used by teenagers. For husband in the kitchen, etc.
Play	For children and teenagers as separate spaces.
Entering	For servants, service, children, etc. with all connected storage space, etc.

Buffers

The list of rooms mentioned in the zone descriptions does not include all of the spaces in a house. Heater rooms, utility rooms, store rooms, and closets of various kinds are left over. They can be used as effective barriers. This use of spaces to achieve privacy, rather than to rely solely on walls and doors, can also extend to rooms actually housing the living activities. There would thus appear to be a sixth zone in the house, made up of rooms so little used that they are not noise hazards in themselves, and of certain other rooms arbitrarily selected to perform the function of separating dissimilar activities. This can be visualized as follows:

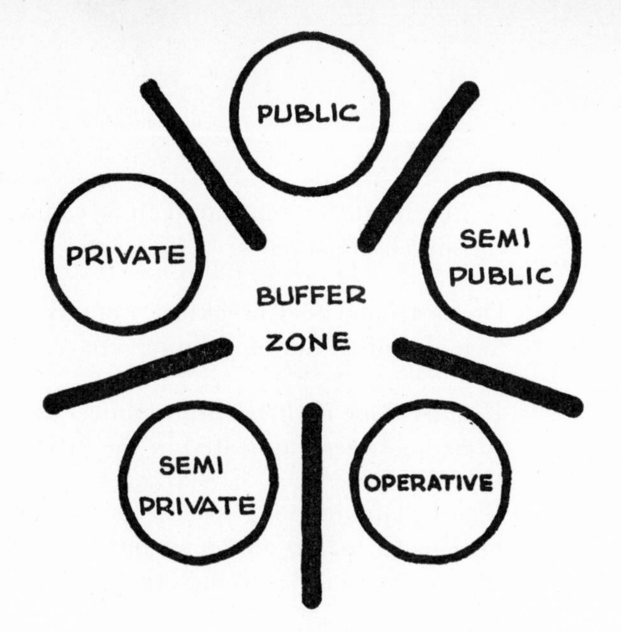

The use of spaces as sight and sound barriers can only be accomplished in the conceptual stage. It must be inherent to the fundamental idea. The requirements for good acoustics, for example, are basic criteria. They must be woven into the very fabric of the plan. The battle against noise is won or lost in the preliminary sketch stage. When working drawings are started, mopping up is all that should be left to accomplish. Knudsen and Harris express this fact with the wry twist of the engineer forever called in too late.

> "Acoustics, no less than structural strength and partitioning of the building, should be planned for at the beginning. It is not good practice to seek the advice of an acoustical consultant after the plans (or even the building!) have been completed, with the request, "Please prepare recommendations, without of course proposing major structural changes, for providing good acoustics in this building." Sometimes such recommendations can be made but more often they cannot."

Exactly the same things can be said of seeing, with all it entails in terms of light, darkness, glare, fatigue, color, and privacy—all of which are human sensations, not architectural features.

The distinction between satisfying human needs by means of

the initial and fundamental scheme of the house, and satisfying them through the use of techniques, cannot be overestimated. The architect's true role is conceptual. The scheme for a house must come from his head complete, as did Minerva from the mind of Zeus. Minerva needed no doctor to bring her in or fix her up. Her only desire might have been for a Five-and-Ten to provide her with bobby pins. The engineer should be in this same relation to the architect.

A concrete example might better describe the two kinds of thinking. The individual, if he is to be ideally happy in terms of sound, must have varying degrees of quiet for the various functions he is to perform. In order to achieve this, the architect must first analyze the noise at the site, locate the house with sound sources and frequencies in mind, locate the zones in successive removal from sources of noise, analyze the functions of rooms in terms of noise, separate them whenever possible by other spaces used as sound barriers, and locate doors and windows with the diffractory and other characteristics of sound in mind. The engineering of a partition or door, or the application of sound deadening material comes only at the very last moment, when the best possible compromise of all factors has been made. In the dynamic environment of the house, with its numerous activities going on at all hours, in winter with windows shut, in summer with windows open, the real solution to the sound, light, ventilation, and other quasi-technical problems will be inherent to the scheme, not to the gadgets.

The use of space and spaces to create buffer zones between incompatible functions can be dramatized. Or they can be so subtly and inconspicuously used as to be invisible except to the inquiring eye. The spaces possible of such use cannot be listed with any degree of surety. The opportunity to use them is usually fortuitous—a matter of skill and opportunism. The usual possibilities are store rooms of all kinds, garages, closets of all kinds, structural features such as chimneys, heater rooms, circulation pieces, etc. The following illustration shows the plan of a house and, beside it, notes on the reasoning behind the use of such features, with descriptions of the way the zones were designed to operate.

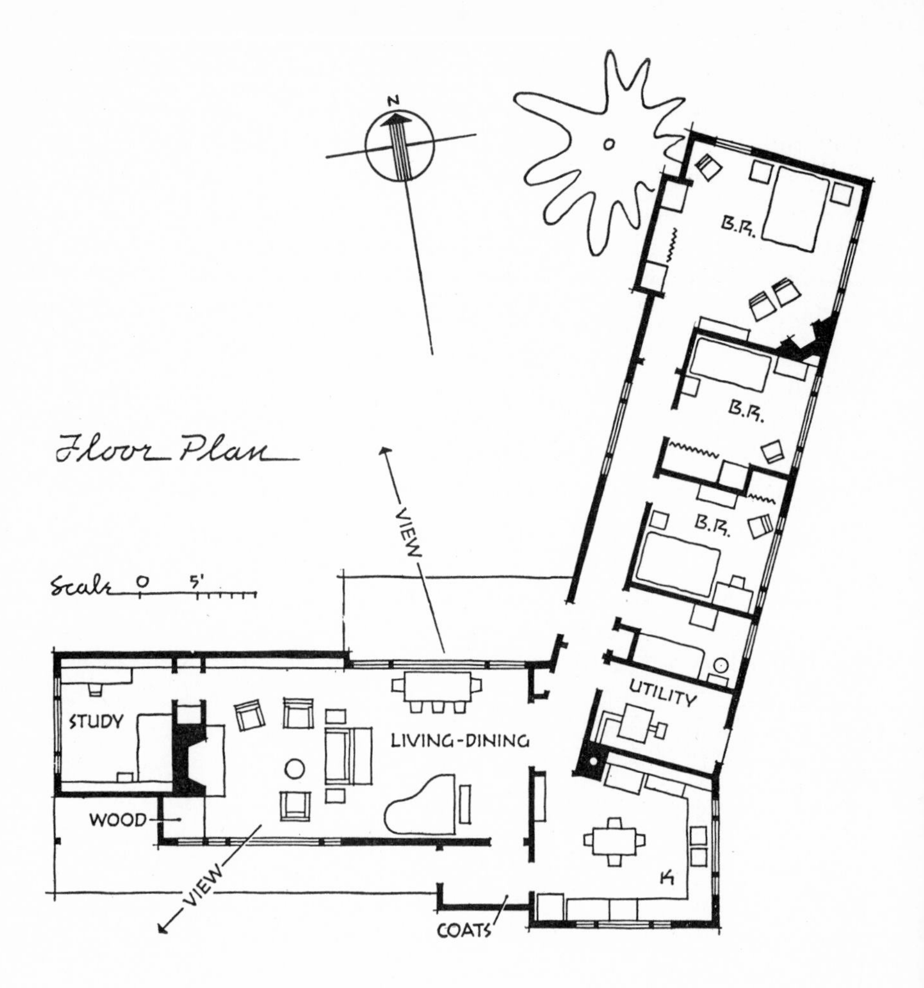

Roberts Woods Kennedy: This is a house for a writer, who works in the study. The study is separated from the living room by double doors through a storage space and by the chimney and wood box. It can be further isolated, during the morning hours, by the living room. This is possible because the bedrooms and entry connect directly with the kitchen. At night the bedroom wing can be cut off from the living room, entry, kitchen group, so that children can sleep while adults have a party. The bath and utility room serve as a further barrier against noise from the front part of the house seeping through into the bedrooms.

Bodies

Livability, thus far, has been considered in the narrowest sense, i.e., only in terms of the class-conditioned needs of individuals, and of the social organization of the family. But livability also involves our bodies.

The problem posed by the relationship of the human body to its housing is so fundamental that one must conceive of the whole of architecture as revolving around it. Architects, like painters, are concerned with the expressiveness of the body. Its beauty and majesty, particularly in movement, are enormously enhanced by the setting in which it is seen. Secondly, architects, like doctors and safety engineers, are concerned with its more tiresome aspects. In order to design a safe and comfortable house for it, one must conceive of it as inept, vulnerable to every sort of accident, disease, rodent, and insect, always reacting to the heat, or the cold, or the light, or the noise, or the ice, or the rain, or the sun, or the mice, or the mosquitoes, or the steps, or the smells, and so on down an interminable list of woes. One purpose of houses is to protect bodies from some of these hazards and to alleviate others. Indeed, there is a school of thought which goes so far as to claim that these functions are the principal purpose of houses. The words "shelter" and "machine for living" suggest an environment which includes all the comforts of the iron lung.

Thirdly, the architect, like the social psychologist, must see the body's strengths and frailties as determined, to a large extent, by social and psychological factors. It would almost seem as though there were no activity which has not been performed in a different way in other times and places, and which does not contain elements which are due solely to social conditioning.

Quite obviously these three views are indivisible. To design for safety, or beauty, or psychic security alone is inconceivable. The building which lacks any one is nothing. As a practical matter however, the body's needs must be examined separately. The conscious mind is not versatile enough to consider such complexities in a block. The architect must break down the material he uses into a series of typical problems, small enough and encompassable enough to be examined rationally. Thus we have heating, for example, essentially the job of solving an equation—thermal physiology + house = climate. Even here distinct differences occur in desired comfort levels, as between North Americans and Englishmen, which are explainable only in terms of social psychology. Each such problem—and there are dozens—contain the elements of art, of safety, of comfort, and of social conditioning. Each can be worked on continuously. Some, like heating, are rather highly specialized. Others, for example the inevitable conflict between the client's budget and the amount of space he wants, are more or less the sole property of the architect. He develops attitudes towards them, or special skills in their solution. The final creative act of design is the synthesis of solutions to all existing problems into a meaningful and efficient whole. Though this is largely an unconscious process a proper solution cannot be achieved without the spade work involved in a thorough understanding of each separate problem.

For a house to be neutral enough to be appreciated for its good qualities it should, ideally, function perfectly as a foil for the human body at its most vulnerable. Whether it is a technocrat's dream of "controlled environment," or a hunting shack with drum stove for heat and kerosene for light is not the fundamental question. Whichever it is, man's physical and mental limitations and capabilities must be recognized. Even the problem of physical safety must, it would seem, be attacked from the standpoint of expression. No matter how safe and comfortable a house is designed to be, it will function well only if its occupants have a will to use it properly. The National Bureau of Standards' "Safety for the Household" notes that safety ". . . conditions in the household appear to be determined largely by the attitudes and practices of the housewife, . . ." These attitudes are in turn capable of being affected by the house. A house which obviously stresses safety as one of its functions is bound, on the average, to be used in a safer way than one which presents an unending series of booby traps.

The N. B. S. also notes: "It may be a jolt to our national pride to know that the number of accidental deaths per 100,000 of population is higher in the United States than in most foreign countries." The average American believes that he should be able to move and go as he pleases, or "naturally," and that obstructions and hazards should not exist. As a nation we suffer from a very real insensitivity towards environment in general, evidenced in a myriad of ways throughout our man-made physical world. This implicit belief in the figment *foolproof*, because it operates regardless of obvious hazards, puts a great burden on domestic architecture to be, in fact, as foolproof as intelligence can make it.

The safety problem, in terms of what happens, can be shown as follows. The relationship of age to death here expressed is fascinating, in that it paints a portrait of everyone, from the rubber ball of 0 to 4 years, including the gun happy and aggressive youth of 15 to 24 years and the pill taking victim of society at 40 years, to the glass fragile grandparent of 65 and up.

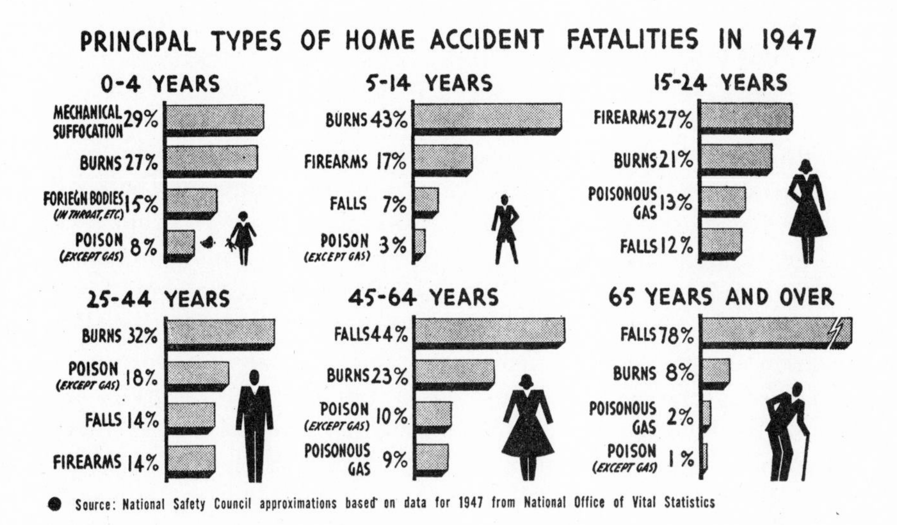

The following figure throws new light on the earlier table. The tremendous importance of disorder is perhaps its most interesting message. The constant complaint of the housewife that she has no place to put anything, a trial on esthetic and on practical grounds, would seem more fundamental than it first appears. Disorder attacks physically as well as emotionally. Closets are one mundane answer to an unromantic death in the afternoon.

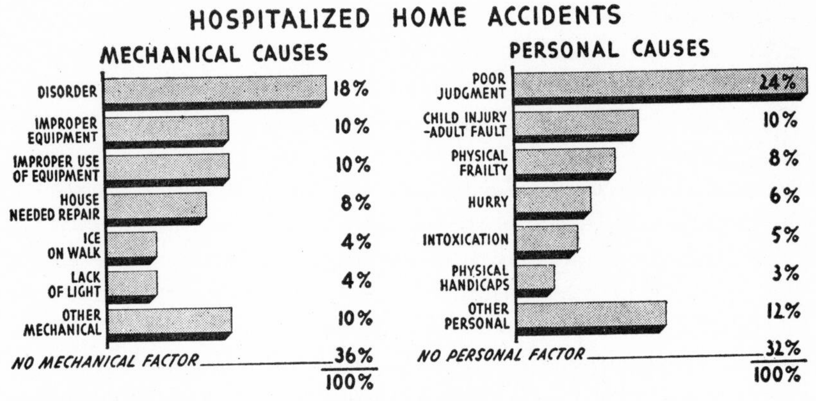

● Source: 4,602 Home Accidents Hospitalized at Cook County Hospital, Chicago

The usual method of approach to the safety problem is an itemized list of where the architect can go wrong. This has its excellent uses. But such lists are perpetually inadequate because the upper middle class house is perpetually changing. Thus in the first instance, certain rather common human attributes, against which every new design may be checked, are the most useful guides. As no one of these is more significant than any other the question of size may serve as an opening. To begin with, as every unusually tall or short person knows, architects should be concerned with people of all sizes. The average heights of men and women are only one factor to be considered. The smallest women and the largest men must also live in houses. Both must get through doors, see themselves in mirrors, cook, excrete, and generally behave like people of average dimensions. Professor Hooton of Harvard University found in a study for Hayward Wakefield, the furniture manufacturers, that the total range in his large sample was from four feet seven inches to six feet eight inches. This is so very great a difference, in design terms, that the architect might be justified in lopping seven inches off the range, i.e., in considering persons of less than five feet and over six feet six as freaks who must abide with all the troubles attendant on such status. In such cases, he must keep in mind some friend who is five feet even in her stocking feet, and her counterpart who is six feet six. The spread between them is one foot six inches; twenty-three per cent of his height, thirty per cent of hers.

Were the elements of houses designed for children, the spread would be much greater. However, children change so fast in relation to the rate of obsolescence of houses, and flexible equipment is so expensive, that they are seldom considered. This is further rationalized by the theory that children need man-sized equipment around in order to "grow into it." In any case, the twenty-three per cent gap is already enormous in terms of some of the functions of houses. Few structures exist where the short woman can sit on the water closet with her feet on the floor, let alone raised as they should be, still fewer where even the six foot man can see himself in his medicine cabinet mirror, or where the six foot six man does not bang his head on the door frames and in the stair wells.

In the design of such things as kitchen equipment, a knowledge of the extremes of height is not enough to be of much use. But we have no really good information as to the average heights of men, or in this case particularly of women, in the upper middle socio-economic group. Professor Hooton found that in samples well distributed among the classes, the median man was five feet nine inches tall, and the median woman about five feet five inches tall. He also notes

> ". . . that individuals from higher economic levels (as college populations) tend to be slightly taller."

How much taller, one does not know. But if an inch were added to the median, that is if the average woman were taken to be about five feet six inches, and the average man to be five feet ten inches, no very great harm would result, though it could hardly be called accurate. Heights of people sitting are equally important. Here we have no better information. Not only does size and posture play a part, but the height of the chair seat is important. Where the problem is to see out of a window slouched down in a comfortable chair, the architect can only guess low.

The common dimensions required as a function of height can be obtained from such references as *Architectural Graphic Standards* by Ramsey and Sleeper, or from *Anatomy for Interior Designers* by Francis de N. Schroeder. But in a general way the principal problems in heights are perhaps as follows:

PART	POSITION	PERSON	NOTE
Door heads	Walking	Tallest man	Must be increased for hat and for increased height while walking
Window heads	Standing	" "	For seeing only
Muntins & Mullions	"	Tallest & shortest	" " "
" "	Sitting	Tallest & shortest	" " "
Window stools	"	Tallest & shortest	" " "
Shade pulls	Standing	Shortest woman	—
Eaves	"	Tallest man	Clearance & view
Risers	Ascending	Average woman	
Stair clearances	Descending	Tallest man	—
Shelves	Standing	Average woman	
Mirrors	"	Tallest & shortest	
Towel bars	"	Average both	
Grab bars	"	" "	
Switches	"	" "	
Pull chains	"	Shortest woman	
Clothes rods	"	Average both	
Evening clothes rods		Tallest woman	Plus step?

In the case of counters, sinks, and lavoratories, (in addition to adjusting for the level of the plane of work) adjustments for height are far less than might be imagined. It may be that people above and below average compensate for their height in some way, and so demand very small increases for tallness, and only slightly greater decreases for shortness. In the housewife's case, one element which allows her to compensate is the freedom she has to vary the height of her shoes. Thus the small woman who eschews high heels and platform soles is a more rock bottom case to plan for than one of the opposite persuasion.

This question raises two issues which seem quite significant to domestic architecture. First, the upper middle class house has, relative to its whole life span, a very short period in which it is enjoyed by its original owners. Thus to reflect their idiosyncracies too obviously and accurately, whether physical or functional, decreases not only its resale value, but its usefulness and safety to succeeding generations. Second, in terms of both comfort and safety, again over a period of years and considering a growing family whose sizes and idiosyncracies are still unknown, the conventional is more often successful than the unconventional but accurate. For example, to lower all of the switches below standard for clients shorter than average probably causes more confusion, more fruitless blind searches, than leaving them where everyone, through habit, expects to find them.

These two notions combined suggest that the sizing of houses should be based fundamentally on averages while always allowing for extremes to operate, and that conventional sizing should seldom be departed from since the surprise and dismay it causes is both uncomfortable and potentially dangerous.

The strength of conditioned responses to the parts of houses is very great. Room doors which open out are difficult to get used to, as are front doors without a step below them, uneven stair treads and risers, and the like. Put in another way the conventions are actually, because of our habit-forming proclivities, aids to movement, and thus contribute to safety. Certain of them however do seem to be one sided, particularly when one considers right-left handedness.

The incidence of left handedness is from four to eight per cent, depending on the characteristics measured. Because we are conditioned to be flexible about the handedness of doors, switches, and the like, such features present, by and large, no acute problems. But the handedness of stair rails and of certain work motions, such as writing and cooking, do. The lefthanded person would like the larger space at his desk to his left, the light over his right shoulder, the kitchen in a left to right sequence, the ironing board with the small end to the left and so forth. Of all these examples the righthanded kitchen may become the most troublesome for the lefthanded person. Kitchens have been designed in the past with such little regard for their functions that we are accustomed to accepting them as they are. However, as devices and work sequences are planned more and more accurately to fit righthanded people they become less and less flexible. Acute problems are beginning to arise in this respect. For example, irons with handles moulded to fit the grip of a righthanded person simply cannot be used by a southpaw. Ideally perhaps, in spite of the small percentage of lefthandedness, alternate locations for its peculiar needs should be considered in certain key areas, such as desk locations, kitchens, and bathrooms.

Danger and discomfort occur nearly always in movement. And here enters, perhaps, the only clearly defined principle of design, that of economy of physical movement. There are exceptions to it, but these are perhaps more accurately variations from common sense which we allow only because they offer us, instead, some very uncommon sensation. Thus they are necessarily limited to areas in which pure pleasure is the goal rather than pleasure in work or in living. Louis Sullivan has expressed this admirably in his comments on the Illinois Central Station in Chicago:

> "My son, here is the place—perhaps a unique spot on earth—holy in iniquity, where to go in you go out, and to go out you go in; where to go up you go down, and to go down you go up. All in all it seems to me the choicest fruit yet culled from that broad branch of the tree of knowledge, known as the public-be-damned style."

The need for economy of movement ramifies itself in all directions. It saves time in work. It saves energy for more useful things. It removes one of the great causes of accidents. We are dealing here with the most practical of matters. A well-arranged kitchen can save an hour's housework a day. Stairs use up about ten times as much energy as the equivalent distance on a horizontal plane. Worst of all, in the crisis situations with which we all must occasionally deal, such as a heart disease or a broken leg, the needless stairs and corkscrew circulations of the average house demand physical and emotional tolls out of all proportion to the flimsy excuses which justify them. To the time and energy elements in this equation we must add another, that of our essentially precarious balance. Even in our middle years we are none too sure on our pins, while in childhood and old age, falls are the rule. The Good Housekeeping Building Forum noting that "The living room is the second most accident-prone room in the house," goes on to advise that furniture be arranged to leave normal traffic paths clear. And again, "many older people die from bedroom falls. Place bed so there is a straight unimpeded path from it to door, with light controls at both places." Such are the minutiae which, in the end, kill us.

Economy can, however, be carried so far as to result in danger and discomfort. The distinction has been ably expressed in "Planning the Home for Occupancy."

> "The word 'economy' does not mean 'closeness in expenditure; reprehensively excessive frugality; stinginess; niggardliness.' That is the definition of 'parsimony.' 'Economy' means 'the management of domestic affairs; the regulation of household matters, especially as to expense.' It is not sound economy to reduce the size of the dwelling below the point at which efficient management of the household is a possibility." (p. vi).

In purely physical terms economy must be subservient to a peculiar quality of our bodies, i.e., to our slow perception of environment versus the speed with which we move. To obviate the danger of steps and changes in direction, we must be prepared for them somewhat in advance. The door opening directly on a staircase, or fixed lights of glass similar to moving lights, present hazards over and above those inherent to them. We approach them at a rate of speed which does not allow us to perceive their peculiar relationship to other parts of their immediate environment. Thus every element of a design must be conceived of as for a fast moving, rather clumsy, rather absent-minded user.

A glance at the safety-comfort problem from an outdoor view increases the significance of size, handedness, and speed in relation to perceptivity, economy of movement, and disorderliness. The Good Housekeeping Building Forum pamphlet previously cited notes: "More home accidents take place outside the house than in any one room. Most of these are falls, due to bad planning or poor maintenance." This importance of the yard as a booby trap again brings up the indivisibility of house and site. The outside is subservient to *uses* in the same sense that the inside is. The only difference is in their nature.

Warmth

The outdoors, in its guise as nature and weather, and as the haunt of inimical animals and people, is the complex of elements the outer shell of the house is designed to exclude. The individual's tolerance for variations in this realm is of the essence. The problems thus raised can be seen as the resolution of a series of opposing forces. On the one hand is the weather, or the burglar, or the rat, opposed on the other by a team composed of house and man. Natural conditions in a given place are fixed. Man is also fixed. House makes up the difference in his favor. Thus, a knowledge of climate, by itself, is not of the slightest value to the architect, unless he constantly equates it with thermal physiology. His goal is human comfort, within a certain set of exterior conditions. We must know what our bodies need in the way of external conditions in order for us to feel comfortable. With this knowledge we can then either modify climate or completely compensate for it, according to the potency of the devices at our command. A pool outside a window in a hot, dry climate falls into the same category as summer air conditioning, though it happens not to be as effective. Lacking such totally effective devices, the whole arrangement of houses, inside and out, and on their sites, must be affected by man's innate thermal mechanism.

The body's temperature is, within narrow limits, (1) constant, (2) the same throughout and (3) maintained at a level quite different from, and independent of, the air. The advantages of its constant temperature as distinct from, for example, the amoeba, whose temperature is that of the water surrounding it, is that it allows the chemical reactions within to go on at a constant velocity. These processes, especially those of oxidation, produce heat. In fact the body produces more heat than is required for its own internal use. Thus in order to maintain its constant temperature, it must get rid of the excess. Internal temperature is maintained through constant modification of these two factors, (1) heat production and (2) heat loss. When they are in balance we are comfortable. When they are out of balance, when we are producing more heat than we can get rid of or are getting rid of too much heat, we suffer. The basic condition of comfort is an appropriate flow of heat *outward* from the body. Our body intensity is approximately 98.6 degrees F. Our skin surface temperature is about 83 degrees F. Because one of the qualities of heat is that it naturally flows from a body of a higher temperature to one of lower temperature, it is obvious that man, who must always be losing heat, will be most comfortable in temperatures of less than 83 degrees F. In temperatures below this he will lose heat. In temperatures above he will gain heat. It is for this reason that we think, off hand and by rule of thumb, of 70 degrees F. as a good temperature—13 degrees F. lower than our skin intensity. It also explains why the temperate climates, which are on the average slightly colder than man, are those in which he is most comfortable and in which he can be most active.

The amount of heat produced by man per hour in Btu for varying conditions is approximately as follows:

ACTIVITIES	BTU/HOUR
Infants	63
Children	240
Adults, sleeping	255
awake, quiet	300
standing at ease	430
at work	480–600
walking 2 mph	760
in violent exercises	600–1400
at maximum exertion	3000–4800

A man doing easy work, generating about 500 Btu per hour, uses his production approximately as follows:

USE OR WAY LOST	BTU/HOUR
Used internally	100
Skin evaporation and exhalation	100
Surface convection to air	100
Radiation to surrounding surfaces	200
Excretion, etc.	Negligible
	Total: 500

He is in the necessity of losing four fifths of his total output, or about 400 Btu per hour. Specifically he is losing it in four quite different ways: (1) by evaporation of water, which brings up the question of humidity, (2) by convection, and thus, (3) by conduction, and (4) by radiation. It is immediately apparent that the rule of thumb assumption that 70 degrees F. will be comfortable cannot be the whole truth. In order to be comfortable our bodies must lose moisture (evaporation), need air movement (convection) and must lose heat from the skin (radiation).

Thermal comfort depends on air temperature, air movement, the average temperature of surrounding surfaces (mean radiation), and relative humidity. Actually comfort can be achieved through a rather broad range of variation in any of these factors because our bodies, if cut off from any one source of heat transfer, can adjust to a certain extent by increasing the rate of heat loss in another way. The amount of heat lost by radiation and convection decreases rapidly as the air temperature rises and humidity goes down, while loss through evaporation increases. In such a case we sweat more and more profusely to make up for our inability to radiate and conduct away heat. Thus there is no absolute optimum condition for comfort but rather a range of conditions, all of which are comfortable. One way to express the interconnection is as follows, where each condition would give the same apparent temperature or degree of comfort:

	TEMPERATURE DEG. F.	HUMIDITY % RELATIVE	AIR MOVEMENT FT. PER MIN.
Temperature Constant	72	10	Still
	72	30	100
	72	78	300
Humidity Constant	70	34	Still
	72	34	100
	76	34	300
Movement Constant	67	98	100
	70	60	100
	72	30	100

Such figures as these are the basis on which the heating engineer operates. They do not consider radiant loss separately. The temperature of surrounding surfaces, that is the mean radiant temperature, is not taken into account as a separate part of the relationship. We have no data as yet with which to equate the four variables at once. In default of exact data the architect must make a series of "informed guesses" as the saying is, and in this realm, as well as in several other unexplored areas, he can make his most valuable contributions or his most fatal mistakes, depending on his sensitivity to the problem. The architect who is not half a magical "wind and water man" must needs be either very conventional or very unsuccessful.

Quiet

To the body's size, movement, and thermal attributes, one must add its ever-alert ear as a factor in comfort. The arguments as to what harm noises do us need not be gone into here. It is enough to know that noise of itself, particularly when it is masking a sound one wishes to hear, is intensely irritating. Thus in houses the most vital problem is that of the attenuation of sound, while good hearing is usually of little importance. Most of the required steps for hearing comfort can be thought of as check list items. But perhaps particularly in the upper middle class house, where on the one hand there is much experimentation in design, and where on the other there is a very high value placed on privacy (of which sound is a function) a more fundamental approach is necessary.

Sound waves are moving layers of compression and refraction in air, set up by a vibrating body of some sort: a speaker, a human, a radio, a string, a wall, or any one of numerous objects. Each complete forward and back movement of the vibrating source is a cycle. The frequency of sound waves and of their sources, is the number of times this cycle is performed per second. Wave length is the distance the sound travels during each cycle its source goes through. Sound waves are, relative to light, very slow indeed. Light travels 982,080,000 feet per second. Sound travels about 1,130 feet per second in air at 72 degrees Fahrenheit, faster in the hard solid materials of building. It is of course this difference which accounts for our seeing lightning long before we hear its thunder, provided we are comfortably far away. On the other hand, sound waves are relatively long. They vary from less than ¾″ for very high frequencies, to about 60 feet for low frequencies. Obviously a short high frequency sound wave one inch long will be materially affected, for example, by a ceiling beam, while a long low frequency sound wave would hardly realize it existed.

Low frequency, long length waves tend to spread out from their source more or less uniformly in all directions. Their wave front in air is thus approximately circular in plan view, and spherical in shape. High frequency, short wavelength sounds tend to confine themselves to a narrow beam in front of their source. One result of this combination of factors is diffraction, that is, the bending of sound waves as they pass around an obstacle or through a crack. Knudsen and Harris describe it as follows:

> "Since the wave lengths of sound vary from about 0.06 to 60 feet, the diffraction may be pronounced for some frequencies and negligible for others. For example, a 3-foot door opening would be small compared to a wavelength of 60 feet. Therefore, such a low-frequency sound would be very much diffracted in going through the door, the emergent sound spreading out almost uniformly in all directions. In contrast, this same door opening would be very large compared to a wavelength of 0.06 foot (a frequency of about 19,000 cycles), and therefore a sound having such a wavelength should be transmitted through the door with little diffraction. Obviously, sounds such as those in speech and music, which are made up of a wide range of frequencies, are selectively diffracted because the low-frequency components will diverge widely while the high-frequency components will continue in relatively narrow beam."

This explains the frequent experience of being able to hear the base notes given off by a distant radio without being able to hear the melody. When sound waves encounter a wall they bounce back or are reflected as light is from a mirror. Their angle of reflection equals the angle of incidence. They can of course go on

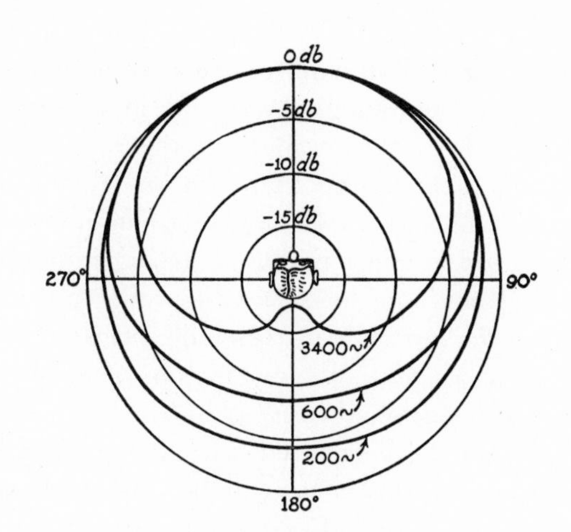

"Relative sound-pressure level around the head during speech. Contours represent levels at a distance of about 2 feet from the head in a horizontal plane for three bands of speech centered at the frequencies indicated (H. K. Dunn and D. W. Farnsworth.)" From Knudsen and Harris.

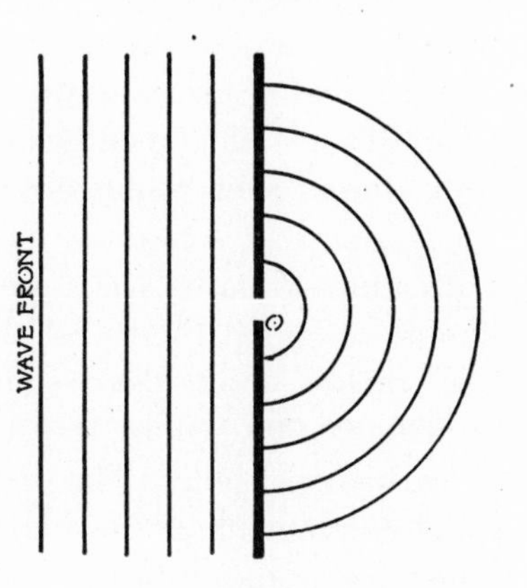

"Diffraction of sound passing through a small opening."

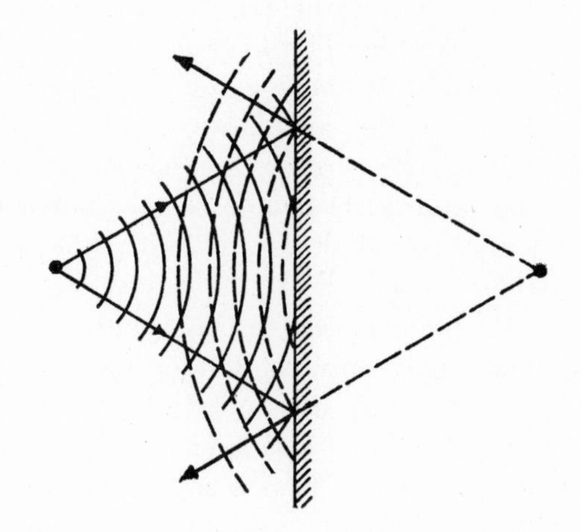

Reflection of sound waves from a plane surface.

doing this indefinitely in a completely enclosed space such as a room, bouncing off one wall after another. After a noise has been made "... every part of the room is filled with reflected sound waves traveling in every possible direction."

The first effect of this phenomenon is that the intensities of sound increase in closed spaces, immediately after they are made, because one hears several reflections as well as the sound itself or the next one in the same series. The degree to which this effect is produced is dependent on the absorptivity of the walls. If they are hard plaster and glass they will send back most of the noise. If they are covered with curtains, and the windows are open, most of the noise will be absorbed or lost.

The second effect is one of reverberation, that is the long drawn out continuation of sound after it has itself ceased. In excessively reverberant halls, for example, a considerable time may elapse before walls, people, openings and furniture finally absorb the last reflections. Such rooms are noisy and hard to hear in.

The loudness of sounds is measured in decibels, db for short. Zero db approximates the minimum hearable sound while 120 db is more or less at the threshold of feeling, i.e. where one begins to feel rather than hear sound waves, and is one trillion (1,000,000,000,000) times the intensity of 0 db. This is a completely arbitrary choice. The decibel scale, like feet and inches, is simply a convenient measuring device. An acceptable noise level for houses is probably in the nature of 35 to 45 db, though lower levels in rooms for writers working at home, or for intensive study, are desirable. The average noise level is made up of a series of sounds from varying sources. These consist, to mention only a few, of traffic, air planes, wind, telephone, radio-phonograph, oil burner, refrigerator, conversation, footsteps, *children*, etc., etc. The noise level in houses goes down about 3 db in winter when doors and windows are shut, thus to a certain extent excluding traffic noise.

People get used to this general noise level and are apt to hear consciously only the louder and intermittent sounds imposed on it, such as an automobile horn, or a particularly noisy bird or truck. On the other hand, it is impossible to shut out a loud noise when trying to hear a soft one. Everyone has this experience on

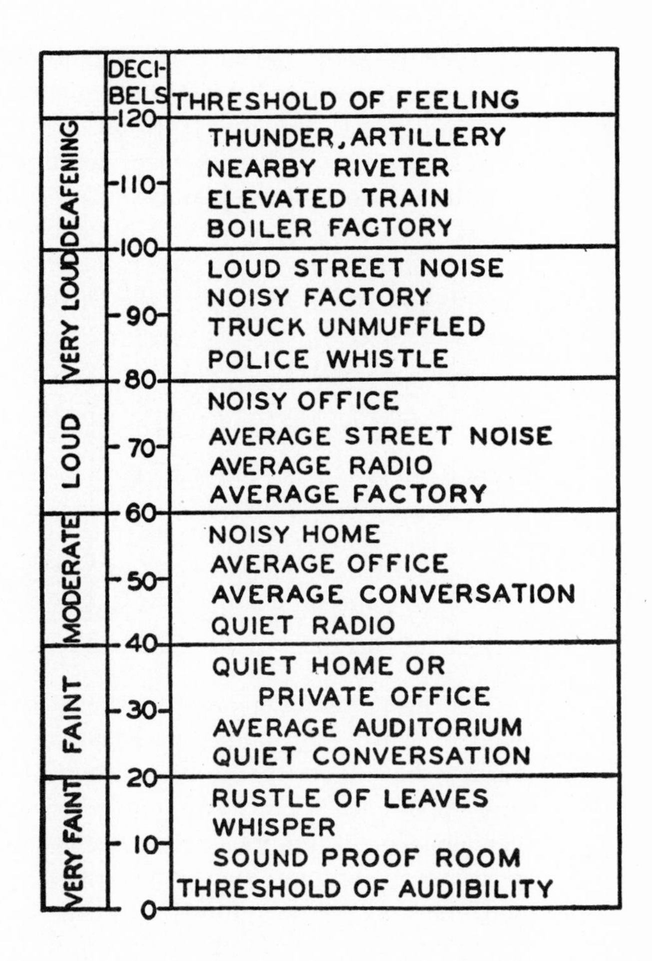

Decibel levels of common sounds.

the telephone. Noise has the effect of reducing one's ability to hear accurately. This effect is called masking. Where two sounds occur at the same time their joint loudness is of course greater than their separate loudness, though not the sum of their measurements in decibels. No room is absolutely quiet and so, in deciding on the amount of noise reduction an author, for example, will need for his study, the starting point is to discover the probable noise level in his room regardless of what can be done in the way of cutting out outside noises. These noises need only be attenuated to the general level of his room to have them disappear. Mr. Sabine explains it thus:

"Usually we do not hear the neighbors' radio through the wall when our own radio is turned on, in which case the wall is 'sound proof.' But if we turn off our radio and are trying to go to sleep, the wall is no longer 'sound proof,' and the neighbor's radio is heard all too plainly."

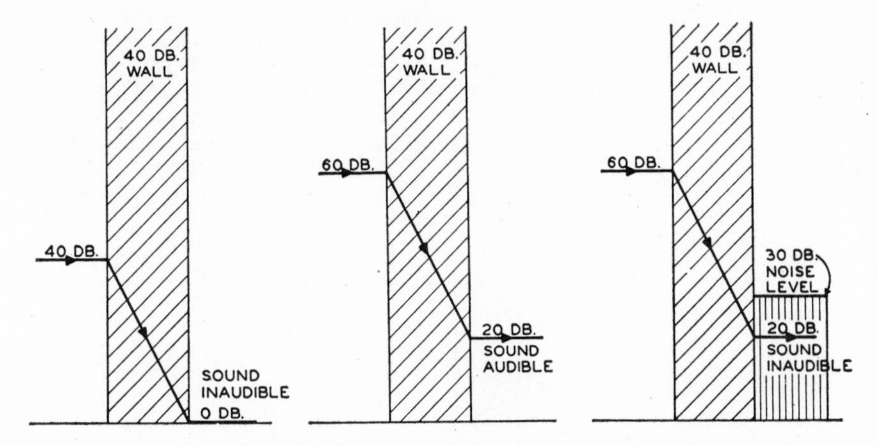

The most common way in which sound is transmitted is of course in air. Continuous air paths in houses, such as openings rather than doors to the living room, the front hall, stair well, and upper hall, or cracks around bedroom doors, are very effective carriers. Open windows, cracks around pipes, electric conduits and particularly hot air ducts and laundry chutes are good transmitters, and are therefore trouble spots. Airborne noise can be attenuated by absorption, that is by catching it in a porous material, where it turns into heat.

A second way noise travels about inside is through partitions. Sound waves striking a wall can force it into the same kind of diaphragmatic movement that originally produced the noise. Sound waves are thus produced on the far side similar to those forcing it into motion on the near side. Obviously the best way to combat this process is to use rigid, heavy walls such as brick and stone. Walls built of thin plywood or wall board on two inch by three inch studs are good transmitters because they are so light and flexible. Double walls help reduce transmission because the two sides are not connected.

Finally, direct impact is a troublesome source of noise. Footfalls, door slams, and things dropped on the floor are carried through the structure of the building with little attenuation. Vibrating furnaces and refrigerators can be heard in the same way. Heavy trucks in the street outside can set a whole house in motion, and thus force it to produce sound. Noises of this sort can best be reduced by discontinuous structure. Cork, linoleum, carpeting, rubber mats under the refrigerator, hung ceilings on springs prevent continuous travel of sound waves between the source and the structure.

Noise attenuation is made necessary by the fundamental desire in people not to be too "surrounded" or "pressed" or "conscious" of those with whom they live. This is not, perhaps, an innate quality in people. Rather it is a result of the society in which we live. It has been argued above that the individual, once he is inside this shell, designed to protect him from the weather and other intruders, lives in a spectrum at one end of which is privacy, and at the other sociality. In between are various semi-states, each of which are cannonized by custom—to a certain extent ritualized—and which contain both personal and social significance for the individual. We experience these states as a function of a more or less specific living activity. The similarities and differences in these activities suggest that if they are grouped in certain ways, and if these groups are then separated, one element of livability is the result. But, where concrete physical environment is the goal, it is necessary to examine these states in the most minute detail, and at the same time in the most all-inclusive way. Structure, equipment, the five senses, thermal comfort, emotion, etc., must all be taken into account. What does working actually mean, in terms of space and equipment? What does going to bed entail, in terms of circulation, artificial and natural light, storage space, the excretory functions, etc.? Livability is also experienced in terms of the shapes of the spaces in which we live, of the locations of light switches, of the height of book shelves, etc., i.e., in terms of the minutiae of life. Thus in order to approach closer to the whole subject, each individual activity must now be considered for itself alone.

Letarouilly: Entrance to Michelangelo's House.

CHAPTER V

Activities

The most interesting dwellings in this country, as the painter knows, are the most unpretending, humble log huts and cottages of the poor commonly; it is the life of the inhabitants whose shells they are, and not any peculiarity in these surfaces merely, which makes them picturesque; *and equally interesting will be the citizen's suburban box, when his life shall be as simple and as agreeable to the imagination, and there is as little straining after effect in the style of his dwelling.* —THOREAU

Entering

ENTERING IS AN EMOTIONALLY DIFFICULT EXPERIENCE. It puts many people at a disadvantage, particularly if it is for the first time. The process at best is fraught with hazards. Invisible street numbers, inimical dogs, unexpected steps and hidden bells can make it immeasurably more difficult. Having braved and conquered such unfamiliar obstacles, the great question remains, "How will I be received here? Will they be friendly?" Most of us as we approach an unfamiliar entrance search for clues to these questions. T. S. Eliot has a character remark:

"But let me tell you, that to approach a stranger
Is to invite the unexpected, release a new force,
Or let the genie out of the bottle.
It is to start a train of events
Beyond your control"

The entrance is a place of signs and portents. This is true even of one's own door, even when the process of getting to and through it has become automatic. The tone of one's wife's voice, the noises of the house, the identity of an unexpected guest, all may mean much for the time to come. Under the impact of the experience the shy withdraw into themselves, the ill at ease make faux pas, the aggressive overplay their role. Surely then, the essential function of an entrance is to make it easy for people to be friendly. The architect cannot hope to determine the course of events through his design, despite Mr. Winston Churchill's famous dictum that "We shape our dwellings, and then our dwellings shape us." Nevertheless it is not too much to hope that a friendly entrance may put the approaching stranger in a warmer and more sanguine mood.

One's first impression of an entrance is made up of a composite of factors. The way it is maintained, its relation to its general environment, its symbolic overtones, the adequancy of its comforts, all play their part. The entrance littered with children's toys and equipment seems messy and distraught. Neatness overdone seems meagre and self conscious. One needs, at entrances, a sense that they are fully used, and that they are commodious enough to absorb all of their functions.

But the sensation of entering really begins on the street. Before one even reaches the house one has formed certain impressions of its environment. The age of the buildings around it, their design, their economic level, the care with which they are maintained make up the background against which the house is seen. If it is much grander than its neighbors it will appear pretentious. If it is less thoughtfully designed it will come as an anti-climax. Such comparisons are not made in terms of style, but rather in terms of elaboration and functional adequancy. They are performed to help answer the question "Are these people neighborly?"

Whether entrances of themselves are inviting or not depends in part on their absolute height and width. A low, wide entrance is infinitely more appealing than a tall, high one. Its lowness suggests shelter, its width generosity. Entrances should be made to walk through arm in arm. The common front door three feet wide by seven feet high is of poor proportion, for it is less wide

Wurster, Bernardi and Emmons.

than half its height. Ratios of $3\frac{1}{2}:7$ or $4\frac{1}{2}:7$ or $5:7$ are more friendly. The materials of the door are equally important. Glass doors into a vestibule are disarming and inviting. Heavy oak plank studded with nails can only mean fortification against an unfriendly world. Flush doors can suggest a strong distrust of germs and emotions. A commodious stoop, a widely over-hanging porch, and particularly an entrance seat, suggest that the owners have anticipated the creature comforts of their guests. The location of entrances in relation to masses and surfaces also contributes to their symbolic overtones. The narrow door poked in the large, flat facade of the New England Colonial house is essentially forbidding. Entrances in the entrant angle of two wings, though hard to arrange, say "shelter" more clearly than they can in any other location.

It is sad but true that the most propitious symbols can be negated by only one of the many physical hazards of entering. If one is half an hour late for dinner because the house was hard to find, no amount of architecture can ease the strain. A good entrance begins with a street number clearly visible from the sidewalk, at night as well as in daylight. Entrances should be obvious, for there are few more frustrating experiences than to wander back and forth on the sidewalk wondering which side of a blank facade to try first. One needs protection underfoot. It is preferable to avoid steps. If they are necessary because a change in grade must be made, they should be very obvious steps, differentiated by color and texture. One also needs a hard, non-skid surface to walk on, sloped to the side so that water will not run its whole length; bushes far enough away so that they cannot be brushed against, particularly when they are heavy with rain. It is during this trip between sidewalk and front stoop that the designer can work on a visitor's sense of security. One way to accomplish this is to give him actual protection on one side, a fence or a hedge, parallel to the walk, with something good to look at on the other side. His apparent physical stature can be increased by minor modelings of the ground surface. Differences in grade, high ground cover, low walls and the like can be used to create a system of minor vertical dimensions against which his own height will seem great.

Once arrived at the front stoop, the visitor is faced with the most dangerous part of his journey. The steps he must climb are new to him; they may be old and wobbly, wet, icy, or hidden in snow. Indeed they can be all of these things at once. He may also be rained on, or drenched in a waterfall off the roof, or crushed by a snow slide, or speared by an icicle. Thus the visitor needs for his well-being, first and foremost, a generous canopy for his protection while he waits for his ring to be answered, or in the case of the owner, while he searches for his key. He needs light for this function, general illumination turned on from inside, and a keyhole light turned on from outside when he comes home in the dark. The canopy can hardly be too commodious. It should protect the steps, accommodate two or three people easily while the out-swinging screen door is open, provide room to haul an occasional bicycle or tricycle out of the rain, provide a seat for the weary. The steps, if there are any, will need handrails on both sides, as do all steps, and should not be less than two in number so that unwary people will be more apt to notice them. Only one riser is absolutely necessary, and that by tradition and common sense is directly under the front door. Because it *is* traditional, it is expected and easy to take. Its function is of course to keep out driving rain and melting snow.

If the visitor is the mailman, he need only put his letters in the slot in the door, which invariably leaks air, or in an outside box which is easy to burgle, or in some more ingenious contraption than either of these. If the visitor is a guest he must give warning. The bell button, if it is to be easily found, must be within an inch or two of the jamb on the latch set side of the door, and should be at the same height as the knob. Because, traditionally, front doors open in, and knockers can only be reached after opening a screen or storm door, they are less easy to find and use. In-opening door hardware is hardest to burgle, and in-opening doors are least likely to freeze shut. In order to hold the screen door open against its spring with one's shoulder, it should be hinged on the same side as the main door. Whether it should be right or left handed seems to depend more on the space available around its jamb than on human factors. We have been trained to be flexible about such things. But for right handed people, a door that opens at the left is the easiest to use.

The driver is perhaps at a greater disadvantage than the pedestrian as far as entering is concerned. While his speed is greater, his abilities are the same. Thus for him the street number or name must be brighter, and the entrance to the driveway more clearly visible over a greater distance than the walk need be. The pedestrian is to the driver as the driver is to the pilot. Each increase in speed requires vastly more room for manoeuvering. The driveway should be clearly visible along the street for a hundred or more yards in each direction. It should have wide radii of curvature leading into it, twenty feet or more, and, if it be marked by posts, they should be twelve or more feet apart. Its grade in icy climates should be nearly level— from one to three per cent. Five per cent is fair, eight poor, ten and over dangerous, or at best uncomfortable. "The driveway gradient of not to exceed 6 per cent is desirable" (National Safety Council). Its surface should slope away from the parking places, *not towards them*, so that stalled cars may be pushed out by hand, rather than towed out by wrecker. The basement garage with a ten per cent ramp leading down into it is perhaps the most dangerous, impractical, and ugly of twentieth century notions.

The driver must leave his tremendous vehicle behind him somewhere; on the street or at the house. Of all the requirements of houses this is probably the most frequently slighted. The reason is twofold. First, the automobile, or horseless carriage, is still conceived of—in design terms—as a smelly, unhouse-broken, barn-living, pesky means of locomotion to be used but not seen. Second, we have not yet realized how great an area it needs for storage and manoeuvre. The first of these reasons points to a curious dichotomy of the American mind. We love our cars, replace them frequently, shine them ourselves on Sundays, or have them shined, talk about them endlessly, consider their make and cost a symbol of class.* Yet, once parked, we feel they should be hidden from view. The fact that they are designed to the lowest common denominator of taste does not seem to enter into this rejection as much as the fact that they have replaced the servant and the horse.

The requirements of automobiles are that they be kept out of the sun, because it dulls their finish; that they be kept from under certain species of pitch dripping trees; and that they be protected from snow, rain, and hail in order to keep them clean and instantly ready to use. In dusty climates a garage reduces maintenance expense. In cold climates there is luxury in a warm car shelter. The automobile's social faults are few: they drip grease, and can roll away if left unbraked on a grade. The first of these can be compensated for by camouflage, that is, the selection of a paving material which does not advertise grease. The second can be guarded against by the proper grading of parking areas, bumpers, curbs, and the like. To relegate the automobile to a barn-like service structure is to underrate it. It needs no hay, no oats, watering trough, manure pit, harness, exercise, nor groom. The car is instantly ready for its driver, and can be abandoned again at the flick of a switch. It has graduated from the service category of the horse to the public category of the sofa.

The owner-driver's first requirement once he has made the

* In the Navy, a tactful way of finding out a shipmate's peacetime economic status is to ask him "What kind of a car does your old man drive?"

House of Lord Ii: Courtesy of Dr. Jiro Harada.

entrance is a clearly defined parking space out of which he can get without too much backing and filling. In any case, "it is desirable to provide a turn around so that a car need not be backed out of the driveway" (National Safety Council). It should be level enough so his car will not tend to roll off if he forgets to brake it. If there is anything dangerous or damageable in front of him as he drives in—the end wall of a garage, or planting, or a change in grade—a bumper is required, far enough in advance of the obstruction so that there will be enough room for the front overhang and for passageway between the bumper and the obstruction. The open doors of an automobile considerably increase its width, and if the driver, now turned pedestrian, is to get around them while they are open, passageway must be provided between their furthest limit and any obstruction parallel to the car. In an ideal garage, passageway should be allowed for at the rear of the car when the door is shut, as well as at the front. This requires a clear depth of about twenty-five feet, exclusive of shelves, benches, storage and the like.

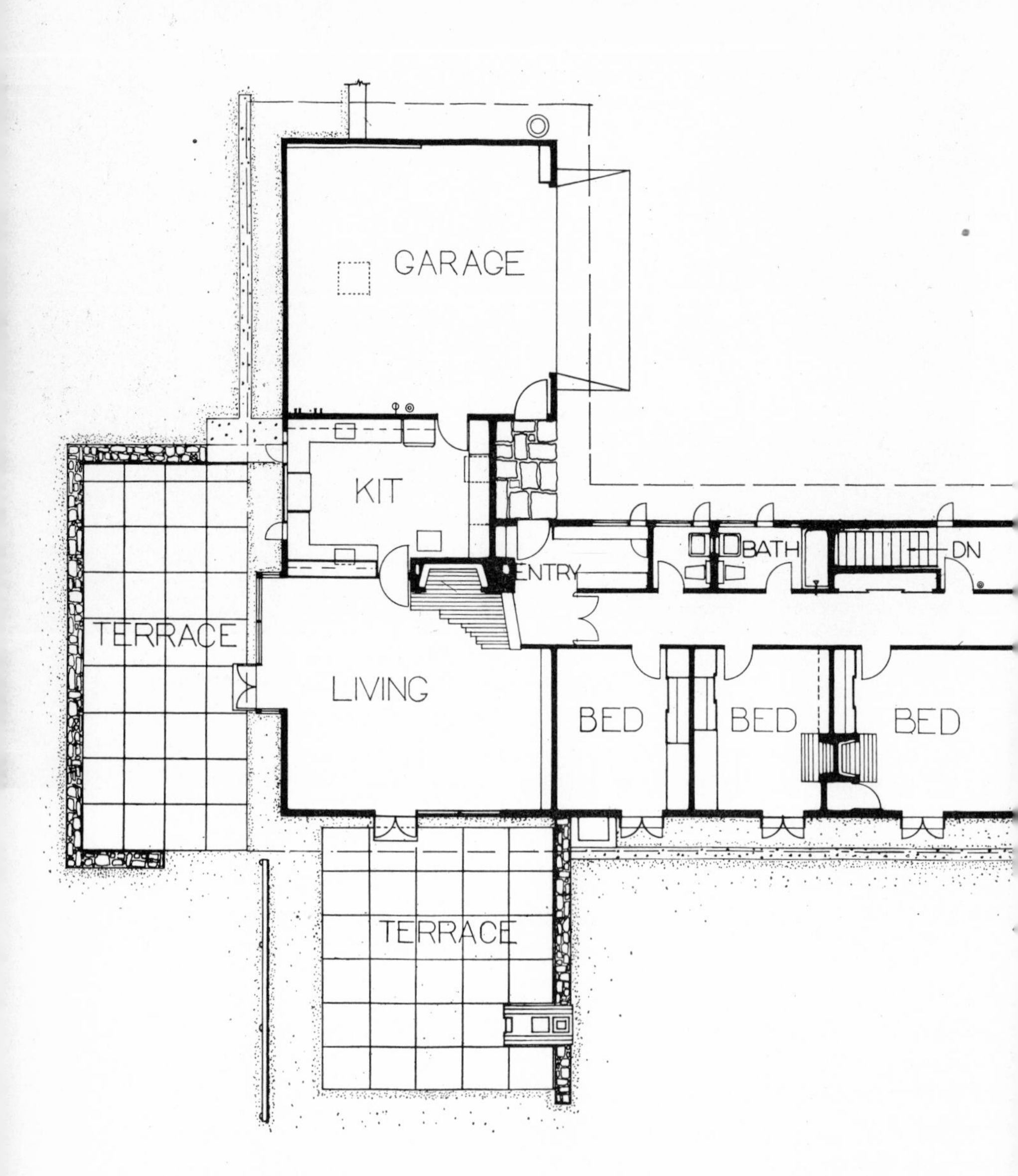

Robert Woods Kennedy: The garage, entrance porch, entry and kitchen are arranged in such a way that one can enter formally, through the front system, or informally through the kitchen. The entrance contains a large amount of storage space for miscellaneous belongings. The fireplace is conceived of as a pivot for the whole house, rather than as a focus for the living room furniture.

Hillmer and Callister.

The driver, because he has arrived almost at the very door in a warm (or cool as the case may be), overstuffed, and generally luxurious conveyance, has a different point of view about shelter than the pedestrian. To travel two hundred miles on a rainy day, dry and in comfort, only to get soaked in the last twenty feet of one's journey is anticlimactic. The driver wants to be able to leave his car and get out his baggage and bundles under a shelter *connected to the house.* Where it connects is a matter of living pattern. Direct access to the front hall, or direct access to the kitchen for ease of bringing in food, are the principal alternates. Such connections can be made equally well either from a garage or a carport. The carport, where it is practical for the climate, seems to offer more possibilities than the garage for symbolizing the scale, functions and public character of entering by car.

The essential difference between the situation of the person arriving at a front door and the person opening it is that the former has had time to consider the action, while the latter is taken more or less by surprise. The bell rings and without further ado he must answer it. The thought that the unknown person outside may just possibly be a burglar or a madman scares the majority of people, particularly at night. Such devices as one-way peep holes, door chains and windows overlooking the front door help relieve tension and can prevent the embarrassment of a too distrustful greeting. Certain visitors, bill collectors, process servers, and irate neighbors can create intensely disagreeable scenes at or just inside the front door. For such occasions a front hall separated from the main living room is invaluable. For upper income groups it is a fixed convention. When one considers the added advantage of entries as weather protection, they would seem highly desirable for all houses in cold climates.

Yet, in spite of such hazards, the greeter is usually in a better position psychologically than the greeted. He is at home; supported by his familiarity with the physical surroundings, and by his sense of his rights of occupancy. He is as sure of himself as he is likely to be. It is also primarily up to him to make a success of the occasion. In this situation he is not seen in a vacuum as he would be on the street, but in a setting: the architecture of his entry. This can support him by corresponding exactly to his sense of fitness. It can be warm and low and cozy and full of objects. It can be large, formal, elegant, and bare. If its character is appropriate he will feel himself to be in a strong position. His guests will be instantly informed as to his esthetic ideas, his socio-economic status, or whatever else the architecture is designed to express. Most important of all, the architecture of entries must shelter the joyful reunions and tearful farewells of families, children, and friends. It is the locus of many significant and emotional occasions, and should somehow suggest that it recognizes the importance of the arrivals and departures it will be called upon to house.

It is very disturbing, both to the greeter and the greeted to have to fuss about dirt. Yet some will inevitably be carried into the house. We no longer put shoe scrapers outside our doors. In fact

Eliot Porter.

only occasionally are special provisions made for wet and muddy boots. The problem seems to be left to the unwilling housewife. She would like a flooring material for the entry which does not show dirt, is easy to clean, and does not stain when wet. In addition a sunken mat either just inside the door or just outside reminds people to wipe their feet, and at least concentrates most of the dirt in one place. A floor drain in its recess is essential outside and handy inside. It allows the dirt in the recess to be flushed away, rather than painstakingly brushed out, and also allows wet umbrellas and clothes to be placed where they can drip.

Greetings and good-byes often involve many people and a good deal of movement, and so require a lot of space. Getting in and out of an overcoat by oneself requires at least three by four feet. If one is being helped by an obliging host an area of about four by five feet is necessary. Children up to five usually have to sit on the floor to get into their snowsuits. Two children in this position can use up about sixteen square feet. Add to either of these functions several more children, adults, and dogs and the space required becomes really formidable. In addition, entries should include a chair to sit in while removing rubbers, and a mirror for adjusting the hat. Very often the telephone is kept in the hall, requiring a chair and table. Indeed the old fashioned hall table has many uses besides visiting cards. It is handy for mail, for notes to members of the family, and to sign petitions and receipts on.

The storage requirements of entries fall into four separate categories. Perhaps the most universally neglected is that for children who need low hooks for clothes, boxes for overshoes and rubbers, and small drawers for mittens, scarves, and hats. These are more manageable, if less handsome, out in the open rather than behind closed doors. Storage spaces usable by the children relieve adults of a tiresome responsibility, and make it much easier to train them to put their own things away. A secondary requirement for children's outdoor clothes arises from the fact that in winter they are usually wet and sometimes covered with frozen snow. The clothes smell, in this condition, as well as drip, and must be dried out somewhere. A ground floor utility room with lines in it, or a large open entry with exposed hooks and a stone or other rough floor are perhaps the best solutions to this problem. Draping such clothes over a hall or living room radiator is certainly the worst solution, not only from the point of view of looks, but also of smell, shrinkage, stiffening, and water drainage into the room. Adults' requirements include a pole for hangers, shelves for hats, and shelves and drawers for scarves, rubbers, galoshes, gloves, etc., and slots for umbrellas and canes. Again all these things may be wet and dirty. A large, warm, airy place with a tough floor is far more practical than a small closet.

Guests present special problems in that they often arrive and depart in groups, causing great congestion. The most common way out of this difficulty is to send them to a bedroom to store their things. A guest closet out of the immediate entrance, so that people taking off coats and overshoes do not block it, is another solution.

The following list of outdoor clothes suggests the desirability of the rear entrance closet for the many work and play items.

Entering

Outdoor Clothes

Husbands

overcoats
topcoats, light and heavy
raincoats, slickers
heavy jackets, mackinaws
lightweight jackets
caps, knitted hats
rubber boots
heavy duty shoes
rubbers
work gloves, mittens
mufflers
overalls
work trousers
work shirts
ski outfits, snow wear
hats

Wives

heavy coats
heavy coats with fur
lightweight coats
fur coats
raincoats
heavy sport jackets
ski outfit, snow wear
hats, berets
scarves, kerchiefs
boots
galoshes, rubbers
mittens, gloves
umbrellas

Boys 2–15 Years

overcoats
light and heavy topcoats
raincoats, slickers
heavy jackets, mackinaws
lightweight jackets
snow, ski suits
leggings
caps, helmets, beanies
school hats
work trousers, jackets, shirts
overalls
boots
rubbers
working gloves, mittens
mufflers

Girls 2–15 Years

heavy coats
heavy coats with fur
lightweight coats
fur coats
raincoats
heavy sports jackets
snow, ski suits
leggings
hats, caps, berets
scarves, kerchiefs
boots
rubbers, galoshes
gloves, mittens
umbrellas

The baby carriage, which appears the day a child is born, is the forerunner of a mass of specialized outdoor equipment for children. Baby carriages are not good things to have in the front hall, or in the garage. They clutter up the hall, unless it is planned to receive them, and are apt to get cold, dirty, and bent in the garage. A really well protected porch can be used, or a commodious back hall, or even a storage shed attached to the garage, provided it is close enough to the house and accessible under cover. The carriage is followed by a succession of tricycles, scooters, bicycles, carts, cars, Irish mails, and the like, all of which deteriorate very fast if left outside. Most children learn to use some of this equipment before they can jockey it up some steps and through a door. Ideally, its storage space should be at grade, with a one inch rise at the threshold only, simply to keep out water. Finally, there are the accessories to the various family activities; golf clubs, cameras, balls, bats, gloves, children's homework, father's briefcase, and a host of other possibilities. Shelves, cupboards, or drawers for this equipment are properly a function of the entrance. Not only are such things easily reached and put away there; many of them are not specifically private property. They are used by several members of the family, some of them indoors as well as out, and thus are best kept in a central location. These requirements of area and storage space will occur whether the designer allows space for them or not. The activities involved can take place in a ribbon, leading from the living room through the entry out to the front door. Or they can be all contained in a proper hall. Whatever their location, living room, hall, kitchen, or other, the things used must somehow be put away.

The process of entering often involves more than simply getting through the front door and out of one's coat. Occasionally it is desirable to get to some part of the house, the kitchen, or the bed rooms, directly from the entry, in privacy. The classical circulation scheme for houses is based entirely on this consideration, rather than on the relationships between the functions taking place every day. In the very common house plan where one enters the living room, off of which is the kitchen with the only other exterior door in the house, and has to pass through this complex to get to bed rooms and bath, one is literally trapped. The only

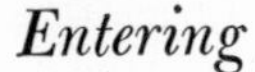

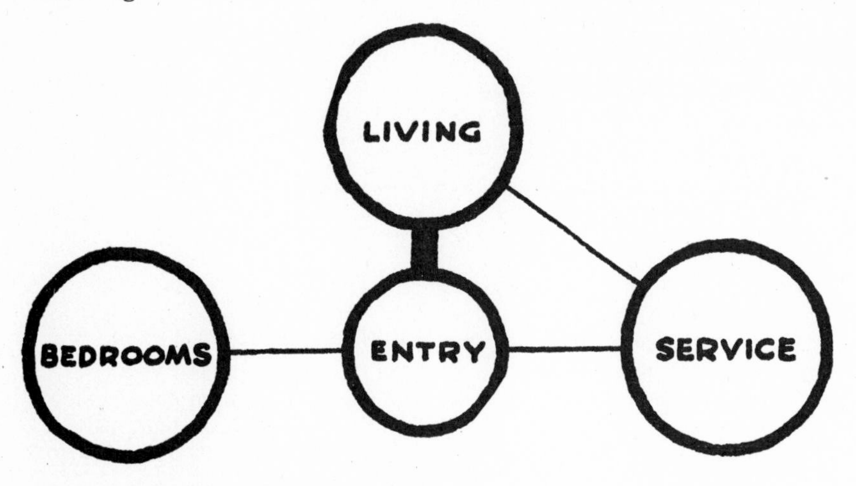

way to avoid an unwelcome ladies' tea or man's poker session is to get in or out of a window. This sort of fix does not occur frequently enough to be worth considering in the very large house, but in small houses it can become a problem.

CHECK LIST

Arriving — who and what —

Good People	
the inhabitants	front and back door
friends, guests, doctors, ministers, architects, etc.	front door
maids, cooks, laundress	back door
mailman	mail box or slot
fireman	doors and windows
garbage man	garbage pail
trash collectors	trash barrels
undertaker	front door
Bad people	
burglars	locks
vandals, rapists	alarms, lights
bill collectors, salesmen, process servers, solicitors, irate individuals	front door
Good animals	
Inhabitants' dogs and cats	front and back door

Bad Animals	
All other dogs and cats	doors
mosquitoes, flies, June bugs, hornets, wasps, spiders, mice	screens
rats, snakes, skunks, squirrels, moles	concrete basement
termites and carpenter ants	termite shields
Transportation Equipment	
owner's car	garage
guests' cars	parking
oil trucks, coal, wood, ice	parking, fill holes
delivery trucks	parking, service door
hearses, ambulances	parking, front door
fire trucks	front door, hydrant, parking
moving vans	front door
bicycles, tricycles	covered porch

Permanent Equipment

Furniture, pictures, lighting fixtures, rugs, draperies, shades, blinds, equipment, kitchen laundry, cleaning

Perishable Supplies	
gas, water	meter
fuel	storage
steam	meter
food	back door
cleaning supplies	back door
garden supplies	garden
medical supplies	back door
ice supplies	back door

Leaving

Except for the perishable supplies all things leaving follow pretty much the reverse pattern of arriving

Gas—unused residuum up fire proof vent through roof
Water—to sanitary sewer by gravity
Fuel—unused residuum up fire proof flue to roof
Steam—condensate returned to supply or wasted to storm or sanitary sewer by gravity
Food—as garbage: to temporary storage outdoors, to pick up for qermanent disposal
as excrement: to water closet, to sanitary sewer, gasses generated in sewer vented through roof
as garbage: ground in sink, to sanitary sewer, incinerated to waste, gasses through fire-proof flue through roof.

Circulating

Rooms in houses develop stable atmospheres. They have assigned functions which do not change often, more or less fixed furniture patterns, and the architecture of each in turn conveys its own special message. We build up different associations for each, compounded of memories of the people who have used it, the scenes which have been played out there, and our own reactions to life. Circulation pieces are relatively free of these overtones. The special quality of moving from room to room, or from one part of a house to another is that it is an extensive experience. One is suspended between the distinct atmosphere of the room one has left, and the room one approaches. Nothing much is done in corridors. They are connections between a task just ended and one about to be begun, or a lull between parts of a sequence of actions. Corridors often catch one in a sort of psychological pause. For this reason, if for no other, they offer a unique opportunity to the architect. People using them are unusually open to esthetic impressions—to the brief enjoyment of a view, or of sunlight, or of a sculpture. Moving from place to place is as much a part of life in a house as dining, and should be clothed in as pleasant an architecture as every other function.

Circulation pieces are by and large very poorly handled in our contemporary architecture. They are treated as service elements on a par with pantries, rather than as the particularly important relaxation areas which they really are. One of the reasons for this is undoubtedly the high cost of construction with the resultant need for efficiency of plan. But a more important reason is perhaps the cult of the "practical" with its negation of imponderable values. We live between, as well as within, rooms. Wide and beautiful circulation pieces are the greatest of esthetic pleasures.

A great part of our pleasure in circulating is quite simply a function of scale. The usually accepted minimum width for corridors is perhaps three feet, the same width as that of the usual front door. Occasionally, as a more or less desperate resort, they are made even narrower than this. Still in terms of minima three and one half feet is considered considerably better. From the standpoint of people, even this larger minimum is far too small.

Corridors, wherever possible, should be designed so that two people can pass easily, which requires about four and one half feet. This width, while it does not give one the sensation of extreme confinement, is still be no means optimum. Corridors become pleasant in scale when one's arms can be held out horizontally in them, which requires about six feet. Over this scale they seem palatial. The small loggias of the Roman palaces of the sixteenth century start at around nine feet in width. Another difficulty with the three foot corridor, aside from the mean effect it produces, is that under certain circumstances of plan it is not large enough for the manoeuvring of large items of equipment such as beds, highboys, refrigerators, deep freeze cabinets, and pianos. The same problem can be even more acute in staircases where such large objects must be turned. When it is necessary to deal in minimum dimensions for circulation pieces, special studies must be made in plan and section to assure that beds, particularly, can be moved about.

Halls, corridors, and stairs, even when of a minimum size, can be made to dramatize the very practicality of their use and conception. A narrow low hall without windows and lined with closets, can carry with it the conviction that efficiency, lack of pretension, and lack of fuss are admirable qualities. The single run staircase engaged between two walls can be expressed as a chute, the easiest possible connection between two levels, and thus a very convincing utility. The expression of minima is as valid and exciting as that of optima. The quality of the saloon in a small yacht, for example, can be very exciting, and is in part a function of limited space. But minima are necessarily cramping both to the body and the spirit. A great wide and beautiful curved staircase is not only valuable for itself but evokes a sense of luxury, scale, importance, and ease. Stairs lend themselves to dramatic effects better than any other element of houses. They can create interpenetrations of space, balconies, long sinuous lines, and great heights, against which people look and feel more significant. They also lend themselves to symbolism. For example, to possess a grand staircase is to consume conspicuously.

Stairs are dramatic forms for four reasons. One is seen and sees people on stairs in motion, which is in itself fascinating. Vari-

Paul Letarouilly.

Charles Sheeler: "The Upstairs."

ations in height are tremendously potent, subjectively as they produce sensations, and objectively as they create interesting effects. Stairs are meeting grounds; they ascend from unseen regions above or descend into unseen depths below, they express the possibility of sudden encounters. And, fourth, the action of ascending or descending is easily translated into other terms, as gayety or gloom, or as emotional heights and depths. It is small wonder that most women want stairs down into their living rooms. Steps provide the ideal setting for entrances, not only for the hostess but for her guests. The elements of surprise; of height, which enhances one's visibility; of slimness, of sense of command; and of motion, are compelling effects and are immeasurably enhanced by long dresses and bare shoulders.

As circulating and circulation pieces can cause great pleasure, so can they cause great displeasure. On one level, that is, where safety and privacy are concerned, the effects are obvious. Parts of a house which are trapped in case of fire are unpleasurable in anybody's terms. The planned, obvious, assurance that one can escape not only fires, but also less destructive occasions, is a great contribution to a sense of ease. It is perhaps for this reason among others that open ended halls are so attractive. To look down a hall and out, or through a house and out a door, is invariably a

Harwell Hamilton Harris: The plan of this house appears on page 15. The fireplace, closely bounded by circulation, precludes the grouping of furniture around it. Part of the fascination of the circulation itself is undoubtedly its treatment as a hole, or slot.

pleasant experience. Sun and foliage and escape at the other end, particularly if there is also width, are almost sure esthetic devices.

Where privacy is concerned the question is more subtle, in that it involves social values. Must the maid be perpetually out of sight, or may she use the front stairs? How far from public spaces should such elements as pantry and toilet doors be located? Here both the client's ideas and the nature of the zone enter in. In spite of the fact that there are no fixed answers to such problems, or perhaps because of it, they involve the most important decisions the architect is called on to abjudicate. Injury to a client's sense of propriety, because it is never ending, is more onerous than most others.

Circulation pieces also present certain technical difficulties in terms of noise control, particularly where the telephone is located in or just off them, as is usually the case. Knudsen and Harris note that:

> "The rooms in which telephones are located should be reasonably free from reverberation. A telephone located in a reverberant hall imposes difficulties on both hearing and talking. If the telephone is located in a hall or separate room, absorptive treatment of the ceiling and upper portion of the walls of the hall is desirable. Reverberant halls are not only noisy and annoying to persons walking through them but they also act as effective conveyors of noise between different parts of the home. If the floors and stairways are tile or hard wood, the ceiling or the walls or both should be treated with an absorptive material having a coefficient of sound absorption at 512 cycles of not less than 0.25. If the hall floors and stairways are 75 per cent carpeted, it usually is not necessary to use additional absorption on the walls and ceiling."

Noise problems in halls and stairs are most severe where children are concerned. Their strong voices, at high frequencies, their propensity to leave toys on the floor, and to skate, tricycle and run about in them, create special conditions. Halls must contain certain safety features for this period. The most essential of these are gates at the tops and bottoms of stairs, which might as well be planned for. They need grounds as well as a place to hook on to.

Balusters should be such that a child cannot fall through, i.e., less than six inches clear between them. Safety on stairs in general might be summarized as follows:

Correct proportion of run to rise
Correct hand rail height
Hand rails both sides, continuous
Sufficient head room
Adequate lighting both day and night
The absence of winders
The absence of shelves and hooks
No doors near stairs
No circulation across top of stairs
No windows high above stairs
Adequate width between rails
Floor covering both for traction and resilience
Three way switches top and bottom
Light color risers to silhouette toys
Adequate length in landings
Uniform risers throughout the house and grounds

Over and above pleasure and safety in circulation there is one other curious human quirk involved. Certain people feel comfortable only when their houses offer alternate ways out of the main circulation scheme. These might be called circular circulators. They abhor dead end circulation pieces, or more accurately, the feeling that a corridor dead ends, even when it does not actually do so. There are sometimes excuses for this. For example some women wish to be able to go from kitchen to bedroom unobserved, to make up and get dressed after guests arrive, and then from bed room to living room via the front circulatory path. Others simply covet two ways around, a feeling which may relate to some archaic provision for safety from enemies. The difficulty which faces the architect here is not a technical one, for circular circulations are not hard to plan; rather it is one of diagnosis. Such clients often do not themselves realize what it is they want, even when they see it in plan, and must be made to realize what they are after by the architect.

Living

The words entering, or sleeping, or cooking, or eating, evoke reasonably clear pictures. One knows within fairly narrow limits just what these functions consist of. This is far less true of the word "living." It means so many things that no one emerges as typical. Furthermore, in terms of house, cooking means kitchen, sleeping means bedroom, and so on. But living can mean not only living room, but study, or library, or boudoir, or hobby room, or music room, or parlor, or playroom, or "all purpose room," or garden, or terrace, or pavilion, or croquet field, or badminton court. What are the actual functions we call living? In order to be able to allocate them to different spaces, they must be analyzed and classified. The following list includes the more frequently performed activities, with some of their necessities, which we tend to lump as "living."

1. READING TO ONESELF AND ALOUD

Comfortable chairs and very good natural and artificial light, thirty or more foot candles, with low brightness ratios. Storage for books, newspapers, magazines, pamphlets and clippings. Wastebasket for used papers. Outdoors, shade is convenient.

2. PLAYING WITH CHILDREN, AND CHILDREN'S PLAY—INDOORS AND OUT

Free area, and storage for toys.

3. DRINKING AND TEA

Side tables at principal sitting positions. Some like to store glasses and certain bottles such as brandy, liqueurs and the like in the living room, i.e., those which do not involve ice and water and mess.

4. LISTENING TO, AND MAKING MUSIC

a. Pianos. Pianos require good acoustics, music storage space, and good light at the keyboard. Their space requirements in addition to that needed for the stool, include free area for groups of singers or instrumentalists, either facing the keyboard or in the hollow side.

b. Instruments require space for from one to four or five people, with their music stands, about 10 square feet per person for the usual instrument, 20 square feet for a harp, 50 square feet for a standard grand piano, and 50 square feet for timpani. Storage space for instruments, music, music stands can require considerable area where bass viols, cellos, drums, bass tubas and the like are involved. Good natural and artificial light is essential. The acoustics of the room should be worked out for both the permanent piano location and the usual instrumentalists' playing area.

c. Radios and phonographs often require, besides floor area and storage space for records, particular provisions for speakers, a large baffle area, either built in or in a cabinet, a long throw in front of the speaker and carefully worked out room acoustics. Provisions for sound isolation of the room for others in the house is desirable if not essential.

d. The practicing of instruments requires besides good acoustics and area, very good sound isolation from other parts of the house.

5. LOOKING

a. Television sets usually focus a limited number of chairs, as in a theater. Rooms where they are used should be planned in such a manner that a bare minimum of change in chair location is required for their use.

b. Views play a part in the business of living, and affect plan and furniture arrangements. As their use is complicated by other and more general considerations, they will be taken up in detail in Chapter Nine.

c. Pictures require wall area and good lighting of a special kind. Light from limited sources such as small windows and lamps reflects off glass as it does from a mirror. In order to avoid reflections and glare, pictures must be located so that they are usually seen from some other angle than that symmetrical to the light source. Storage space for pictures in a dry, well ventilated spot is often required.

d. Moving pictures require storage for stereopticon, screen, projector and film, slides, etc., free area for setting up chairs, good acoustics and the ability to darken the room completely.

6. SMOKING

Ventilation and storage for tobacco, pipes, cleaners, humidor, cigarettes, cigars, extra ash trays, etc., and end tables for boxes and trays.

7. CONVERSATION

Comfortable chairs, end tables for smoking and drinking, good acoustics, a quiet location, a dead end location, i.e., freedom from people passing back and forth, pleasant surroundings, i.e., colors, views, etc., interesting, not necessarily "good" lighting, i.e., with marked contrast. Perhaps the most important single factor is a proper relationship between people in the conversation group. They should be not too far away from each other, they should also not feel too pressed together. A single focus, such as a fireplace, a view, a flower window, greenhouse, or a table has a unifying effect. Group identity is fostered by the knowledge all face the same direction or surround the same simple perimeter.

8. DOING NOTHING

Nothing, for many people, is the hardest thing to do gracefully and with moral assurance. Its requirements are similar to those for conversation. Beauty of surroundings, views, comfortable chairs with end tables and accessories, a fire, a low illumination level with high contrast, flowers, pictures and, particularly, a beautiful flooring material, are all important aids. The latter requirement, a handsome floor, is enjoyable because people look downwards more often than out or up. The color, texture, and finish of floors can do more to create atmosphere than walls or ceilings and perhaps even more than views.

9. PLAYS AND CHARADES

The drama needs a room in which one section has a separate identity, so that it can be seen as a frame or stage. This section should be towards the halls and bed rooms for ease in the hasty collection of costumes and props. The living area, ideally, should be capable of facing the playing area without any, or with a minimum of chair and table moving. This need for wide opening into another space, or for some less obvious separation, is similar to that often desired for dining and subsidiary seating areas. Whether or not duality of form has a specific reason, it is often wanted for its own sake, for it is essentially dramatic.

10. ROMANTIC COOKING

The living room fireplace is sometimes used for toasting marshmallows, popping corn, mulling wine, baking potatoes, and broiling meat, no matter how complete the kitchen. Marshmallows, forks, pop corn, and the like can be stored nearby. A crane built into the fireplace for pots, or even a built-in recess into which pots can be swung when not in use, is sometimes required. If the fireplace is near the kitchen the whole process is that much more convenient.

11. GAMES

Storage for card tables, and game equipment, and free area for setting them up without moving too much regular furniture. Good light.

12. DANCING

A smooth flooring material, waxed, large free area, good acoustics, separation from quiet parts of house.

13. PAINTING AND DRAWING

All children if given the chance, and many adults, do a considerable amount of painting and drawing as recreation. Blackboards, papers, colors, tables, easels, and water may be required. When painting is done as a family, or as part of entertaining, it may take place on the floor.

14. ENTERTAINING

Parties may involve simply sitting and talking to two or more people, or they may involve an afternoon outdoors playing croquet, badminton, etc., or they may involve music, drinking, dancing, conversation, smoking, playing instruments, games, cooking and even painting all in one session. Aside from the specific space requirements, equipment, and storage area for these activities, parties put other demands on the house and garden. Large numbers of people require greater space and more furniture than daily living. The rooms and terraces where parties are given must be able to absorb extra people, chairs must be easily available, and so forth, yet they must not look like hotel lobbies when in normal use. Free areas, secondary furniture groupings, and storage space for equipment must relate to and be in scale with the primary conversation group. Crowding during a party is not always objectionable, and may even be desirable. It proclaims an unusual and festive occasion. Noise, novelty, and forced physical contacts add to the excitement up to a certain point, but are tiring and harrying beyond it.

15. STUDY

Study habits differ widely but at one end of the scale quiet, privacy, and good light together with a desk and comfortable chair are required. As study becomes more social its requirements in terms of planning become less stringent.

16. ACCOUNTS AND WRITING

Letter writing, accounts, and various other kinds of home paper work require a desk, chair, and sometimes a file. Good light is important.

17. COLLECTING

Collections vary so that each one must be planned for itself.

Stamps may not involve much more than a little storage. Cut glass or pictures may affect the whole concept of the house. In any case most families have things they keep and add to which must be kept out of harm's reach, and whose value is that they are brought out in the open only on special occasions.

18. MEETINGS

The requirements for meetings are similar to those for entertaining. They may include movies, or slides, or refreshments, involving large areas and many chairs.

19. MAKING THINGS

Perhaps the most common hobby requirements are tools and a work bench. Making things for and with children, maintaining the house and its equipment relate to the wood working, metal working and electrical hobbies.

20. MENDING AND KNITTING

Very good light, forty footcandles or more, without glare or contrast. A comfortable chair and storage space for work, tools, and materials. Sewing, as distinct from mending, is a large scale and delicate operation. Mending can be a more or less social affair, and can take place nearly anywhere.

21. TELEPHONING

Quiet is here important, as is privacy, storage for books, pads, pencils and ash tray.

By design, or because of economic necessity, certain more or less extraneous activities, over and above these just mentioned, also take place in living spaces. Dining is one of the most common of these. There are several reasons for this combination. The volume of the room becomes that much greater and more impressive. The omission of one separate space saves money. The housewife is that much nearer the living room and is not as excluded from what is going on there. The dining room is not generally used

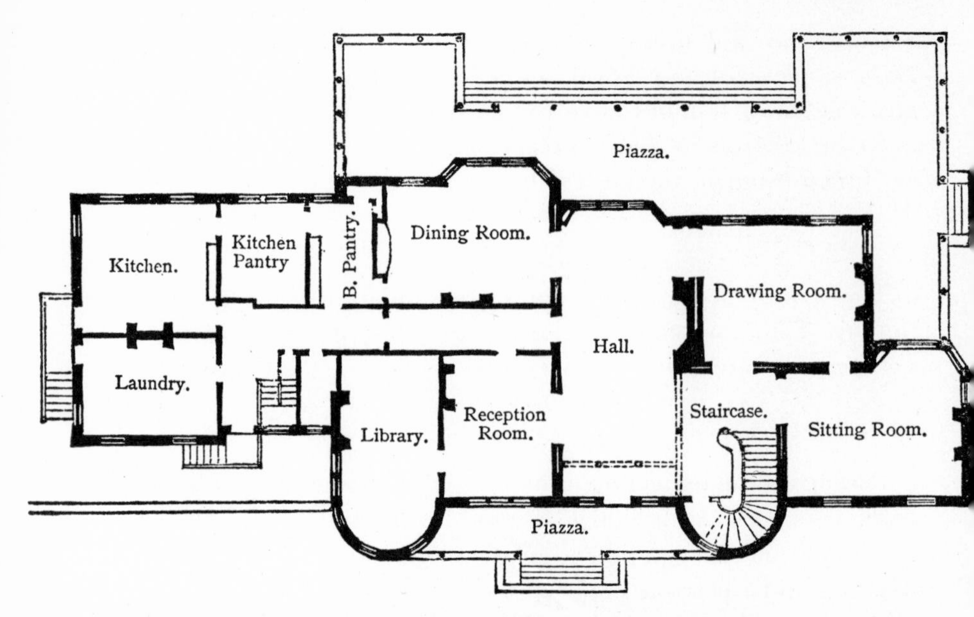

"Southside" in Newport, Rhode Island. Here the living activities are spread over six separate spaces.

except for that function and thus seems a waste. The disadvantages of the arrangement are that it introduces an active, noisy, and messy function into a room which should probably be free of such things. By bringing the kitchen closer it also increases the likelihood of noise and smells from that quarter. In practice it also seems usually to increase the amount of circulation in the living room.

The combination of entering and living has little or nothing to recommend it but economy. In northern climates particularly, it can only be seen as a last and desperate expedient in the interest of saving money.

The living room occasionally must serve as a guest room. Where this is inevitable because of lack of space elsewhere in the house, it should be planned with that in mind. It will need a door, and if possible, a nearby toilet, and should include storage for the guest's suitcases, pillows, blankets and linen. Without this it is difficult to make rapid shifts from one kind of atmosphere to the other.

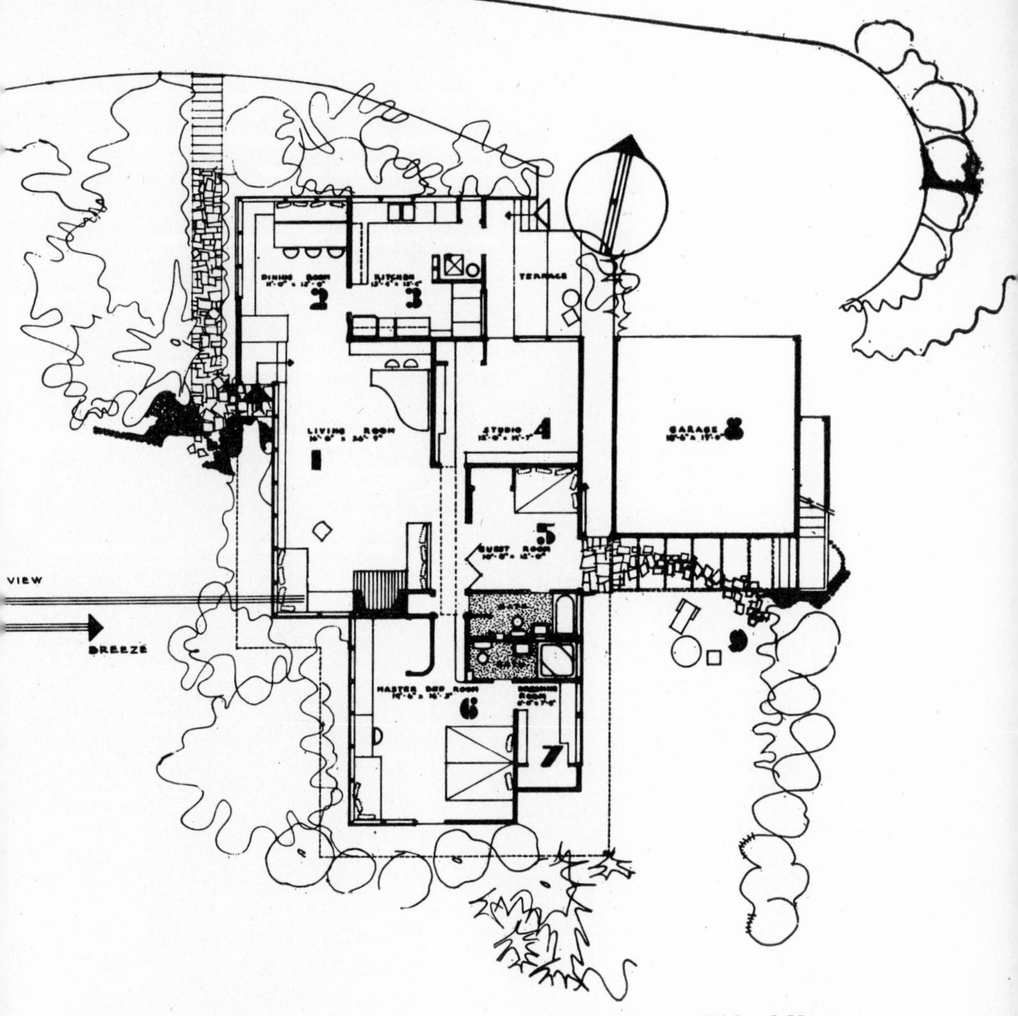

Richard Neutra.

In the very small house, some or even all of the twenty odd separate activities we call living must take place in the living room. They are so dissimilar in many respects, however, that this can never be truly convenient. Such a room exhibits use overcrowding. It is hard to keep clean. People compete for its use, and become disagreeable when they cannot have it, or when it is being used by others for an activity inimical to theirs. At the other extreme, these functions can be spread over a dozen or more inside and outside spaces. How they are allocated is a matter of cost

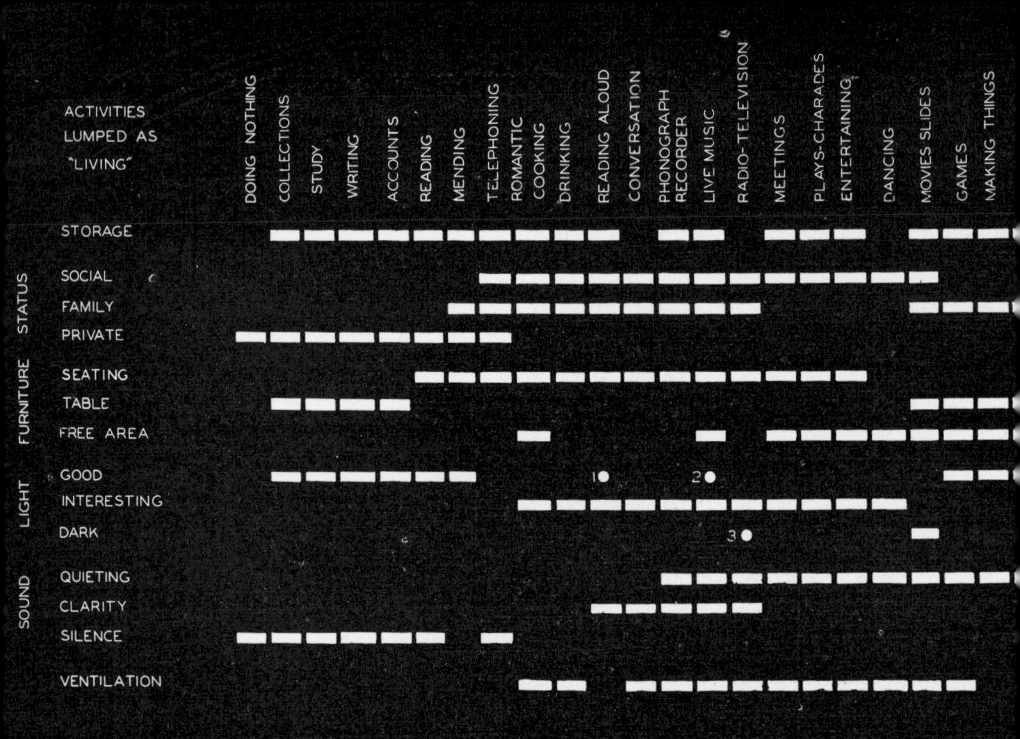

1 GOOD LIGHT NEEDED FOR READER ONLY.

2 GOOD LIGHT NEEDED FOR MUSICIANS ONLY.

3 DARKNESS NEEDED FOR TELEVISION ONLY.

LUMPED — LIVING ROOM

ZONED — BED ROOM / LIVING ROOM — LIVING ROOM — KITCHEN / DINING- PLA

DIFFERENTIATED — BED ROOM / BOUDOIR / LIBRARY / STUDY / DINING RM — LIVING ROOM / LIBRARY / DEN-STUDY / PORCH-TERRACE / SEWING ROOM — KITCHEN / DINING / LIVING / GAME RM. / NURSERY / ALL PURPO

CLASSIFIED BY FUNCTION — PRIVATE — QUIET-PRIVATE OVERLAP — QUIET — ACTIVE-QUIET OVERLAP — AC

CLASSIFIED BY NOISE — PRIVATE — QUIET — NOISY

ACTIVITIES LUMPED AS "LIVING"

DOING NOTHING / COLLECTIONS / STUDY / WRITING / ACCOUNTS / READING / MENDING / TELEPHONING / ROMANTIC / COOKING / DRINKING / READING ALOUD / CONVERSATION / PHONOGRAPH RECORDER / LIVE MUSIC / RADIO-TELEVISION / MEETINGS / PLAYS-CHARADES / ENTERTAINING / DANCING / MOVIES SLIDES / GAMES / MAKING THINGS and taste. But they must all take place somewhere. The purely indoor activities are arranged in the figure opposite according to their needs in terms of storage, social status, furniture, light sound, and ventilation. The need for storage is most significant, in that virtually all of these functions require it in the room where they occur. Living rooms need a large amount of small-article diversified storage, either in furniture or built in.

Except in the largest house there are bound to be incompatible functions assigned to the same room. In real life this overlap is usually compensated for by the fact that groups of people are apt to do the same things at the same time, if not because of the herd instinct, then in sheer self-defense.

On the other hand, the more complex the family, the greater the possibility that differing functions will be performed simultaneously. Broken down to their simplest requirements the living activities group themselves as follows:

PRIVATE	FAMILY AND SOCIAL	FAMILY
Storage	Storage	Storage
Table or desk	Seating	Table
Good light	Some free area	Large free area
	Interesting light	Good light
	Good acoustics	
	Ventilation	

These groups of activities can take place in one living room, or in a study, a living room and a play room; or in a bed room, a living room and a kitchen-dining-play room. There are many ways in which they may be assorted. Wherever they take place, the resulting rooms must be sized, arranged and expressed as multi-function spaces.

They also can all take place out of as well as indoors. A summer afternoon involves numerous shifts back and forth, from outdoors to indoors and out again. Outdoor living, in the immediate vicinity of a house, is largely a sort of expansion of the usual activities out into outdoor space. Because their principal locus is indoors, their outdoor requirements are less complex, and can be summarized as follows:

FUNCTIONS	REQUIREMENTS
Reading Drinking and tea Doing nothing Smoking Conversation Entertaining Mending and knitting	Terrace: The usual outdoor furniture must be stored someplace. Such storage is handiest immediately adjacent to the terrace itself. Its seasonal use allows it to be stored elsewhere, provided there is a covering or very wide eaves under which it can be pulled in wet weather. Terraces must be over sized to seem in proportion to our expanded sense of scale outdoors. As they also are in effect outdoor living rooms, great area is actually necessary. They should always be as large and spacious as imagination and the budget will stand. Electric outlets and telephone jack plugs are in order. Porch: The screened porch, essentially a wall-less room for the enjoyment of shade and air circulation should be on the coolest side, in most climates. To place it in the sun for sun's sake, is to invalidate its real purpose.
Lawn games, as tennis, croquet, badminton, etc., catch, touch football	Level area and a hardy ground cover, well drained.
Flower gardening	Outside: As the imagination wills Inside: Greenhouses from the smallest window variety to the magnificent Victorian domed sun traps are perhaps the most luxurious of all luxuries. The damp smell of earth and the scent of flowers indoors is one of the most pleasant of all sensations.

Wurster, Bernardi and Emmons.

The spaces used for living, whether outdoors or in, are inevitably the most important expressions of the owner's taste and status. The entrance makes a flash impression. The living room must make that impression stick. The furniture, the books, the pictures, every element of the room helps tell a story. It may not be read consciously, but it is always fully sensed and understood. The enormous living room so many people desire is in part required by living functions. Small rooms, as well, set up an unconscious claustrophobia. But a large room also indicates that the owner can afford to consume in the grand style. Social status is most easily expressed by size, and by luxury of materials. And there are, of course, other symbols. Some furniture arrangements, for example are seen as desirable by certain socio-economic groups while others are not. The degree of privacy surrounding the various living functions increases as one goes up in the social scale. This is particularly true where guests are concerned. Many of these symbolic messages are given maximum expression by furniture. But an appropriate background atmosphere for them must be suffused by the structure. The basic atmosphere—simply friendly, or stylish, or recalling a certain period, or place, or suggesting a formal or informal way of life, or based on some very personal intuition or reaction—is more or less a matter of pure design feeling. But the story must be accurately told, nevertheless. Otherwise there is very little point in having one's own house built.

Almost everyone agrees that one of the most potent devices for the creation of atmosphere is the fireplace. The "almost" is a necessary qualification because it has been the fashion of late, among the pseudo-practical, to attack the fireplace as a useless and extravagent sentimentality. It will take several centuries of attrition, however, to lessen materially its supreme symbolic importance. The equation "fire + hearth = home" needs no proving. Fire satisfies us in too many ways, on too many levels, to be easily cast out of the house. Its light, like that of candles, is fascinating. It is full of color, movement, brilliance and gloom. People look far more interesting in its glow than under any other circumstances. Its heat, largely direct radiation like the sun, has the same quality of embracing and caressing one's skin. Lighting a fire provides an extraordinary primitive and ritualistic pleasure. One inevitably suffers certain consequences for lighting a fire in one's host's fireplace one's own way rather than his, and vice versa. Getting in the firewood for the winter is part of the rites of fall. It carries with it the satisfactions of providing with forethought, and premonitions of long, warm evenings. If all these pleasures are significant for adults, they are ten times as significant and intense for children. The fire for them is a marvelous ritual, which they are eager to learn and willing to master step by step. Getting the wood, laying the hearth, lighting the fire and tending it is the first work they eagerly perform. It is one of the easiest ways to quiet them down when they are bored, tired, and obstreperous. Mrs. Field, in her very sensible housewife's view of architecture notes that:

> "During the winter months, when the children are often confined indoors for their play, it often happens that around four

o'clock or a little after they become cross and grumpy in their playroom, or wild and almost hysterical with boredom. Then I light a fire in the living-room fireplace, and send the children in there to watch it; if the fire were not lighted they would continue their quarreling and perhaps try to turn the quiet room into another bedlam, but with the burning flames on the hearth, they relax into easy interest. They see things in the fire, someone tells a story that interests the whole group, they quiet down, leaving me free to prepare the supper and serve it. It has a definitely hypnotic quality that can be turned to good account. The fireplace, therefore, while practically speaking it may be totally unnecessary in the modern home, may from the psychological point of view be a very definite tool in the management of children."

The essential quality of fire is perhaps its element of mystery. Children are particularly involved in this aspect of it. It is their first intimation of consumation, that things and therefore even people can completely cease to exist, can be reduced to a handful of ashes. This central mystery deserves the most noble expression.

But the significance of the fire would by no means seem to end here. In fundamental terms the house is a symbol of women, hollow, womb-like, commodious, and warm. It is also run, managed, cleaned, and tended by women. It contains this one masculine symbol, the chimney. Its tall rigidity, its flue, its heat, are all inescapably phallic. The man of the house, if he does nothing else, is apt to insist on making fires, that is, on tending his own symbol. And, during the design process, it is the husband who inevitably is most concerned with the design of the fireplace. The male client, casting about for an exact expression of what he wants in the way of a fireplace, is a most common architectural office scene. The importance of the symbolism involved makes most men approach the subject very conservatively. They are apt to be shocked by novel designs, and need a great deal of mulling time, and selling, in order to accept them. They feel that the architect has no business to proffer his own solution to the chimney problem—that they themselves should create it.

It is curious that despite this great concern with fire, very few houses provide wood storage near the hearth. Such storage is by no means difficult to arrange. A small door near the hearth, a larger loading door from outside are all that is required. In addition to wood, kindling, and paper must be stored someplace. A cupboard next to the hearth is very useful. Fire tools, the paper, tongs, brush, and other such items, again are seldom provided for. Clips to hold them can be built in to the masonry. If nothing is provided they either lean against the trim, falling down periodically, or must be stored on a stand which clutters up the hearth. Cape Cod lighters are designed to sit on the hearth and need no special provisions. The other things occasionally found at fireplaces, chemicals to produce colored flames, pine cones, very long matches and the like, also need storage in a nearby shelf or cupboard. Spark screens are perhaps the most obnoxious interference with the whole business of fire, yet they are a necessary safety device. They can be built in, and traversed, which solves the storage problem. The cost one way or another is not too different, while storing the movable kind when not in use is a nuisance. Getting rid of ashes can be simplified by the provision of ash dumps in the hearth. The cleanout door, and therefore the floor of the ash chamber below, should be high enough to take a standard ash can three feet above the floor. There is no point in shoveling ashes up into the barrel. Dampers are much easier to adjust if they are controlled by a knob on the face of the fire place. Few people will remember to get down on their knees with a poker, reach up into the fireplace, and feel around for the lever, after the fire is out. Yet if this is not done the flue becomes an excellent heat waster.

Fireplaces, with all their paraphernalia, are traditionally used as the focus for the fixed living room furniture. The value of this arrangement is purely psychological. The heat and light gained are far less perfect than that provided by modern heating and electrical systems as a matter of course. Indeed, in order to enjoy fully the special qualities of fire, the heat and lights may have to be turned down or off, and the windows opened. Practically speaking, the one thing which can be said in favor of the fireplace, ordinarily a great heat waster, is that it provides ventilation and air movement. But in every other way the fireplace has great

Pietro Belluschi

value. It unifies people because they are all directed at the same object, more or less equidistant from it, and the circular seating form thus provided suggests that everyone is equally a part of the whole. There is no pecking order, no hierarchy expressed. Each individual has the opportunity of participating. A good furniture arrangement is one which expresses this condition in a beautiful way.

The planning problems involved arise from this essential expression. There should be no passage, no opportunity for other than casual movement between the group and the fire. People moving back and forth between the two separate them psychologically, and thus break the spell. In order to give each position in the circle equal opportunity, the fireplace must be fairly large. Small fireplaces seem awkward not because they are less efficient, for they are not, but because they deprive one of full participation. Ideally, perhaps, there should be no doors beside the fireplace. By suggesting the possibility of circulation they separate the two elements. Great width for furniture on either side of the fire is also required in order to be able fully to complete the circle. Finally, distance from the fire to the furthest chair plays an important part.

Conversation is one of the greatest of all arts, and one of the most difficult for which to plan. What are its space and furniture requirements, if any? Thoreau tells us that his Walden Pond house was too small for it.

> "One inconvenience I sometimes experienced in so small a house, the difficulty of getting to a sufficient distance from my guest when we began to utter the big thoughts in big words. You want room for your thoughts to get into sailing trim, and run a course or two before they make their port. The bullet of your thought must have overcome its lateral and ricochet motion, and fallen into its last and steady course, before it reaches the ear of the hearer, else it may plough out again through the side of the head. Also, our sentences wanted room to unfold and form their columns in the interval. Individuals, like nations, must have suitable broad and natural boundaries, even a considerable neutral ground, between them . . . . In my house we were so near that we could not begin to hear,—we could not speak low enough to be heard, as when you throw two stones into calm water so near that they break against each other's undulations. If we are merely loquacious and loud talkers, then we can afford to stand very near together, cheek-by-jowl, and feel each other's breath; but if we speak reservedly and thoughtfully, we want to be farther apart, that all animal heat and moisture may have a chance to evaporate . . . . As the conversation began to assume a loftier and grander tone, we gradually shoved our chairs farther apart till they touched the wall in opposite corners, and then commonly there was not room enough."

For us ordinary mortals an area of somewhat less extent than Walden Pond is more comfortable. To be too far away from one's interlocutor is to be excluded. If the circle is too loose, voices must be raised and intimacy is lost. The largest comfortable diameter is probably twelve to fourteen feet.

Fireplaces, however, do not necessarily have to fit into this traditional arrangement to retain their satisfactory quality. Indeed, they have certain qualities which make them a poor focus a

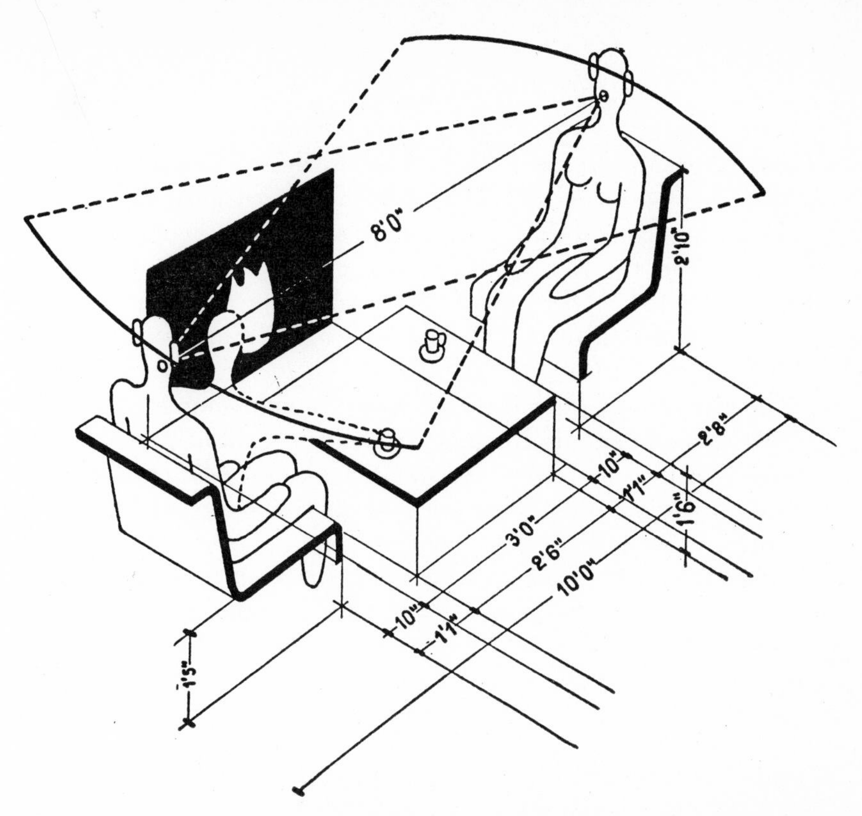

Francis de N. Schroeder: "The arc of conversation."

great deal of the time. Not in use, in summer particularly, they can have a dirty, abandoned look. With the ashes removed, and sometimes replaced with a paper or floral decoration, the hearth no longer carries much conviction. Living groups must of course be focused in any case, but other things will serve equally well. A flower window is a wonderful focus because it is beautiful at night, if well lit. A view will serve, though it has the disadvantage, unless it is a city view, of disappearing at dusk. A private garden which can be lit is also delightful and varied. Where such an arrangement is proposed, the fireplace becomes an incident in the room rather than a focus. It should still be glimpsed, it should still be part of the experience of moving around, but it need no longer be in formal relation to the living furniture. In order to keep its most dramatic value, it must, if not a focus, become the core of the whole situation. From a dead end location it must be shifted to the very most central crossroads of the house, where one may partake of it wherever one is bound. And there is still a third alternative. One of the greatest luxuries a house can provide is flexibility to focus furniture towards the outdoors in summer, and on a fireplace in winter. Removable fireplaces, like the Franklin stove and the Acorn, make such a plan easier to achieve if space is limited. Where great space can be provided, it is not a difficult matter to plan differing furniture arrangements for the two seasons.

The living-group-furniture problem is not completely stated until the requirements for making music are added. The proper integration into the circle of a readily usable radio-phonograph-record collection, often a largish item, is the most usual demand. Ideally, one should be able to use such equipment without getting up. Constant trips back and forth are tiresome to everyone concerned. The piano presents an even more fascinating and difficult problem. Unless it is an upright, it is a great space user. Its volume

Robert Woods Kennedy: A window for flowers is next to the fireplace, as alternate focus

is large and ungainly. In order to bring it into scale with the rest of the furniture, it must be placed in such a way as to minimize its mass. Placing it in front of glass emphasizes its bulk. In addition, this location exposes it to changes in temperature, causing it to get out of tune. Constant exposure to sunlight deteriorates its finish. It is best located against a bare wall and away from small scale furniture. The curved side is better-looking than the straight side because it is more interesting, looks smaller, and has both an enfolding and directional quality which can be used to advantage in laying out the spaces and circulation patterns around it. Because the curved side opens, the hinges being on the flat, it should of course face the listening area. The elephantine proportions of the piano can be further disguised by visually relating it to the next largest piece of furniture, the sofa. The most common volumetric sequence is thus from least to greatest; glass outside wall—space—lightest furniture—space—medium volume furniture—space—sofa—space—piano—no space—interior wall. Where the sofa is the last step before an interior wall, its lesser volume is still further decreased by allowing circulation space behind it. But such spaces must be explained, i.e., must be usable for getting at books and the like.

The proper volumetric arrangement of furniture is sometimes handicapped by a peculiar client pecadillo. Many people feel that the principal furniture in their houses must be backed up by a wall or a corner. There must be no circulation behind them, or even the possibility for circulation, no matter how infrequently it might occur. Some are so deeply disturbed by the idea of being unprotected from behind that every room must be arranged so that chairs, sofas, and chaises longues may be backed up by entrant angles. This need, whether it is a throwback to a primitive fear of enemies creeping silently up behind, or a manifestation of a neurosis, is sometimes very consciously understood by the person involved.

There is another reaction to the placing of seating areas, less frequent in occurrence than this, but equally strong when it does occur. A minority of clients like their living groups to float in space, preferably near large openable glass areas, and away from walls. They enjoy the freedom, the airiness, the flexibility, the luxury of a sense of great space, sensations akin to those we feel lounging on a beach. The architect must find out to which of the two categories his clients belong, if the information is not volunteered.

If there were any rules to go by in planning houses, the most probable would read as follows: *Living spaces for quiet and passive occupation must be dead-end rooms.* Besides the freedom from interruption required by the majority of living functions, there should be an accompanying feeling that the living circle is one with its focus. Listening to music, conversation, reading, doing nothing, games, charades, meetings, and many of the other activities called living, are detracted from by people coming and going on other errands. From the point of view of freedom to concentrate, privacy, and protection from dirt and drafts, the living room should not be an entrance, nor should it be sandwiched between sleeping and eating, and used as a passage between the two. In such case, but particularly where children are involved, the corridor living room can only have the character of a club lounge or a waiting room.

Not only should living spaces be set apart, they should also, particularly in houses for bringing up children, be capable of being closed off. There should be doors or sliding partitions between them and both the noisy activity areas and the sleeping areas. The open plan of the Victorian era, abandoned for a while and now once more in vogue, is a particularly poor arrangement for families. Sounds reach the living room from all over the house. Sounds made in the living room—music or a party, for instance—disturb the sleeping areas. This latter condition is particularly acute in houses where the stairs are in the living room, or adjacent to it without separation. Open planning is only successful when the areas thrown together are similar in their requirements for privacy and sound isolation.

The common processes of living, whether indoors or out, which we perform daily and without much excitement, would perhaps become unbearable if they were not occasionally heightened, given symbolic or ritualistic significance. Such occasions occur in three ways: periodically as Christmas or Yom Kippur; with forethought, as a party or wedding; and spontaneously. Everyday life and these climactic moments alternate as calms and storms. The storms are the memorable times, the ones we date our memories by. The planned occasions such as Christmas absorb our energies for weeks ahead of time, and our memories for years after. The setting in which they take place, primarily the living room, but usually the whole living area of the house, have a tremendously important effect both on the atmosphere of the moment and on our memories of it. It is no accident that the architecture of churches, the other building type in which significant social events most often take place, is usually as dramatic as the talent of the architect and the building budget can make it. The character of the various rites, festivals, and orgies we engineer are quite different. Christmas, the children's apogee, with its tree, candles, masses of presents and family, is the central festival; the one most in need of a grand and significant architectural background. Its essential requirements are space and light.

The cocktail party, a modern counterpart of the ancient orgy, is quite different. Its character and fascination are enhanced when, besides the excitement of alcohol and conversation, it is noisy, crowded, confined, dark, with spots of light only here and there for contrast. Spotlights shining on the undersides of leaves, or Japanese lanterns hung in the trees are its most appropriate illuminations. Birthdays, dances, and parties are between Christmas and cocktails. They need more space and light than the latter, often less than the former. This whole group of occasions is primarily festive. The anniversay of birth, whether it be of Christ, Lincoln, or an as yet anonymous three year old, does not seriously engage one's sense of mystery or inevitability. Weddings and funerals do. They demand of living areas still another kind of atmospheric adaptability. All such events are immeasurably enhanced by calmness, height, vistas, and balconies. These are the forms against which people seem most significant. The same kinds of architectural elements satisfy all our dramatic needs. Their lighting plus the emotional charge inherent in the occasion itself is enough to accomplish the necessary change from one mood to another.

A second kind of service which must be performed by living spaces is almost diametrically opposed to the climactic. Festivals and orgies in one sense do renew one, but they do it as a result of satiation. The kind of everyday relaxation and renewal required by most people must be calm and socially confined. The family seems to be the largest unit in which this can take place. Everyday renewal for most people consists simply in "living." Even when "living" becomes as active as, for example, carpentry performed as a hobby, this exertion is still as essential to renewal as sleep, or as, in other times, the bath. Architecturally speaking the significant aspect of renewal is delight in the products of culture; in books, music, pictures, sculpture, conversation, furnishings, and architecture itself. Because such things are inherently beautiful, their essential qualities, plus the delight of seeing them well set off by their environment, is a most subtle and all-embracing pleasure. The primary purpose of art is personal delight. The pleasure to be obtained from its objects and repositories is, to a certain extent, cumulative, perhaps in the same way that two sounds are louder than one, but not as loud as the sum of both. Music heard in a beautiful room both gains significance itself, and lends it to the room. The atmosphere created by a book can alter that of the room in which it is read, and in turn, be altered by the room. Pictures can change character markedly under the stress of differing emotions and light conditions.

This constant flux, the ability to perceive objects in quite different ways is of course in us, not inherent in objects themselves. For this reason the kind of dramatic quality required of living spaces must lend itself to atmospheric change. It must not be typed. The qualities we have come to associate with religious feeling, (verticality), financial success (monumentality), nostalgia (the cult of the antique), etc., are obtrusive. They force us to react in certain set ways. They lack atmospheric flexibility. The architecture of living rooms, in order to meet fully the various emotional demands which are made of them, must be somewhat neutral. It cannot ignore the past, yet it cannot partake of history. It must be contemporary, yet it must not be simply another example of the latest style, no matter how avant garde. Neutrality of this sort is perhaps the most difficult atmosphere to achieve because it conforms to no formula. It must partake of the past, present, and future at one gulp, and do it inaudibly.

Cooking

While it is possible, in terms of function, to separate the actual acts of cooking and eating, in terms of house planning they must be considered as a unified sequence of operations. The problem which faces the person trying to choose between the various cooking-dining combinations is an extremely delicate one. Socio-economic status is nowhere more convincingly expressed than in a plan which is predicated on the use of servants. To choose an arrangement which does not express dependence on service is forever to shut the door on this possibility for display. Most upper middle class families, whether they have servants or not, cannot get over the idea that eating in the kitchen is "common." It is seen as a lower income and therefore lower cultural pattern. Nevertheless, the trend is away from complete separation. There are several potent reasons for this shift. The change from a servanted to a servantless society, increased emphasis on child care, gourmandism, high building costs, nostalgia for things past, and a gradual acceptance of the fact that cooking is intermixed with a variety of other functions, all force the contemporary family towards new cooking-dining relationships. Because our living patterns are undergoing a gradual evolution, the average house suffers from the lack of a clear attitude on the subject. The old formal relationship is too expensive in first cost, too onerous a work pattern, yet it cannot be easily abandoned because of its honorific overtones. As a result, most current houses exhibit various compromises between the two extremes.

Many of these compromises, particularly where they also involve very small areas, simply do not work. For example, to plan a minimum corridor kitchen separate from a minimum formal dining room, with the laundry as a separate utility room, or in the basement, so complicates cooking-washing-child care, let alone the seven or eight other functions paralleling them, that the housewife's work is made both more hectic and more time-consuming. Because of use-overcrowding of the various spaces, the grandeur supposedly inherent in the plan is not only missing, its atmosphere may even approach squalor. Each relationship makes its own special demands on area, finish, circulation, separation and the like. If the essential concomitants of the particular scheme are not fully developed, it will fail miserably in use. The choices available go somewhat as follows:

COMPLETE DIFFERENTIATION

The kitchen is seen as a pure service function, entirely relegated to servants, and seldom entered by the adults of the family. It must be separated from the dining area by a pantry, because dish washing and pot washing are separated, because extra storage space is needed, and to confine smells, noise, and servants' chatter. Drink mixing is done in the living room or library, the ingredients having been brought from the pantry well ahead of time. The kitchen in this scheme is the servants' social center and must be planned with this in mind. Dining is done in state. This is the upper class pattern par excellence.

SEPARATION

This is to all all intents and purposes the same as complete differentiation, though on occasion the pantry may be omitted as a separate space. Its function remains, and may include drink mixing. The length of the service path may be seen as important whether servants are involved or not. Dining is still done in state, or in a close approximation thereof.

COMPROMISES

a. Separation, but with a service opening or slot between kitchen and dining room through which china, glass, and silver are passed by the diners to the cook, and vice versa. Dining may be done in a dining room, in the living room, or in a dining alcove. In the latter case it is recognized in plan though not differentiated from living room.

b. Dining and living are part of the same space but very completely screened off from each other. The kitchen opens completely into the dining alcove, or can be closed off completely, with folding doors or the like.

c. Visual separation only. The kitchen flows freely into the dining space, the table being an extension of the cabinet work, and the dining space flows into living space.

d. A breakfast room, a table in the kitchen for "informal" dining, and a formal dining room, with, of course, a separate kitchen. Of all the schemes, this is the most expensive, the most difficult to plan, and shows least ability on the part of the client to reconcile functional and socio-economic pressures.

COMBINATION

The cooking-dining process is seen as one and undifferentiated. No movable screens are set up between the two, though the equipment is arranged to hide mess from the dining or living-dining portion of the room.

In addition to making this decision, that is, as to the relationship of cooking to eating, the location of those functions commonly accompanying cooking must also be settled on. Cooking is only one of a large number of connected activities, all of which are essentially operative in nature, and all of which share a good many common characteristics. It is inevitably complicated by the addition of any one or all of the following parallel and simultaneous functions. As these are all described elsewhere, they need only be summarized for reference here.

1. SERVANTS

Servants are relegated to the kitchen, and, when they have no facilities elsewhere, must eat, rest, and entertain there.

2. SNACKS

The midnight snack can occur at any time, but it is perhaps a favorite of teen-agers and very usual after drinking parties. It usually takes place in the kitchen, as much for the change of atmosphere as for practical reasons.

3. CLEANING

Breakage of china and glass, and spilling of food are inevitable during the process of cooking, eating, washing up, etc. Floor cleaning equipment, particularly wet mops and the like, can most conveniently be kept in the kitchen zone.

4. WASHING CLOTHES

Washing is increasingly done in the kitchen. Automatic equipment is not difficult or time-consuming to use. It is clean and relatively odorless. Cooking, washing and child care can go on at the same time, and take less total hours to perform because no waiting is involved.

5. DRINKS

Drink mixing is almost always done in the kitchen in that it involves glasses, water, ice, and sometimes such other food as sugar, cream, cherries, olives, etc. Where drinking cocktails or highballs is a common living pattern, it should be considered in planning, and space allowed for it in the serve center.

6. MAINTENANCE

In almost every house, and particularly where children are involved, the kitchen serves as a minor work shop. Many creative activities involve water, or heat, or various kitchen utensils, or easily cleaned surfaces. Water color painting, gluing, oil finishing, soldering, inevitably flow over into it. Certain tools should be kept there or end up there, such as oil, hammers and screw drivers, etc., used for opening crates, oiling equipment and so on.

7. ANIMALS

"Undoubtedly there should be room in the kitchen for the family dog because there he will be, whether or not there is space for him."

8. IRONING

The inclusion of washing tends to centralize the subsidiary processes: drying, sorting, ironing, mending, with their necessary storage and equipment in and adjacent to the kitchen.

9. GROWING THINGS

Plants of all kinds, with their necessary paraphernalia, are frequent and delightful kitchen accessories.

10. ENTERING AND LEAVING

This function is an almost essential concomitant of the cooking-dining process.

11. CHILD CARE

A great deal of the feeding, training, supervision, entertainment of and own play of children necessarily takes place in the kitchen during cooking hours.

12. THE SOCIAL HOUR

Husband-wife-children get together before dinner or breakfast.

13. STORING

The variety of equipment, food, clothes, tools, little used utensils, gadgets stored here is very great.

14. CONNECTION WITH OUTDOOR LIVING

Secondary circulation patterns may be necessary, though they are not always essential.

15. CONNECTIONS WITH THE OPERATIVE OUTDOOR ACTIVITIES

These may be the same as 14 (above), or where privacy requirements are complex, they may be quite separate.

In spite of the fact that any or all of these activities may be going on while one is cooking, it seems highly important that cooking itself be considered as an absolutely self-contained function, and that none of its parallel activities should in any way interfere with its performance. They should surround it, rather than penetrate it. The whole process of ordering food, receiving it, storing it, cooking, setting the table, eating, clearing the table, washing up, putting away, and finally garbage and waste disposal, cannot really be separated from architecture. Cooking is not only a work function, but a social affair, and is inextricably mixed up with the other aspects of living. However, it is possible, and really necessary if one is to be able to cook easily, to isolate the pure process.

It is dangerous to generalize about these matters, but it would seem to be true that the space and equipment required for cooking by the urban-suburban upper middle class family can be pretty well pinned down, and need vary by a few feet only, depending on the amount of extra equipment which is desired, plus slight adjustments in space standards for the various work centers. There is a minimum below which cooking is uncomfortable, and a maximum beyond which a lot of extra movement is involved. Cooking equipment should exist only in relation to the work motions and materials involved. To separate the various work centers with doors and circulation, or to shape the total equipment in any way other than for its own needs, is sheer bad planning. With this in mind, the first decision which faces client and architect is how to arrange the whole process in undifferentiated space. This is by no means, however, true of the kitchen as a room. The individual family has a wide latitude of choice as to what functions other than cooking shall go on in the kitchen. Its area, shape, and volume must be increased as each additional function is added.

The distinguishing characteristic of the cooking-eating-cleaning-up cycle is that it has a definite beginning, middle and end. Each time it is performed, one knows, in a general way, what is going to happen. It may be repeated anywhere from two to six times per day, and the preparation and clean-up will take an average of three to four hours per day. Certain days such as before feasts, when canning, etc., will be entirely devoted to the process.

Ordering, which in a way starts the cooking activity off, is not in actuality a part of the process. In most houses it is done not from the kitchen, but from wherever the telephone happens to be. Kitchen cabinet manufacturers have of late recommended "plan desks" as part of the equipment for cooking, outfitted with paper, pencils, cook books, telephone, telephone books, files for menus and receipts, a chair, etc. For the housewife or couple who take food so seriously that it spills over into the realm of gourmandism, such a facility may be well worth while, in that such cooks are in constant need of more or less rare ingredients. In the average case, a place for cook books, paper, pencils, receipts, is enough. A list, particularly if it is only in one's head, is not difficult to transport around the house. Also, where a telephone extension is obtained, its preferred location is usually the master bedroom, for obvious functional reasons, and a third outlet in the kitchen seems warranted only under exceptional circumstances. Finally, an appreciable number of women order and make a series of other telephone calls each morning lying down if they can—a sort of rest period between breakfast and the day's activities.

Where food is marketed for, and brought home by automobile, a short, covered, easy connection between the garage or carport, or parking place, and the kitchen door is invaluable. Whether food is delivered, or brought home, a place to put it close to the back door and between the refrigerator and the rest of the work sequence is essential to comfort. Again, in the average suburban case, the delivery boy opens the back door, often without knocking or ringing, dumps his carton, and leaves. If the arrangement is such that he automatically puts it in the right place, a minor source of discomfort is eliminated. Where for various reasons the door is kept locked, a delivery port is useful. The usual arrangement is an unlocked self-closing door on the outside, followed by a large compartment, followed by a locked door on the inside, opening into the kitchen at a convenient place. This arrangement is peculiarly adapted to the regular deliveries such as milk, cream, eggs, bread, etc. In cold climates where things freeze between the time they are left and the time they are taken in, it has more to recommend it. In any case, some spot must be provided for such deliveries, under cover, within easy reach and in a location which does not involve an unnecessarily long path of approach for the delivery people.

Finally, there is the business of distributing these goods received to their storage places. This is, perhaps, the real start of the cooking process. In order to achieve maximum convenience, they should always be stored where they are first used. Storage, mixing, washing, cooking and serving are absolutely inseparable. The location and type of storage needed, therefore, must be planned in the context of the operation to be performed.

In most families, the housewife and her extension, the maid, do nearly all the storing, cooking, serving, and washing up. It would seem obvious that the equipment should be sized exclusively for their physical convenience. This can be done with great accuracy where it is to be designed for the specific job. Where stock cabinets and equipment must be used, only minor adjustments can be made. Because stock equipment is so uniform, there is little point in discussing it here. Accurate sizing, on the other hand, is still somewhat of a problem because of our lack of specific knowledge. The architect has two possibilities open to him. He can design to the actual dimensions of his client, or to the average dimensions of the income group involved. In both cases, it is of course only women who need to be considered. Men, by and large, have too little to do with cooking to make them worth while taking into consideration. We think of the current kitchen as presenting a working place of uniform height, usually thirty-six inches. But this is not really the case. The cook is actually faced with a series of heights. The level of the tops of bowls and pans is from two to eight inches higher than the counter. The level of the bottom of the sink is from six to eight inches lower. A study made at the University of Oregon indicates that the working height preferred by the average woman for the mixing surface is thirty-two inches, and thirty-two and one half inches for the bottom of the sink. In the latter case the counters around the sink will be at least thirty-eight and one half inches in height. Although this is too high for most operations, especially that of mixing, it is acceptable for stacking dishes and serving foods. These findings strongly suggest that for the average woman both the mix and range centers should be at the thirty-two inch level, while the sink and any counter space in the serve center should be at the higher level. In the sample studied by the research team, there was a variation of twelve and one half inches between the shortest and tallest person. It is interesting and significant that the variation in desired working heights varied only two and one half inches—from one and a half inches lower to one inch higher than the average. Thus a scale such as the following might produce the most comfortable working conditions for the whole range of housewives.

HEIGHT OF HOUSEWIFE WITH SHOES ON	BOTTOM OF SINK	SINK AND SERVE COUNTERS	RANGE AND MIX COUNTERS
5–0″	31″	37″	30½″
5–3″	31¾″	37¾″	31¼″
5–6″	32½″	38½″	32″
5–9″	33″	39″	32½″
6–0″	33½″	39½″	33″

Such dimensions are easy to achieve provided a unit range can be used. The same study indicated that a comfortable working area at counter height is about sixteen inches deep and forty-eight inches wide. The stock counter depth is twenty-four inches, eight inches deeper. There is some question as to whether the extra eight inches is not useful as temporary or even permanent storage for toasters, mixers, and the like, though this is felt to be messy by some.

For the right handed person, the easiest sequence of work centers is from right to left. The proper order saves work motions. The relationship of the centers is perhaps happiest as follows, though they may be arranged differently, provided each center is complete in itself.

4	3	2	1
SERVE	RANGE	SINK	MIX

The mix center starts with the refrigerator, which is thus on the extreme right of all equipment. Its door should be hinged on the right. The mixing center with its incidental storage is immediately to the left of the refrigerator, and is first used to put down food just arrived while it is being distributed to its proper storage spaces. The unit, excluding refrigerator, should be thirty-six inches to forty-eight inches wide. It needs sixteen inches clear over it for an electric mixer, and a duplex convenience outlet for that as well as the refrigerator, on the right hand side. Helen McCullough notes that "this is the center where a lower counter, or a sturdy pull-out shelf or table is desirable." If no special facilities are provided for ordering, cook books and so forth, they may be kept here, in addition to the materials and equipment listed below.

TOP LEVEL

Foods — Packaged and Canned	
1 cocoa 4 fish 3 puddings, starch base 1 cake flour 1 cornmeal 1 cornstarch 1 tapioca 1 prepared griddle-and-waffle mix 1 prepared biscuit mix 1 prepared fudge mix 1 junket tablets 1 shortening 1 baking chocolate 1 baking powder 1 cream of tartar 1 baking soda 1 each brown, confectioner's, cubed sugar	On closely adjustable shelves
Foods — Bottled	
1 molasses 1 syrup, corn 1 syrup, maple 3 herb vinegars 1 sherry 1 vegetable oil 1 salad dressing 1 vinegar, cider	On shelf
Shallow Utensils	
2 layer cake pans 1 piepan, 7″ 2 piepans, 9″ 1 piepan, 10″ 2 cookie sheets 1 muffin pan	On closely spaced shelves, or in vertical slots, with frequent divisions

INTERMEDIATE LEVEL — *from bottom shelf to top of counter*

Spices, Extracts and Flavoring	
1 salt 1 chili powder 1 onion salt 1 garlic salt 1 coconut 10 spices 7 herbs 2 food colorings 1 vanilla flavoring 1 almond flavoring 1 maraschino cherries	In open shallow shelves just above counter

Rolling, Mixing and Cutting Tools	
1 set of measuring cups, 4 1 measuring cup, glass 1 sifter 1 grater 1 grinder 1 pastry blender 1 rolling pin 1 rotary beater 2 cutters	Can be hung on specially located hooks etc. just above counter, or kept in drawer just below counter level

COUNTER LEVEL AND IMMEDIATELY BELOW

Accessories	
1 electric mixer	Can be stored on counter or in large drawer below, with accessories. 16″ clearance for use

Small Tools	
1 tablespoon 1 teaspoon 1 set measuring spoons 1 spatula 2 mixing spoons, wood or metal	In small drawer immediately below counter level

BELOW COUNTER TOP

Large Utensils	
1 pie pan (casserole cover) glass 1 casserole, round, large 1 casserole, small 1 loaf pan, glass 1 loaf pan 1 baking dish, glass 1 ring mold 1 cooler rack 1 baking pan, large 1 cake pan square 1 angel-food pan 8 custard cups 4 mixing bowls 3 cannisters	In large compartmented drawers, or pull-out shelves, or on adjustable shelves closely spaced
Bulk Food	
1 granulated sugar 1 all-purpose flour	In metal lined drawers, just below counter with scoops left in drawers; or in cannisters (see above), on pull-out shelves
Refrigerated Foods and Refrigerator Dishes	In refrigerator or freezer to right of mix counter (right-handed people)

The fundamental character of the storing and mixing center is exotic. Here, in a few cubic feet, and in little bundles, are materials from all over the world. Corn meal from the mid-west, lobsters from Maine, cheese from Switzerland, spices from India, oil from Italy, wine from Spain, fruit from Central America, milk from Vermont or Wisconsin, fill it to bursting with very special and romantic connotations. All this bounty is, furthermore, consumable. Much of it is also perishable. It lacks the sense of preciousness typical of permanent things. The storage center smacks most, perhaps, of an Eastern bazaar.

The sink, on the other hand, is folksy, homey, and down-to-earth. People are always throwing out "everything but the kitchen sink" and treating it tenderly in other locutions. How could one exist without it? It is used incidentally in just about every process having to do with eating, let alone for garbage, washing things, hands, babies, children, watering flowers, making drinks, and a host of minor processes. There is always some question as to which way it should be used when washing dishes. The usual procedure for right-handed people is to put dirty dishes on the left, stack clean ones on the right, and for convenience's sake, to dry and store them on that side. (Left-handed people may want it the other way around.) Thus it is most conveniently located to the right of the circulation from the dining table. The amount of space on each side varies, but about thirty-six inches per side is perhaps minimum, some of which can be for a dual purpose, that is, part of the mix center to the right and the range center to the left. As the left hand side takes hot and dripping dishes, there should be a drainboard on this side, if not on both. Based on various studies made at the Universities of Oregon and Illinois, the things to be stored here, and the way they may be stored, are as follows:

Foods — Packaged, Bottled and Canned	
3 milk 3 soup 3 gelatine puddings 1 dried peas 2 navy beans 2 shell fish 1 rice 2 noodles 1 prunes 1 raisins 1 currents 3 bouillon cubes	A base counter to the right of the sink. Adjustable shelves.
Foods — Fresh, Non-Refrigerated	
4 vegetables, and fruits	In ventilated drawers or bins to right of sink, or on both sides.

Item	Storage
Small Tools	
1 measuring cup, 1 cup 1 potato peeler 1 apple corer 1 utility knife 2 paring knives 1 French or butcher knife 1 scissors 1 sieve 1 can opener 1 bottle opener	Shallow, compartmented drawer to right of sink. May be over linen and accessory drawers. Can also be hung on wall or from underside of shelves, or in open racks just over the counter.
Kitchen Linen	
12 dish towels 6 dish cloths 6 hand towels 6 pot holders 1 roll paper towel	Shallow drawers to right of sink — may be under or beside cutlery drawer.
Accessories	
1 juicer 1 can or bottle opener 1 knife sharpener	Attached to wall to right of sink when in use. Stored immediately below in shallow drawer under or beside drawers for linen and cutlery.
Waste Disposal	
1 wastebasket 1 garbage pail	Under sink.
1 strainer, triangular	In sink, or under it when not in use.
Cleaning Supplies	
2 abrasive 1 bleach, liquid 1 drain cleaner, powder 2 soap, white 1 soap, yellow 1 soap flakes 1 soap powder 1 household ammonia 1 scouring pad (package of eight) 1 washing soda	Under sink in wire racks or pull-out shelves, or trays.

Cooking

Empty Bottles	
1 carton carbonated beverages (six bottles) 2 gingerale bottles 2 milk bottles	Under sink, or on shelves near service door.

Silverware	
12 dinner knives 12 dinner forks 12 salad forks 12 dessert or soup spoons 24 teaspoons 1 tomato server (open disc) 1 cold meat fork 1 sugar shell 1 gravy ladle 1 set salad fork and spoon 2 sets pepper and salt shakers	Shallow partitioned drawer to left of sink, below counter.

Utensils	
1 stewpan, 6 qt. 1 saucepan, 5 qt. 1 saucepan, 4 qt. 1 saucepan, 3 qt. 1 saucepan, 2½ qt. 1 saucepan, 2 qt. 1 kettle, 10 to 12 qt. or 1 pressure cooker 1 double boiler 1 colander 1 coffeepot 1 funnel 1 sieve 1 utility pan 1 measure, 1 qt., 1 pt.	Below counter to left of sink, in graduated drawers, pull-out shelves, or in tall narrow full-height unit.

Complete Service for Twelve	
China (Stock set of 95 pieces) 12 dinner plates 12 salad or dessert plates 12 bread-and-butter plates 12 soupe, cream, or flat soup dishes 12 fruit dishes	

12 cups 12 saucers 2 vegetable dishes, uncovered 1 vegetable dish, covered (2 pieces) 1 small platter 1 large platter 1 sauce or gravy boat (2 pieces) 1 covered sugar bowl (2 pieces) 1 cream pitcher *Glassware* (stemware, 36 pieces) 12 goblets 12 sherbet glasses 12 juice glasses 24 cocktail glasses *Additional pieces* (china, glass, or metal) 1 large pitcher 1 medium pitcher 3 jelly or condiment dishes, assorted sizes 2 cream pitchers 2 sugar bowls 3 sets salt and pepper shakers 1 vegetable dish 1 chop plate 1 center bowl 2 flower containers 2 candleholders	Above counter, so that they may be put away as soon as dried. Shelves adjustable or very close together. Cups, saucers, butter plates on lower shelves. Stacks of plates and glasses above, large bowls and pitchers on top.

Where the housewife likes to sit at the sink, garbage, cleaning supplies and the like must be put in the spaces on either side, in order to leave knee room and space to store a stool under it.

The range, with its attendant storage, is the third unit in sequence from the right. In comparison to the other units, its storage requirements are small. Its modest needs are fortunate because of the fact that it should usually have nothing over it but a hood to catch grease. This hood should have in it a fan of sufficient capacity to ventilate the kitchen in hot weather as well as to carry off cooking odors at all times. Ideally, the cooking top should be sixteen inches to eighteen inches deep, and the burners

Saul Steinberg

Carl Koch

should be in line. Under it should be one large slitted tilt-out drawer for pans and covers, another large drawer for food, a small compartmented drawer for tools and a compartment for an electric coffee maker, or large and seldom used pans. The oven should be to the left and above it, its front set back from the face of the counter. The bottom of the oven can be placed some ten to fifteen inches above the cook top, or from forty-two to forty-eight inches from the floor. It may also be set directly on the counter, of course, if this does not interfere with the serve center. Ranges and cook tops designed for this purpose are currently available.

The storage requirements of the range center are as follows:

Item	Storage
Foods — Packaged, Canned and Bottled	
1 tea 1 malted milk 1 coffee 1 coffee substitute 1 decaffeinated coffee 1 tea balls 1 meat 7 vegetables 4 cereals, uncooked 1 noodles 1 spaghetti 1 macaroni 1 vegetable soup, dried	On shelves above and to right of range, immediately to left of sink center. Shelves should be adjustable and close together. Where space does not permit, they can be kept in a drawer immediately under right hand side of cook top.
Utensils	
1 skillet, large 1 skillet, small 1 saucepan, 2 qts. 1 griddle, large 6 lids	In large drawers under range, slotted and pivoted to tilt out from bottom.
Tools	
1 turner 1 ladle 1 spoon, wood or metal 1 spoon, perforated 1 masher 1 fork, 2-prong, long 1 fork, case 1 tablespoon 1 teaspoon 1 set measuring spoons 1 spoon, large bowl	In small compartmented drawer under range.
Accessories	
1 electric coffee maker	On counter to right or below range in compartment with door. Convenience outlet to right.
pot holders	On hooks, over cook top, to right.

The range itself and its accompanying somewhat greasy utensils is, symbolically, the very center of the kitchen. Here is heat, fire, steam, smells, usually wonderful but sometimes awful, and a mysterious chemical process which, because it is superintended by women, makes her into a sort of genie. Here is the female symbol of creative heat, which she can only regard with the greatest of awe—even as her husband regards his fireplace.

The most appropriate character for a range is a difficult question. Symbolic objects are always visualized in a relatively obsolete form. If one asks a child to draw house, he produces this:

The basic image kitchen stove is probably a black iron range, with a high back, perhaps built into a brick niche in the Victorian manner, or standing free before the brick work, on iron lion's feet. Such stoves are often resurrected and equipped with gas, simply because of their symbolic connotations. They are, some-

JEWEL GRAND.

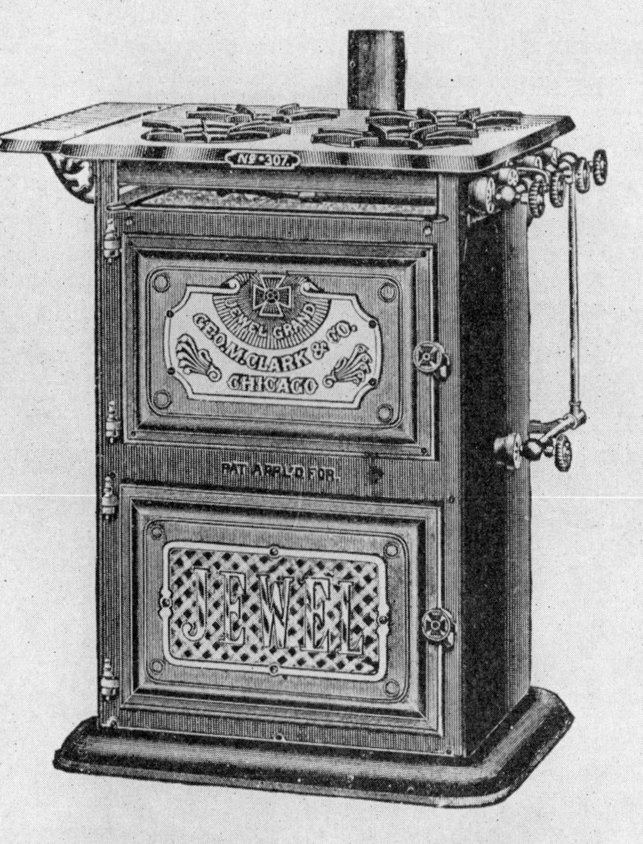

No. 307. Without Water Back, $30.00

FOUR BURNERS ON TOP.

OTHERWISE LIKE RANGE ON PAGE 16.

Jewels are High Grade, Interchangeable, Right.

how, appropriate to the function cooking. Will the stark white, streamlined current equivalent, which becomes in its most luxurious form a cross between a dissecting table and a juke box, ever accumulate such rich connotations? It seems unlikely. Like so much industrial design, it is in reality packaging. The enameled steel straight jacket in which it is physically imprisoned also imprisons its spirit. The architect must bring that spirit out in other ways—through the design of its hood, and through color.

The serving area, immediately to the left of the range, again involves a change in character. Here one begins to deal with the more formal, valuable, permanent, honorific utensils of eating. This is where, out of the steaming witchery of the stove, there materializes those good things consumed at the dining table. The serving area is the simplest of the four units, in that it is the only one which does not need any equipment other than storage. Its surface may best be heavy, laminated wood, as sandwiches and the like are often made here. It should have a duplex convenience outlet to the right, for toaster, waffle iron, etc. Its width can range from eighteen inches to forty-two inches, depending on the number of items desired. Its storage requirements are as follows:

UPPER LEVEL

Foods — Packaged, Canned and Bottled	
4 fruits, #2 3 fruits, #2½ 2 fruit juices, qt. 2 fruit juices, pt. 1 fruit cocktail 1 vegetable juice 2 sardines 6 cereals, dry 4 cookies 4 crackers 1 ketchup 1 Worcestshire sauce 1 mustard, prepared	Adjustable shelves to 72″ above floor.

Cooking

INTERMEDIATE LEVEL — *above counter*

Items	Storage
1 cucumber pickles 6 jellies and preserves 1 peanut butter 2 sandwich spread 1 pickles, sour 1 ripe olives 1 olives, stuffed 1 mints 1 ginger, candied	Narrow shelves immediately above counter. May be open.

IMMEDIATELY BELOW COUNTER

Items	Storage
Foods — Fresh, Non-refrigerated	
3 bread or rolls 1 cake 1 date-and-nut bread 1 doughnuts	Metal-lined drawer to left of unit. Should be large and deep with cover.
Utensils	
1 slicing knife 1 wax paper, roll	Small drawer at right of unit.

LOWEST LEVEL

Items	Storage
Equipment	
1 waffle iron 1 electric toaster	Adjustable shelves, open or behind doors, at left of unit.
Accessories	
2 trays 1 cutting board	Slotted compartments, open front to right of unit.
Linen (everyday table use)	
2 sets of 6 place-mats 2 luncheon cloths 3 sets of six napkins 1 pkg. of 80 paper napkins	Drawer or drawers to left of unit. Paper napkins are better stored above.

The other serving problem in the typical upper-middle class house is that of drinks. As the only function of alcohol is delight and relaxation, there would seem to be every reason to make serving it as pleasant as possible, a foretaste of the pleasant occasion to come. The kinds of liquor used, and the places where the various ingredients are kept vary tremendously. But it seems reasonably safe to say that most families store beer, gin, whiskey, two kinds of vermouth, and some wine, and that these are used mostly for making cocktails and highballs. Vintage wines, old brandies, etc., of course, should be kept in a wine cellar, while table wines and liqueurs may be kept in the dining area. For the ordinary family, mixing the ordinary drink, the bar should certainly be near the refrigerator and the sink, because water and ice are usually needed. A drink center thirty-six inches wide, with the following facilities, would be ample in most cases.

UPPER LEVEL

Gin	kummel	Adjustable shelves to 72″ above floor.
vermouth	rum	
chartreuse	cointreau	
dubonnet	brandy	
grenadine	fruit brandies	
whiskies	sherry	
creme de cacao	benedictine	
creme de menthe	curacao	
absinthe	amer picon	
sloe gin	anisette	
	creme de cassis	

INTERMEDIATE LEVEL, *above counter*

jiggers	Narrow shelves, immediately above counter, may be open
3,4 bitters	
syrups	
glasses	
sugar	
olives	
cherries	
honey	

Cooking

COUNTER LEVEL

Items	Storage
Squeezer Bottle opener can opener cork screw, attached to counter	Stainless steel or heavy wood counter, with small sink, high faucet

JUST BELOW COUNTER LEVEL

Items	Storage
coasters glass jackets strainer bar spoons paring knife swizzle sticks bottle caps	Shallow drawer, compartmented

TRAYS — Open slot next to drawer

LOWER LEVEL

Items	Storage
Mixes tonic soda water beer, cans and bottles colas ice bucket	Large fixed or pull-out shelves from which bottles can easily be slipped into refrigerator

The serving of food and drink may involve a walk, more or less devious, as it involves crossing pantries, other circulations, etc. Or it may be through a port. Or it may simply involve shoving things from the serve center directly on to the table. The decision in each case hinges on the question of privacy, and isolation from the cooking process, versus the number of steps and motions necessary for serving and clearing. The greater the privacy, the greater the amount of work involved. The port system, which theoretically seems so ideal a compromise, in practice actually involves an appreciable amount of backing and filling. It also produces a variety of embarrassment, perhaps because of the caged look of the housewife, when viewed through the peephole-like opening, in the litter of her kitchen. The fact that the family and guests literally toss her bones through the slot does not decrease the zoo-like illusion.

Decisions as to which system to use are inevitably made not on grounds of utility, but on those of propriety. This is as it should be, for except in extreme cases of bad or honorific planning, the extra energy required by greater privacy is very slight in any terms. The ability to enjoy and digest one's food is certainly affected by the appropriateness of one's surroundings, and is more significant than the mere saving of a few steps.

Whatever the connection, or lack of it, between cooking and eating, when the latter process is complete, the flood of food, accessories, and utensils which originally emanated from the kitchen returns to it, like the tide, and brings, like many tides, a litter of waste materials. Garbage, cans, empty bottles to be returned, paper, etc., need temporary storage inside as well as out. The various centers contain these necessary spaces. Outdoor storage for their second resting place is, however, too often neglected. A corkscrew circulation, through a back hall, back porch, garage, down steps and around corners, makes the unpleasant task of getting rid of waste still less pleasant, Ideally, garbage should be kept in a cool place, tightly covered, and ungetatable by dogs. The underground can is about as good and as inexpensive a solution as can be imagined, other than the sink disposal unit. Waste paper in watertight cans out in the open, where, unless they are covered, they fill with water and snow, and where their contents are apt to blow away, seems less than adequate. A hard surface to put them on, protection from above, a hose bib nearby ready to use in cleaning them, seem desirable accessories.

The "rationalization" of any process always involves very great dangers, first because people develop personal and often highly suitable and original ways of doing things for themselves, and secondly because the limitations of the human mind being what they are, something is usually forgotten. The client with a strong and well worked out cooking system is the least of the architect's worries. Forgotten details are the worst of them. These often involve that general category of things known to yachtsmen as gadgets and gilhickies. They include, for example, can openers, orange juice squeezers, paper towels, towel drying racks, and match supply and disposal for gas stoves. Opinions vary as to whether such things should be out in the open, and available for instant use, or hidden for purposes of appearance. In the former case they must be easy to get at, and need grounds or surfaces to which they can be screwed. And they must not get in one's way, particularly at eye and waist level. Such things, when unplanned for, can cause great sores in the plaster, rip clothes, and generally become a terrible nuisance.

The kitchen is, in any case, second only to the bedroom as the locus of most fatal home accidents, and is the most dangerous as far as all others are concerned. It would undoubtedly be first on both lists, were it not for the fact that the aged build up the figure for bedrooms. It is small wonder the kitchen ranks so high. It involves fire, hot liquids, poisonous gas, poisons, wet and greasy floors. Burns, scalds, explosions and fires are very apt to occur here, with falls, and bumps against drawers and cabinet doors a common occurrence. It is possible to decrease the possibility of some of these accidents through planning. The absence of breaks in the working surfaces; non-slip flooring materials, horizontal sliding doors; low top shelves; a handy step ladder; ranges away from opening windows where the wind can blow curtains into their flame; locked cabinets for poisons, rounded corners wherever possible—all help to make a safer kitchen. As noted earlier, the most important safety precautions are those for little children. While provisions for their safety cannot sensibly interfere with the cooking process, the equipment must be related to their needs, just as it is to those other functions which parallel cooking. Finally, dark kitchens are a menace. Light is an important aid to accident prevention. It may also affect our health, in that a dark kitchen will probably never be kept as clean as a bright one. General illumination in kitchens should reach at least 10 footcandles, while the work surfaces should reach at least forty.

The kitchen as the center of a great deal of noise, both from pots and pans and children, is usually in need of quieting. The shape and volume of the room can play an important part in this, but treatment is usually needed as well. The only safe material is an absorptive blanket covered by a perforated, washable, metal or asbestos surface. Knudsen and Harris note that:

"This same material can be applied also to the ceiling of the

kitchen, especially in large homes. Most acoustical plasters available at the present time are not suitable for use in residences since they offer difficulties in cleaning, washing, and decorating."

As in everything having to do with cooking, there is a remarkably wide lack of unanimity on the subject of the character of the kitchen. The same cultural factors which operate to confuse the cooking–dining relationship also affect the kitchen's atmosphere. We are all familiar with the poles of opinion on the subject of "the farm versus the laboratory kitchen." Both ideas seem somewhat false in that the kitchen for the typical urban-suburban single family house has nothing to do with either farms or laboratories. The real argument is perhaps between the warm and the cold kitchen. The cold, or stock, kitchen is undoubtedly a reflection of the same complete lack of humanity which characterizes most of our industrial design. The farm kitchen, on the other hand, is a sentimentalism. Mixtures of the two, such as the combination of natural wood and the snow-white streamlined ice box, usually leave something to be desired. Separated burners

Wurster, Bernardi and Emmons

and ovens, in stainless steel, designed so as to fit into ideal work patterns; refrigerators built on the job; or the usual white coffins reenamelled some gayer color; all tend to free the architect from the physical and esthetic limitations of stock equipment, provided he can spend enough money.

This leaves us still with the true character of the kitchen in doubt. What does the housewife really want? The message imparted by the laboratory kitchen seems most unpleasant. It says in effect: "This business of cooking is time consuming and boring, and should be accomplished with a minimum of motion and emotion." It demeans the art. In so doing, it demeans the housewife, who becomes an almost mechanical adjunct to the equipment, rather than the sorceress of the steaming pot. The farm kitchen is simply a stage set, an artificial make-believe world. Here the housewife play-acts the role of cook. Neither atmosphere suggests the solid dignity of an important work function, the magic in cooking, nor the delights of its products.

The problem should be approached, perhaps, from the point of view of the essential character of the various work units. Each part of the kitchen contains, latent in it, very strong and attractive qualities: the oriental bazaar of the mix center; the rich mess of the sink; and the steaming cauldrons of the range. The inherent beauty and formality of china and silver needs only to be brought out, in order to give the kitchen the richest and realest of atmospheres. In addition, the building materials most appropriate to its uses are inherently handsome. Cedar, cypress, black linoleum, stainless steel, birch and cherry for counters, quarry tile, Keen's Cement painted, all go beautifully together. The aim in putting them together, over and above that of solving accurately the functional requirements of the room, is a sense of *living*. The housewife cannot be expected to enjoy cooking as long as it is thought of and expressed as a duty which interferes with life. It must be a part, an important part, of life itself. That is why fireplaces, and flowers, and children, and dogs, and husbands also belong in the kitchen. Life is never one pure unmixed occupation. Life in the house is, and must always be a kaleidoscopic sort of affair, in which the fact that one has gone around three hundred and sixty degrees is the least of one's worries.

Encyclopedia Britannica Films Inc.
Diners from "A Giant People."

Eating

The meals, snacks and drinks we consume, have great variety of kind and of atmosphere, as well as of social and other distinctions. The basic division is of course between family and servant. The latter must have full facilities in the service area of the house. Secondarily, little children are best fed in the kitchen. Indeed it is often some years before they graduate to the status of eating all of their meals with their parents. In the meantime the servant may eat with them, increasing the space needed for dining in the kitchen. The adults may, after a day of household and family activities, very much desire to eat together alone and in complete privacy. And finally, the sick and elderly may, through force of circumstance, have to be fed regularly in their bedrooms. The whole gamut of ordinary meals involved might be summarized as follows:

Meal	By Whom	Location
Picnics	Family and guests	Outdoors
Romantic cooking	Family and guests	Living room and porch
Outdoor cooking	Family and guests	Garden and terrace
Snacks midmorning midnight	Family, servants, guests	Kitchen
Tea	Family and guests	Living room, terrace, porch,
Cocktails	Adults and guests	Living room
Breakfast	1) Family	Outdoors, kitchen, dining room, breakfast room
	2) Parents	In bed
Lunch	1) Family	Dining space; outdoors
	2) Wife and guests	Dining space; living room; outdoors
	3) Family, guests on Xmas, Fourth July, Thanksgiving, etc.	Dining space
	4) Children, husband	Eaten out
Dinner	1) Family	Dining space, outdoors
	2) Children and maid	Kitchen
	3) Parents and guests	Outdoors; Living room
	4) Parents and guests	Dining space
Supper	Parents and guests	Living spaces
All meals	The sick or aged	In bed

Equipment	Storage	Nature
Baskets, thermos, blankets, etc.	Largely kitchen	Festive
Forks, grills, cranes, etc.	Fireplace & kitchen	Romantic
Grills, forks, etc.	Largely kitchen, shed	Festive
No extra required; usually eaten standing	In kitchen	Utilitarian
Tray, china, etc.	In kitchen	Homey & social
Tray, shaker, etc.	In kitchen	Festive & relaxing
		Humdrum
Bed tables	In bedroom	Luxurious
		Humdrum
		Social
Large, seldom used utensils. Extra table leaves.	In kitchen	Climactic
Lunch box, thermos	In kitchen	Extra-familial
		Humdrum
		Humdrum
		Informal relaxed; or formal alfresco
Fountains, flowers, candles, extra chairs		Festive and social
		Alfresco social
Trays, etc. Bed tables	In kitchen In bedrooms	Lonely

The order of frequency of the various kinds of meals is of course very subject to individual patterns. But, in the usual household, the humdrum comes first, tea and cocktails second, with outdoor meals and sick room meals vying for third place. This again suggests the utility of short circulatory paths between the kitchen and the terrace, bedrooms, and living room. It also suggests new needs for storage. Such items as bed tables, outdoor cooking equipment, fireplace cooking equipment, picnic equipment, lunch boxes and the like must be tucked away somewhere.

From the architect's point of view, once the functional demands for eating are decided upon, the principal question is not the humdrum occasions, but the festive ones. An atmosphere which will rise to these can only inform all of the others, provided that it is not so thick as to be cloying as an everyday diet. These special occasions are, of course, Christmas, New Year's Eve, Thanksgiving, and the Fourth of July. The menus for each are traditional. On a more even beat, the dinner party, of several people, with several courses, cocktails, wine, evening clothes and candle light, is probably the most ambitious, formal, and exciting occasion.

These special meals require extra space, not only for a large number of people, but for service around them. Lack of interruption is another essential. The spell of such occasions cannot brook telephone conversations or farewells and goodbyes in their midst. Audibility is also of the essence, though, as in all parties, a slight din, a slight crowding, is not amiss. Knudsen and Harris note of dining room acoustics:

> "Large areas of highly absorptive material in a dining room are very desirable. If the floor is completely carpeted over a ½-inch felt pad, and if the windows are draped with heavy hangings, absorptive material for the walls and ceiling may not be necessary. In one dining room designed for good acoustics, the entire ceiling is treated with an acoustical tile having an absorptivity of about 0.50, the entire floor is heavily carpeted, and doubly lined draperies are used for all windows and for one large door opening. The social conversation of as many as 12 persons sitting at dinner in this room does not produce the usual din of

Robert Woods Kennedy.

noise that would result if this same conversation took place in untreated room. In fact, it is easy to converse at one end of the table while general conversation is in progress among the other guests in the room. In like manner, the playful chatter of children is reduced to a level that can be readily tolerated, whereas this same chatter in a reverberant dining room may be well-nigh intolerable."

An even more significant atmosphere evoker is light. The continuing use of candles, despite that new-fangled invention, electricity, is an indication of our love of romantic settings. Candle light, because it flickers and makes everything move, because its radiance is limited, because of the deep and mobile shadows it makes, because it is fire (rather than hot tungsten), creates a potent mood unaided. The best substitute electricity has so far been able to offer is the ceiling pin-point fixture, sized in such a way that it illuminates only the table top. Its disadvantage is that it is inflexible. Its advantages are an extremely sharp and brilliant and contrasted lighting scheme, with many reflections off the table and silver up into people's faces. The day lighting of dining spaces is often uncomfortable because of the sun. Direct sunlight in the eyes while eating is harder to combat at table, where we cannot move, than in the living room. Sunlight which floods the table, and which therefore must be totally excluded, is of less than no value.

Finally, these special meals involve certain equipment which is usually thought of, for some curious reason, as "extra." Actually it is not extra to the house, it is only extra to the humdrum occasions. Additional chairs, additional leaves for the dining table, extra large pots, platters, etc., as well as table ornaments, candles, candle sticks, and the like, must be stored. As many such items do not need cleaning after every meal, or are cleaned in the dining space, side boards, built in or otherwise, are still of great use.

Relatively few present-day houses do this category of things justice in terms of storage. The tendency of the innovating part of the upper middle class is to underplay them. Yet they have not been abandoned. The very great cost of cubic feet must be blamed in part, whether these feet are for storage or living. And the tendency, at least for men, to dress formally less and less often, may make these "extra" things seem less important. We take an increasingly dim view of the unhealthy preoccupation with possessions typical of the Victorian era, as well as of their initial cost, and of the work involved in maintaining them. Whatever the reasons, to inhibit the expression of these aids to romantic entertaining does seem to rob the house of one of the principal evidences of a friendly spirit.

Whether a meal is humdrum or festive, candle lit or sunlit, every family feels that their own way of doing it has unique and individual importance. It is never so face to face with itself as while eating. Its manners, the gusto (or lack of it) with which it attacks the food, the fact that father, mother, and guests take ritualistic positions around the family board—all conspire to put it on show. The father is never more commanding, the mother is never more the woman of the house. The children are never more regulated according to age. Many families increase this ritualistic

Wurster, Bernardi and Emmons.

atmosphere by making specific meals into family conferences. Others stress the social graces of the occasion.

Because of ritualistic importance of meals, the family's relationship to the guest, and particularly to the unexpected guest, becomes very touchy. Most people seem to dislike to eat while others watch. The guest must eat too, if the family is to be at ease. The food eaten, the way in which the table is set, the family's manners are all highly potent symbols of class status. "Nice" people have "refined" table manners. The family feels that the guest will necessarily watch for the little indications of culture and refinement, while the guest feels embarrassed to have unwittingly invaded the family's privacy. Thus dining spaces located where they can be viewed from the entrance are anathema for most people. They should be as private as the family feels; their atmosphere should suggest that degree of ritual which the family enjoys; and their appointments should be the most elegant.

*"The Princess bathes" from a Balinese manuscript.**

Bathing, Washing and Excreting

Because of the remarkably large number of euphemisms for bath room, ranging from "can," "head," "John," and "Jane," to "Rhett" (Butler) and "Scarlett" (O'Hara), it would seem necessary to start with a few definitions:

Lavatory: A basin used primarily for washing the hands and face
Sink: A basin used for cleaning food and for washing dishes
Tray: A basin used for washing clothes
Bath room: A room which houses a bath tub and/or shower, a lavatory and a water closet
Toilet: A room which houses a lavatory and a water closet

* Reprinted from *Island of Bali* by Miguel Covarrubias by permission of Alfred A. Knopf, Inc. Copyright 1936 by Alfred A. Knopf, Inc.

Saul Steinberg.

It is common European practice to separate the water closet in a compartment of its own, usually without a lavatory, and to include a bidet. European water closets are sometimes flush with the door and designed to use in a squatting position. One occasionally sees bath rooms with two tubs, or two lavatories, or both. Tubs are sometimes recessed, square, built on the job of tile or wood, and so forth. In fact, our conception of the subsidiary purposes of bathing, and consequently of bathing facilities, has undergone many changes. There is nothing either inevitable or sacred about the tub, water closet and lavatory combined within one horribly hygienic space. Bath tubs can logically and indeed have been located in direct conjunction with dressing and sleeping facilities. The fact that they are more frequently connected with washing and excreting is perhaps primarily for technical reasons. Water, waste, water vapors, and certain accessories and equipment such as towel bars, towels, and soap seem to tie the bath to the other fixtures. The connection is not as inevitable in terms of function. One can take a bath without the need for a lavatory or water closet. One can use either or both of the latter fixtures without using the bath. Indeed this experience is very common, occurring several times each day. The common Japanese house provides a large and often very beautiful bath compartment and a small toilet compartment similar to ours in size. The same arrangement might be adaptable to our own houses. It may indeed be a better variation from the norm than to connect the bath compartment to individual bedrooms.

Because of the more frequent use of the water closet, and the multiplicity of functions connected with the lavatory, the toilet is perhaps better connected with bed-dressing rooms than with the bath. Also, many families see no need for privacy among themselves where bathing is concerned. Where this is the case, a large and elegant bath compartment with small lavatories connected to bedrooms could be pleasant and workable.

But there is no reason why any of these fixtures have to be in bath rooms at all. The close connection between dressing and undressing, bathing, and clothes storage make the bath-dressing room an ideal combination. Over and above the obvious convenience of the arrangement, there are two other points in its favor.

Bathing

First, when people sleep cold, the bath-dressing room can be kept warm, and dressing as well as bathing can be accomplished in comfort. Second, the fact that couples share a bed room does not necessarily mean that they always get up at the same time. When the bath-dressing room has an entrance from outside the bed room, the earlier riser can prepare for the day without disturbing the later. The bath-dressing room, in this case, needs inherently warm floors, carpets, or cork tile. Radiant heating also offers the right kind of warmth, even though the air temperature may be low. The room should, perhaps, have sufficient radiation to keep its temperature slightly over that of the rest of the house. Steam from bath and showers, which is not good for clothes, must be taken care of by mechanical ventilation.

Courtesy of Dr. Jiro Harada

In the average case, the lavatory and water closet are used most frequently during the day, once while going to bed, occasionally after going to bed, and once on getting up. Where the budget allows, the obvious solution to this use pattern is to provide a toilet in the day use zone of the house, and a bath room in the night use zone. When a single bath room is mandatory, standard practice is to place it in close proximity to the bed rooms and living room, and in such a way that people can visit it from the bed rooms without being seen from the living room. This latter arrangement is fundamental. The Federal Housing Administration requires that:

> "The bed room in one-bed room living units and at least two bed rooms in all other living units shall have access to a bathroom without passing through another habitable room."

This saves much embarrassment for those who are in the habit of nipping into the bath room without clothes, and for those who do not like to be seen unless fully dressed.

There are, in addition to the more or less common alternatives for the location of bath room fixtures just mentioned, numerous others which have been tried lately. The alternatives might best be suggested in list form, as follows:

1. Three fixture bath, separate
2. Bath compartment with separate toilet
3. The three fixtures grouped but compartmented
4. A toilet with a compartmented bath-lavatory
5. A lavatory in the bed-dressing room
6. Dressing room with bath and lavatory, water closet compartmented
7. Bed-dressing-bath rooms, with bath and lavatory, water closet compartmented
8. Bath-dressing room combined, with no compartmentation
9. Bed room, dressing room, and bath room in suite form

A shower can, in any of these cases, be in the tub, replace the tub, or occur as a separate entity.

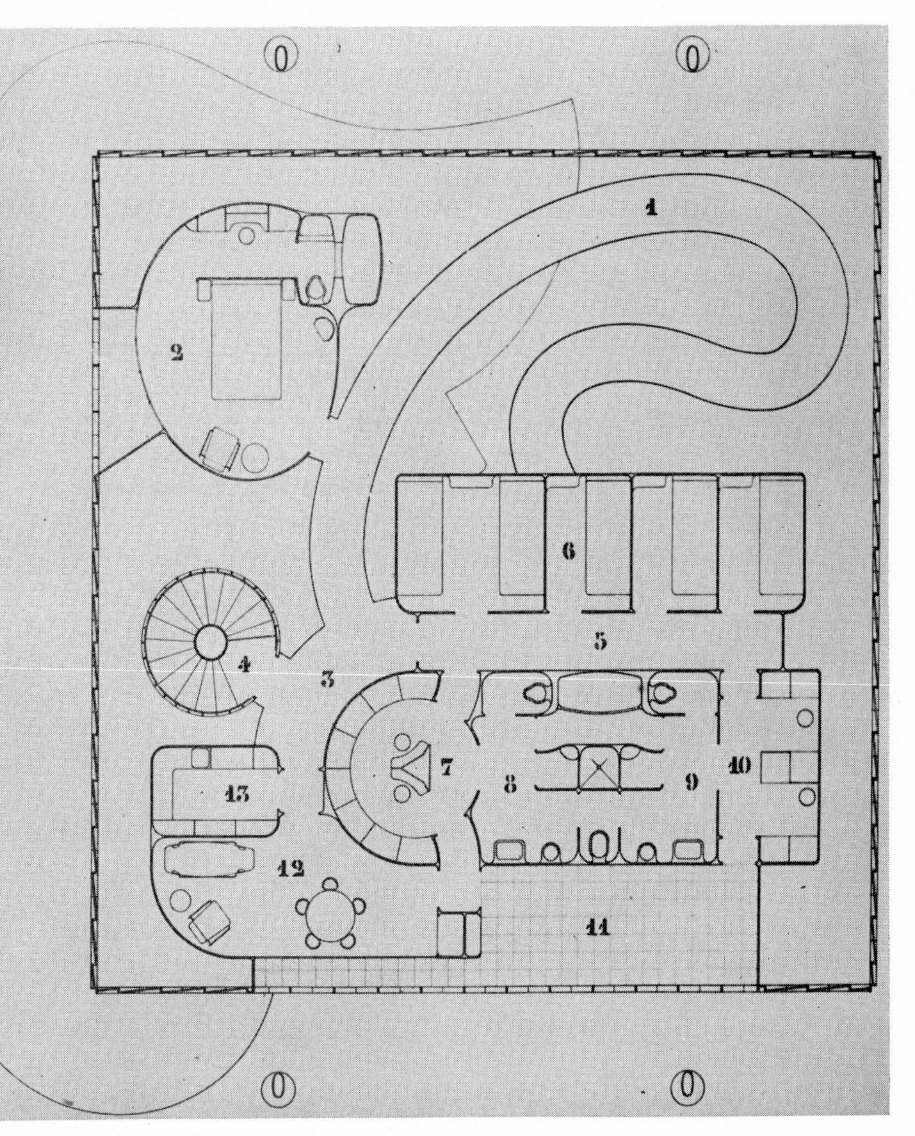

Paul Nelson: The Suspended House: Top Level: 1. Ramp. 2. Bedroom with dressing space, bath (Fuller), and porch. 3. Landing. 4. Main stairway. 5. Passageway. 6. One double and three single sleeping cabins. 7. Dressing room (women). 8. Toilet and bath (women). 9. Toilet and bath (men). 10. Dressing room (men). 11. Porch for calisthenics and sun-bathing. 12. Children's playroom. 13. Linen and cleaning utensils. The originality of the plan is due as much to the way in which activities are allocated to spaces as it is to the forms and construction used.

However one arranges the bath room fixtures themselves, the real combination of activities involved in their planning is as follows:

1	2	3	4	5	6
Dressing Undressing	Storing clothes	Washing Excreting	Bathing Shaving	Sleeping Sex	Child care

The location of the fixtures and of the spaces which contain them, and the circulation patterns between these spaces must be governed by the privacy requirements of the combination of functions involved. In the average house, these activities are so compartmented, and privacy is lent such an air of prudery, that pleasure in them is materially reduced. The bathroom is usually too small and dark. In its more pretentious forms, its colored fixtures, walls, and floors are gaudy. It seldom seems to include sufficient storage space for linen, towels, medicine, bathinette, and toidy seat. Even less frequently does it carry the conviction that the activities it houses are anything but a germ-ridden service function, to be got through with as quickly and unobtrusively as possible. The idea that a bath can be a regenerative experience, that the body has dignity and beauty, that the excretory functions can be satisfying, is seldom expressed. Dr. Sigfried Giedion has pointed out that our conception of the function of bathing has undergone many changes.

"Bathing, in whatever fashion performed, is concerned with care of the body. To maintain the balance of this delicate instrument, to dwell in harmony with our organism, is a prime necessity of life. Some periods have viewed bathing as part of a broad ideal: total regeneration. Other periods have seen it as a mere ablution to be performed in swiftest routine. One age may weave bathing into the well being of the whole man. Another age may see it as an isolated act, or neglect it almost altogether.

"The role that bathing plays within a culture reveals the culture's attitude towards human relaxation. It is a measure of

how far individual well being is regarded as an indispensable part of community life."

Obviously, in our age, bathing has become by and large a "mere ablution to be performed in swiftest routine". The reasons for its present low repute in terms of regeneration need not concern us here. But, even though bathing has fallen from grace in the eyes of our culture at large, there is no reason why the individual, aware of its regenerative possibilities, cannot make some better use of it. The mechanized bath tub must be used, for practical reasons, and it surely is a sad object: hard, cold, hygienic, uncomfortable, awkward, dangerous, and suggestive more of excretion than regeneration. But again, the circumstances surrounding its use, both operational and physical, can make of it a far more significant object than is usually the case. The bath, rather than the excretory function, should set the atmosphere of bath rooms.

The essential condition to taking a bath is nudity. For some, this is a shameful and disturbing state to be avoided wherever possible. For others, it is delightfully exhilarating. No matter what the individual attitude, convention demands that under certain circumstances bath taking shall be private. Houses must afford the possibility of privacy, even though that possibility is not taken advantage of at all times. The most universal of these special circumstances is privacy from outside. Bath windows must be curtained continuously. This is an important consideration because curtains cut down the amount of light in a room that requires high levels of illumination when a lavatory is also involved. Privacy and light can be achieved in other ways: by skylighting, clerestory windows, high windows, opaque glass, etc. All of these methods suggest some objections. They advertise the location of the bath to the outside. They are unpleasant inside because they preclude the enjoyment of views, give the room the atmosphere of a cave or a high-walled box and, by stressing the idea "decency" in its worst sense, rob bathing of the practical, pleasurable and dignified role it should play. Another solution is to provide a relatively very large window, big enough to admit adequate light after it is curtained from outside view. The low intensity per square foot will be compensated for by the large number of square feet. A large window also provides better diffusion and expresses the fact that one is in desirable, not shameful circumstances. The requirements of privacy inside are simple in comparison. A door with thumb latch to the space where the tub is located is sufficient.

A second corollary to the absence of clothes is the need for an increase in the amount of apparent heat. Drafts are obnoxious; high mean radiant and air temperatures, and high relative humidity are pleasant. The latter condition is taken care of automatically because of the large amount of hot water involved. Ideally, the temperature in baths should be between eighty degrees Fahrenheit and eighty-five degrees Fahrenheit, i.e. about that of the skin, with the other factors adjusted to temperature. One way to achieve this is to provide locally operated radiant electric heaters, built in or in the form of infra red lamps which can be turned off and on as needed.

Faucets for tubs are usually too low and sometimes unreachable. They should be easy to reach. One must not only turn them but adjust them until the water temperature is satisfactory. For this purpose, the bath room floor plan where the water closet is next to the bath is convenient because it allows one to check on the water temperature sitting down. When the bath is compartmented, space for a seat at the foot of the tub is useful. Faucets for showers are usually higher, and easier to reach. It is important to have them near the opening to the compartment. It should be possible to reach the faucets without getting wet. Water for domestic use should be less than one hundred and forty degrees Fahrenheit, otherwise it will scald. Where for some reason it must be higher than this, automatic mixing valves help prevent accidents. In any case, mixing faucets for both hot and cold water are far superior to separate ones for baths, lavatories, and sinks because they allow one to check water temperature before it is in the basin. Low water temperature, quick recovery, and thermostatic valves are particularly useful where children are involved, because the latter seem to scald so often. Built-in containers for soap are essential for both tubs and showers. Soap holders in showers should be well drained or in a dry location so they do not get full of water and allow the soap to get soggy and even liquid. It is convenient to be able to reach the soap easily either in or out of the fixture. Tubs, shower stalls, and bath room floors can be very slippery. "Bath tubs should be of the flat bottom type" (National Safety Council). Falls and scalds are the most frequent bath tub accidents. Non-skid surfaces under foot are the obvious solution to the former but since tubs should also be easy to clean a smooth surface best fulfills this requirement. Grab bars at several locations help to compensate for this difficulty. The typical fully-recessed tub-shower combination, for example, can well accommodate three bars, one at the shower location five feet high, and two at the sitting location, one low and one high to help one down in and out of the tub proper:

> "A metal pipe extending from floor to ceiling and erected at the front edge of the tub to be used as a hand grasp upon entering and leaving the tub is an additional safeguard strongly recommended." *National Safety Council.*

Towel bars, which often serve as grab bars, need to be strong enough in themselves and firmly enough attached to bear the sudden weight they occasionally have to take. Grounds for such bath room accessories are a primary safety precaution.

Hot baths and showers heat the air in bath rooms, incidentally introducing large amounts of water. Because this happens quickly, the walls remain cool long after the humidity has reached a peak, and visible condensation appears on mirrors, windows, tile, glass tile, and similar "cool" surfaces. Given appropriate conditions, all the materials will collect large amounts of condensation. If decay is to be prevented, this moisture must be retained on the surface of the walls, floors, and ceilings and allowed to evaporate before it penetrates. Impervious materials, or oily woods, are thus the most appropriate. Porous materials such as plaster are to be avoided. A foggy bath room can be avoided by exhausting the air mechanically from a location immediately over the bath and shower stall.

Many people spend the happiest and most mentally productive hours of their lives in the bath tub. Some like to read in it, others to smoke or drink cocktails, still others simply like to relax and look at a view. This habit creates a problem in cold climates. Glass over a tub sets up a falling column of cold air which gives a sense of chill to those parts of the body not under water. Double glazing and a heat source directly under the window, between it and the tub, or simply a hole for the cold air to fall into are required for comfort. Cigarettes, ash trays, matches, books, and glasses require a shelf or space beside the head of the tub for a low table. Scales are frequently a part of the bath room equipment and need free floor area. It is often handy to have at least one towel bar close enough to the tub or shower so that it can be reached quickly when soap gets in one's eyes. Towels should be hung away from the tub or shower, however, to insure that they will not fall into the water or get splashed. Towel bars should be far enough away from the wall for ease of use, and they should be long, thirty inches or more, because bath towels are often very large and there should be room to accommodate a face cloth as well. There should be space to store clean bath linen, bath mats, and a ventilated hamper for used towels. Storage space for soap, bath salts, shampoo, bathing caps, bath oil, talcum powder, water softener, etc., is also required. If it can be reached from the tub as well as the floor, so much the better.

As in all rooms where people are wet, electric outlets, telephones, switches and other electrical equipment should either be high or outside the room entirely. Electric outlets which children can monkey with while wet, or in contact with plumbing, are dangerous. Switches should be outside the room, and outlets for electric showers should be high and away from the tub. Radiators, in particular, should be so arranged that they cannot be touched by bare, damp skin. Few sensations are more shocking.

Beyond these functional needs of bathing, and in addition to the delight of a view, and of places for books and drinks, flowers are the most rewarding addition to the bath. The dampness and perfume they add to the air are particularly pleasant and appropriate, and they are the best complement of the nude figure.

These are the factors which should set the tone of the bath room, if it is not to be in reality a toilet. But, while the tone is set by the function, bathing, each of the other other fixtures demand certain unique facilities. By far the most complex is the lavatory, for it constitutes a center for several related activities. Because of this fact, and because of the variety of its other uses it needs far greater storage space surrounding it than it usually gets. Some of the common uses of a lavatory with their resulting requirements are as follows:

1. HAND, FACE AND HAIR WASHING

   Towel rods and storage for towels and face cloths for each individual using the lavatory, plus one for guests. A place to hang up wet face cloths and paper towels. Soap holders and storage for soap, shampoos, pumice, sponges, and brushes. A mirror with good light, and space for a hand mirror. A ventilated basket for wet and dirty towels.

2. DRINKING WATER

   Tumbler holder. Occasionally several tumblers are required.

3. TOOTH BRUSHING

   A tooth brush holder located so that brushes will dry. Storage for tooth paste, mouth wash, dental floss. A tumbler.

4. HAIR COMBING, BRUSHING, CURLING

   A mirror, good light, storage for combs and brushes, a waste basket, electric outlet for curlers, vibrators, dryers, etc. Space for hair tonic, hair pins, clasps, etc.

5. MAKING UP

   A mirror, good light, storage for cosmetics, a place to put out several jars, etc., storage for disposable tissues, and a place to dispose of them, either waste basket or water closet.

6. TAKING MEDICINE

   A tumbler, spoon, storage space for medicines, band aids, eye cups, thermometers, etc. A waste basket for disposal of wrappings and boxes. A lockable medicine space for poisons and medicines dangerous to children, in addition to a regular medicine cabinet.

7. SHAVING

A mirror, storage for shaving things, good light, an electric outlet for shavers, waste basket for wrappings, towels, face cloths, lotions, soap, etc. "Some provision for the safe disposal of safety razor blades should be included in the bath room design" (*National Safety Council*).

8. BABY WASHING

Flat surfaces at the side of the lavatory to sit and dry baby on. Towels, face cloths, soap; storage for apron made of toweling, counter space to put diapers on, pins, clothes, etc. Storage space for pins, powder, oil.

9. CLOTHES WASHING

Soap storage and a place to hang things up to dry in an out of the way spot.

10. MANICURING

Storage for manicure equipment, scissors, nail polish, emory boards, etc.

11. MISCELLANEOUS USES

Hot water bottles, douches, contraceptives and the like are connected with the lavatory, and require storage near it.

12. CLEANING

Most lavatories need readily available rags, floor mops, etc. for emergencies and quick cleaning.

One of the most important demands on the lavatory is that the mirror immediately above it be placed so that one is able to see oneself in it. Many men have never been able to do this except in a stooping or semi-crouching position, and many women can see themselves in certain mirrors only by standing on a stool, a scale, or on some thick books. A very large number of men fall in the height group between six feet and six feet three, and an appreciable number in that group between six feet three and six feet six. Many women are as short as five feet one and a few are five feet or slightly less. The range of height between the neck of a short woman and the top of a tall man's head is about two feet three inches. Obviously then mirrors should be no less than two feet six inches high, with their tops located six feet six inches above the finished floor. The same effect can also be achieved by a low tilted mirror, over which a window can be placed, for view and light directly on the face. Such mirrors, however, are hard to keep clean. A second requirement is a high level and good diffusion of light at the mirror. One needs to see well not only the top of one's head, but the underside of one's jowls. A general level of at least thirty foot candles of quality illumination is desirable. A single ceiling lighting outlet over the mirror is rarely adequate. Outlets on either side of the mirror, either of the ordinary incandescent point source or of the linear type, are preferable. Because of the necessity to gauge color in make-up, the color of the lamps should be the same as in the living rooms. Fluorescent lamps, if used, should be color corrected and instant starting. Natural illumination for most lavatories is poor. Not only should its window be large—it must also be well placed. One of its jambs can be flush, or nearly so, with the wall on which the mirror and lavatory are located. Several examples exist of windows on either side or right across the top of the lavatory in which the mirror becomes simply a silvered section of the general glass area.

The area around lavatories is particularly subject to splashing, spotting from things spilled, splatter from tooth brushing, etc., particularly when children are about. The materials in back, to the sides, and under it should be impervious to moisture, easy to clean, and should not be of a color or texture which readily shows stains. The most troublesome problem is, of course, the point between lavatory and wall. One solution is to avoid the joint altogether, that is, to hold the lavatory off the wall enough to allow its back side to be cleaned. The wall can then be plane, waterproof, and cleanable. Where a top or lavatory counter must touch the plane of the wall, hangers, caulking, mortar joints, and back splashes continuous with the counter, as in kitchens, offer the only sensible solution. The sides and ends of fixtures should always be held well away from walls for cleaning when they are not actually built in.

Lavatories are by and large too low, because the working level is not at the top but down in the bowl. Finally, the lavatory, because of the things stored there, is the usual focus for such activities as cutting toe nails, paring corns, shaving legs, etc., all of which are done sitting down. When the water closet is not adjacent, a chair is needed for these functions, or they must be moved to other spaces.

The water closet, unlike the lavatory with its multiple functions, is relatively easy to rationalize. First of all one should be able to lock the door. Second, there should be enough space to move around in, and to sit in comfort. The water closet itself should have at least one foot six inches of clear space on either side. One of the most common faults is to squeeze it in too tightly between a wall and another fixture. Boy children take a long time to learn to urinate accurately into the bowl. Men urinating in a standing position cause very appreciable splashing which moistens the floor and rim of the water closet. Condensation on its under side in hot weather can be extreme, flooding the floor under the tank. The flooring material around the base of a lavatory should therefore be very impervious to water and easy to clean.

The use of a water closet involves certain noises which are, for many people, the most embarrassing and painful experiences foisted on them by house architecture. The principal source of noise is the flushing of the closet. This very recognizable sound adds nothing to life at any time, and can be avoided. One-piece and close coupled closets are seldom audible outside the compartment, and where the budget allows, are highly desirable. In any case, the more sound-proof the room, the better. Knudsen and Harris make the following recommendations:

"The insulation of bath rooms from the other rooms in the home is a difficult problem. Great care should be exercised in the selection of bath room fixtures. The architect should obtain data and make careful observations of the amounts of noise produced by the different types of toilets and bath tubs. In order to prevent turbulent flow, water pipes should be large enough to allow relatively low speeds of water. The more noisy pipes should be wrapped with a fibrous blanket covered on both sides with tough paper, and they should be insulated from the rigid frame of the building by means of flexible connectors. Wherever practical, the entire bath room floor should be insulated from the rest of the building by means of flexible chairs or by means of felt, mineral wool, or cork board. The floor and ceiling section under the bath room should have a sound-transmission loss of not less than 45 db."

Ventilation to remove water closet odors is also essential. A window for this purpose leaves much to be desired, particularly in cold climates. Odors can be blown into the house rather than out, and an open window in a bath room or toilet in severe weather is uncomfortable. Frozen pipes, caused by carelessly leaving bath windows open too long, are not uncommon in northern climates. The positive ventilation of a fan drawing air from other rooms and exhausting it to the outdoors has much to recommend it. Many people like to read and smoke while on the water closet, and as a result spend a considerable amount of time there. Good light for reading, and even a view make the process of defecation vastly more pleasurable. Storage for books or magazines to the right of the seat, and a low window overlapping the fixture location, are easy to provide in any but minimum housing. Storage for sanitary napkins, toilet paper, enema bags, bed pans, etc., as well as the paper holder for daily use, should ideally be located low and to the right of the water closet, or at least within arm's reach without getting up.

Because it is hygienically desirable to wash one's hands before or after using a water closet, a lavatory in the same space is more or less essential. From this point of view, it would seem less good to have it even in an adjacent compartment, as the hardware,

Le Corbusier

doors, or walls may be touched before it is used. Where a bidet or sitz-bath is also planned for, it can be placed immediately adjacent to the water closet, or near at hand but in connection with dressing space and lavatory.

The toilet training of children can begin as early as ten months, and can go on for several years. During the first part of this process, a "toidy" seat in the bath room can take the place of the bathinette. Later on, as the child grows larger, a small toilet seat which attaches to the regular seat is needed. This can be con-

Le Corbusier

veniently hung on a long metal peg, or put in a metal pocket next to the water closet. It is a frightful nuisance if there is no provision for getting it out of the way, particularly in a one-bath room house. Children often need to be helped on and off the water closet, and there should be enough room to do this in comfort. Another seat to wait on while they are getting through is a great convenience. Children and very sick adults occasionally lock themselves in and then are unable to unlock the door. Sometimes they become hysterical, thus making it difficult or impossible to calm and instruct them from outside. Thumb latches for bathrooms are made with a safety device allowing them to be turned back from outside with a key, or, in a pinch, with a screw driver or nail file.

The proper character of bath rooms, like all the other rooms in the house, must be a function of the peculiar combination of activities which the client elects to combine in its space. Obviously the sybaritic atmosphere, designed for pleasure in warmth, steam, nudity, sex, flowers and alcohol, cannot appropriately combine with the bathinette, the toidy seat, and the diaper pail. On the other hand, the well-designed family bath, large, commodious, practical, somewhat ascetic, can be a magnificent thing, not only in terms of utility, but also in terms of its expressive message. Ideally perhaps, every family should have one of each. But where for practical reasons this is impossible, a little of each, a compromise, is certainly possible, and a great challenge to the designer.

Sleeping

During the night people are tired, they cannot see without help, their enemies are on the prowl, and once they go to sleep they are absolutely defenseless. They are apt to create sinister and demoniac forces even where none exist. Children and maiden ladies, are, by tradition, supposedly most scary at night. There may exist a few strong men who have not been similarly excited. In any case, night fears are so real, and such a waste of true emotion, that houses should certainly do what they can to alleviate them. Small bedrooms seem to make the majority of people more fearful than large bedrooms. Blum, Milton and Candee note:

> "Discomfort in small spaces may be related to mild forms of claustrophobia. It is entirely possible that bedroom design must allow for a somewhat larger space than is actually necessary in order to overcome this fear on the part of many people."

Squeaking floors, stair treads which ride up on their nails, and other sources of ghosts can be helped by good design and detailing. But it is impossible to design against howling winds, storms, and just plain loneliness. Burglar alarms, fire alarms, and lightning rods may help to alleviate fears, but burglar alarms at least have severe limitations as far as houses are concerned. Perhaps the easiest way to reassure people is to install two or three outdoor flood lights capable of being turned on all at once from in bed. Very few animals or prowlers will wait to find out who flicked the switch.

But a sense of safety in bed is only the end step. The process of getting there becomes so automatic that one forgets how many separate moves it entails. Once the decision is made, the first of these moves is usually to close up the house for the night. This may require visiting almost every room. Doors must be locked, thermostat reset, windows latched, lights turned off, children visited to make sure they are covered, cats and dogs let out and in, etc. During this trip one should be able to turn out lights behind one, yet leave lighted the rooms and halls still to be visited.

Thus one's first requirement is a switching system which will allow lights to be turned out from the door of the room as one leaves, and to be turned on for the next room at the same door, and so on, until one reaches the bedroom. As it is usually the owner who performs this nightly task, the master bedroom, if not all bedrooms, should certainly be at one end of the chain.

Another going to bed problem involves the requirements of couples. When one spouse goes to bed earlier than the other, the later one must fumble around for his clothes, the bathroom door and light, etc. etc., in the dark, always afraid of disturbing the sleeper. Where this is a problem, the bedroom should obviously be in a circulation scheme such as this: Entrance door—dressing room and bath room—bedroom door—bedroom. Such an arrangement allows the later retiring spouse to get completely ready for bed before entering the bedroom proper, in this case reduced to a sleeping room alone.

The volumetric requirements for dressing and undressing are, like those for most other human functions, subject to so much variation that no rules maintain. One can undress in the lower berth of a sleeping car. A dressing room in a Newport mansion may reach heroic proportions. An optimum volume for the movements involved is probably a cylinder seven feet in diameter and eight feet high, large enough to allow free movement of the arms out and up, without having to put one's feet exactly in the center of the circle. In addition, room is required for a chair to sit on while removing shoes, socks, stockings, and garters; a full length mirror preferably with two movable leaves; a horizontal surface for such things as brushes and cosmetics which can be left in the open because they are frequently used (a second mirror may be needed here); a storage place for clothes; and storage for dirty clothes. From the standpoint of the process alone, these six elements should be closely grouped. There is no point in moving around, while dressing, any more than is absolutely necessary.

The most important of these elements in terms of volume, aside from space to move in, and the only one which cannot intrude upon that space, is clothes storage. Again, the volume requirements are a matter of income and personal habit. In designing storage, clothes used together or in sequence should in fact be planned to be together. Ideally, trousers should be with jackets, mules with nightgowns, ties with shirts, bras with panties, etc. Again ideally, if the small items of equipment, such as handkerchiefs, handbags, gloves, and even shoes can be stored above two feet high and below four feet three inches high, bending and reaching can be avoided. The items of clothing usually needing storage are as follows, the number of articles in each category of course being highly variable.

INDOOR CLOTHES

Husbands	Wives
Summer and winter suits	Dresses
shirt-pants outfits	suits
separate trousers	separate skirts, jackets
separate jackets	blouses, jerseys
bathing trunks, sun suits	sweaters, cardigans
gym suits, costumes	aprons, smocks
T shirts	slack suits, slacks
sport shirts	jeans, overalls
dress shirts	play suits, bathing suits
dress hats	gym suits
sweaters	costumes
undershorts	slips, petticoats and vests
undershirts	panties
union suits	brassieres
pajamas	girdles, garter belts
nightshirts	nightgowns
bathrobes	robes and housecoats
heavy work socks	pajamas and bedjackets
socks	handbags
shoes and sneakers	belts
slippers	handkerchiefs
handkerchiefs	street shoes and sneakers
ties	long hose and anklets
belts	house, work dresses
jewelry	jewelry
hunting, fishing clothes	hats

Boys

Summer, winter suits	undershorts
shirts-pants outfits	undershirts
separate trousers and jackets	union suits
bathing trunks, sun suits	pajamas
riding, fishing clothes	nightshirts
gym suits	bathrobes
costumes	slippers
T shirts	socks
sports shirts	heavy socks
dress shirts	sneakers
sweaters	dress shoes
ties, belts	heavy shoes
jewelry	handkerchiefs

Girls

Dresses	panties
suits	brassieres
separate jackets and skirts	girdles, garter belts
blouses, jerseys	nightgowns
sweaters, cardigans	pajamas
aprons, smocks	slippers
slack suits, slacks	robes
jeans, overalls	housecoats
play suits, bathing suits	long hose
gym suits	anklets
costumes	street shoes
slips, petticoats	handkerchiefs
vests	hats, belts
	jewelry

In the average case, the architect can find out what his client needs in the way of clothes storage space. When he is in doubt, some sort of an average must be used. Francis de N. Schroeder, in an interesting estimate of men's clothes, credits them with the following personal belongings, which can be stored in a space five feet six inches by six feet four inches by two feet, or 29.63 cubic feet.

18 ties
2 brushes and a shoe horn
1 pair of slippers
1 pair of boots
4 pairs of shoes
6 suits (season)
3 coats (season)
2 hats (season)
1 derby or straw hat
1 top hat
12 shirts
3 dress shirts
3 sports shirts
12 undershirts
2 sweaters
12 shorts
6 pajamas
1 umbrella
1 stick
48 handkerchiefs
12 stiff collars
12 soft collars
24 pairs of socks
scarves
gloves
garters and braces
3 small drawers of little affairs
plus miscellany

Mr. Schroeder estimates that the amount of space required by women's clothes is three cabinets, each three feet nine long by six feet six inches high by two feet deep, or 146.25 cubic feet. The difference between men and women seems amazing, particularly when the weight a woman wears at any one time is only about one pound eleven ounces. But who knows a man who does not complain about the way his wife usurps his closet, if he is lucky enough to have one he can call his own in the first place? The average woman's wardrobe was estimated as follows:

2 suits
1 jacket, one skirt
3 sport dresses
3 daytime dresses
2 afternoon dresses
4 blouses
2 negligees
2 bed jackets
mules and slippers
6 hats
2 fur muffs
1 fur jacket
1 fur scarf
2 dinner dresses
2 evening dresses
1 evening wrap
2 housecoats
6 handbags
6 slips
6 panties
6 bras
4 girdles
6 nighties
6 pajamas
6 sweaters
6 scarves

2 fur coats
3 coats
1 raincoat
1 umbrella
overshoes
rubbers
belts
2 brushes and shoe horn
8 pairs of shoes
12 pairs of stockings
6 pairs of gloves
48 handkerchiefs
accessories
jewelry
plus large amount of miscellany

In all cases where for the sake of efficiency, neatness, or looks, a design is made which very accurately reflects the items to be stored, a certain inflexibility results. Thus the fitted closet must always take very large account of miscellany. Everyone seems to store, along with their clothes, certain little oddments of a personal nature. These may include medals, old engagement books, statuary, photographs, a flask, a screw driver, in short almost anything. At a minimum, a large drawer should be provided for such collections, in that they also include such bulky items as a large box of sanitary napkins, a hat box, small trunk full of papers, etc.

It is impossible to view clothes storage, dressing and undressing, washing, bathing, excreting, sex, child care, etc., as unrelated. The business of going to bed at night, and getting up again in the morning involves, inevitably, a host of related functions. Going to bed means washing, urinating, tooth brushing, contraceptives, miscellaneous applications of cold cream, and the like. Getting up means shaving, urinating, excreting, tooth brushing, make-up, hair combing. It also involves, for many people, exercises. In such case the ceiling height in the bed room or dressing room or bath—wherever exercise is taken—must be high enough to allow freedom to stretch upward. This must be particularly remembered in the case of dancers, who need really very great heights, no matter how small they look in an architect's office. In any case, and no matter what the personal pecadillos of the client, a bath room is always involved.

Somewhere in these two processes, of going to bed or getting up, baths are taken. But when? The most likely times for adults are in the morning; late in the afternoon (after work and before dinner) and before going to bed, that is, fairly late in the evening. Children usually bathe before they go to bed, in the early evening. It would seem that bathing patterns are often as much affected by an inadequate supply of hot water as by any other factor, this inadequacy having nothing much to do with the size and luxury of the house. Another determinant is congestion. Bathing, plus the numerous other activities which go on in bath rooms, use a considerable amount of time. In under-bath roomed houses, this creates the kind of congestion beloved of the cartoonists and comic strip artists.

During the winter in cold climates the next to the last act of the day is to open the window. The last is to turn out the light. Ideally, one should be able to turn on lights in a bedroom from the door, turn them off from in bed. The reason this is seldom achieved is that most bed room plans provide flexibility of bed location, which makes it impossible to locate switches and bed lights permanently. For this situation we need portable bedside lamps with three way switches which can be plugged into receptacles connected with the other three way switch at the entrance door to the room. Many adults prefer a low intensity light for love making rather than total darkness or the brilliance of ordinary bedside lamps. Fixed night lights will serve for this purpose if properly located, as well as for those occasions when a small amount of light is needed momentarily. If an electric blanket or pad is to be used, it is plugged in on going to bed. Because a fan, radio, and clock are also very frequently used at the bed location, a duplex convenience outlet is insufficient for one person, though two of them usually do for a couple.

Almost everyone gets up during some nights to look at children, to shut windows during a storm, to go to the bath room, to drink, or excrete, etc. A very low intensity light for this purpose is invaluable. Stumbling around in a dark room, trying not to wake someone up, is undignified if not dangerous.

> "A small blue light installed near the baseboard is of value in the sleeping rooms of elderly persons for indicating the direction of the bath room or exit door." (*National Safety Council*).

When one considers that about twenty-five per cent of fatal home accidents occur in the bed room, the small cost of adequate electrical devices seems well worth while.

Josef Frank

Once one has closed the bed room door, the first need is that of visual privacy for undressing, love making, and sleeping. The first way to achieve this is to design the door to open in, and in such a way that it comes between the person entering and the bed. A night latch is essential. For privacy from outdoors, one also needs some way to close off the glass without reducing the ventible area of the window.

A second kind of isolation is needed to permit noise to be made but not generally heard. It is almost impossible to suppress the noises we make snoring, loving, dreaming, and getting up at night. It seems desirable to isolate bed rooms acoustically as much as possible. Partitions with good sound loss characteristics, and a plan arranged for acoustic isolation are as important for sleeping as they are for any other function. This isolation of course militates against the parents' requirement of hearing small children during the night. However, as the parents' door can always be left open a crack, or as a radio nurse can always be used, sound insulation should probably always be planned for between bed rooms.

Tolerance for noise from without varies tremendously. However, as the majority of people are relatively sensitive, houses should be planned for this group rather than for those individuals who can sleep through an earthquake. Knudsen and Harris remark that:

> "No one has determined the price we pay in loss of sleep resulting from avoidable noises. Several years ago, one of the authors kept a record of the number of times he was awakened each night. Approximately three fourths of all awakenings could be attributed to noise. Among the most frequent offenses were the honking of automobile horns, barking of dogs, the screaming of ambulance sirens, the late arrival of some members of the family, and the chirping of birds. The wearing of ear plugs, which attenuated these noises about thirty db, reduced the total number of awakenings to less than one half. Important factors in determining the disturbing effects of noise are its over-all level, frequency distribution, and time pattern."

All of these noises emanate from the outdoors. It is unfortunate that the sleeping period is just that in which windows are kept open, for they are the principal means of entrance for sound. Thus bed rooms, first of all, need to turn their backs on the worst sources of outdoor noises, streets, railroads, etc. A second defense is to locate bed rooms remote from the entrance and the garage, thus guarding against noise made by other residents of the same house coming back late.

Light is as important as noise in its effect on sleep. The darker a bed room can be kept until getting-up time, the better. In rooms used primarily for sleeping, the glass area should be limited by this consideration. Shades, curtains, and blinds are hard to make tight. They leak around the edges, and when there is a wind, they flap, and let in light and rain. This is most acutely annoying during naps. A large proportion of children, and many adults must sleep during the day. East-facing bed rooms are, for this purpose, the poorest. Low and brilliant morning sun is the most difficult to keep out, and makes all but the most opaque shades glow. Automobile headlights are very disturbing, in that they are intermittent and moving. Fixed street lights, in just the wrong location, can also make it hard to keep the windows dark. City and town fathers are sometimes obliging enough to shield street lights if requested. But the combination of hazards to sleep from noise, headlights, peeping Toms, and street lights, suggest that bed rooms should face away from streets if at all possible. Certainly beds should not face directly into windows, as this position is bound to aggravate any light problem which does exist.

The third element required for sleeping comfort is relatively low temperature and fast air movement, humidity being less important except in summer. However, it is precisely in summer that, without air conditioning, the three factors which influence thermal confort are least controllable. Temperature being equal, the more the relative humidity increases, the more air movement is required. Thus bedrooms need small glass but large ventilating areas, or about the reverse proportion offered by the most commonly used windows. Air conditioning and attic fans designed to promote positive circulation modify the need for large openings and cross ventilation. But natural ventilation is still the most useful and pleasant device. Falling columns of air on beds, induced by cold walls and windows, are to be avoided. Those who enjoy the romantic aspects of sleeping next to a window, where they can see the stars and feel the night, can so arrange their beds. But to plan a bed room so that the only bed location is under a window, or along an exterior wall with a low u factor, is to assure discomfort for most of the sleepers who will use it. Where possible, beds should be located along interior partitions.

Richard Neutra.

These requirements, i.e. for darkness, acoustic isolation, ventilation, visual privacy, and rain exclusion are poorly solved by our present window types. The best solution so far is probably the fixed light of glass, with louvered screened vents below it. This sort of window is good acoustically, excludes rain, and can be curtained without reducing its ventilating opening. It obviates the mad midnight rush around the house whenever a thunderstorm comes along.

The double and twin beds, either side by side or separated only by a bed table, suggest that the occupants of a room are married. Rooms planned for two boys or two girls should be arranged in such a way that each person can consider the part of the room around his bed more or less his own. Such rooms should tend to fall naturally into two invisibly defined areas. Rooms planned in this way can perhaps ease such problems as are created by differing possessions and living patterns. If they can provide for even slight variation in the amount of daylight, enough separation to ease night reading problems, variety in distance from ventilating openings, and a certain freedom from the other person's belongings and body, they are apt to be more successful.

A desirable feature in bed rooms is flexibility to place beds in several locations. Many people enjoy the variety they can achieve by changing over rooms seasonally, or even more frequently. In addition, the amount, size, and kind of furniture varies so much that at least two theoretical bed locations are necessary to assure one practical arrangement for a given set of furniture. Freedom to make beds easily is a tremendous convenience. Corner locations make this difficult. Many people sleep best with arms or legs extended over the edge of the bed—another reason for keeping beds out in the open.

Resting, sleeping and loving are only three of the many functions of beds. Leisure-class women are apt to breakfast in and to spend the first hours of the morning telephoning, ordering, and receiving in bed. Many people read in bed before going to sleep, just after waking, and during the day. Others like to sew, write, listen to the radio, and eat in bed. For the sick there is no choice. Storage for the numerous accessories involved, such as lamps, clock, cigarettes, ash trays, books, newspapers, food, candy, flashlight, telephone, paper, pencils, magazines, tissues, waste baskets, glasses, teeth, tumblers, medicines, radio, and for children toys, paper, pencils, crayons and paste are a necessity. Most people also keep slippers and bathrobes near at hand. Storage for such things behind the head of the bed has certain innate disadvantages. It is out of sight, hard to reach, covered with pillows when sitting up, and wastes the space below the level of the mattress. The top of such a piece is, however, useful for lamps, infrequently used books, and the like. Side tables, or recessed shelves on one side of a corner bed are easier to use, and the latter device can be more commodious. Where storage is planned behind the bed, the depth it adds to that of the bed must be considered if the dimensions of the room approach a minimum. An essential part of the storage

Carl Koch and Robert Woods Kennedy.

area is space for fan, electric pads, electric blankets, and outlets to connect them to.

The average family trains the children in the rites of privacy in bed rooms from the day they are born. The child is put in his room for a certain number of minutes or hours each day, and is expected to enjoy his time alone with his own toys and thoughts. Rooms for little children should be especially planned and equipped with this in mind. Of course, as children grow older, their rooms slowly evolve, take on a different atmosphere and contain different equipment. But the basic safety and storage requirements which they need when very young do not unfit rooms for the changing patterns of a child's development. To begin with, convenience outlets should be out of reach, or of a type which can be locked shut when not in use. Little children stick pins, nail files and the like into every crack, slot, and hole, and can be injured as a result. Later on, they begin leaning out of windows. As they have at this stage no sense of the danger of long falls, and are often injured as a result of this lack of awareness, windows must be especially protected. Guards, or limit devices, can be attached to them so that they will open only at the top, or if they swing, so that a five and one half inch crack is the largest possible opening. Screens are not adequate protection unless they are well made, maintained, and installed in such a way that they cannot easily fall out.

Toys present one of the most difficult storage problems that exist. They are hard to classify, numerous, vary greatly in size, small things being predominant, and by and large give the general appearance of so much junk. They should obviously be stored near the floor so that children can put them away and get them out again without help. They should also be separated enough so that certain things can be chosen without getting everything out. Chests do not live up to this requirement, and cause more mess than they prevent. Open shelves starting at the floor, recessed, about fifteen inches deep, or shelves covered with horizontally sliding doors are permanently useful and ideal for toys. A deeper recess, with large openings at floor level for tricycles is also convenient. In any case, the floor should run under the whole stack because of the convenience of being able to push in and pull out rolling stock without lifting it. Children, particularly at four, begin to admire their drawings and paintings, at least for short periods, and like to have them up. Later on they sometimes like to put up pictures by others. A bulletin board in their rooms does much to save the walls and door from pin pricks and the residue of scotch tape. They also very much enjoy blackboards to draw and practice their letters and numbers on. The blackboard will be outgrown, but the bulletin board is permanently useful to some children. And as little children often crayon on their walls, and tear off wallpaper, it seems sensible to give them washable walls, even at greater first expense, because it will save both money and fury in the long run.

Getting children into bed presents a special problem. Gesell and Ilg note that they are "especially likely to show disturbance of sleep . . . when growth changes are most actively taking place."

Sleeping

Very often during these periods children feel the need of light in their room, or even refuse to go to sleep without one. "Leave a dim light on in his room, or the next room, if that makes him feel safer," says Dr. Spock. A night light has great advantages at such times. It obviates the need for hasty and possibly dangerous improvisations, can be switched off at the door when the child is asleep, or, because of its low cost, can be left on all night.

Night awakenings are one of the most trying of a parent's problems, and because of their patterns suggest the need for several planning devices. Gesell and Ilg describe the situation as follows:

> "The four year old usually awakens by himself if he needs to be toileted during the night. A few children are able to go to the bathroom by themselves, but they usually tell the mother first. They may need only verbal help, and the most difficult part of this procedure is usually getting back into bed. Sometimes verbal suggestion is not quite enough and the mother may need to get up and help the child back into bed. By five years he is ready to carry through the entire process without the parent's help."
>
> "There is much less wakefulness caused by dreaming at four than there was at 3½ years; but by 4½, the child may again have a period of dreaming about animals, especially about wolves. He may be especially sensitive to any light stimuli coming in to the room and therefore may need to have his bed in a dark corner. If the child is afraid of the dark, a light on in the hall is often sufficient to allay his fears."

The multiplicity of activities which we allocate to the bed room brings up the problem of just what kind of a room it is. Because the bed room is the most logical place in which to be private, it is more than a mere sleeping compartment. It tends to become a sort of private living room. In it are kept the things which are peculiarly its occupant's, not only his clothes, but those little things each person has which are his alone. The bed room, its arrangement, furnishings, degree of neatness, etc., gives an in-

Saul Steinberg.

sight into its occupant's character quite different from that of the living room. In the latter, he is on his metal; in the former he is apt to be much more himself. It is a curious fact that the average person is relatively unaware of the possibilities of self-projection in his bed room's basic architectural design. One "fixes up" one's bed room to suit oneself. It is a creative act with a minimum of social overtones. One "arranges" the living room with a whole series of ulterior motives in mind. Perhaps this is as it should be. But to start the planning process with the almost standardized American bed room is not necessary. There would seem no more appropriate place to get exactly the personal peccadillos, no matter how wild, that one has always wanted. A bed with a view, a bath tub one can open into a garden, a private place to sun, mirrors to suit, the expression of a certain mood conducive to the enjoyment of privacy, and similar purely personal desires should somehow get into the bed room plan, because it is the least tied to the necessities of social convention.

Because one of the bed room's most important functions is love making, part of its emotional impact must inevitably derive from our typically American attitudes towards sex in general. These are unquestionably shifting from a more prudish to a less prudish view. Contraception, as Mumford points out

> "has vastly increased the erotic possibilities of marriage . . . there is no comparison whatever between a married pair of the sixteenth century, whose sexual life would normally be interrupted by a series of pregnancies right up to the menopause, and a married pair of the twentieth century . . ."

Sexual intercourse can now usually be accomplished as often as desired without fear of pregnancy. Perhaps because of this fact, but also because of an increased awareness of the role sex plays in mental and emotional stability, the frequency of sexual intercourse and the duration of sex play have undoubtedly increased and will continue to do so. Taboos against sex with all they entail in terms of fear, shame and abstinence, are on the wane. Delight in sex play, nudity, and all the rites of the bed seem to be on the increase. Mumford goes on to draw this conclusion "every part of the dwelling must be arranged equally with an eye to sexual privacy and untrammeled courtship. Private bed rooms alone are not enough; soundproof partitions are equally important, and in communal units soundproof floors. One of the reasons that the poor are so inept at using contraceptives is that the sanest and simplest devices a woman may use still require, if sexual joy is not to be changed into a sordid mockery, such facilities as go only with a well-equipped bath room. Sexual intercourse must not forever be doomed, except for the luxuriously rich, to take place only, like burglary, under cover of darkness, in that part of the day when the energies are fast ebbing away; but before it can occur at any other times many weaknesses in house design will have to be rectified. Even at some little extra cost in corridor space, the architect must eventually learn in house and apartment design to separate the children's wing from the adult's wing."

A bathroom, as Mumford points out, is an essential requirement for love making. It is needed not only as a concomitant to contraceptives. Urinating and drinking are frequently performed as a by-product. To have to get dressed and leave the bed room for any of these three functions adds nothing to what should be the pleasantest of occupations, and can be irritating or result in extreme embarrassment. It goes without saying that privacy from without and within, freedom from interruption, are also essential. The full enjoyment of nudity cannot be realized without some light. It is a visual as well as a tactile sensation. Making love, whether for its functional purpose of reproduction or not, is pure pleasure. Like other activities in the same category, for example listening to music, it both informs and is informed by its physical environment. Making love or listening to music in beautiful surroundings is far more pleasurable than in drab and ugly ones. A beautiful bed room, or a beautiful garden, adds a great deal to the inherent joy of sex play. In addition to the factors which go to make any beautiful space, love making can be enhanced by several others. As part of its pleasure is seeing, the room should create a good background for the nude body. Its color and texture should be designed to compliment the body's modeling and soft-

Robert Woods Kennedy.

ness. Its lighting need not, in fact should not be good. Interesting lighting is essential. Candles, fire places, or low incandescent lighting are preferred. Most people want a fireplace in their bed rooms, and one reason for this desire is undoubtedly its beautiful and warm light, and the radiant heat it emits, so pleasant to the nude skin.

Our culture, and both our functional and nostalgic architecture tend to suppress direct appeals to the senses such as those just suggested. Nevertheless, when such appeals are made, by happenstance or by design, the houses concerned are seized upon with the greatest of avidity. They *work* esthetically, in the only way of any real importance, that is, as background and foil for the human body motivated by love. This is far surer ground for stimulation than history books or the current architectural magazines which, after all, present any life which they do happen to contain at several removes.

Housekeeping

Just what housework consists of is rather difficult to specify, even though it is everyone's experience. In general, it certainly includes child care, cleaning, outdoor work, neating up, washing clothes, bed making, ordering-cooking-washing up, shopping, and mending clothes. In addition there are certain seasonal activities, such as getting fire wood, putting on storm sash, spring clean ups, canning, and the like, which are in addition to the general everyday work load. This is in outline, the work which the upper middle class housewife tends, increasingly, to resent. Obviously, certain of the household tasks have their creative side, and are often very much enjoyed. Cooking can not only be performed as an art; it can be surrounded with much ritual and mystery. But washing the dishes is enjoyed by few. It is simply a chore to be performed quickly. The only pleasure to be derived from it is the sense of having done it well and efficiently. Any chore, no matter how burdensome, can be made more tolerable in two ways. It can be planned for so skillfully and accurately that its performance is made physically easy and thus speedy. It can take place in an environment so delighful that its onerous quality becomes diluted. A very efficient machine has great fascination in itself. If it is also beautiful it is a delight to use in all but the most difficult circumstances.

The most serious conflict the housewife must face is that between the demand for good housekeeping, and that for good child rearing. They are by no means compatible. Both take a great deal of time, and the hours when each is performed overlap. Both the lower and the upper classes are apt to solve this dilemma by personal withdrawal from their children. In the former case they are simply put out to roam. In the latter they are given to servants. The upper middle class tends more and more to neglect housework in favor of the children and a modicum of leisure time. Thus it is in the upper middle class house that ease of maintenance is most urgently needed. Spit and polish not only take time, they are directly contradicted by children's inherent messiness and boisterousness. With less than the required amount of time available to keep up the standard of maintenance the family still desires, housework must be made as easy to perform as possible. Most parents would like at least one room to be always tidy, appropriate, and quiet, not only to get away to, but to receive guests in and to calm the children down in. In past times this was the parlor, the kitchen-dining-living room offering the contrasting atmosphere. One was neat, sacredly so. The other was as ordered as the occasion demanded, and required no apologies for its state. This earlier division of functions and atmosphere seems an excellent solution to our current living patterns where they must occur in minimum areas. As a scheme it has inherent variety and contrast, and is thus easy to dramatize. Why was it abandoned? Perhaps the principal point against it is that it was a farm house kind of zoning, and thus carried connotations of the hick and the hayseed. The parlor was also rather brutally and arbitrarily used. It still suggests restraint, punishments, Bible reading, and unbearable boredom. Its furniture was stiff, uncomfortable, too delicate, and too neat.

The current fad for a big friendly living room, and a small efficient kitchen is undoubtedly in part a reaction against the old kitchen-parlor zoning. But it also reflects the desire to consume conspicuously. Such a living room apes that of the very rich. Yet the middle class house cannot also afford the multiple service and living spaces which are necessary to support such a room. The big living rooms of the English country houses and of our own great New England and Southern houses are reinforced with boudoirs, studies, libraries, and with many servants, and are used almost exclusively for entertaining. Living takes place in the smaller spaces, and children are relegated to nurseries in separate wings. Because the large living room in the small house is not backed up by either adequate storage, or a large kitchen, or subsidiary living spaces, it frequently exhibits use overcrowding. It is impossible to keep clean or to put things away in. Competition for its space causes irritation and friction. It does not meet the housewife's desire for neatness, nor the father's desire for peace, nor the children's desire for a free play space. If they are allowed in at all, they are always being reminded to keep it clean, or quiet. When they overstep the limitations, they are sharply reprimanded or banished. The living room has become the catch-all for a host of functions it cannot and was never intended to serve.

The desire for great space and long vistas in the small house, plus a purely esthetic desire on the part of architects, has resulted in the free plan. Such open planning was the hallmark of the great Victorian houses, and is appropriate to their size and scale. They were heavily furnished, voluminously rugged, draped, and overstuffed. As a result they were neither too noisy nor too public. This kind of plan applied to contemporary houses with few and very light rugs, drapes, and furniture is not only impossibly noisy and lacking in privacy; it is also difficult to keep in order. Uses are not adequately separated, with the result that entering-playing-living-dining-cooking functions tend to spread away from their planned locus. Children's clothes drift into the living room, and their toys turn up everywhere, as do adults' sports equipment, cameras, games, etc. Outdoor dirt also tends to get tracked throughout the house, although dirt is perhaps not as great a problem as the thousands of individual items which must be kept out of sight for neatness's sake, yet be readily available when they are needed.

Many people feel that the esthetics of buildings and of rooms affect the degree of maintenance required. The "laboratory" kitchen somehow insists that it be kept clean and spotless. The "farm" kitchen, because of its darker surfaces and easy going atmosphere, makes less stringent demands on maintenance. This sense of correlation between character and standards of neatness is applied to every room in the house. Hard, bright, uniform surfaces do in fact demand more washing and polishing, if they are to retain their essential qualities, than do the soft, dark, and variegated materials. The sort of hard, "clean", exact architecture typical of the International style seems to be complimented by orderliness of furnishings and belongings. By the same token disorder in such surroundings is felt to be more disorderly by contrast to its intrinsic order. Of course this kind of comparison has nothing to do with fact. Rooms get equally dirty no matter what their character, and the impervious surfaces are the ones most easy to get really clean. But the important thing is to be able to let go certain aspects of house work, at times, without having the

Joseph Nash.

resulting effect cry aloud for correction.

Just where the desire for inconspicuous deterioration, orderliness, and polish are balanced is an extremely difficult question. It varies from person to person and from room to room. Certainly it is between the two extremes: it is not where orderliness and mess accentuate each other, nor is it where disorderliness and mess compliment each other. The middle ground may be such houses as Joseph Nash's beloved "Mansions of England in the Olden Time" or more contemporaneously in the easy going Bay Region style. Such houses tell one a story. They state quite clearly that they are not uncomfortably neat, nor uncomfortably formal. They enjoy a mild amount of mess, and adapt themselves to it because it is human to be disorderly—pretentious to insist on neatness.

More important, they manage to convey the feeling that they delight in harboring other activities than house work: music, books, conversation and drinks. There is enough time left over to live in them.

The housewife invariably asks her architect for time to live. She does this seriously, and with an air of faith in his ability to make a miracle. She really puts it to him. How can he reply? The subject is so complex that there is no single attack on it. Ease of housekeeping must be a part of the very fabric of the house. The principal considerations involved are as follows:

1. Optimum floor area for the kind of life the family needs. Too little or too much both increase the work load.
2. The separation of active-messy from passive-neat activities.
3. An esthetic which does not place a premium on spit and polish.
4. The choice of realistic (i.e. easily maintained) colors and materials.
5. Proper functional provisions for such frequently performed activities as cooking, dressing children, and mending.

We have considered in some detail the various activities which create the necessity of housework. For each in turn those provisions which might ease the business of cleaning up after them have been considered. There remain two subjects, washing clothes and sweeping-vacuuming-dusting-neating up. The first of these, washing clothes, is most logically done in the kitchen. It no longer takes a very great amount of continuous time and this can be squeezed in between other housework activities. Provisions for it are logically built into those of connected activities, and share some of the equipment of these other activities. The hamper or bag where dirty clothes are collected is most conveniently located where one dresses and undresses. Hampers for dirty bed clothes are best located in the bottom of the linen closet. A built-in collecting hamper is needed next to the washing machine, to hold laundry for a while, and the large basket in which it is carted around. A space—the kitchen counter, or table, is needed on which to sort them, and on which to put them again after they have been through the washing machine. The collecting hamper can again be used to store those to be ironed. The built-in hamper, the washer and dryer and ironer or ironing board are all logically located near the back door and the cellar or utility room door. Just outside the back door is the clothes drying yard. In the cellar or utility room are clothes lines for wet weather. Over the equipment involved there is storage space for soap, bluing, iron, clothes pins and the like. Mending can also be concentrated in a single unit, including a holding hamper immediately adjacent to the laundry equipment. Washing clothes, like cooking, is a more or less predictable and periodic process, which need only be thought out to be easy of accomplishment.

There remains that final and most perplexing of subjects—dusting-sweeping-neating up. Here there is no easy solution. One cannot reduce the area of the house simply in order to have fewer square feet to clean. The job can be helped, but not to any great extent by well located, well fitted, and commodious cleaning closets, one for each zone. Proper materials, washable papers and paints, mop boards and the like all help. This is about the end of the list. The real problem is neating up. One cannot neat up if there is no place to put things. The basic aid to housework is the right kind of storage in the right place. In the small areas we are faced with today, it is uneconomical to provide this in furniture. It must be built in. The smallest house needs an amount of storage not incommensurate with the next to the largest. Thus the total area of the smaller houses should include what seems, on the basis of current practice, a disproportionate amount and number of storage spaces. The difficulty here is, of course, money. Adequate storage requires a large number of expensive cubic feet. Small, specialized closets, drawers, and the like cost considerably more per cubic foot than most of the living spaces. Another reason may be that we take maintenance so much for granted that we fail to see it, much as we forget a too familiar view. The hundreds of little things involved are bewildering. Furniture will take care of them, we hope they can be tucked away, or thrown out, or stored in a warehouse. The desire to make a show also plays its part. When the budget cannot absorb both storage and the desired symbols of conspicuous consumption, the former is apt to be pared to a minimum. Whatever the reasons, or combinations of reasons, adequate storage space in contemporary houses is unusual in spite of the fact that in realistic terms it is far more essential than the imponderables which often limit its scope.

The housewife's basic problem is the conservation of wealth. Toys stepped on and broken, a vase left out and smashed, clothes eaten by moths, bicycles rusted in the rain, shoes mildewed in the basement, bread eaten by mice, are examples of the loss of wealth through inability to keep objects in a suitable thermal and physical environment. Even when storage spaces are supplied which accurately reflect the needs of the objects to be preserved, they are still not adequate unless they are properly placed in relation to the functions they serve. If they are too difficult to get at, they will not be used. A dry warm space for the baby carriage in the attic might as well not exist for all the use it will get. Where children are concerned the problem is infinitely acute. Not only do they possess a host of belongings which must be conserved, they cut down the amount of time the housewife has available for maintenance, increase the amount needed, and must themselves be trained to store and conserve things. The housewife faced with lack of storage is quite literally prevented from accomplishing her basic economic function.

The amount of storage space required by families is almost impossible to assess. The lower income groups would seem to require more storage than the others because of their necessity to save, re-use, and make things. Upper income families also often require vast amounts of storage, not only for things purchased currently, but for heirlooms and inheritances which they wish to keep and pass on. Mrs. Field notes

> "Families in the middle-income group are usually in uneasy transition either from the lower-income group with its economy of saving 'things' to the higher-income group with its economy of saving cash; or from the higher-income group (the well-to-do young girl who marries the boy on $25 a week) which is ignorant of the possibilities and techniques of saving 'things' to the lower-income group which has no money to save. The most expert keep a nice distance from both extremes by very

delicate juggling. Their houses reflect this juggling in their uncertain attitude toward the question of how much storage space is economical, efficient, adequate, properly located, in other words 'functional'."

While it is impossible to assess accurately the amount of cubage any one family will require for storage, it would seem to be a fairly safe guess that they will have at least something in most of the following thirty-seven categories.

1. *Vehicles*
   Automobiles, tires, tools, cleaning equipment
   Bicycles, tools, tires,
   Boats, motorcycles, etc.
   Babycarriages, strollers

2. *Outdoor Games*
   Nets, posts, wickets, bags, gloves, rackets, mallets, bats, balls, clubs, golf bags, skates, skis, outboard motors

3. *Outdoor Clothes*
   Coats—wet raincoats
   Gloves—wet gloves and mittens
   Umbrellas—dripping umbrellas
   Dirty work clothes
   Footwear—wet and dirty footwear
   Snowsuits
   Hats

4. *Garden Tools*
   Wheelbarrows, spray trucks, rollers, lawn mowers, etc.
   Hoses, string, stakes, flower pots, seeds, sprays, fertilizer
   Clippers, pruner, gloves, hoes, rakes, shovels, forks
   Ladders

5. *Garden and Porch Furniture*
   Chairs, tables, chaise longue
   Swings, hammocks

6. *Storm Sash and Screens*
   Screens, screen doors, storm sash and storm doors

7. *Tools*
   - Wood working tools
   - Bolts, nails, screws, parts, etc.
   - Replacement parts, wood, screen cloth, repair tools, etc.

8. *Indoor Games*
   - Card tables, ping pong tables, etc.
   - Cards, rackets, sets of games, paper, pencils, etc.

9. *Recreational Equipment*
   - Records, music, music stands, instruments, tapes
   - Projectors, screens, reels, cameras, developing and printing equipment, slides
   - Books, papers, magazines, clippings, etc.
   - Pictures, paints, paper, pencils
   - Fire tongs, brushes, long forks, pokers, wood, paper, kindling
   - Collections, hobbies
   - Cigarettes, ash trays, pipes, tobacco, cleaners, etc.

10. *Toys*
    - Carts, tricycles, scooters, Irish Mails, sleds, cars
    - Models, electric trains, bulldozers, steam shovels, farms
    - Erector, construction, Lincoln Logs
    - Paper, pencils, glue, scissors, cloth, wire
    - Costumes
    - Water toys
    - Tools

11. *Festival Accessories*
    - Christmas tree ornaments, tree holder, lights, etc.
    - Hallowe'en masks
    - Flags
    - Punch bowls

12. *Papers*
    - Correspondence, letters, bills, stamps, writing paper, etc.
    - Documents, birth certificates, insurance, service papers, etc.
    - Check books, receipts, etc.

13. *Drinks*
    - Wine
    - Whiskey, gin, liquers
    - Beer
    - Shakers, strainers, trays, muddlers, straws, fruit, etc.
    - Mixers

14. *Daily Food*
    - Perishables, butter, milk, meat, etc.
    - Spices, condiments, seasonings
    - Dry groceries, boxes, cans, etc.
    - Vegetables
    - Bread
    - Beverages
    - Frozen foods

15. *Preserved Food*
    - Jams, jellies, food in jars, home canning equipment, etc.

16. *Kitchen Equipment*
    - Knives, forks, spoons, mixers, etc.
    - Collanders, strainers, grinders
    - Mixing bowls, measuring cups, etc.
    - Pots and pans
    - Cook books, receipts, etc.
    - Dish cloths and towels (see 22)
    - Pot holders

17. *Cooking—Accessory Equipment*
    - Toaster, Coffee maker
    - Juice extractor, can opener
    - Grinder, mixer, beater
    - Timer-clock
    - Grill, waffle iron
    - Baby bottle sterilizer and warmer
    - Miscellaneous, including roasters, ice cream freezer, hot plate, vibrator, corn popper, broiler, egg cooker, deep-freeze, coffee mill etc.

18. *China and Glass*
    Plates, cups, saucers, bowls
    Tumblers, serving dishes, cocktail glasses
    Vases

19. *Silver*
    Knives, forks and spoons
    Plates, bowls, tumblers
    Vases, candle sticks, etc.

20. *Table Linens*
    Table cloths, napkins, place mats, bibs, etc.

21. *Serving Trays*
    Flat trays for table, bed, etc.
    Wheeled carts for cooking, drinking, serving

22. *Dish and Pot Cleaning Equipment*
    Pans, strainers, dish towels, soap, mops, steel wool, polish

23. *Waste*
    Waste paper storage
    Garbage storage
    Outdoor-waste storage, leaves, garden refuse, etc.

24. *Medicines*
    First aid kits
    Miscellaneous drugs, lotions, etc.
    Eye cups, thermometers, hot water bottles, ice bags etc.

25. *Lavatory Equipment*
    Washing materials, soap, brushes
    Hair tools, curlers, pins
    Tooth brushing equipment
    Make up, cosmetics
    Shaving equipment
    Baby equipment
    Manicuring equipment
    Towels, face cloths, bath mats
    Dirty towels

26. *Bath Equipment*
    Soap, shampoo, towels, face cloths, bath mats, mits, sponges, crystals
    Bathinette and equipment

27. *Water-closet Equipment*
    Toilet paper, bed pans, toidy seats, enemas
    Sanitary napkins, contraceptives

28. *Cleaning Utensils*
    Vacuum cleaners, polishers
    Mops, brushes, brooms
    Pails, rags
    Soap, wax, cleaning fluid

29. *Poisons*
    Garden insecticides
    Ammonia, spot removers, disinfectants, bleaches, drain solvent
    Medicines, sleeping pills, etc.

30. *Weather Modifiers*
    Fans
    Heaters
    Vaporizers

31. *Bed Linen*
    Sheets, blankets, bed spreads, pillows, cases, comforters
    Dirty bed linen
    Electric blankets and pads

32. *Clothes*
    Suits, dresses, coats, etc.
    Underwear, shirts, blouses, sweaters
    Socks, stockings, shoes
    Ties, belts, headwear
    Jewelry, studs, cuff links, etc.

33. *Sewing and Mending*
    Sewing Materials, thread, scissors, patterns, buttons, trimming, etc.
    Things to be sewed, materials

Sewing machines, and cutting boards

34. *Clothes Cleaning Equipment*
    Spot remover, rags
    Shoe polish, cleaner, rags, shoe rest
    Iron and ironing board
    Soap, detergent, starch, bluing
    Clothes pins, baskets, hampers, line

35. *Travel Equipment*
    Bags, hat boxes, cases, food baskets, thermos flasks, lunch boxes
    Crates, barrels
    Trunks

36. *Furnishings*
    Chairs, tables
    Rugs, curtains
    Lamps, etc.
    Miscellaneous

37. *Fuel*
    Wood, paper, kindling
    Oil, coal, bottled gas

Obviously, the kind and the location of the spaces designed to receive these storagables will vary in every individual case. As storage is not a primary function, it is highly influenced by other considerations. And opportunism enters in. It is always possible to eke out extra cubic feet; over the hood of the car, at the end of the garage; over stair wells; or along one wall of corridors. At least three kinds of spaces can be used year around, but differently according to season. Storm sash replace screens, winter clothes replace summer clothes, and skis replace tennis racquets. The location of storage space for storm sash, for example, in an inaccessible location such as a basement, is justified because it is used only twice a year. But to locate a wheel barrow and lawn mower in the basement is, because they are used so frequently during their season, frightfully inconvenient. One even wonders why storm sash, at least, are not redesigned so that they fold back against the wall when not in use, just as blinds used to.

Many of the things stored need protection against animals and insects. Garbage is subject to dogs; clothes to moths. Relatively tight cedar closets are great boons to the housewife. Other sorts of things are affected by weather. Humidity takes the press out of clothes and makes them feel clammy. Bicycles rust outdoors. Still other things are dangerous when they can be reached by children. The medicine, cleaning, and other poisons around the house are, sensibly, locked up. Finally, another series of things need air circulation, such as vegetables, towels, and bed linen. The best conditions for the various household belongings are well known, so well so in fact, that it seems redundant to mention them. Yet there are very few houses which provide enough storage, let alone adequately located, fitted, and protected storage. Is there a house in the United States which can get along with, for example, the standard medicine cabinet?

The architect and client bent on achieving livability in the broadest terms must ask themselves why it is not more frequently achieved. Houses are everyone's experience. The business of rationalizing their functions is not too onerous. Why is it then that there are so few adequate entrances, so few pleasant kitchens, so few beautiful living rooms? The obvious answer to this question is a list of lacks; lack of money, lack of talent, lack of a rounded approach. That "practicality" mentioned earlier also plays a destructive role. But every architect has seen jobs fail where architect and client were generously equipped with all of these aids and qualities. What got in their way? It seems more than likely that in most cases they got in each other's way; that in the process of dealing with each other the goal they both desired, livability, got lost sight of. We carry the seeds of our own destruction within us.

Every architect has seen a job, for a good client, started with great verve and a will to make it work, get slowly and mysteriously less and less adequate as it went along. Such jobs seem to have a gradual, creeping, fatal, disease, which never gets accurately diagnosed. The architect blames the client. The client blames the architect. Which one is right?

When I think of acquiring for myself one of our luxurious dwellings, I am deterred, for, so to speak, the country is not yet adapted to human *culture and we are still forced to cut our* spiritual *bread far thinner than our forefathers did their wheaten. Not that all architectural ornament is to be neglected even in the rudest periods; but let our houses first be lined with beauty, where they come in contact with our lives, like the tenement of the shell-fish, and not overlaid with it. But, alas! I have been inside one or two of them, and know what they are lined with.*—THOREAU

CHAPTER VI

Relations

Architects and Clients

The atmosphere in which decisions are made is so important to the success of the house that it absorbs a great deal of the architect's time. Yet little or nothing is known about architect-client relationships, nor about doctor-patient or lawyer-client relationships for that matter. The professions and the schools assume that the ability to deal with clients is inherent in the individual practitioner. And, certainly, it often is. On the other hand architects tend to agree that house work is the most demanding and discouraging of all specialities because of personal difficulties with clients. The architect probably does not exist who has not sworn never to do another house. Next day he will probably be dreaming of a new, a bigger, and a better dwelling; and one cannot help but suspect that the fascination of these same "impossible" personal relationships plays a large part in his regression.

It would be unrealistic to deny that some clients are quite literally barbarians. It is equally futile to ignore the fact that architects, particularly the better ones, tend to be pigheaded; that they arrogate to themselves omnipotence in esthetic matters. Thus one often hears that so and so "is a pretty good architect but he does not know how to get along with people"; or that so and so "is a pretty weak architect but he sure does know how to bring in the clients." Such comments come from the public. Within the profession the most touted questions revolve around "ethics"; i.e., around the question of salesmanship versus excellence. How far can one lead a client on? Where does personal salesmanship get out of bounds? How poor a job can one let a client force on himself? As in all dealings between someone with a body of specialized knowledge and someone who needs that knowledge applied to a personal problem, be it a disease, a question of civil right, or a building, the foundation of the relationship must be professional ethics.

The ethical code of the profession seems to be very nearly meaningless. Furthermore the way in which it is used by some Chapters of the Institute—as a tool with which those in power prevent those not in power from competing with them—makes the whole subject somewhat distasteful to the thoughtful practitioner. The very notion of a list of dos and don'ts seems unrealistic. The kind of integrity demanded of the architect is so complex and often so subtle that it must be one of his most constant preoccupations. Because professional ethics are so integral to every action the architect takes, they will not be considered separately here, but rather as an aspect of all his relationships.

What is the fundamental situation between client and architect? Very few professional or social meetings of architects end before someone has bewailed the "place" of the architect in society at large, and therefore vis-a-vis his clients. Architects consider themselves to be without public respect and without channels to public opinion. They labor under a distinct inferiority feeling. Like all psychological states, this is compounded of numerous elements. In support of the notion that they are, as a rule, treated in a manner most unlike the other professions, the following analysis by Rosow is most interesting:

> "The fundamental distinction between the architect-client situation and other professional relationships may be traced to factors of client attitude and participation. The client becomes the significant variable in this situation. In other professional roles, the client's initiative is minimal. The professional specialist is relied upon for technical judgment, execution, and advice. And this essentially functions as a 'take-it-or-leave-it' package. If a client fails to accept professional judgment, he is implicitly assuming full responsibility for the consequences. And his decision—whatever it may be—is seldom presumed to be made on technical grounds, but always on the basis of nonprofessional criteria. But the architect relationship allows much broader scope for the play of client preferences. As a result clients define the planning situation as one where the architect is simply taking directions. They assume not only prerogatives of personal taste, but arrogate to themselves competence of

architectural judgment in highly technical matters (whether of engineering or aesthetics). Unlike a doctor or lawyer, an architect's recommendations are extremely susceptible of client criticism. While many clients have only the vaguest ideas of what they want or an understanding of how to achieve it in architectural terms, they frequently insist upon 'telling the architect his business.' Consequently, architects often feel that the structure of their role leaves them highly vulnerable in crucial areas and that they have relatively little institutionalized defenses such as bulwark the authority of physicians, lawyers, or engineers."

The implicit assumption by the average client that he is in command evidences itself throughout the relationship. An interesting corollary is stated by Mr. Charles Luckman in an article called "The Client's Point of View." (Progressive Architecture, Oct. 1951, p. 63.) After qualifying himself as a "buyer" of many buildings, he lists the fourth of four things a client wants as: "The designing and building to be done in a manner which will protect him against his own inexperience." The implication is that the client will make the decisions and that his architect's job is to let him know when he gets off the beam. The architect is here endowed by the client with a role somewhat resembling that of a nursemaid. His job is conceived, by the client, who casts himself in the role of a "buyer," as a cautionary one. "Don't do that, you may be sorry," he is supposed to say whenever the client seems to be going too far for his own good.

But, while this situation might be thought of as average, there are of course other types of relationships. Every architect has experienced pleasure, despair, and surprise at the roles in which he is cast by his clients. The most flattering is that of the wise and sensitive divinity, whose every word must be taken seriously, whose every esthetic whim must be considered, lest the job be in some way tarnished. The worst role is perhaps that of handy man, whose function is to be ordered to draw blue prints and whose suggestions are made for the express purpose of being contradicted, thus proving the client's infallible taste and judgment. The most wearing role is that of the keg of delectable spirits which must be drained absolutely dry and then broken up so that no one else will be able to use it. It is with clients who put him in this position that the architect is apt to have hour-long telephone conversations in the middle of dinner and six-hour sessions breaking up at two in the morning. A rare client treats his architect with strict professional decorum. There remains the ideal client, a subject which will be treated with the most careful attention, for the client is as important a factor in the creation of a good house as the architect himself.

While the architect's impression that the average client does not hesitate to tell him his business is unquestionably correct, his feeling of being looked down on generally is not borne out by the facts. W. Lloyd Warner, Carson McGuire, and others concerned with systems for measuring social status place the architectural profession in that group most favored by the public at large. This high value placed on architecture is borne out by another interesting study, Strong, in his measurements of liking for 114 occupations by men in general, ranks them as follows:

> "The occupational items are listed . . . in the order of their being liked, according to the weighted averages. The occupation of explorer stands at the top, liked by 60.5 per cent; next comes inventor (50.3 per cent), and musician (49 per cent), followed by manufacturer, architect, editor, and scientific research worker—all liked by 46 per cent. At the bottom of the list are street-car conductor, (0.8 per cent), steeple jack, (2.8 per cent), and undertaker (3.2 per cent), lighthouse tender (3.8 per cent), and floorwalker (4.7 per cent). A perusal of the list will arouse some surprise as to the placing of certain occupations and many speculations as to why occupations are arranged as they are."*

He also found that while most professional men become less and less interested in their occupations with age, architects became more interested. This is perhaps the greatest recommendation the profession could receive.

The tendency of the people Dr. Strong studied was to overestimate the profession's rank order as far as income is concerned.

* A further comfort to be derived from the Strong findings is that decorators are approximately 77th on the list, just behind auto repairmen and just ahead of automobile salesmen. Real estate salesmen are even less well thought of, placing about 84th.

Dr. Strong placed it 16th, a control group estimated it at 12th, while the sample put it in 8th place. Their liking may have been influenced by an overestimation of the amount of money architects make. Architecture might not seem so attractive if the truth were more generally known. On the other hand, its very desirability might lead people to overrate it financially. One is apt to attribute to a beautiful girl a far better character than she usually deserves. In any case, the impression of affluence is there. Among money-conscious and status-conscious people, it evidences itself in charges of profiteering. A frank explanation, before the question of fees is gone into, might, in some cases, do much to clear the air. Houses in particular are not famous for the profits involved. If gossip in the trade is any true indication, the better the house, the more money is lost.

The high value placed on the profession by society is thoroughly consistent with the individual client's belief that he can direct the building of his house. He grasps at the experience as, at long last, an opportunity to be an architect himself. He wants, very urgently, to make it his own creative act, particularly if his creativity is thwarted elsewhere. He believes he can direct the architect because design seems very easy. Unlike a surgeon's job, for example, it is pleasant and well understood. Almost anyone can sit down and produce a buildable design. Many people, particularly in such professions as engineering, which involves a knowledge of drafting, actually do design and build their own houses quite free of architectural "interference" and are well satisfied with them. There are several generally-held beliefs and likes which contribute to the client's self-confidence. Dr. Strong's studies indicate that most men (93 per cent at 45 years of age) feel they "can discriminate between more or less important matters." A large proportion (78 per cent at 55) expressed liking for museums and art galleries. Artist, architect, and musician are included in the first 23 occupations by order of preference. As every artist and architect knows, the vast majority of the public subscribe to the theory "I don't know anything about art, but I know what I like," brought in to clinch any argument involving esthetics. The architect, faced with such odds, can only sigh and wait for some client like the hero in this cartoon by James Thurber.

"He knows all about art, but he doesn't know what he likes."
James Thurber: Copy. 1939 The New Yorker Magazine, Inc.

Behind these more or less explicit drives there is another which accounts more fundamentally for the client's desire to do it himself, for his feeling that all he needs is "just a little help with the blue prints." The neighborhood and the house in which one lives rank with source of income and occupation as the prime indications of social status. The house is inextricably bound up with one's social relationships. The natural tendency when dealing with something so personal, individual, and important, is to go it alone if one possibly can. One tends to distrust the capacity of another to be as vitally interested and concerned as oneself.

The public's liking for architecture and their concern with houses suggests that the design stage be as cooperative—as joint an enterprise—as the principals can make it. The client must be let into some of the "secrets" of the profession. He should be "used" creatively in the process of design. The question of degree must be decided individually for each case. Inadequate distance between client and architect can result in the architect's having to design or specify things which he knows are unsuitable. Too great a distance usually results in client dissatisfaction.

The Professional Hierarchy

The solution of the distance problem between architect and client depends in part on the professional goals of the architect. And these, in turn, have reality only as they are compared to other goals, i.e., as they exist in a hierarchy. The mean position typical of the profession today seems discouragingly low. Up to the twenties the general standard of house design was trapped in a descending spiral. Lack of public understanding of good design led to lack of demand for it, which led to a scarcity of good architects, which led to low standards of professional competence, which led to a poor calibre of person entering the profession, which led to a lack of examples of fine architecture, which finally led back to an increasing lack of opportunity on the part of the public to understand. This downward spiral is, perhaps, being checked by the modern movement. But in the meantime, the plant of good design must struggle in a thin atmosphere.

The downward spiral took place during the long reign of the "Traditionalists." It began and gained impetus during the period in which nearly all work followed revivalist theories. While the Traditionalists still retain control of building, if not of the schools, magazines, and museums, they are now under attack. This assault is from a minority and is in the nature of a reform, factors which give the modern architect his peculiar characterological and professional make-up. The movement was given impetus and homogeniety (as Modernism) by the writings of Sullivan, increased by Wright, increased again by export to Europe, increased still further by reimportation. It was spurred on by a growing realization among intellectuals that American architecture was on the rocks. Mr. Lewis Mumford's "Sticks and Stones" is an example of the dim view taken of architecture by its most intelligent friends. Finally, while important buildings continue to be built "traditionally," the very businessmen, college presidents, insurance company executives and mayors who commission them constantly denounce their inadequacies. This stream of criticism levelled at architects and architecture is by no means wholly reasonable. But there is surely a drop of truth in each gallon of it.

The Modern reform must of course counteract the downward spiral. It must, in its turn, also avoid calling forth such criticisms as are levelled at the Traditionalist. As a result, the value placed on good work becomes a driving compulsion for the Modernist. He must prove himself competent in the face of a strong public distrust of all architects. He must sell his reform. He must make his point of view felt. This drive is far too fundamental to confine itself to creative quality alone. His work as a whole, his client's best interests, and the public's view of the competence of the profession become obligations which often outbalance money and status considerations. A natural byproduct is a strongly critical view of the Traditionalists, based on esthetic, moral, and ethical concepts. These drives, reformist and idealistic in nature, are apt to spill over into the practitioner's private life. His interests include anything from the preservation of natural resources to the dissemination of birth control. As a result, the modern architect suffers from greater insecurity than is generally typical of the profession. A limited number of clients are available to him. Of these, he must refuse some. Others will take much of his time and money in his efforts to educate them. Thus the conflict most modern architects must resolve is between a desire for economic security on the one hand and for untrammelled creativity on the other.

The way an architect solves this problem places him in the professional hierarchy. It also determines, to some extent, the degree of distance he maintains from his clients. There would seem to be five levels of adjustment. The first three are oriented primarily toward the production of good architecture. The last two are oriented towards the making of money. As in all hierarchical systems there is an increasing envy for successive positions above one's own in the scale and increasing contempt for those below. Thus the top man in our U. S. architectural totem pole delights in insulting, publicly and loudly, all of those below him, while the bottom men affect to despise "art" and boast of their earnings.

The characteristic adjustments in the five levels may be summarized as follows:

The Professional Hierarchy

1. HIGHEST CREATIVITY AND INDEPENDENCE

The most desirable goal for architects in this category is to be able to achieve complete work independence. This involves being able to accept only modern jobs and only from people who indicate the ability to recognize good work. For complete happiness, all but the interesting problems would be refused. At the present time it is possible to practice architecture in this way only under two circumstances. First, architects of national and international reputation gain complete work independence through the job-drawing power of their work and name. Second, the architect may be wealthy. Or, he may teach, practicing less than full time. This last liability is counteracted by the opportunity a school affords to keep up with one's profession, to gain current design experience, and to force the objectivization of experience. Among doctors, school or hospital affiliations are considered essential to continuous professional competence, and this is perhaps no less true of architects.

2. HIGH CREATIVITY AND INDEPENDENCE

This group, larger than the top, but still comparatively minute, achieves independence through work of an industrial or social nature usually outside the residential field, where the problem of thwarted creativity is not too pressing or where the limitations on it are well understood. Its members will only accept modern houses, though they may take on the less promising clients on occasions. Again, as in the first category, teaching or job security with an organization or great professional prestige are sometimes required to support the design independence achieved.

3. MEDIUM CREATIVITY AND INDEPENDENCE

This group might be characterized as having strong interest in good work but as willing to do "modernistic" jobs when under pressure. They are unwilling to do eclectic work. They do jobs which they are ashamed of, yet they also send clients away who obviously will cause only trouble and produce little satisfaction. They will protest bad decisions and fight for their views but, because of temperamental and economic pressures, will go very far into artistically undesirable compromises.

4. BUSINESS AND LOW CREATIVITY

This group includes those who "would like to do one of those modernistic houses" but who would never lead a client into

Clifford McBride: Napoleon and Uncle Elby.

one. Some might, when choosing the style, mention "modernistic" but at the first sign of client resistance or indecision would advise against it.

5. MERCHANT-ARCHITECT

This group will design anything that a client wants. Their chief interest is in making money. Their only professional maxim is, "The customer is always right."

The architect's adjustment in this scale gives him, at the high end, the ability to withstand the average client's arrogation of competence. The "uppity" client can be turned down or educated or, in the case of the very top men, simply brutalized into submission. From the client's point of view, his architect's position in the hierarchy is of great moment. At the top of the scale he will get a house with a strong proprietory flavor. It will excellently

express and contain his needs and desires. But he will not be able to participate personally in the process to any great extent. At the bottom end of the scale he will enjoy full participation but will get a vulgar house. In the middle he will get a more or less standardized and "central" version of modernism, without much personal insight. He will participate, but the reflection of his needs will be subordinated to style. A great many of the gyrations which clients go through when shopping for an architect are the result of their efforts to discover intuitively exactly what the relationship of process to self expression to end result is for each different architect. The much touted business of discovering whether one "likes" an architect is in large part an effort to guess how much he will let one get away with. Obviously, the most desirable architect is one who can not only express himself but who can also drag out of his clients what *they* want to express.

The situation which has created the architectural hierarchy and the prerequisites enjoyed by those at the top has an adverse effect on architects' behavior. The best clients believe, with more than a little justification, that architects are stubborn, demanding, and condescending. They leave out necessary spaces and equipment for ulterior and arbitrary esthetic reasons. They are snooty about their taste and wish to exert their influence to the extent of seeing that the forks are in tune with the *gestalt* of the house. They arrogate to themselves the right to veto their clients' dearest activities or to force them into new and undesired living patterns via their houses. Thus goes the myth. No architect ever lived up to all its details. On the other hand, few clients who have dealt with the top modernists have failed to run up against a stone wall at some point, or have failed to resent it, or have failed to make a good story of it later.

In defense of the architect, if not of his worst behavior, it must be admitted that even with the above average client he must often fight all the way in order to achieve a distinguished result. And the client is by no means his only adversary. The real estate man, the decorator, the surveyor, the contractor, the subs, etc., etc., down a long list of people, usually fail to understand what he is trying to do. They tend, through sins of omission rather than commission, to vitiate the job, as it progresses, in a series of small ways. Faced with this array, the architect tends, like a horse dealer, to ask for too much freedom in the hope that he will get enough with which to achieve his goals. The fact that this effort spills over at times into downright "temperament" is an unfortunate but inevitable result of the pressures to which he is subjected, and of the counter pressures he must always have in readiness in order to maintain his standards.

The Effects of Art

"They can do without architecture *who have no olives or wines in the cellar."*—Thoreau

Boiled down, architect-client relationships might be described as follows: At the top of the hierarchy, client arrogance is met by architect arrogance (whether or not justly), which results in a certain reluctance on the part of the average client to take on the top people, which results in the architect's need for some extraordinary economic bolster, such as a job, a great reputation, or a rich wife. At the bottom of the scale, client arrogance is met by architect permissiveness, a popular quality, which results in some economic security. Given the theoretical constant that any location in the hierarchy is open to anyone, the real point at issue is the quality of the end product. For obvious reasons those talented architects who have arrived at the top adjustment enjoy the greatest all-around security, i.e., financial, personal, and professional, and thus have more time and energy available to concentrate on the job itself. These factors combine with a synergistic effect to produce more of everything.

The drive for money, or the drive for pure art, the characteristic goals of the bottom and top of the hierarchy, are both, in terms of all around human adjustment, extreme phenomena. Such single-mindedness cannot but reflect unusual and very personal goals. The architect's adjustment *to* his profession on the other hand, as distinct from his adjustment *within* it, is largely determined by client goals.

The person commissioning an architect makes three demands. He wants his house to be well designed, both functionally and esthetically. He wants it to be structurally sound. And he wants his money-dealings with architect, contractor, and subcontractors to be well run. Because of the human tendency to specialize, these three demands tend to operate as magnetic poles. The architect is pulled in three directions, and he is faced with one of his most difficult problems in professional adjustment. This might be visualized as follows:

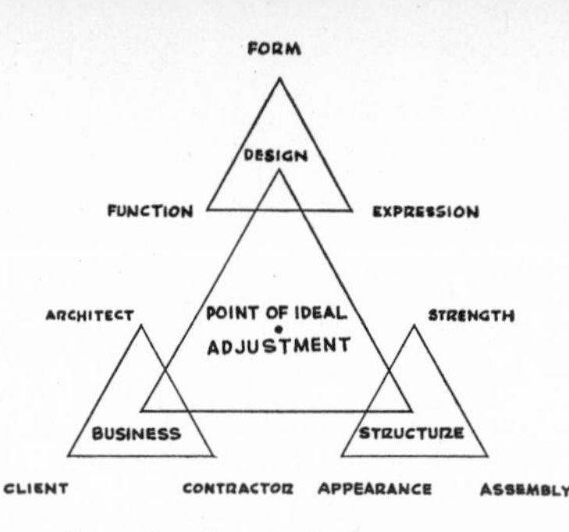

It is quite obvious that architecture cannot be practiced solely from the vantage point of any one pole. But it is possible to practice perilously close to either the Design, Business, or Technical apexes. Theoretically perhaps, the point of most stable adjustment would be equi-distant from all three. But in practice this point seems, as often as not, to result in mediocrity. The individual is just far enough away from the pull of the three magnetic fields so that he neither designs, manages, nor engineers his work with snap. The largest number of successful practices are off center, heavily weighted toward the Business-Technique axis.

Each of the three typical positions is, of course, thought of as ideal by those architects who are located in its vicinity and by all those who have been or will be their clients. The most challenging design is produced from the "Artistic Architect" point of adjustment. The best architecture is not. The exact distances from the poles which an individual deems meet and proper is entirely a matter of talent, breadth, and judgment. Looked at in the obverse, the location in which the individual finally comes to rest is a function of his limitations. The business of deciding just how far the ideal is from each pole is a fruitless task. The individual can only strive in all three directions and hope for the best.

Among modern architects, the artistic element bulks large. The Traditionalists are thought of, and even think of themselves, as businessman—technical types, who get their "art" by osmosis. Their true ware is a sense of conventional security. Modernism, a reform movement, naturally stresses the element—art—principally lacking in its progenitor. Thus the modern architect must add to those problems which are in any case inherent to the profession certain others which badger the artist no matter what his medium. The modern architect's rather typical paranoid attitudes may be motivated by this factor as much as by the general distrust of Modernism.

It is the norm rather than the exception among artists to feel that the world misunderstands them, passes them by, and under-

Picasso: "The End of a Monster." Could it also represent Art (personified), and the artist?

values their contribution. There is no need here to explore this situation in detail. A few of the factors which, perhaps, create and perpetuate it are worth mentioning however. It seems probable that to adopt an unpopular goal, such as art, is the mark of a deviate individual in the first place. Dr. Fisher notes that:

> "Rank, bless his far-sighted soul . . . beheld in the neurotic individual a strong similarity to the creative individual—if, in fact, the two did not actually overlap."

Whether or not this apparent conjunction is true, the Modernist, revolutionary as he had to be in the period preceding the second world war, usually exhibits a strong urge to set himself against society. Society itself scorns the sensitivity essential to artistic creation. Artists are looked down on as "impractical," particularly in the more or less rough and ready world of construction. But whatever his medium, the artist is frequently subject to what appears to be gratuitous attack. W. H. Auden has noted that "the odd and frightening thing about the provincial middle-brows is the intensity of their hostile interest in the high-brow." The artist lives in a state of siege, Mr. Auden says, and if he is a person of talent and integrity, if he meets the enemy head on, he pays a heavy price for his defiance. In the same piece, Mr. Auden, addressing the young person considering a career in the arts, warns him, ". . . of the iron nerves and strength of character he will need, for, lacking them, no matter how great his talent, he is doomed to failure." Over and above the general social handicap of being an artist, cyclical fluctuations in the building industry, plus periods of political tension, plus wars, plus defensive rearmament, plus shortages of materials, inhibit fine building for long periods, during which the architect must change his occupation or reduce his standard of living. It would seem that the fine architect, like the artist, can avoid his sense of paranoia only at the price of poor work.

Fine architecture, like the other arts, is taken to be an expensive luxury, about which one must exercise a kind of extra caution. Furthermore, the more "artistic" an architect is, in the popular myth, the more extravagant he is supposed to be. It would seem that a myth of this sort (there are several within architecture) must, in order to survive, fulfill two conditions. First, there must be, from time to time some outstanding instance of it, in real life. Second, it must in some way exonerate the person using it from responsibility. The "architects are extravagant" myth is kept alive by such reminders as the following letter from Stanford White to Col. Oliver H. Payne about decorating the house of Payne Whitney (the Colonel's nephew).

> "I know" he wrote, "that all kinds of small extras have crept in and that the changes I made in the treatment of the smaller rooms have added over a hundred thousand dollars to the price of the house, and I have dreaded to speak to you about it until the house was far enough finished for you to see the result, as, although I feared that you would be angry at first, I thought if you saw the money had been wisely spent and that I have given Payne and Helen a house to live in which was really of the first water and could stand in beauty with any house in the world, that you would forgive me and I believed in my heart that you would in the end approve of what I had done, but

your saying to me yesterday that you could not see where the money has gone has taken all the sand out of me and made me very unhappy, for I know from the character of the work and in comparison with other houses that it is not extravagant. However, I must not say more until you receive and go over the accounts tomorrow, but I am sure you will not find it as bad as you think."

Extravagance of this sort is unquestionably rather rare. But to the public it probably appears to be quite usual. Such examples as that quoted by Mr. Andrews are so spectacular as to be very engaging and worthy of repetition. There are other reasons for the myth's perpetuation. Building costs have a habit of increasing rapidly in short periods of time compared to the length of time it takes to build a house. This situation produces stories of overruns which are actually caused by incompetence or by "acts of God," or both, rather than by "artistic" extravagance.

The uses of the myth are very real. The client who wants the luxury of fine architecture but is unwilling to face the fact that he must pay for what he wants can absolve himself of responsibility by blaming the architect for "unwarranted" extravagance. Unwarranted in this case is defined by the client as "implicitly but not explicitly ordered." It sometimes happens that the architect who fails to be extravagant arouses his client's wrath in that the latter must take full responsibility for an expenditure.

A natural extension of the myth—to the effect that architects are lackeys of the rich—also contains a modicum of truth. Building statistics indicate that while most structures of any size, cost, or pretension are architect-designed, the vast majority of small jobs are not. The architect depends largely on wealthy clients for his livelihood. Houses done for the middle income groups almost invariably involve a loss and must be subsidized by the architect's more affluent clients. The same situation is prevalent in medicine and even to some extent in the law. But there are far more poor men's lawyers and doctors than there are poor men's architects.

The client who wants the extra values an architect can provide but who, for various reasons, does not wish to pay for them is quite naturally apt to be cantankerous. The more ingenious usually pose this question: "Joe Doaks, the speculative builder, can sell me a house my size for twenty per cent less than the cost of your building me one. Of course I couldn't live in his house. It's badly planned and I don't like the location. But why can't you build me a house for the same amount of money? Just putting the rooms in the proper order shouldn't cost me twenty per cent, and anyway you're supposed to be a smart architect, and I don't see why you can't save money by using better techniques than Joe Doaks." The question actually involves two elements. The first is fairly easy to scotch. One has only to point out that the speculative builder puts up many houses at once, on cheap land, usually of poor design, sometimes with poor materials and techniques, and also that he is in continuous business and can buy when things are cheap. The custom house, on the other hand, must be built when, where, and how the client wants it. It is a single operation, well planned, of good materials, supervised by the architect, etc., etc. There is obviously no comparison between the two. The second, "better techniques," part of the question is based on the belief that there are marvellous new methods and materials available which are just about to cut building costs appreciably. This notion involves a childlike faith in the ability of the architect to produce technical miracles. But it's parentage is advertising. It acquired new impetus during World War II, when the government allowed producers a certain amount of tax-free space in consumers' media. As the companies involved had nothing to sell, they used it to paint rosy pictures of the benefits science would bring to the post-war world, such as radar ranges and cheap aluminum houses. The dream is most real to those ignorant of the archaic, handicraft, trade union, character of the building business. The client who says "Can't you use the newest and most up-to-date materials; I don't care how they look as long as I get the area I want and as long as they are as good or better than wood, stone, and brick," throws down a challenge the building industry, let alone the architect, is not strong enough to accept.

Another type of client reaction to the "architects are extravagant lackeys of the rich" myth is to maintain the true size of the budget a secret. One such case, told by a New York architect, had to do with a very rich man and a very large house. The client specified a budget and left for Europe. When he had returned and moved in, his architect called on him to find out how he liked the house. The client was disappointed. Why? Because the house was "cheap." The architect explained that no greater luxury could have been achieved within the budget. The client then broke down and told him that he had heard that architects always spent much more than they were asked to and that with this in mind he actually had available some sixty per cent more than his specified budget, which he had expected to spend, and for which he had expected to receive a much more luxurious house.

Reactions such as these are of course extreme in that they involve an inability on the part of the client either to face facts or to trust his architect. Where, and this is the more usual case, no such difficulties exist, the rational view of the benefits of fine architecture are perhaps as follows:

1. The materials and methods of assembly used in the house will be superior. This is a very concrete benefit, worth money in the pocket.
2. The plan of the house will facilitate the everyday drudgery of housework and child care and provide for privacy and communication, both spacially and structurally. Because we *can* live in a cave, this verges on an imponderable value.
3. The house, over and above its practical utility, will be a work of art and as such will inform and respond to the life in it. This is an entirely imponderable value.

It would be fruitless to claim that fine architecture costs nothing. It need not cost much. It can cost a great deal. Certainly it costs something. The real question comes down to this: "Are the imponderables worth money out of pocket?" The client must give an unqualified *yes* answer to this question if he is to be happy with the fine architect. If his answer is hedged, he then can seek someone on a level in the hierarchy corresponding to his own. If his answer is "no," the speculative builder is the sensible solution to his housing problems.

Clients, "Ideal" and Otherwise

"What of architectural beauty I now see, I know has gradually grown from within outward, out of the necessities and character of the indweller, who is the only builder—out of some unconscious truthfulness, and nobleness, without ever a thought for the appearance; and whatever additional beauty of this kind is destined to be produced will be preceded by a like unconscious beauty of life."—Thoreau

The existence of a hierarchy among architects implies that clients come similarly assorted. Theoretically at least, the five types of adjustment cut across both architects and public. The business of selecting an architect on the one hand and of "promoting" clients on the other is almost sure to take place within a given horizontal slice of society. By the same token unhappy experiences are probably caused as often as not by the accidental matching of an architect and a client who do not share similar goals.

To place an architect on one or another level is not too difficult. His reputation for integrity and sincerity, his design ability, and above all, his work, are comparable factors. The canons of taste used in the classificatory process are set by magazines, museums, and critics. While these canons are inevitably vague and subject to much question, they do create a kind of yardstick. The client on the other hand is subject to no such easy pigeonholing. His taste, ability to cooperate, creativity, volubility, and accuracy of judgment all have the most profound effect on the house. But how to measure these qualities? Eventually perhaps the social-psychologist will be able to provide typologies for clients of various sorts. Today the finest distinction made is simply "good" or "bad."

Rosow, in his study of modern houses in Detroit, distinguished two types of houses and two types of clients. One sort of client (Group A) had built semi-modern houses which were compromises in every sense and which showed little understanding of the goals of contemporary architecture. The other sort (Group B) had built successful modern houses. They are described as follows:

Group A (Semi-Modern) consisted mainly of business men with a mean high school education and a largely nouveau riche orientation: status striving, "sophistication" aspirations, prestige organizational affiliations, leisure-time stereotypes of sedentary home life and commercial recreation activities. Personal participation interests were unintensive and narrowly defined beyond immediate social interests. Life goals approximated middle-class social mobility aspirations and prestige identification.

"Group B (Modern) consisted primarily of professional people with a mean college education, diversified interest areas (including intellectual-esthetic fields), group associations of personalized interests, patterns of high creativity in participation activities. They had strong 'self-expression' and personal response goals. Life aspirations approximated 'self realization' and personal satisfaction aims in individuality rather than socially defined terms."

It is obvious from this that excessive concern with status makes for a poor client. There are few exceptions to this rule. On the other hand, as every architect knows, his most fascinating and perceptive clients are often those in transition from group to group. Such families are difficult to deal with only when they are socially uneasy. In order to make sure they are conforming properly, they tend to exaggerate certain characteristics of their new class. If they are entering the middle-middle class, they may be excruciatingly neat, clean. sound, and expensive. If it is the upper-middle class, they may be tiresomely messy and intellectual. Usually there are physical symbols as well—in the first case, a cut glass chandelier or a pine-panelled den; in the second, a display of books or a certain kind of fireplace. But it is also true that they sometimes create, out of new and old patterns combined, a fresh and valuable approach to the living activities.

Social stability would seem on the whole to be a better recommendation than its counterpart. While it may in some cases tend to make people want exactly what their parents had, it is more likely, particularly when combined with education, to have a freeing effect. The stable person does not need to prove to anyone that he either is going places or has arrived. He takes his place more or less for granted, and is thus under very little obligation to see that his house expresses anything but himself. The average modern client is well enough stabilized so that his energies can be utilized in creative ways rather than in the search for prestige, security, and personal aggrandizement.

From the architect's point of view one of the factors which seems to inhibit some of the more secure and better educated clients is their lack of "good taste." By the same token, some less secure and less well educated clients seem to be naturally gifted with that quality. But taste is an acquired characteristic, not come by easily. Furthermore, good taste is not confined to one segment of the art of our time. To pick contemporary architecture out of the welter of "available" styles requires much more than taste. It presupposes an understanding of the goals of the new architecture and an ability to deviate from the conventional norm, in short—the ability to make up one's own mind on the basis of one's own judgments. Thus the architect's best clients are apt to be rugged individualists. Many of his problems arise from their independent drives and self-reliant qualities.

A better view of the client can be obtained in terms of goals. His motives for building, stripped of make believe, have profound effects on the house. They determine the types of pressures, monetary and personal, which he will exert on the architect. They can be directly translated into expression, i.e., the story told (inadvertently or through artistry) by the house. What are clients' goals? The Detroit clients' motives for building, and their rank order as reported by Rosow were as follows:

> "The most significant ownership goals were *emotional* (psychic, family, and ego) which included almost one-half the replies. *Status-prestige* aims and desired *living facilities* ranked next in importance. *Financial* considerations appear less significant than commonly supposed (although it is usually a strong motive when it does arise). Several family and financial reasons emerged partially as rationalizations of prestige motives."

This order seems highly significant. To suffer psychic, family, or ego frustrations because of a lack of money is one of the most horrible situations the middle class American family can be faced with. In order to avoid bruises in these areas, budget stretching to the very brink of financial insecurity seems worthwhile. Money for itself becomes unimportant. Furthermore, it is generally held that emotional security and prestige are part of the equipment necessary to make money. Thus the rationalization can always be made that the house and the ever-present opportunity, implicit in the American dream, to make money and to rise in status will combine to increase a man's income. Whether or not this is true, it is probably a fundamental reason for the client's tendency to spend more money than common sense indicates. It is thus at the root of many architect-client difficulties.

This problem would not be so hard to resolve if it involved only the two-way split described above. Actually, the average number of motives per client varies from four to five. The secondary motivations vastly complicate the business of reaching a solution to the cost-area-luxury problem. It is sometimes further complicated by unresolved husband-wife disagreements which may range from problems of whether to buy or to build, choice of lot, choice of architect, etc., to fundamental disagreements about the whole character of the house itself.

Money and marital felicity are, of course, everyone's problems. It is the way they are handled which counts. The bad client is unable to resolve them and thus needs ego reinforcement from his house. The good client works in the reverse direction. Rosow describes the ideal modern client as follows:

> "The family is largely of the equalitarian, democratic type with a high degree of family harmony. Authority, responsibility, and prerogatives do not rest upon rigidly formal role relations. The parents recognize the needs and rights of children as individuals and the children are expected to respect those of the adults.
>
> "The unifying characteristics of the typical modern client must be borne in mind if he is to be understood. The modern

client is vital, physically active and energetic, mentally alert and curious, sensitive to the world he lives in. He is intelligent and rather intellectual. He has a broad range of intensively developed personal interests. He places a strong value upon the individual, the development of his interests and capacities, the growth, the expression and the realization of his ability. He is less concerned with middle class social judgments than he is with directing his life pattern toward his personal satisfactions. There is little social pretension. He is easily stimulated by many things and he wants to explore those stimuli. He is not self-sufficient, but he is independent."

The bad client exhibits opposite behavior patterns. He is highly status conscious, has few interests over and above the newspapers and his business. He is authoritrian, his childrens' social and emotional needs are not well taken care of, and his wife's principle preoccupation is housework and "society."

From the architect's point of view an unfortunate element enters in here. The good client whose goals are, in essence, happiness for himself and family, is usually not too concerned with earning power. As a result he is poorer, on the average, than the bad client. The latter's money-status drives, his acceptance of the Horatio Alger American dream, his single-minded concern with business, all pay off in cash if not in a relaxed family atmosphere. This is the lead lining in the silver cloud. It accounts perhaps for the house architect's concern with his smallest jobs and for his not infrequent and very irrational desire to subsidize

William Juhre: "The Orbits."

his poorer clients.

To place the good client in the lower income, better educated, more liberal segment of the middle or upper middle class does not, of course, imply that all members of this group are easy to get along with. One might, on the contrary, hazard the guess that if people, regardless of socio-economic class, contain the same modicum of original sin, then the upper middle class, because of their stability and creativity, can express and project this sin with extra thoroughness and fervor. Every practitioner with experience recognizes certain types known as "architect killers." But they come in such assorted sizes and at times so well disguised that he can not be sure of spotting them before they have commenced their dire work.

The most common type is the non-building client. The best of these comes into his architect's office, year after year, has plans made, pays for them, and then year after year, for more or less plausible reasons, decides not to build. This paying non-building client is apt to be pleasant, reasonable, and a great help with the overhead. He is usually a person who enjoys a good deal of leisure. The fault he is most apt to have is simply that he talks too much.

The bad non-builder on the other hand is apt to be the dynamic business man, with many deals on the string, demanding, pretentious, and suspicious. He arrives in the office with a set of fixed misconceptions and exhibits a kind of genius in his ability not to hear any contrary evidence. As time goes on, an increasing number of "misunderstandings" occur. The architect has not followed

his orders, has not told him of this, has not warned him of that. As he begins to realize that the client is impossible to communicate with verbally, the architect begins to lean on the "legal technique." He confirms conversations by letter and insists that plans be signed. This is quite useless however. When such written evidence is referred to, the client claims that it was not a proper interpretation of the actual fact, or that other circumstances not mentioned alter its whole complexion, or that he had not been informed of some corollary fact which negates the whole thing. At some point prior to construction the client often breaks off the relationship. He goes to another architect or buys a house. At the same time he either demands that the architect's bill be cut in half because, as he is not building, the drawings are of no use to him, or else he refuses to pay at all because the architect is incompetent and untrustworthy. His file sometimes ends up in a lawyer's office, and after a lot of palaver he usually pays, though sometimes not in full, the effort required for full payment being incommensurate with the amount owed. He may go through the same process with several architects. If he is an old hand at the game, he considers himself a sort of expert on their ways, which he professes to scorn and despise.

This sort of client arouses the architect's most extreme wrath. The indecisive type of architect killer, on the other hand, wrings his heart with pity. The indecisive killers are often attractive, sensitive, intuitive, and thoughtful of others. Their only difficulty is that it is impossible for them to make up their minds. They agonize for years over the build-or-buy problem and then over which neighborhood, street, and lot would be best for them. They bog down completely on preliminary sketches, demanding as many as twenty, each of which is discussed and compared ad nauseum. If this sort of client is a woman, she may cry over the architect's drafting board because she is being such a nuisance, doing great water damage to any originals which may be under her at the time. She is apt to decide that there is some subtle current of understanding missing in her relationship with the architect. She then goes off to another with, of course, many tearful backward glances.

Because such clients are born suckers, they sometimes get

outrageously gyped. Whether they are gyped or not, they usually come back to their first love, who, if he is smart, persuades them to design the house themselves, with the help of a nice contractor or a nice draftsman or a nice architectural student. A minority of such clients exhibit very alarming post-building behavior. One variety turns on his architect like a tiger at the end of the weaning period and for years thereafter never fails to tell every visitor to the house that the architect is a sinister and incompetent character. The verbal lashing is sometimes accompanied by a conducted tour so that the visitor may view the horrors for himself. This sort of client sometimes remodels every few years or in extreme cases tears the house apart bit by bit, all under the heading of improving it. In a relatively short time it begins to leak, squeak, and droop in a hundred places.

The largest group of architect killers are the practical people. They want to get more house for their money than anyone ever did before. They believe themselves competent to perform both the architect's and contractor's jobs. They are usually ingenious and hard working. They are gadgeteers and are often semi-modern in taste. Occupationally, they occur with greatest frequency in engineering and the physical sciences, in the more tangibly oriented branches. Some of them drift in and out of architects' offices, usually seeking some bit of advice rather than plans, specifications, and contracts. When they come in for the full treatment, they do so unwillingly and with little grace. They make it a point to let the architect know his place. The building industry, they say, is a farce and a thousand years behind the times. Good design is fancy pants. Architects are incompetents, dreamers, illiterates, etc., etc., etc. Such clients are great checkers of dimensions and specifications, while their wives "check it for beauty." If they irritate the architect, they enrage his draftsmen and specification writers, and the contractor needs a rest cure before he is finished with the last detail.

Fortunately most of this sort do not engage architects. They draw plans themselves, or seek out a poor architectural student, or buy plans from a lumber company or mail order house, or build a house exactly like the Jones's with a few "individualistic" changes, or try to have their program given the students at the local architectural school. Or they try to persuade some architect to give them a sketch, or to help them with their sketch, or to draw up their sketch. They may also get the house started through the use of employees or of materials available at their business. Still others are great shoppers for second-hand bargains. The bargain may be a whole house to be moved and remodelled or a barn to be torn down for its lumber. The distinguishing feature of such deals is their technical and operational complexity. The extreme type would rather engineer something complicated than save money. He will pride himself if, after spending a year or more of his own time, the deal turns out to cost only slightly more than a new house. The following quotation, from a circular received in the mail, illustrates the type of operation:

> "In the recent restoration and reconstruction of an 18th Century house in . . . for my own use it became necessary to acquire and disassemble another 18th Century house in . . . , as well as other similar materials of a slightly later date . . . (from another state). Consequently, I now have on hand for disposal a considerable quantity of scarce old oak beams, a few pine ones, original panelling, and more than 25,000 antique chimney bricks, all of which I am ready to sell for a fair price, as a whole or in part.
>
> "A summary of the beams and boards at . . . will be of interest! . . ."

This sort of client has, in addition to his delight in the process, a strong element of connoisseurship of the antiquarian variety. There are, of course, also connoisseurs, or Friends of Modernism, who make, at their best, the most vital clients. At their worst they are sometimes known to the trade as "commonsewers." Whereas the Friend (to keep the distinction) enjoys the evolving architectural scene and takes great interest in relating it, after the fact, to its corollary cultural phenomenon, the commonsewer thinks of himself as a commander directing the course of Modernism. He knows that one of its some twelve directions is "the true one." He also has all of the architects of his knowledge taped, usually in three categories—for example, "designers, practical, and screwball." In choosing an architect he wants someone who combines all three qualities and keeps urging him on in all three directions at once.

The types just described are extremes, the shooting stars in the firmament of bad clients. They cause a good deal of anguish but are fortunately few and far between. The most common type exhibits none of these bad qualities. He makes but one demand. "Traditional outside. Modern inside." If the architect goes into a state of shock, he may compromise to the extent of "Traditional front, Modern behind." The unfortunate connotations of this desire worry him not at all. Perhaps because the architect conceives him to be suffering in his conflict, such a client usually arouses the architect's reformist zeal. They seem to cry aloud for free education in the folklore of modernism. To let him go his blind way, thinks the architect, is a sin, and that is where the client's troubles and the architect's education begin.

Aline Louchheim has dramatized this moment as follows:

> " 'We don't really want a modern house,' such a cornered potential client as Sally Sherman says. 'That is, we like lots of sunshine and windows and air and gadgets and conveniences, but modern is so stark and ugly. A friend of ours has a house that looks just like a chicken-coop . . .
>
> " 'We want a functional house that doesn't look functional,' her husband explains bluntly.
>
> " 'We want charm . . . a gracious home,' his wife picks up.
>
> " 'I know exactly what you mean,' John Miller interrupts, recognizing Hurdle No. 1. 'You want a pitched roof, not a flat one, and white shingles and something that will harmonize with the countryside. Well, why shouldn't you have it? Modern architecture,'—he slows up slightly, preparing for the cliché explanation which is the modern architect's first defense—'has the advantage of suiting your individual needs, building from the inside out. Let's plan for you and let the roof take care of itself.' "

The Shopping Client

"Often we are forced to deal with a tribe of medical shoppers who are not only looking for bargains but who prefer shoddy to real goods. That is where the quack steps in and the charlatan, with their false claims and high-pressure salesmanship. For each quack there are many suckers who are driven by a need and a will to believe."—Binger

The ban on advertising typical of all professions tends to make the architect's house clients come from the circle of his friends. Whether or not he promotes jobs, in a roundabout way, through a consciously developed, extensive, and directed social life, a natural element of selection enters in. The client is more apt than not to share some or many characteristics and attitudes with his architect.

The good client follows a rather standardized shopping procedure. About half go to architects with whom they are personally acquainted. Half of these have inspected some of his work in order to assure themselves that they like his personal idiom. Another third go as a result of his being recommended by a friend. Like the first group, half of these will also inspect his work before or after seeing him. The smallest proportion, about a sixth, will go to an architect of reputation. The significant aspect of the good client is that from the very beginning he is apt to look on the relationship as being one which might best develop on a friendly and informal plane. The less personal the method of choosing an architect, the less good the client is apt to be. The doubtful client is apt to go to an architect recommended by a friend, seldom inspects a job beforehand, very seldom knows the architect, and never goes to an architect of reputation. The way in which clients arrive suggests of itself some characteristics of the good client. He must be fairly gregarious in that he is apt to know one or several architects of high caliber. He must be of the thorough type as well as vitally interested in this new experience in order, as he does in many cases, to inspect several houses by several architects before making up his mind.

The Shopping Client

The client who has inspected an architect's work and has sold himself on it, or has been sold by a former client, presents no problem. He likes the architect's idiom and is willing or anxious to have more of the same. Not all clients come thus blessedly equipped. There seem to be four general types of initial reaction:

1. Enthusiasm for the architect's work in general or for the architect as a person with complete trust in the outcome.
2. Appreciation of one or several architects' work, but an inability to find any one job with which they can identify themselves, resulting in a lack of certainty that their ideas can be properly materialized.
3. Identification with one job which they want repeated "with a few changes" to make it suitable for their needs. At their worst, these clients appear with a plan clipped from a magazine which they want adapted, without change, to their needs and site.
4. General distrust and fear of the architect and of the whole process of building.

This last reaction is not, evidently, confined to architects. Dr. Binger in *The Doctor's Job* admonishes a hypothetical patient

> ". . . if you doubt the honesty of all doctors then you had better try to find out why. But if you go to another doctor to find out why, you will probably end up by questioning his honesty too."

It is best, perhaps, to turn such clients away. When they are attractive, in spite of their distrust, one might well quote them Dr. Binger's advice for choosing one's doctor.

> "Pick a man who is well trained and whom you trust. Then trust him. Don't shop around and bootleg and play fast and loose and expect miracles. All you will get is bills. If you proceed on the principle of ten cooks are better than one you will only spoil the broth of your remaining years."

The doubts of the client in the second and in the third categories have to do with expression. The client believes his wants to be personal and unique. At the same time, he may wish to see a house reflecting these wants before he can be convinced that any one architect is his man. The architect who has built a variety of different kinds of houses for a variety of different kinds of people, may still be unable to convince him that, since he has expressed personal wishes before, he can do it again. To be completely happy, the client needs a sense of identification with his architect's work or with some particular job. The personal-subjective nature of this need for identification may account for the lack of tact, sometimes approaching brutality, that architects frequently encounter in new clients. Were they buying a picture from a painter, they might indicate greater or less liking, but they would be apt to refrain from outright criticism. It is not at all uncommon, however, for architects to have their work described to them as a "chicken coop," or as a "shack," or as "no better than a back house." In such a case the client is saying in effect that the job does not correspond to the image he has of a proper symbol for himself and his family. He is not looking on it as architecture, designed for someone else. He views it solely as a "home"—for himself. He is blind both to its intrinsic merit and to its relationship to the client's needs and desires. The distinction between personal-subjective judgment and judgment based on the reality of what he sees can sometimes be pointed out with beneficial results. When clients are able to understand it, forms which they had liked on the basis of emulation may suddenly be seen by them in a truer perspective.

Because the forms used in any given house largely grow out of the functional needs of the client, this understanding is of vital importance. Once the process is appreciated, the client's real decision is whether he likes an architect's expressive mode. It is, perhaps, impossible or even undesirable to "sell" a resistant client on a personal mode—undesirable because he is likely to become unsold during the long gestatory process. But in the case of doubtful clients the rational element in an esthetic is "salable" through understanding of its motives and its relationship to function and structure. Such are the hazards of building that the architect usually has to continue to convince his client throughout the whole process.

But first of all he must create a climate conducive to the discovery of his client's needs, to good design, and to efficiency of operation. This climate must be established with the utmost speed. One must try to persuade a new client to like one's work and to trust one's abilities, must talk fee and contract with him, must disillusion him as to building costs, must get a sense of what he wants and of how he should be handled—all in the preliminary conversation. The way various architects go about solving these problems seems to vary tremendously. Not a few, consciously or unconsciously, make personal friends of their clients. This may involve endless and difficult discussions in which all of the building conflicts and often others, more basic to the client's personality, are aired. Other architects limit the depth of such friendships, largely through an innate ability to take and keep the center of the floor. Another type limits his clients to a friendly, businesslike relationship. Because personality and prestige have so much to do with such dealings, no single basic description seems possible. But the architect's effectiveness both in discovering and in resolving his client's house problem must depend in part on the inwardness of their relationship, whether this is reached in business surroundings or not. This inwardness cannot be achieved without frustrations on both sides. It is bound to invoke love and hate. No matter how reasonable it may appear on the surface, it is essentially irrational. It is this factor, perhaps, which makes the personal relationships in house design so difficult. The architect must be lucky enough to enjoy either iron emotions or a well-perfected technique of emotional preservation. His aim must be empathy, or a feeling into his client's life, rather than sympathy, or a feeling with him. This is most true for the less rich client, who needs much more than he can afford. The architect, as a matter of sheer self survival, must look on him from a somewhat Olympian height.

The great majority of people live with a very unrealistic idea as to how much house they can get for their budget. Their ideas as to what they can afford are always on the grandiose side. The cost situation in building is constantly in flux, usually moving

Claude.

in an upward direction. Because the client is not in constant touch with costs, his data are likely to be out of date. Prices have always gone up since his last bit of information. His notions of costs are often based on the prices of speculative houses. Finally, he has been, for years, in the grip of a dream and has gradually winnowed out those starkly real considerations which would have made it not a dream but a discipline. It is this dream of a house with the latest equipment, very large and spacious, dignified, cottagy, or whatever, which the architect finds—humanly—so difficult to destroy. In fact, it would seem likely that a large proportion of the accusations leveled at architects are the result either of failure to make the dream a reality or of casting it out too brusquely.

Reproduced by permission. Copy. 1947 The New Yorker Magazine, Inc.

The client is about to pay the largest bill of his life—for the most obvious symbol of social class. He must, he absolutely and positively must, wring out the very last ounce of house for his money. The two most common reactions to this unpleasant squeeze play are to try to save money inconspicuously or to chisel. The person able to resolve the problem with dignity and economy of emotion is a supreme client. To be very rich as well helps enormously. Such people, whether they are rich or poor, are a delight to design for and pose the architect no disagreeable problems. Not so the chiseler.

The degree to which a client will go to get a Cadillac for the price of a Ford usually becomes apparent early in the preliminary conversations. The characteristic sign of the chiseler is his habit of directly equating house with dollars to the exclusion of all other values. Thus it does not matter how rich he is. Getting things cheaper even if poorer is a way of life with him. The question is not how to recognize him, for he is easily discovered. He will usually open the second conversation with some such remark as, "Come on, now, how about giving me a twenty per cent cut in your fee, to give me an incentive to get started with the house," or "How about giving me a break. I have lots of friends, rich friends too, who want to build, and if the house turns out well, I could send a lot of business your way." These are his heralds. The difficult part is the summoning of enough strength of mind to turn him down. When he is taken on, the architect must expect multiple troubles. And, in their turn, the contractor and even the workmen on the job will be badgered out of their wits. It is not uncommon, for the workmen at least, to retaliate against such types, with the most dire results for the architect. The irate masons who built one of America's most beautiful houses revenged themselves on its owner by constructing a brick shelf closing three quarters of the living-room fireplace flue, located so as to be nearly undetectable and so as to permit some smoke to escape, but in such a way as to cause the fireplace itself to smoke hopelessly.

The client who simply wishes to save money inconspicuously almost invariably appears with a predictable list of devices. He will get his stove and refrigerator wholesale. Or he will buy Sears, Roebuck plumbing fixtures. Or he will do all the painting himself. Or he will suggest that the architect go out and find second-hand doors. Or, he has a relative in the plywood or lumber or lighting business and can get such materials wholesale. He then sits back with a delighted gleam on his face, waiting for the architect to say, "Oh, in *that* case we can add at least another two rooms to the house!" This is when his second and final disillusion as to building costs occurs. The first is when he finds he cannot get his ideal house for his ideal budget. The second is when he finds there is nothing much he can do about it but cut the house or increase the budget. In such cases, for example, where the client has some second-hand lumber only fifty miles away—"All you have to do is get it and take out the nails"—to explain that this will cost more than the normal way of doing things is like turning the knife in the wound. When the crisis has been passed successfully, that is, when the client has not marched out of the office to find a "cheaper" architect, the real problem still remains to be solved. The client must be acquainted with the amount of area he can purchase for his budget, within some understood framework of luxury or economy.

These body blows perforce leveled at prospective clients usually come at the same time that the most delicate of subjects is also being discussed, namely the architect's fee. The fact that they come together is unfortunate. The client feels he is under financial pressure from all sides. He often cannot see why architects' fees are so high. He has been brought up in a culture in which it seems proper and fundamental that artists should live in garrets and that architects should "make blue prints" (what a blue printer does in this scheme is a mystery). When he comes face to face with the twelve per cent fee which most good architects have to charge, it is small wonder he is shocked. The architect must get his client over this painful emotional-financial hump without losing him. He must justify the months of work which go into a good house against a background of disbelief on the part of banks, the Federal Housing Administration, and the general public. He may, himself, feel guilty about the size of his bill. This is mitigated by his knowledge that it is all too easy to lose money on even the largest house. Nevertheless, he is tempted, when faced with a fixed budget, and a wonderful client, to cut his fee and put the difference into the job. He must often fight for his pocket book against his own deepest desires.

Curiously enough, the contract problem is sometimes more difficult than the percentage of the fee. Many people are by nature contract shy. They are convinced that all legal documents are a snare and a delusion and that they are written for the sole benefit of their authors. They hold that A.I.A. forms A-102 and B-102 are no exception. Because it is the first document they must sign, it symbolizes their involvement in the whole terrifying process. "Now," they say, "I'm in for it." The feeling in signing is that they have gotten themselves into some very deep water. Conversely, by putting it off, by bargaining, and by insisting on revisions in wording they hope not only to delay the fateful hour but incidentally to save some money and some face. They will at least beard this great behemoth of a building industry, if they can not subjugate it.

It is the opinion of most architects and lawyers that a contract per se is not of much value. Nevertheless, some architects insist that one be signed. The process separates the sheep from the goats. It proves that the client really means business. But in the case of clients who grow genuinely hysterical at the idea of signing something, an appropriate letter of intent is, legally, just as binding and not half as scaring.

Forms A-102 and B-102 do not mention time, but the average client need not be probed on this subject. One of his first questions is, "How long will it be before we move in?" Few clients fail to be shocked by the answer. Most underestimate the time it takes to construct a house. Most have entirely left out of their calculations the fact that the architect also needs time. When they learn that they cannot hurry the building process without undue expense, they start to hurry the architect. Thus another of the architect's initial problems is to dissuade the client from hurrying the design. This is often difficult. The client is panting in anticipation. He must move out of his present house, or go to Europe, or must do any one of a hundred other things which indicate the desirability of great speed. The trouble is that great speed and great architecture are apt to be incompatible.

The architect who promises speed has, usually, no way of assuring himself that he can perform. Unless he already knows his client very well, he has no idea how long it will take to sign a contract, jell the program, and approve sketches. These three steps can be completed in a week, but they can also use up six months or a year of shilly-shallying, misunderstandings, new starts, and second thoughts. Even if he is sure that he can bulldoze his client into keeping to a schedule, speed is still to the architect's disadvantage. He cannot be sure that he can bulldoze himself into turing out a good design in a hurry, or his office into developing and refining that design according to schedule. Buildings, like large and long-lived animals, require proportionately long periods of maturation. A cat takes nine weeks to be born, a man nine months (even then, he is not legally mature until he is twenty-one years old), and an elephant nine years.

The average client cannot know, unless told, that after the program is complete the architect needs his so-called "inspiration time", which is of variable duration. If he does not allow enough time for the architect to use his conscious and unconscious design ability, he is quite simply not getting his money's worth. The architect who allows himself to be unduly hurried is forfeiting the opportunity to do his best work. This identity of client-architect interest continues through the working drawing period. The pushy client will suggest that this stage, "which is purely mechanical," "just like squeezing toothpaste from a tube," etc., etc., be speeded up by working overtime or by putting more men on the job. But overtime, or more men, or both, not only cost more, they also increase the number of hours involved because of the concommitant decrease in efficiency. Mistakes, omissions, and unthought-out areas are more likely to occur.

The average conscientiously designed and developed house requires about two man months for its working drawings. To this must be added a two weeks' bidding period, plus time for a little haggling with the successful bidder, plus time to sign the contract, plus a few days for the contractor to organize the job and move in. These steps, which take so few actual hours of work, nevertheless usually manage to use up the better part of a calendar month.

It is quite fruitless to suggest to the client that, over and above these two calendar months, he can speed up the process by being reasonable and by making decisions fast. He naturally thinks of himself as reasonable and decisive and will promise anything when it is put on this basis. The fact is that he would be highly unreasonable if he hurried himself so much that he failed to get what he really wanted. Thus when it comes right down to it, he will take the time he needs to assure himself that he has thought out his problem and understood the architect's solution of it, regardless of the schedule. Too much money, too much prestige, too much future living is at stake for him to act—reasonably—in any other way. The architect therefore can only try to persuade him to allow an optimum period of time for his particular job, and to shun minimums like the plague.

CHAPTER VII

Process

From "Anatomy for Interior Designers," by Francis de N. Schroeder.

Programming

AT THIS POINT IN A PERSON'S CAREER as a client one can only view his position with the utmost empathy. He can, without disrespect, be likened to a hooked fish. He has been teased by a fly, personified by the architect, but which is, as Robert Dean has pointed out, really a cultural lure. He has struck. He is now about to be landed. Later, after thrashing around in the boat for a time, he will escape into his own element again, wiser for the experience but nevertheless bearing a scar. Thus in the end he, in effect, wins. And as no one really loses, the story is a comedy rather than the tragedy it appears to be during the act in which the hooked fish is still in the water.

The client at this point has indicated by his actions that he is at least willing to talk about his future living patterns as they are affected by physical environment. The architect becomes his counselor. Riesman has noted:

"This function is . . . evident in the work of the domestic architect for the upper middle class client. True, like the decorator, he still counsels his clients in providing the correct public facade, and his current lesson of conspicuous retreat from display may for many be only a change in style of display and not necessarily a decline of architectural or decorative exhibitionism. But a generation ago he would not have dreamed of counselling his clients about the functional interior relationships in the dwelling in terms of anything more avocational than 'gracious living.' Today, however, the architect, by interior and exterior planning, can lead as well as follow the play patterns of his clients. Through him and his views there filters a variety of tastes, inclinations, social schemes (as in easily rearranged living rooms), leisure-time ecologies that scarcely existed a generation ago. The architect—and, beyond him, the city planner—brings together play opportunities that might otherwise remain subdivided among a score of specialists.

"We all know how little use Americans have made in the past of the architectural avocational counselor in disguise, how they have fled into some historically standardized solution from the autonomous possibilities of designing a house to fit their individual needs. Increasingly, however, many Americans seem to feel they must build "modern" houses, without knowing whether they really like them, because it would be stuffy and reactionary to do otherwise; in other words, out of the same kind of compulsive liberation that drives many people to other guilty choices in friends and consumption goods. Nevertheless, with the architects' encouragement and help, it is possible that people are becoming willing to have a house fit them. This requires that they find out who they are."

To find out who one is strongly suggests the need to destroy conditioned attitudes, as a first step, in order to get at a genuine and creative nexus. In the average client's case the artificial overlays are developed and kept alive by the "Dream Magazines."

Programming

House clients usually appear in the architect's office only after years of thinking about building. During this time they have usually subscribed to a "Dream Magazine," have usually read a book of the "How To Do It" variety, and have collected a file or scrapbook of pictures and plans. One recent "Design Your Own Home" book even had large envelopes bound in at the end of each chapter in which to file these "ideas." The magazines from which the client's clippings come are one indication of his general approach to architecture. Warner and Lunt discovered that certain magazines were more popular with one socio-economic group than with others. Figures for the four house-home magazines on their list were as follows:

THE DISTRIBUTION OF THE PURCHASERS OF EACH MAGAZINE IN THE SIX CLASSES; THE PER CENT OF THE PURCHASERS IN EACH CLASS BY MAGAZINE (TOP, BOLD FACE); AND THE PER CENT OF THE TOTAL BY MAGAZINE (BOTTOM, ITALICS).

	UU	LU	UM	LM	UL	LL	TOTAL
5 Better Homes and Gardens	**0.56** *0.77*	**3.89** *4.46*	**32.78** *7.09*	**42.22** *7.38*	**14.44** *4.82*	**6.11** *5.19*	*6.21*
23 American Home	**3.03** *0.77*	**21.21** *4.46*	**36.36** *1.44*	**33.33** *1.07*	**6.06** *0.37*	**0**	*1.14*
26 House Beautiful	**8.70** *1.55*	**17.39** *2.55*	**52.17** *1.44*	**17.39** *0.39*	**4.35** *0.19*	**0**	*0.79*
62 Arts and Decoration			**100.0** *0.12*				*0.03*

The more a magazine is oriented towards lower middle class patterns of thinking, the less apt it is to offer any material which might explain the architect-client relationship. Clients who have been exposed to only such magazines are apt to come in with a plan to be "adapted." The whole tone of the material they have been studying glorifies the juggling of existing conditions, style as a commodity, and "do-it-yourselfism." This is the antithesis

to the creative approach to design. At the present time none of the dream magazines provides the prospective home owner with much of a clue to the connections between living and style. The editors themselves are usually only dimly aware of the issues involved. Furthermore their purpose is not to prepare people to build. It is to sell magazines. The eye catching house and the pretty picture are the first requisites. The reader must be shocked month and after month, into feeling *"I want this."*

Haddon Hall: A real dream castle. The photograph is copyright by Country Life.

Each issue must have a more perfect, more unusual, more striking house. Because the magazines' medium is photography, it is the photogenic house which is first in demand. Just as a beautiful actress who does not photograph well has no place in the movies, a beautiful house which does not photograph well has no place in the dream magazines. Unfortunately the subtler, more refined, more expressive face often fails to photograph, and the same is true of houses. Photogenic houses whether by accident or design

Robert Woods Kennedy: A house as the magazine readers see it.

are not, of course, necessarily thoughtfully planned. And in any case the magazines seldom publish any data which might allow the reader to correlate problem and solution. The "dream" aspect of these magazines absolves them of the responsibility of publishing houses for the economic bracket which includes the majority of their readers. They assume that the reader wishes to see "homes" typical of the socio-economic classes above him, either for emulatory purposes or as material to use in escape dreams. The editor of one such magazine specifically tells the architects he commissions to design a house catering to the readers' desires, rather than to their economic capabilities. Thus any reasonably photogenic house for the upper three per cent in terms of income, will be published. No matter what the cost of the house, competition for the reader's eye puts an ever greater emphasis on com-

The same house as the owners and their friends see it.

pleteness of finish. Each photograph must be perfect in every respect. The house must look as if it received limitless maintenance in the upper-upper class tradition. The more arbitrary, set, and formal it looks, the easier it is to photograph and the more it suggests "high class" to the middle class mind. As none of these qualities is very typical of a house that has a real and full life going on inside it, the magazines must conjure them up. If the furniture, for example, is unsuitable to the picture the magazine wishes to create, the photographer will bring in certain key pieces in the ruling taste to place in the foreground of his shots. Even when the furniture is found suitable, it is still rearranged, often in completely unlivable and inappropriate patterns, for the sake of a striking picture. The magazines give the photographers certain rules. The table must be set in a characteristic way and the beds must be made thus and so. The photographer comes with an assistant and usually takes two days to do a complete job. Most of this time is spent turning curtains inside out, rearranging things on shelves, moving furniture from room to room, cutting branches to spread around as foundation planting or to hold over the camera in order to frame a shot, with the inevitable dusting and sweeping such rearrangements always involve. The sensible family moves out while all this is going on. In a house where child care, music, and books take more of the housewife's time than housework, the photographer's assistant may spruce it up considerably.

With such devices the magazines build up a picture of an architecture which by and large does not exist. The client who arrives steeped in this mythology frequently makes demands which cannot be satisfied within any sensible framework. The glamorous images in their mind's eye obscure the fundamental values they should seek if they are to operate comfortably on a day to day basis. Such is the force of this composite image that even the most sensitive clients are sometimes not immune to its radiance. And, certainly, there are architects who design with photographs as the goal, and who find this technique so successful that no other promotional devices are necessary to them. Thus the problem is to persuade the client involved in the dream magazine myth that beauty and livability are experienced in time and space rather than in pictures. Rosow describes the Detroit Architects' reactions to scrapbooks as follows:

> "Most of the architects found these scrapbooks comparatively useless in specific terms, although occasional items appeared which were found helpful and practical. For the most part, the clippings represented a diversity of unrelated elements, and only a fraction of them at best might be incorporated into any one house, often at an expense prohibitive to the client. Most of these scrapbooks represented impractical pet client notions which architects handled in various ways. Some rather bluntly dismissed or ignored the clippings while others diplomatically tried to recanalize the client attention and thought. Some architects made a 'careful study' of the scrapbooks with the

This picture of an Hungarian thatched farm hut originally appeared in Life. *It formed part of a client's scrapbook with the note pencilled in the margin, "Style of house—combined modern and rustic." This scrapbook also included R. M. Schindler's cabin for Gisela Bennati near Lake Arrowhead, California, which is identical in form—that is, the steep roof pitches form the walls. The client, a painter, also indicated in his written program that he wanted a maximum of wall surface on which to hang pictures!*

client present to establish an ostensibly 'considered' rather than 'arbitrary' basis of judging the ideas. Some architects indulged clients with a permissive technique."

There are of course, exceptions to the generally small value of the scrapbook. Artist clients, in particular, are able to choose pictures which tell a general story rather than suggest a detail. But in the usual case the architect must discover his client's needs in other ways.

Clients arrive varyingly equipped. The amount of preliminary thinking they have done can be classified roughly as follows:

1. Client presents only the names of the rooms he would like and a total cost.
2. Room and cost, plus some ideas as to decoration, or luxury of appearance, or looks (in terms of style).
3. The above, with specific material and equipment in mind or for question.
4. Rooms, cost, decorative scheme, etc., materials, equipment, plus such planning ideas as rooms or zone relationships and a general idea of the atmosphere they wish to achieve.
5. Same as four (4), but with the addition of a house plan of a rudimentary sort, usually lacking stairs, heater room, etc., and unrelated to the site.
6. Same as four (4), but with a floor plan related to site, and with orientation taken into account.

People in the last three categories are ideal clients. The last two differ from the fourth only in the extent to which they have carried their preliminary thinking. Such clients are almost always apologetic about their plans. The myth is that such sketches enrage architects. Certainly they do enrage when the client insists that they be "made into blue prints." But in most cases they should be welcomed by the architect with open arms. They are a symbol of the client's creativeness. They often serve as an excellent straight man to the architect's lead. In this role, the better they are—i.e., the better the client's understanding—the better they serve. And—let no architect claim that they do not—

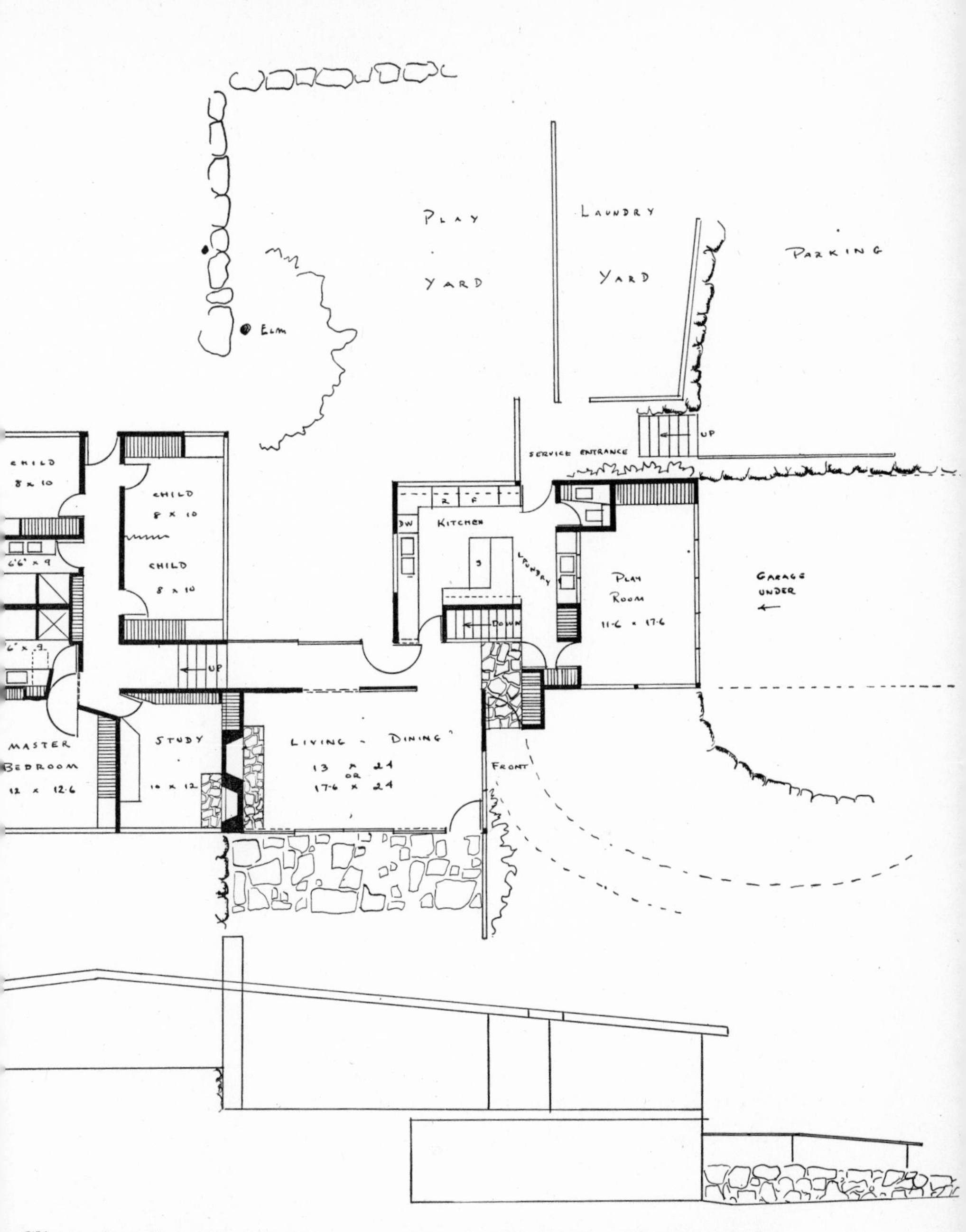

Clients plan: Here is a plan of very unusual merit. The client has taken topography, orientation, circulation, and the heights of rooms into account. Play yard, laundry yard, terrace, driveway, front walk, etc., are all related to the plan in three dimensions. When contrasted with the client's plan on the following page, this one seems of professional competence.

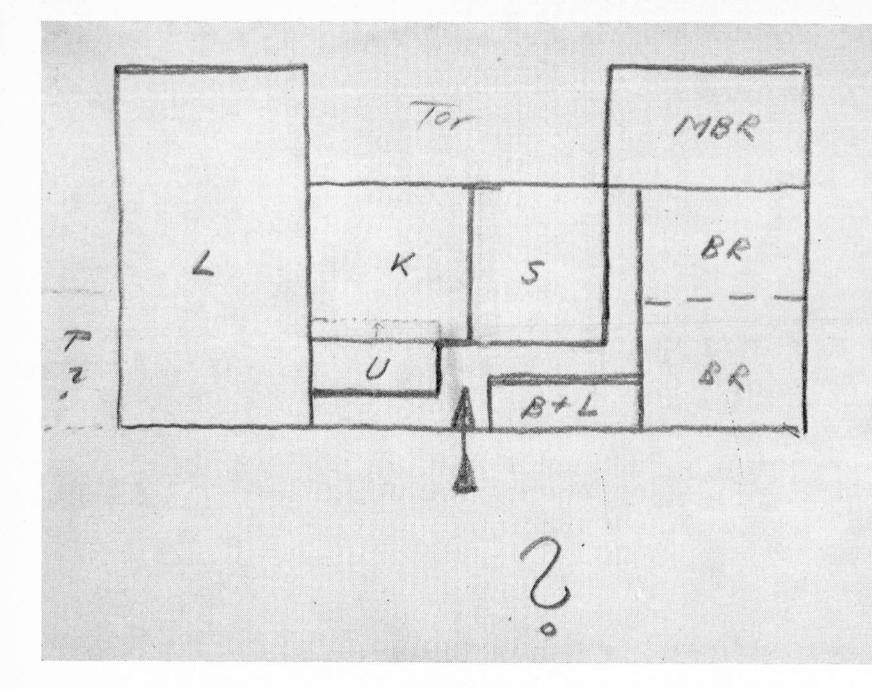

occasionally contain ideas he would like to have thought of himself.

On the other hand the client's plan can never take the place of a written program. The surest way to pin down all of a client's desires and to avoid later misunderstandings is to write up a complete, detailed program, which takes as its scope not only the house and its equipment but the whole site. Very few clients present such a program of their own accord. Its development is necessarily the architect's responsibility. It is usually not as easily come by as might be imagined. Not only does the number of people's individual desires vary from just about none to a complete, if naive, visualization, but their ability to express these desires varies equally drastically. Some clients seem to have a new and brilliant idea each day, two on Sundays. Others are as voluble as fish. Still others refuse to write out their thoughts. But most are grateful that the idea was suggested. To write a program forces careful consideration. In the process, many clients reach conclusions which might not otherwise have materialized until much time and money had been spent on useless sketches, or even on working drawings. Such a program, in full, follows (courtesy of its author and of Mr. E. B. Flowers, Architect):

Certain Specifications for a House

In the first place, as an introduction, I think I ought to say that the relationship of an architect to a client like myself must be something spiked most richly with difficulties! Because not only do I know—far too explicitly—what I want, but the reasons for wanting it seem to me thoroughly valid reasons: rooted in experience. Having lived, since childhood, a nomadic sort of life, I've been able to feel at home in an English cottage and on a desert ranch; in a Bavarian inn and a Canadian cabin; in London flats and New York studios, and a 12th-century castle in Northumberland. I've lived in brick houses and stone houses, plaster ones and wooden; all sizes and shapes, primitive—elegant; beautiful and quite ghastly and altogether humdrum. And if there's one thing I've found it is that one's own *concept of living* can, essentially, go on almost anywhere. It isn't something derived, or created by, a house. Although a house, obviously, can facilitate its expression.

At which point I should like to mention briefly a warning experience in Carmel, California. A house was rented for me there by some friends—a house especially designed, I was told, "for a writer." (I happen to be a writer.) It was smack on the beach; it had a charming patio; there was the inevitable huge window at which (presumably) one sat, inspired, in a fever of creativeness. And from the very first moment I loathed that house! It seemed to me—if I can manage to put it into words—dogmatic, doctrinaire; somehow both naively and arrogantly presumptuous. I felt as if I were living in someone's mentality; or in an objectified theory. "Go on! Write!" everything, at every turn, appeared smartly to dictate. And I couldn't write a word. I couldn't wait to get away. It was, I believe, the only time in my life when I've felt personally antagonized by an arrangement of wood and stone and glass. . . .

And so I know, from experience, that I don't want a house that asserts itself; a domineering house; or an over-artful one, either. I don't want rocks cropping up in the living-room; or self-conscious dramatizations of space; or the introduction of new materials simply because new materials now happen to be available. In brief, I don't want guests, when they have gone away, to say, "We were in such an interesting house last night," but, "Last night we had such an interesting time."

This is not only important; it is absolutely basic. My sense of a home (whether cottage or castle, studio or cabin) has always been a place to which people come, simply and freely, for comfort, for companionship for the sharing of ideas; nearly always it has been a kind of focal point for a diverse group of friends. Therefore, the accent must clearly remain on the quality of living; not the place itself.

And when I come into my house I want to have a sense of really coming *into* it.

This, I realize, is lamentably un-modish! Nevertheless, I want to have a sense of coming *in*, of being *inside*. And for a reason that is quite simple.

This house would be situated in the country; therefore the whole out-of-doors would be everywhere around. I should, as I've always done, spend quantities of time in the open. For I don't happen to be one of those for whom the country is "scenery." (Several contemporary houses I've been in seem to me to be occupied by people who have a quite spurious sense of being associated with "nature" because they live behind glass walls instead of brick or wooden ones!) On the contrary the country for me is something to be experienced actively and intimately: to be tramped across, and climbed, and smelled, and picked, etc., etc. In all kinds of weather. Not something to be stared at safely from an aquarium. And I love, after hours outside, in sun or rain or snow or wind, the sudden and significant contrast of coming into a house: the firelight and books; the gaze that has been widened to all earth and sky now deepened to the immediate, the intimate, the warm interflow of whatever one means by the word "home." I don't want the out-of-doors to intrude upon the in-doors. Any more than I like the in-doors to intrude upon the out-of-doors—as aggressive and elaborate "landscaping" seems to me to do. Each, it seems to me, should supplement, and heighten the values, of the other. So that one opens a door and goes out with a feeling of "Oh!—" and opens a door and comes in with a feeling of "Ah—".

As to rooms:

The main one would be the living-room—large, with three exposures (east, south, and west) because I like the afternoon sunlight, and the room would be much used at tea-time, and oriented towards the fireplace. And when it comes to the fireplace I have certain prejudices! I don't want a great thrust of stone, or anything spectacular. I should like it to be quite plain, with a broad shelf above: its beauty in the rightness of proportions; its drama in the fire itself. An equally dominant feature will be books. There would have to be space for a steadily growing library; this is most important. The fireplace and books would be the heart and substance of the room. . . . And instead of a fashionable flood of light, I'm afraid that I would want long narrow windows, from ceiling to floor—all of which *open.* There would be panels of garden and countryside, and shafts of sunlight, which I happen to love. And the room should open on to some sort of grassy space, or terrace; and, at another point, should have a door into the kitchen. I see this room as having space and dignity and grace and warmth of tone; a sense of rich inwardness, accented by the outside. . . .

The kitchen would also be important. And of all things it must not—should not—be clinical in atmosphere; none of that hospital operating-room look of some modern kitchens. It should face east and south; have one large window among several, intimately related to garden or terrace; should have an air light and gay and sociable and not cleverly contrived—the closer it felt to a farmhouse kitchen translated into contemporary terms the more I should probably like it.

There should of course be a bathroom downstairs; and I think a guest room. And this, the guest room, could have one wall of glass. For, again, a quite simple reason. Guests for the most part would probably come from the city; therefore the contrast, for them, would be between what they have come from and what they have come to—city and country. Therefore, this contrast should be dramatized. Living in the country, as I've already said, seems to me to shift the contrast into outside and inside.

My own room, bedroom and workroom combined, I should like to have upstairs, with, perhaps, a balcony. It, too, should have three exposures. East, south, west. Also, it should have a fireplace; and more bookshelves. And the working corner should be highly private in feeling. (I've always enjoyed working under eaves, for instance!) It should not be decked out with a fine, inspiring view! I've seldom met a non-writer who didn't suppose that writers love to sit looking out grandly upon vistas galore. And I've never met a writer who loved to do any such thing. The assumption that a "view" helps or stimulates this order of creativeness is, I think, grounded in a complete lack of understanding of what the writer is up to. If you're creating a whole inner world in a novel, say—or burning at poem-heat—you are seeing, experiencing, something inwardly that bears no relationship to the immediate scene and is a thousand times more real, for the time being. Therefore a view is either an imposition, or a dead loss. I myself happen to like to be able to look across a room, with a window or windows to be glanced towards, but not stared out of. On the other hand, to go to sleep and wake up with the out-of-doors well at hand is, I think, wholly to be desired; so I'd like my bed bang against glass. . . .

This, I perceive, could go on forever! But there should, I think, be two more rooms; and perhaps an area, looking west, for sunsets—where one could have a big, round table for supper parties in spring and autumn. (Summer one would out of doors; winter by the fire.) No dining room. Breakfasts and lunch in the kitchen.

And quantities of closets. And a garage, rendered miraculously unobtrusive. And perhaps two terraces, or garden spaces—east and south, and south and west—so that there would always be shelter from wind in early and late seasons.

But most of all, over and above everything, a house that doesn't demand to be accepted as a dogmatic entity, or an exercise in theories, apart from the quality of living, the arrangement of values, that it houses.

The value of a program such as this is that it expresses the criteria the design must meet while in no way suggesting a concrete solution. The architect must avoid semi-demi-solutions, dreamed up before all the requirements are in. His aim is first to get all of the data, and only then to let his unconscious go to work on a solution. Pre-determined partial solutions will stick in his mind like glue. Once there, they are almost impossible to get rid of. Incorporated in a scheme but not of it, they may require endless spade work before they can be made to seem integral. Obviously it is as much to the client's interest as to the architect's to start the process off with a bare slate. A client's floor plan does not affect the slate, provided he does not require that it be taken literally. But if he insists on a certain form or set of related forms, all is lost. The design process becomes, instead of a fresh synthesis, a painful accretion of elements around the given factor—a remodeling job rather than a new house.

Preliminary Sketches

"However, if one designs to construct a dwelling-house it behooves him to exercise a little Yankee shrewdness, lest after all he find himself in a workhouse, a labyrinth without a clew, a museum, an almshouse, a prison, or a splendid mausoleum instead. Consider first how slight a shelter is absolutely necessary."—Thoreau

The written program sets the stage for a sketch. There are a good many points of view among architects as to the best method to use at this moment. The requirements of the situation are perhaps as follows. The client wants something which will give him an indication of what he is going to get. The architect wants something which will satisfy his client and which will expose the fundamental principles on which he is working. At the same time details and petty items should not be too apparent. Because the client is inexpert, he is likely to get confused by them and to miss the real point. If his understanding of the basic design is delayed too long and if, when he does understand it, he objects, a great deal of time and money will have been wasted. As all the details of a good house grow out, like branches, from the trunk of its fundamental concept, the client's real need is to understand and accept that. When he does, he will be able to tend and prune it intelligently. When he does not, he may, through ignorance, spoil an increasing amount of fruit as the tree grows. The obscurantist architect forfeits his client's help and deprives him of that joy in creation which is his due.

The average upper middle class client is competent to deal with the fundamentals of planning. Such matters as siting, orientation, circulation, zoning, and furniture arrangement are not mysteries. He is not able to deal with details nor, usually, with esthetics. This latter handicap is more often than not the result of an inability to visualize. Not a few clients seem to go blind when faced with an orthographic projection. Some of these, particularly women, pretend to understand, as if ashamed to admit their inability. Thus, as the drawings and then the house proceed, they are let in for a series of rude shocks. The house does not correspond to the view of it they had in their mind's eye, that view

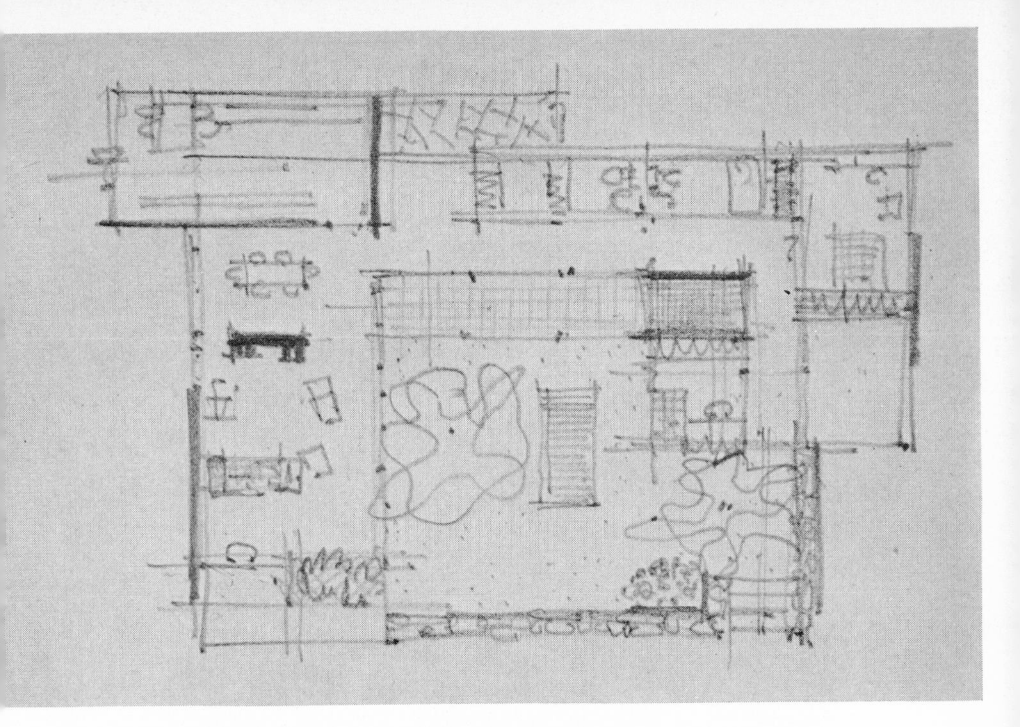

being quite different from what was shown them in the first sketches. If they are strong minded, they may insist on drastic changes. If they are dishonest, they will bitterly accuse the architect of deceiving them. As the number of people with training or with an innate ability to visualize are comparatively few, the architect's first desire is to make sure that his client is seeing the same thing he is.

These are, roughly, the requirements which the preliminary sketch should meet. The sensible architect, even though he is about to show his client a seemingly rough sketch, designs the whole house, down to the last bed table, on the back of an old bill. He then abstracts from this synthesis of all elements only those issues he wants his client to understand first. The architect who does not see the house whole, at the very beginning, is simply designing by accretion. His result is apt to be an undigested assortment of parts. This is not to say that months of study and refinement are unnecessary. But architecture is first and foremost a total synthesis. The only way to achieve this is with a bang. It cannot be built up like a patchwork quilt.

It is this fundamental truth which makes the claim of many architects to "design research" so questionable. The very words are meaningless. Design is not research, it is a creative process,

Robert Woods Kennedy: Sketch of a house and, on the facing page, the house itself.

guided, as is fine writing, painting, and the other arts, by the unconscious. The architect who "explores all the possibilities," who makes several designs for the same job, would seem to have few inner convictions. He is apt to follow slavishly the accepted canons of a certain style. Work so laboriously achieved lacks freshness and individuality, and the process wastes a tremendous amount of time.

The architect who shows two or more designs to his client is in effect proclaiming his incompetence. The sensible client faced with such a choice says: "You are an architect and presumably an expert in design. If *you* can't make up your mind as to which of these schemes is the best, how in the world do you expect *me* to." The gullible client will get hopelessly lost in a maze of comparisons and will usually demand a compromise.

In the average case, then, the client gets most from one sketch. Before the architect presents it, he must be sure that he himself likes it. He cannot change his mind later on without some loss of prestige. If it is not liked, architect and client must go back over the program, site, budget, circulation patterns, orientation, and zoning schemes, and start again. The architect must usually wait for the old scheme to recede from his mind before making a new sketch based on his fuller understanding of his client's needs.

The actual form the first sketch takes depends on the client's ability to deal with drawings. The sophisticated client can be shown the wheels going around from the very beginning. To exclude him is to miss a potentially useful partner. The client, if he is capable, can help collect data. He cannot help in the synthesizing process. But as soon as the synthesis has taken place and a scheme is produced, he can be let in on its evaluation, just as it stands, on the back of the unpaid bill.

The less creative client must be kept at a greater distance. The first sketch in such cases is usually a plan of the house, on

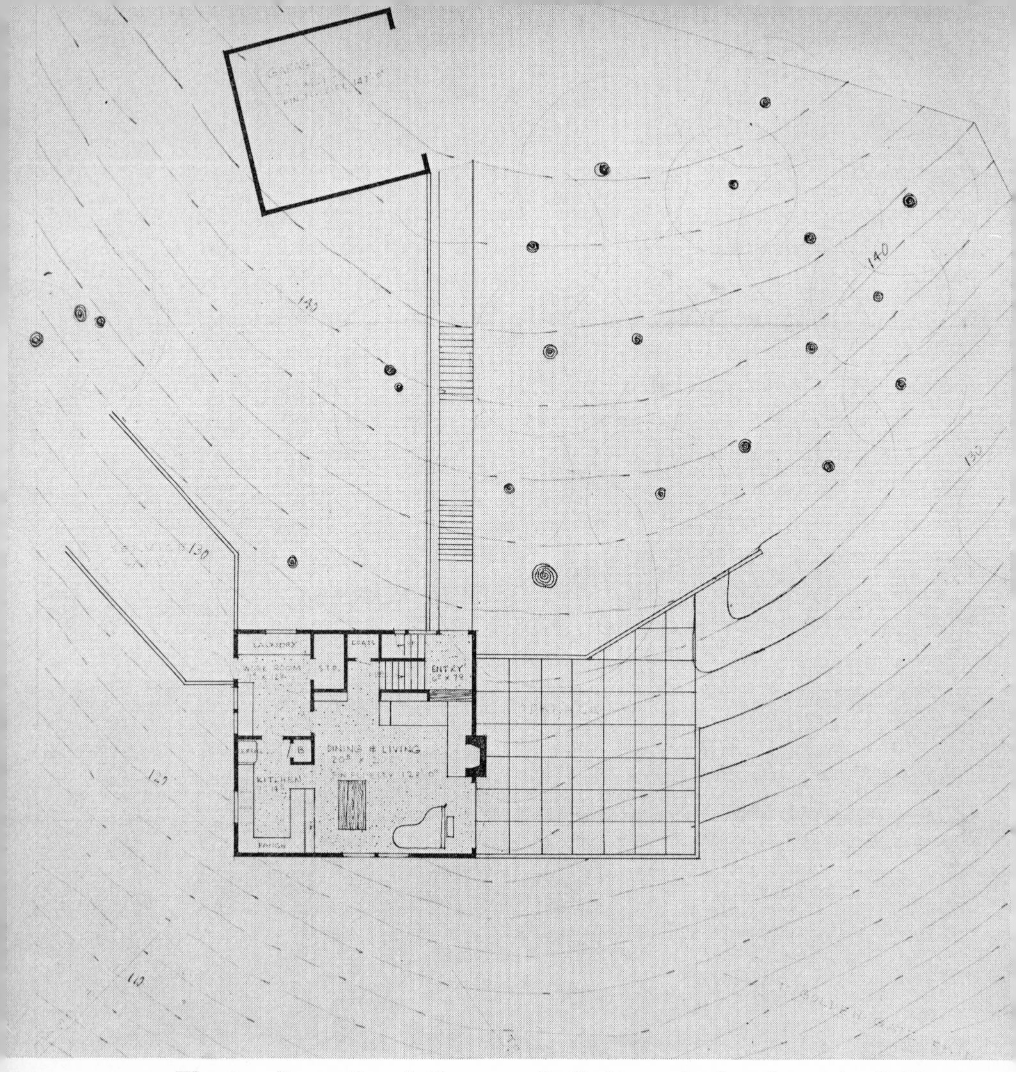

Wurster, Bernardi and Emmons: Preliminary sketches, house in California. (Fragment) See Mr. Wurster's photo of a house in Massachusetts, page 389.

its site, complete with furniture and graphic indication of insolation, ventilation, etc., but without elevations or perspectives. Detailed arrangements of bath, kitchen, heating, or other equipment may be omitted, as can all indications of materials other than those mentioned in the program or essential to the conception. This sort of sketch sets the stage for a discussion of the fundamental concept of the house. Discussion of the location of the can opener or of the fire extinguisher can be avoided by making it obvious that little or nothing is as yet known about such details. They belong to a later stage of development.

Preliminary Sketches

In the usual case, perspectives need not be shown until the fundamentals are accepted. Elevations, to begin with, are hopelessly abstruse. The appearance of the house must grow out of the more basic decisions, and the client will not actually feel this to be the case unless he sees it happen. Some architects start the visualization process off with a high vanishing point perspective showing massing and site relationship only, that is, without windows, doors, or other secondary details. In the early stages such sketches can be distorted to bring out the *aimed at* esthetic char-

acter. The client cannot be shown a finished product off the bat, and at the same time he may not be able to see the potential character in the preliminary sketches. The architect needs to show his intention. Once this esthetic intention is understood and accepted, the client need not be shown elevations or perspectives again until they are well along. In the meantime he needs to see, one after another, the detailed arrangements, such as kitchens, linen closets, bath rooms, and fire places, if these were omitted from the original sketch.

This process usually involves a continuing effort towards client visualization of the interiors and of certain key exterior views, such as the entrance. Quick thumbnail sketches are perhaps most effective here and are less apt to cause trouble than are properly set up, detailed, perspectives. Details can be tyrannical. The uninitiated allow them to guide, and therefore to distort, fundamental concepts. It takes a large amount of will power to prevent them from usurping control over design. The process of visualization is made easier if the client can be persuaded to take an active part. If he himself will make models or sketches, his understanding, and pleasure, is the greater.

The fundamental problem which the preliminary sketches set out to solve is that of some equable adjustment of space to budget. The client almost invaviably wants more house for his money than it is possible to give him. There are several ways in which the problem can be approached. The most common is, perhaps, the "ostrich technique." In such case the architect prepares a sketch which incorporates all his client's desires, regardless, and presents it with an estimate of cost. This method seems open to question, except in the hands of the most skillful psychologist. It faces the client with a highly disagreeable choice. The architect is saying; "Here is the house you would like. You see I can design it for you, but as you cannot afford it, you must give it up in favor of something less svelte." There is more than one danger involved. The architect who prepares such a sketch, suspecting that it is destined for the wastebasket, has two alternatives. He can knock it out any old way and run the risk of his client's disliking it. In such case the client may lose trust in his architect's ability. Secondly, the architect can develop his client's dream as conscientiously as he would a scheme destined to be built, and in so doing, lose money. On the other hand, for the occasional client who is convinced that all architects are extravagant with other people's money and who does not frankly state his budget, the "ideal house" sketch may sometimes have the advantage of bringing out the real economic picture.

A dislike of coming to grips with the money question is not an uncommon characteristic. The client wants the kind of a house he wants very badly indeed. He also has a gnawing suspicion that it will cost more than he can afford. He would rather suffer the financial consequences than not get the house he wants. But he cannot, himself, make a decision involving such an extravagance. He therefore refuses to really tackle the financial problem. This position allows him to put on the architect full responsibility for spending more money than he knows he should. In such case, the ideal sketch, all other things being propitious, is sometimes accepted off the bat.

This reaction to the cost-income equation poses the architect a curious problem. His urge is, of course, to design the best, the biggest, and the most beautiful house he can. He may also bank on the fact that, if all goes well, his client will be tremendously proud and pleased with the result. On the other hand, the client may proclaim to all comers that the house is much more grand and expensive than such an unostentatious and humble person as he himself could ever wish for and that the architect's extravagance was the sole reason for its luxury. Some architects try to forestall this poor publicity, after allowing the client to get in so far he cannot back out, by proving, with carefully saved documents, that the client had only himself to blame. This does not work because the client is quite justified in his point of view. His architect could have forced him to a sense of reality (and perhaps out of the office). The fact that the house might not have been built or might have been built in its luxurious form by another architect cannot, and morally need not, influence the client's belief that he did not make the decision to spend so much money. All he did was want something. The architect who enters into this comedy of avoidance is actually doing what his client desires and may get a good house out of it. He must balance this advantage against the adverse publicity he is apt to receive and against the possibility that he may lose the job. It is small wonder that most architects plunk for what the client really wants rather than for what he says he wants.

The ostrich technique, obviously, can involve serious financial crises. It is also essentially obscurantist and is thus not professional in the best sense. The real professional, for his own satisfaction if not for that of his client, needs to have every decision rationally thought out and fully understood. One of his functions is, certainly, to make sure that essentially irrational personal relationships are not "immortalized" in building materials.

The poorest way of maintaining a logical thread of thought through the building process is, perhaps, the "legal technique." This consists of voluminous contracts, letters confirming every step, letters protesting every decision disagreed with, the client's signature on every drawing, the saving of every scrap of paper connected with the job, and so on. It is "playing safe." The architect involved seems to be scared of his own jobs. He does not object to terrorizing his clients. His documentation is geared for his day in court. The technique, far from keeping the decision-making process open and clear, tends to obscure and muddy the issues. The fact that the architect writes a letter absolving himself of guilt for a certain decision does him little good in the long run. He may have his letter, but the client has the mistake and will never forget it. The excuse for the "legal technique" is that clients are so irresponsible that the architect needs thorough documentation for his own protection. But in many instances this appears to be a rationalization which allows the architect to avoid true professional responsibility. The irresponsible client should have been turned down in the first place, or at least after the first bitter experience.

With a strong minded and cooperative client the best way to keep all decisions above board starts with a frank description of the realities of building costs and the presentation of as true a picture as possible of what the client can expect for his budget. The architect continues to keep decisions above board by insisting that anything which might cause an overrun be eliminated from the very beginning.

This sort of approach might be called "rugged collectivism." Because it is uncompromising, it involves certain very real difficulties. Some clients do not want to be acquainted with the realities. Others are easily scared. Still others assume that the architect who starts this way is "expensive." Others will accuse him of "not wanting the job." Some of these will get up and leave—to find a more "cheerful" architect, by which they mean a liar. Some of them return later on, sadder, wiser, and often considerably poorer. Those clients who are completely lost are probably well-lost. To build a good house involves an ability to be uncompromising.

The emotional tone set up by architect-client dealings on a basis of strict reality is hard on the client. The architect is saying to him, in effect, "You must cut rigorously." No one likes to do this. The client usually takes the line then, that the architect "won't let him have what he wants." The architect is cast in the role of a father who is taking things away which his child needs and deserves. Such accusations are the forerunners of complete trust and understanding. The client who gets a good house, which meets his budget, and who understands how, why, and where his money was spent, is almost always happy and grateful.

The only effective way of meeting the average house budget is to save everywhere. This is often a difficult concept to get over. It takes the client some time to realize that very few of the thousands of items which go into a house can be omitted, and that none of them cost very much in themselves. The only way significant savings can be made is by chipping a little bit off a very large number of small parts. It is essential that the client understand this, for it brings the space-money conflict into focus, and provides the only way of solving it. Furthermore, the SAVE EVERYWHERE motto produces certain secondary and very happy results. The tone set up absolves the architect of any last remaining suspicion of extravagance. Increases, when they occur, are understandable. Luxuries earned through the saving of money somewhere else take on a particularly pleasant connotation. They are little indulgences, like a cocktail before Sunday lunch, and thus carry a greater emotional impact than if they had been expected as a matter of course.

Working Drawings

Ideally, the form and arrangement of every detail should be accepted by both the architect and the client before working drawings start. The client should not need to see them, nor should he need to make any but the most minor decisions while they are going on. Design done in the working drawing stage is apt to be poor and expensive. Actually, the first of a series of crises occur in this stage, due to delayed visualization, or to improper programming, or to muddy handling of the space-money conflict, and also, alas, due to plain cussedness. If the preliminaries have been conscientiously carried through, such crises can only be seen as Acts of God. Because in many cases they are more or less unforeseeable, the architect does not have ready defenses against them. The most he can do is to point out to his client the financial, practical, and esthetic horrors of changes, these horrors being more drastic the longer changes are delayed. In most cases clients will not believe that they, personally, would ever be tempted to cause so much trouble, and it is therefore necessary to hammer the point home. Most architects have seen an apparently very minor change set off a chain reaction of mistakes and extras. Such stories, or certain sections of *Mr. Blandings Builds His Dream House* contain salutary lessons for the client prone to numerous second thoughts.

On the other hand, second thoughts, particularly those of the good client, often do have great value. Unlike the architect, whose nose is in the working drawings, the client retains some perspective. He is uninfluenced by the pressure to get the job technically organized. Every design, every office, and every architect should be flexible enough to absorb a few second thoughts without undue stress. Unfortunately most architects are resistant to changes, good or bad. They have acquired, quite justifiably, the reputation of being arbitrary. This reputation is most true in the case of the best architects, least in that of the businessman architect for whom the client is always right. Because the reasons for professional pig-headedness are not too creditable it behooves the architect to force himself towards leniency in client relations. It is too easy to justify resistance to change first because his precious design might be spoiled, and, second, because the effort involved in tracing down the effects of the change is too much like work. The first of these reasons, particularly in the case of strict stylists, carries the emotional charge of the Ten Commandments. The more arbitrary an architect is about being an Internationalist, or a Colonialist, the more arbitrary his personal relations become. The doctrinal overtones in much contemporary architecture are as unpleasant there as they are in the architect-client relationship. The second reason is, of course, only laziness.

If changes are the emotional hazard during the working drawing period, then the commonly accepted division of the fee into twenty-five per cent for sketches, fifty per cent for working drawings and twenty-five per cent for supervision is the financial hazard. A good set of sketches needs, and should ordinarily receive no major design decisions during the working drawing period. This means in effect that the sketches cost much more than twenty-five per cent, while the working drawings cost less than fifty per cent. That division is based on the business man approach to design, not on the requirements of the creative architect. A division such as thirty-five per cent–forty per cent–twenty-five per cent would be more accurate in the latter case. The present scheme is incorporated in the A. I. A. forms of Standard Contract, and is thus very difficult to change, particularly in the case of greedy or contract shy clients. It leaves the conscientious architect in the position of losing money on sketches, and if he is lucky, making it back again on working drawings. However, when the job is called off at the end of the sketch stage, and a large percentage of jobs are, then the architect sustains a permanent loss. The serious practitioner, because he works on such a small margin of profit per job, must usually develop his own contract for this reason, despite the obvious psychological advantages of the A. I. A. printed form.

Supervision

"At this point the clients transfer their allegiance, dependence and respect to the builder, or, more specifically, to the superintendent, the carpenters and masons on the job. The wife "goes out to the job" frequently, watching with astonished eyes the skills of the workmen. The architect's lot is not abetted by the fact that the superintendent always has a habit of shuffling through the blueprints and muttering in the presence of the client some such remarks as "These guys ought to get out and build for themselves and they'd know you can't hang a door that way."—Louchheim

The completion of the working drawings heralds the client's most difficult period. The question of who shall bid on his house again opens up the money-space conflict, adding new facets—those of workmanship, and of client-contractor relations. Client and architect have reached some sort of a compromise between space and the quality of the materials to be used. But the client has not had to face the question of how well these materials are to be installed, or of how well his job is to be run.

These new complications are sometimes aggravated by the client's belief in one of two myths, to the effect that contractors are either crooks, or divinely practical supermen. The architect must discover and modify such attitudes. In the case of distrust, the contractor may react by neglecting the work or by retaliating in some way. Faith and trust are the priceless ingredients of the construction period. In the case of worship, the contractor and client, waltzing together, may blemish the job, if they do not spoil it altogether. As the architect can not control his client in the sense that he can, under certain circumstances, his contractors, his relationship with the latter is of the essence.

The architect's best defense against unpleasant client-contractor deals is a continuing relationship with a group of builders whose integrity he is sure of. The next several jobs are a powerful factor in his favor, in any three cornered row. This group of contractors is best made up of people who do not, at one extreme, fall in love with each new client, or at the other, get fed up with client and job before the punch list period, and neglect the finish-

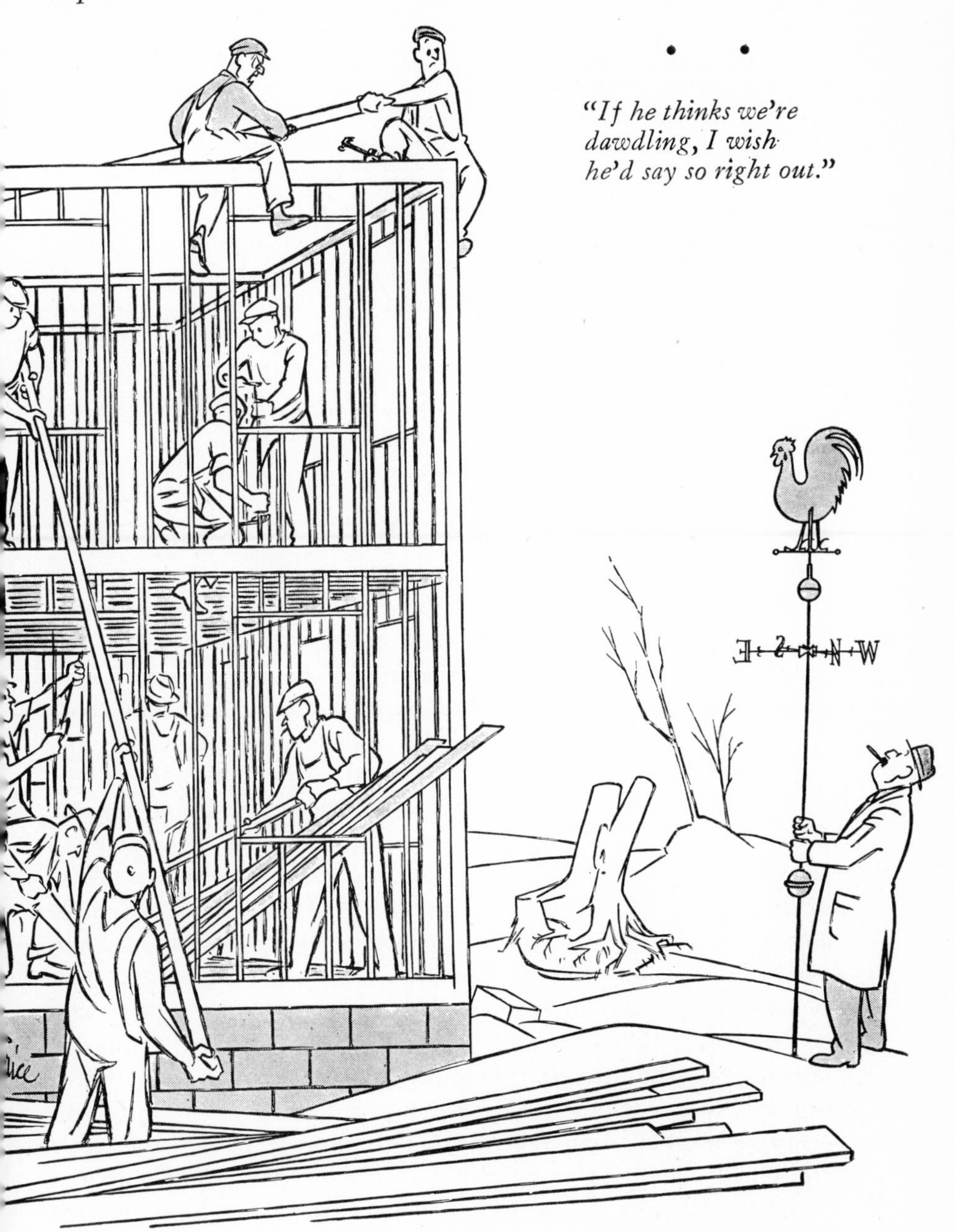

"If he thinks we're dawdling, I wish he'd say so right out."

George Price: Reproduced by permission. Copy. 1949 The New Yorker Magazine, Inc.

ing touches. For the architect, fairness and impartiality are the priceless ingredients of such relationships. To let a contractor "get away with something" or to make him correct an architect's mistake at his own expense are at best questionable practices. Architects who pay for their own errors derive long term benefits which far outweigh the short term losses.

From the architect's point of view a contractor who understands and sympathizes with his goals is ideal. Unfortunately there seem to be very few builders in the United States with any real understanding of contemporary architecture. Most of them were brought up on copies of the traditional styles. They are likely to have worked their way up to entrepreneurship through a building trade, and thus have little understanding of design goals. Some have been to college, but the curricula of even the best construction engineering schools are deficient in general education. Finally, most builders come from the upper working or lower middle classes, and are conditioned to be suspicious of, and hostile towards, high artistic standards. The architect who has available a builder whose judgment in such matters he can trust is unusually lucky. In default of builders who can act as co-partners, "stick to the blueprints" is the order of the day. The client needs to understand the reasons for this irksome discipline.

Contractors arrange themselves, as do architects and clients, in a hierarchy. At one extreme is the conscientious, able, expert, professional builder, who runs a beautiful job, sees it through to the bitter end, and who costs a lot of money. His overhead is necessarily large. The subs he uses are the best. His foreman is able and expensive. At the other extreme is the slipshod one man operation, without office or sometimes even a telephone, whose accounting system consists of his left and right pants pocket, who is always a little bit behind on his bills and therefore wants his money fast. The presentation and collection of his monthly bill is usually the only thing he does do fast. He rarely finishes a job to everyone's satisfaction. The ideal contractor, from the architect's and client's point of view, combines the advantages of both the extremes. He is very cheap, has no overhead, and does a superb job of management and workmanship. Such is the versatility of the human race that such characters actually do exist.

Supervision

Most architects know one or more builders of every type. Were an identical set of plans and specifications given to a representative of each category in the hierarchy, the bids received would vary from cheap to expensive according to the bidder's place in line. Thus the best contractors will not bid against those lower down in the scale, for they know they will be too high, while the low bidders have no objection to competing, moneywise, with their betters.

The average client wants to believe that the plans and specifications describe one product of one quality. When they realize that the human element plays so large a role in the quality of the finished product, they feel completely adrift. "What," they ask, "is to prevent the less good contractor from rooking me four ways to Sunday." The explanation that, because he is less of a perfectionist than the best does not mean that he is dishonest: that the quality of his workmanship and management is well understood by himself, his subs, and the architect; and that he maintains this less than ideal quality at its own level, is not, in the client's particular circumstances, very reassuring. The client is in the grip of a very strong surge towards the best. He is deeply involved, financially, emotionally, and socially. It is small wonder that he wants this new baby of his to be perfect.

To the two client fears already mentioned, the fear of being gypped and the fear of poor workmanship, must be added a third; that the house is too small. This is a further stage in the visualization problem. It takes, for example, considerable professional experience to be able to visualize how a house sits by looking at the bare foundation. Most clients will take that relationship on faith. However, when they walk into a frame house just studded up, they are apt to claim that the builder has made all the rooms several feet too small, or that the architect has been deceiving them as to sizes. The incredible beauty of a house before it is closed in, the delicate tracery of its studs against the sky, is usually totally lost on them. This is a pity, for the average house never looks better than at this moment in its development.

The apprehensive client should be prepared for this moment in advance, in that it is one type of crisis which can be foreseen and averted. The fundamental principle which causes the *tromp d'oeil* must be taken into consideration in the early planning stage, as it affects the relative sizes of garden rooms or living rooms versus terraces, gardens, yards, walks, drives, gates and the like—wherever the scale of the outdoors and indoors can be readily contrasted. The simple explanation that the indoors is reduced in scale, when compared directly with the vastness of the sky, can be of help. It is the same principle which makes a very small and feminine woman so effective on the arm of a large and masculine man.

These three types of fears, when they are all operating together, can make supervision one long hell. Rosow notes the following in a summary of architect-client relationships:

> "During construction, while the house is in essentially a fluid state, the greatest client apprehension appears. All sorts of fears develop, largely from client inexperience, and these must be mollified. For many clients, the construction period becomes one major crisis after another. Since the architect has a better understanding of what is going on, the client rather than the house frequently becomes his main headache."

The architect has several devices over and above those already mentioned with which to alleviate the crisis nature of supervision. Extreme fears of being gypped can sometimes by allayed by the assumption, on the architect's part, of extreme competence to deal with dishonest practices. In this case he assumes the policeman's role. The best start is perhaps to put the contractor-client relationship on a more or less social level through properly staged conferences, in which the contractor's identity as a human being is the *piéce de resistance.* Such conferences are by no means always easy.

It is not unknown for a builder to start the first meeting with some such remark as "Couldn't you give your poor client a better looking job than this. It looks to me like one of those barns we used to have in the old country"; or "There's no accounting for tastes," or "Some people sure do have queer ideas. *I* wouldn't be seen dead living in a shack like that." This sort of dialogue can sometimes be smoothed over by explaining to the client that the contractor is either a "diamond in the rough," or a "character." One comfort is that such comments are most likely to come from a builder who has not yet built a modern house. When, during the process of building, he becomes slowly convinced of the logic of the job, the client and the architect consider it a triumph, and see great cause for mutual congratulation.

The average contractor's tendency to pride himself on his practicality is more difficult to deal with. Faced, as he most often is, with an architect and a client who are college graduates, who function in a mysterious realm of taste, and who are "high class," or even "fancy pants" he is apt to contrast himself as the competent, realistic, rough and ready "graduate of the college of hard knocks." When he carries this role over into action; when he attempts to engineer "practical" changes in the plans, he must be curbed. The real practicality, i.e., a thoughtful adjustment of each newly added element to the reality of what has gone before, and to one's plans for the future, must be constantly guarded and defended. When the client as well as the contractor, confuse opportunism and practicality, the job is almost sure to suffer.

This point of view can be explained, in terms of the meaning of a particular design, and of how that fundamental meaning is reflected in the details. However, many of the small problems which occur during the course of the average job cannot be obviously and rationally tied back to general principles, unless the architect happens to be a spell binder. They are of small consequence in themselves, and are decided on "taste," or on a "feeling" for the unity of the job, or even on irrational whim. Such petty details, if they become symbols of the architect's or client's or builder's power, can cause much trouble. Unless the contractor exercises proper professional discipline he can easily create this situation. If he arrogates to himself the competence and the right to decide on such things, or sides consistently with or against the client, one cause for a three cornered row has been created.

The drawings, specifications, and details, plus supervision, are the only devices we possess for describing a desired result. These, along with a contract which states that the job shall follow the documents and interpretations strictly, should be enough, ideally at least, to assure concordance. But as every architect knows, this is far from the true case. It is all too easy to change a job many times during construction and some houses go through an almost complete metamorphosis. In order to defend his design, the architect must create a psychological climate, in both client and contractor, which gives the documents the sanctity of canon law.

The most usual device is to set up chains of command, or, as the Armed Forces have it, channels, through which all requests and decisions must go. Changes initiated by either the contractor or the owner must go to the architect first, be reduced to paper, and finally be signed by all three. This or some similar device is, to some extent, unavoidable. But like all systems depending on red tape, it is irksome, slow, inefficient, and sometimes breeds as much trouble as it obviates. There is no substitute for team work. The real need is good will, sincere attempts at mutual understanding, and self discipline.

The client is the strongest force for good or evil in this three-cornered team. If he bosses the contractor, orders changes himself, and vetos the architect, he will spoil both the house, the atmosphere of the relationship, and spend a lot of money needlessly. If he goes through channels to the extent of never actually ordering a change without prior agreement, if he treats the contractor as the honest and sincere person he is apt to be, he is sure to get more from his contractor, simply because he is a nice guy. The ideal client is a person who understands and enjoys team work. Some people seem to be naturally endowed with this ability. Others learn it, through experience in business or government. Such people, from the architect's and contractor's point of view are blessed. Unfortunately, something like one third of all clients are unable to function adequately in this particular circumstance. Some of these suffer clearly from a lack of experience with complex operations. The majority of failures seem to go back to a desire on the part of the client to get more than his money's worth, with the inevitable concomitant, a distrust of people and a fear of being gypped.

The architect must, himself, exercise, vis a vis the contractor, the same discipline of doing things through channels that he expects of his client. He must also prevent the contractor from being too generous in the early stages lest he be too niggardly at the end, and must see to it that the contract is really fulfilled. This can only be done adequately if the architect maintains, and has maintained over a period of years, the strictest personal integrity. He can not accept presents or free corrections of his mistakes and retain his control over the men who do his jobs. The claims often made, particularly by eclectic architects, that their strokes of genius are delivered during the construction period, would seem to be sheer nonsense. To make drawings on shingles, or to tell Joe, the carpenter, how to do it, as he does it, is to admit that the architect himself has not been able to visualize the job. It is also obvious that such a procedure costs someone money. Architects seldom pay for these delayed flashes of understanding, so it must be assumed that the contractors who know them pad their bids, while the new contractors take it out of the job somewhere else.

Rosow found that:

> "Almost half of the clients stated that in building another house they would take more definite steps to tighten responsibility for construction in order to eliminate difficulties and dissatisfactions."

He found that this point of view was more prevalent among the Semi-Modern than among the Modern clients, but the percentage in the latter category was appreciable. When nearly fifty per cent of such a broad sample as Rosow's were dissatisfied on this score, the need for better handling of the supervision period is obvious.

This need has been sensed for some time, and various schemes have been tried, usually involving an architect-builder, in an attempt to correct some of the faults in the traditional system. Such schemes are branded as unethical by old line architects on the ground that there is no middle man involved who can protect the client's interests vis a vis the contractor. Logically, this may make good sense, but practically it would seem to be meaningless. There is no operational way of assuring competence and integrity. Both schemes work well when they are guided by these qualities. Both fail when competence and integrity are absent.

The Weaning Period

The client is the architect's chief headache during supervision. But, during the weaning period, their roles are often reversed. The client thinks of the architect as a headache. Except in those cases where intimate mutual understanding exists between architect and client, the client usually has some feeling that he is being pushed around. The architect knows exactly what he wants. He is more expert and more at ease, and thus is in a superior position. To have a close relationship with a superior is, for many people, rather irksome, be it doctor-patient, teacher-student, father-son, or officer-rating. The person temporarily in the inferior position is apt to go through stages of awe and dependence, disillusion and criticism, revolt and flight, ending, in the good cases, with tolerance and understanding. This cycle can be very pronounced and obvious. The period of revolt and flight can be compared to the weaning period for infants. The architect must, in self defense, wean his clients. He wants, like a good mother, to do it in the least traumatic way. Some clients take it very hard—in fact, hang on for dear life. They will drop into their architect's office four years after the house is finished to discuss a change in the color of the curtains in the small north bedroom. They are worried because they feel that their choice may offend the architect's superior sensibilities. At the other extreme is the client who weans himself prematurely. People of this sort begin to discard the architect as soon as the house is far enough along to visualize more or less completely—usually just after it is plastered. They can finally see their baby. They are tired of the architect, with his "You better do this" or "I wouldn't do that if I were you." They feel terribly grown up. They begin to want to live their own lives in their own way. They do not realize how much work is still involved nor how important this work is to the success of the finished product. The architect's nagging falls on deaf ears. The client is off in a cloud of dust. The contractor, because he has always been excluded from design decisions, doesn't care what "they" do as long as "they" let him get on with the job, and pay him on or about the twelfth of the month.

Whether the weaning period is traumatic or blissful, it involves a transfer of the house from architect to client. During programming and sketches the client thinks of it as his house. But during working drawings and early supervision, he loses his feeling of identity with it. The architect refers to it as "Your house" (the client's) while the client refers to it, humorously or bitterly as "Your house" (the architect's). The client is usually right in this. Many architects refer to their jobs as "*My* house in Doetown, or "*My* house in Roetown," except when speaking to the client involved. The client senses that he must somehow get his house away from the architect. The perceptive realize this, are amused by it, kid their architect a little, and sooner or later the house is theirs. Others feel they must take more drastic steps to accomplish the same thing. They may make a host of small decisions exactly contrary to the architect's recommendations. Or they may tear out some feature particularly dear to him, or they may add an element which will spoil it in his eyes.

The client who is unable to visualize the house until it is virtually finished, has the worst time at this period, particularly if he is also subject to any of the extreme attitudes described above. The rude shock experienced by someone who suddenly realizes that he has spent some tens of thousands of dollars for something entirely foreign to his expectations, is hard to take. This reaction is probably more common than most architects realize. The client is apt to hide it, acting on the same impulse which makes people hide a defeat. It is usually of short duration, for as he begins really to understand, he also begins to accept and appreciate. Furthermore his attitude, pendulum like, is apt to swing towards a kind of euphoria—he has a romantic affair with his house before he settles down to the humdrum business of marriage.

The love affair takes several forms. The most common is the attitude that the house deserves every attention which can be lavished on it. The client's old furniture isn't good enough for it. Numerous little things have to be done for it, involving either money or personal labor. Other types of clients literally play with their house as if it were a baby. Such play should make the architect very happy, in the same way that the stork who brings babies must be happy. Occasionally, however, it goes too far. Reasonably frequently the client, either just before or soon after he moves in, gets what is known in architectural circles as an "inferior desecrator." He does this with the best will in the world. He wants his house to be perfect, and he does not want to overwork his architect. But the desecrator rarely fails to create a nuisance, and sometimes spoils the entire interior.

One of the most curious quirks of client psychology, from the architect's point of view, is the casual way in which the desecrator is chosen and dealt with, particularly in contrast with the careful screening the client performed before choosing the architect. From the client's point of view however, there is sense in it. He has been struggling with the house for a year or more, and at long last it is ready to move into. He is in a fever of expectation of requited love. The desecrator cannot effect the house in its role of investment, nor in any fundamental way. Spurred on by his sense of urgency the client acts fast. Because this development is apt to hit him like a bolt from the blue, it behooves the architect to do a little client education in advance. The periods when furniture arrangements are discussed, and later when finish schedules are drawn up, are both natural opportunities.

It is unfortunate that there are so few decorators who have any feel for the modern house. It is more unfortunate still that they usually fail to realize it. Their assumption of competence is sanctified by one of our society's most deeply believed myths, that "art" and "culture" are perpetuated only by women. Thus most women believe themselves to be competent in artistic matters, as do most feminine men. Actually, the confusion here is between art and craft. In most cultures women do the craft work, just as in ours they by and large do the decorating. The average woman's claim to craft competence *is* backed by tradition. The new element in our culture which makes it impossible for her, lacking education, adequately to perform this role is eclecticism. She is no longer plunged at birth into a consistent tradition, with conventional ways of doing, which have been improved and refined by generations before her. Unless she goes to a school she has nothing, and the average school, in its turn, cannot adequately prepare her without the backing of a consistent tradition. Furthermore, while the average U. S. house is, of course, a craft product, the upper middle class modern house attempts fine architecture. In order to deal with its interior, artistry, rather than the craftsman's conventionality, is needed.

The situation would appear hopeless were it not for the fact that in recent years a few schools have developed courses in "interior design" (a new and less invidious name for the old craft) which introduce students to the fundamentals of modern architecture. A generation of interior designers who can be accepted as partners by the architect, rather than avoided as parasites, will usher in a new millenium.

The client's romantic affair with the house does not, of course, stop with its interior. One of his first moves is to landscape it. In the average case he does this himself, but he may also hire a "landscrape garbeler," and again it sometimes happens that the architect is unaware of this move until the damage is done. The landscape situation is as serious as the decorating one. The real truth of the matter is that there can be no differentiations made between landscape and architecture. Together they create a single environment. Mr. Garrett Eckbo has expressed this as follows:

> "We (landscapers) work in from the natural periphery toward the refined core, the architects and engineers work out in a reverse direction, and we cannot stop where we meet without establishing a boundary that defeats our objective. We must overlap as a beginning, and become increasingly collaborative as we proceed. We must become sensitive and appreciative of the forms of architecture, and the architects must become sensitive and appreciative, not only of the forms of nature, but of the forms of landscape design which can come out of the meeting of architecture and nature."

This suggests that the house architect must either combine the two skills in his own person, or work closely with someone in the other discipline. There is no dividing the two. The practical difficulties in the way of good landscaping, however, are very real. The client's initial drive is towards a maximum of enclosed area. In the average case all of his then available cash is spent on house. There is nothing left over for landscaping, nor for landscape design. If the architect does not, as a regular part of his services, supply this, he can only expect the client to do it himself.

When the client does do it himself he is most apt to start with that most horrible of devices, "foundation planting." There is, perhaps, no more elegant or satisfying effect in our environment than the clean junction of grass and wall, but its peculiar beauty is almost unknown. The excuses for foundation planting, i.e., "to dress up the house" or "to make a transition between house and ground" are so universally believed that, without a prior understanding of house-ground relationships, the row of bulbous and stunted evergreens is almost bound to appear.

Again, where the client has been failed by the architect, and sets out to get help somewhere else, his chances of receiving adequate advice are no better here than in the case of decorators. The average landscaper, an employee of a nursery, is primarily concerned with selling a maximum of material. He also favors foundation planting (it moves a lot of stock) and feels "artistically" the need for a "softening of the lines." Unfortunately this same poverty of understanding applies to most of the more truly professional practitioners. Eckbo asks "When architecture moves from Vignola to Frank Lloyd Wright and Le Corbusier, how can landscape design stay with Repton and Le Notre?" The sad state of the profession, which includes less than a handful of distinguished designers, cannot, however, be considered as entirely its own fault. Architects have tended to stick, myopically, to their "refined core" and to let the periphery get along as best it may. Just as H. H. Richardson created a generation of craftsmen skilled in Romanesque stone cutting, contemporary architects could, by demanding appropriate landscape design, create a new generation of garden architects.

Front family entrance, Mr. Yagi's house, Kyoto. Courtesy of Dr. Jiro Harada.

Love, Hate and Architecture

The trouble with thumb nail sketches of extreme behavior patterns is that one never meets a person who fits into any one pigeon hole. Every architect has had business men clients who were sensitive to esthetic values, ethical in their approach to others, and who paid their bills with grace. By the same token he has dealt with professionals who behaved in an exactly opposite way. Categorized descriptions can only help one's general understanding. They are but a small part of the broad frame of reference used by the individual architect face to face with the individual client.

It is beyond reason to expect this relationship to be "professional," that is, impersonal, clear cut, and rational. That is an ideal. Actually, as a single goal, it would be highly undesirable. The purposes and end products of the relationship are too varied to allow of any single behavior pattern.

It is also beyond reason to expect the relationship to be uniformly pleasant. When a group of architects get together there is always a gnashing of teeth over their sufferings with clients. The wonderful experiences, the rewarding and illuminating times, are seldom touched on. Nor are those clients discussed who come in various neutral shades, and those whose jobs create hardly a ripple on the emotional lake of the office. The black hearted clients get all the attention. But they are more or less rare, and take on importance only because they are so excessively disagreeable. White hearted clients are more frequent and make life worthwhile. Far from presenting problems, they create solutions.

The question is, then, what quality does the architect need in order to carry him through the bad and boring times. There is only one answer. He must love people. This does not mean he must fawn over them, or get all starry-eyed just because clients are human. Dr. Carl Binger, at the end of a description of the "ideal" doctor added this, which might apply to architects as well:

"This much is sure, that stylishness and elegance, expensive equipment, attractive chintzes, stream-lined limousines, high fees and social position, membership in clubs, brilliant dinner-table conversation, even general reclame and notoriety are not in themselves hallmarks of the good doctor (architect). He should be an honest, upright man whom you instinctively trust. He cannot always be brilliant. It is far more important that he possess integrity in a high degree. There is no one kind of personality that is the perfect one, but his personality must suit yours. I have seen excellent doctors (architects) who could pass as floorwalkers or ham actors, dapper stockbrokers, homespun farmers or ascetic saints. I know some who fraternize with their patients (clients) and others who are aloof, some with urbane bedside (conference table) manners and others gruff and uncompromising. There is no patent of nobility on their sleeves."

The client looking for an architect, if he is sensible, is in search of this deep concern with human nature. For the humane view is reflected, as inevitably as the dawn, in an architect's every job. The character of the house is a reflection of the client from off the surface of the architect's vision. It is clear or distorted exactly as the architect's vision is clear or distorted. The architect who distrusts people is easier to recognize in his work than in his person. His jobs are regimented, inhuman, cold and uncomfortable. He punishes his clients by placing them in bare white cells, or behind west facing walls of glass, or by forcing them to play out every scene, to perform every function, to display every motion and every weakness in public.

The fawning architect is equally discernible in his work. His jobs are designed to satiate the esthetic appetite, just as a good chef's dishes are designed to satiate the palate. And like the chef's concoctions, they are pot pouris, collections of a little of this and a little of that, appropriately blended, and served hot. Both kinds of architecture must be alternated with rest cures, or as the Victorians had it, with a "taking of the waters."

The clear vision of people is essential to good architecture. It is only by seeing human faults clearly that they can be decently suppressed. It is only by seeing human strengths clearly that they can be powerfully expressed.

CHAPTER VIII

Style

2. He answered and said unto them, "When it is evening, ye say it will be fair weather; for the sky is red.
3. And in the morning, it will be foul weather today; for the sky is red and lowering. O ye hypocrites! Ye can discern the face of the sky; but can ye not discern the signs of the times?

MATTHEW XVI 2-3

Security and Innovation

THE MOST TOUTED ARCHITECTURAL QUESTION of our time is: "Traditional or Modern?" It seems absolutely necessary to take a stand on it. Traditionalists call modern houses "freaks." Modernists call traditional houses "mausoleums." The variety of traditional styles on any one street is obnoxious to the Modernist. The variety of modern splinter groups is bewildering to the Traditionalist. The vast majority "pays their money and takes their choice"—of Traditional.

In Traditional circles, architects are blamed for Modern. The possessor of a modern house is commiserated with. The feeling is "You poor thing. That architect certainly put it over on you." On the other hand, in Modern circles, the public is blamed for Traditional. And the architect is commiserated with. "You poor thing," they say, "That client certainly gave you a ride, didn't he?" About all this proves is that the war between the two camps cuts across both the profession and the public. Traditional architects get along better with their clients than with their fellow, but modern, professionals. And vice versa.

This is so fundamental that it is taken for granted. But, in terms of other public-professional relationships it is unparalleled. True, in medicine, there are osteopaths with their following, and homeopaths with theirs. But by and large there is a main stream in which nearly everyone swims. It is generally agreed that if one wants to get well, its waters are the safest ones to drink. The American Medical Association, or the Bar Association, or the Society of Civil Engineers may all be stuffy, but they are believed in. There is no large segment of the public questioning their professional position. The individual practitioner, in such case, can be thought of as operating in two spheres. His professional circle is cohesive, and more or less in agreement as to standards and goals. Its traditions, its literature, and the research it undertakes all feed and support his skills. The doctor, or lawyer, or engineer is, so to speak, at home when he is among his fellow professionals. His other sphere is the public one, within which he operates, and where he uses his peculiar skills. In this realm he is backed up by his profession as a whole. When a conflict develops between uninformed public opinion and informed professional opinion, it is fought out *between* the two spheres, not within them. This can be visualized as follows:

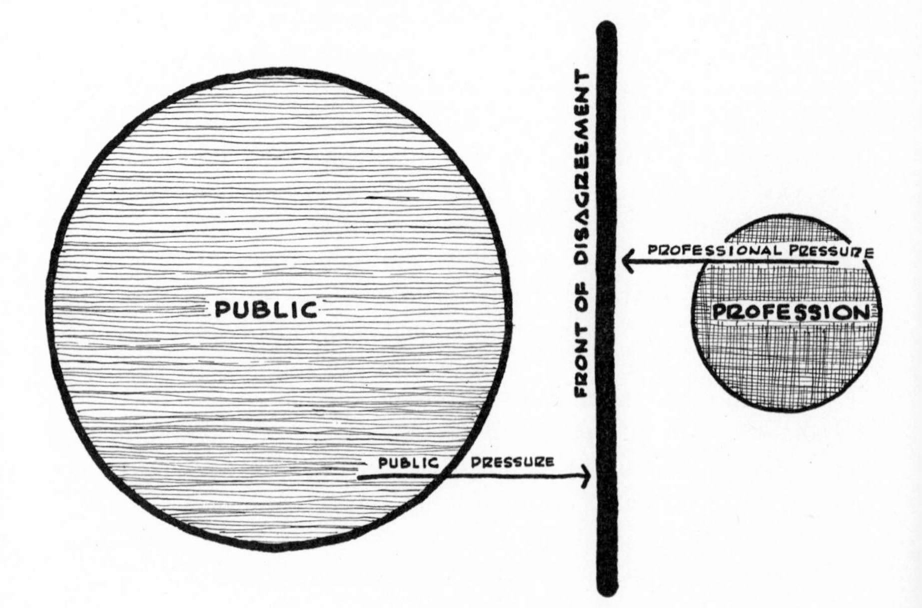

The obvious advantage of this relationship is that it tends towards the creation and maintenance of a high over-all level of competence and integrity.

The situation in architecture is quite different. Here both the public and the profession are split. There is a Traditionalist and a Modernist camp in both. The architect does not have a unified profession to back him up—to create standards and to undertake research. The disadvantages involved are very real. For example, one of the most thoughtful commissioners of public buildings refuses to take his problems to the A.I.A. He does not wish to antagonize either faction and feels sure, quite justifiably, that such a move would cause dissension. The average non-architect exercises no such restraint however. He is more or less solidly behind one or the other group. As a result, architects are peculiarly subject to public pressures of all sorts. Conflicts over what should be matters of strict professional standards are fought out *within* profession and public rather than in between them, as is generally true. High general standards are impossible to maintain in such circumstances. This situation may be visualized as follows:

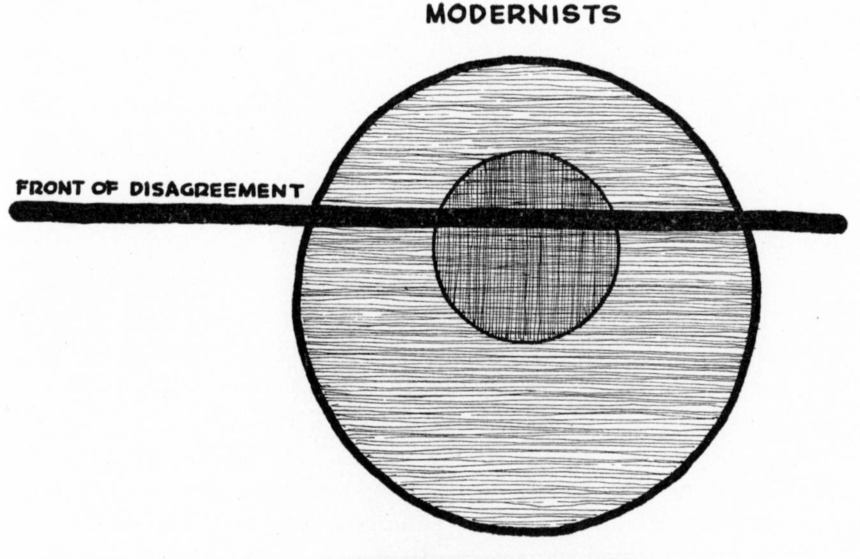

These public pressures on the architectural profession arise from the fundamental relationship between a man and his house As has been mentioned earlier, to build a house is to make a very strong statement. Its style, size, luxury, architectural merit, location, all impart messages to friends and neighbors, to superiors and inferiors. An obviously rented house allows of a certain symbolic vagueness. But the person who builds his own must accept full responsibility for its message. "This," he is in effect saying, "is what I aspire to be." One reason he builds a new house is to be able to make such a statement himself, rather than to buy or rent someone else's. The other reason is that he is able to arrange the business of everyday living exactly as he, personally, likes it. The Traditionalists are largely motivated by the former reason; the Modernists by the latter.

However, no one's motives for so drastic an action as building, could be limited to a single goal. The average client is motivated by from four to six. Rosow found that they correlated with the type of house desired as follows:

GOALS	GROUPS	
	(*Semi Modern*)	(*Modern*)
Status-Prestige	28	2
Living Activities	6	20
Psychic Security	15	7
"Self-Expression," Creativity	3	13
Aggrandizement, Pride	8	3

These contrasting groupings of goals and, more particularly, the differing symbols through which they are achieved by each group, are the underlying causes of the Traditionalist-Modernist split. By the same token, they are the primary sources of those client pressures on the architect having to do with style.

It is obvious from the above chart that the semi-modernist feels great need of a bolstering of his social position, and of his own opinion of himself. This is equally true of the Traditionalist, for they are in fact the same sort of people. Semi-modern bears the same relationship to the International Style that Neo-Classic bears to the Golden Age, or that Suburban Colonial bears to Bulfinch. In all such cases of compromise or commutation, style is being used as a commodity, i.e., for other than its real purpose. In the Traditionalist's case, driven as he is a by desire for generalized and personal prestige, style becomes purely and simply a security symbol.

Prestige is a social gift. It must be conferred on the individual by a large number of people. One way a person achieves it is to be as like the group whose respect he desires as is possible. This involves strict conformity to all their known likes and dislikes. It also involves numerous compromises with his own and with others' desires. It is "keeping up" rather than "striking out." The logical choice of style, in such a case, is one which is commonly enjoyed by those in the group to which one wants to belong. Old families live, as we have seen earlier, in old style houses. The older the style, the more it suggests belongingness. To belong socially is, in the Traditionalist's case, to be secure. It is for such reasons that the Traditionalist blames Modernism on architects. He cannot conceive of a sensible middle class man spending his money on a style the security symbolism of which is unknown.

The Traditionalist uses the old styles as symbols not only of belongingness, but also of an idealized family life. He is even apt to prefer the word "home" to "house," forgetting the immortal words of the poet, to wit: "It takes a heap o' livin' in a house t' make it home." (Edgar Guest) More important still, from the architect's point of view, he also symbolizes home in picture form. For the lower middle class the dreamy vine-covered cottage is the goal. For the upper middle class, solid brick Georgian is the preferred image, at least in the Northeast States. Both types of security symbols refer to that complex, demanding and frequently difficult social affair—the family—as well as to its house. Quite obviously a sentimentalized distortion is being perpetrated. This is thoroughly consistent with the lack of personal security indicated by the Traditionalist's goals. Dr. Otto Fenichel remarks that:

> "The use of symbols is a falling back into an earlier primary stage of thinking, by means of which intended distortions are brought about. In dreams (in this case of belongingness), symbols appear . . . as a characteristic of archaic pictorial thinking, as a part of visualizing abstract thoughts."

The fear of not belonging, the necessity for conventional features to reenforce one's sense of security, lead inevitably to comforting clichés, both verbal and pictorial, in lieu of logical or creative thinking. In such circumstances innovation is, of course, impossible. Dr. Fenichal remarks that:

> "Logical thinking presupposes a strong ego that is capable of postponements, tolerant of tensions, . . . and ready to judge reality according to its experience. If the ego is weak or tired or asleep or without confidence in its own ability . . . then the pictorial type of thinking becomes more attractive than objective intelligence.

The person whose goals are subjective and hidden insists that his architect build him a reasonable facsimile of his dream house. He trusts that he will achieve thereby not only a sense of belongingness, but also, miraculously, a better family life. The person whose goals are objective and stateable thinks his problems through logically and is more than likely to achieve his stated aims.

The Modern clients' motives would seem to indicate that he is personally secure. He does not need to advertise the fact that he has arrived, or is going places socially. He is not greatly concerned with what the neighbors think, because he knows what he himself thinks. His first goal is better living. In order to achieve it, he must use to the full our constantly expanding technical advantage and our constantly expanding insight into humans. He is literally forced to innovate. But he is also influenced by the need for security. Thus his definition of security is at the root of the difference between himself and the Traditionalist. The latter defines it, passively, as social status, and symbolizes it as "home." The Modernist defines it actively as an harmonious and creative approach to life, with personal fulfillment as the goal. This definition is not directly symbolized. The Traditionalist buys a ready-made symbol. The Modernist creates a structure designed to increase his pleasures in living and at the same time to express and abet those pleasure. He is after a life symbol—expression—rather than a security symbol.

This desire to express his life has the effect of freeing the Modernist to think logically about architecture. The form of security symbols is necessarily predetermined. In order to achieve them, every other factor must be compromised for the sake of their fixed outline. When one simply wants to express one's life patterns, no fixed image must be achieved. The functional and esthetic goals merge. Thus the Modern client carries his ideas, unhampered by the need to conform, into every nook and cranny of his house. Because he is following his own, rather than a social scheme of things and because in order to get the best, he is using new techniques, materials and theories, he is bound to innovate. This does not war with his desire for expression. The technical and intellectual advantages we enjoy are the very things he wants expressed.

In the Traditionalist's case, the architect's job is to materialize a day-dream image in bricks, stone, and mortar. It is significant that the Traditionalist architects are expert at what they themselves call "pretty pictures," while the typical Modernist rendering makes no concession to sentimentality. The currently most fashionable Internationalist rendering seems, in fact, to go out of its way to show people in a supposedly humorous, but actually quite hateful light. The architect is saying, in effect, "We are above all this gooey sentiment. We're hard-boiled logical thinkers, and we look reality straight in the eye." But this approach is extreme, as well as extremely disagreeable. In the ideal case, that is where no wedge is driven between thinking and feeling, the architect's job, as conceived by both himself and the client, is to express in building materials the charm, warmth, and humanness of the living activities.

While the Modern client comes to the house building experience very well equipped, it is new to him. Thus the architect must further him, and guide him, in thinking out his own functional problems and in feeling out his expressive desires. This is very much in the architect's professional realm. He is helping his client, who, while he is creative, is not the active member of the team. The architect is. The client may set the tone of the house, i.e., its social message. The architect endows it with its deeper symbolism, gives it its unique message. This third, or personal kind of symbolism, is the function of the artist, no matter what his medium. It is responded to intuitively—very seldom verbalized. Though it refers (as must all symbols) to universally shared sensations, it is by no means universally understood or desired. This subject will be examined in greater detail below. In the meantime, the important fact, from the point of view of the practicing architect, is that the Traditionalist client is apt to recoil in horror before personal symbolism, while the most intuitive Modernist, apparently stimulated by his own kind of creative expressiveness, welcomes it as the fulfilling element in the expressive content of his house.

One reason, perhaps, that the Modernist is not alarmed by the consequences of functional and symbolic innovation is that he is apt to know from experience that this new thing he is helping to create will, all in good time, itself become traditional. The traditionalization of Modernism comes about as a result of interaction between the conservatives and the innovators. The process (which can be visualized as in the following figure) starts with the person who wants above all else a better design for living. He looks towards the newest techniques and social theories for help. Because these are in constant evolution, he inevitably turns up with something new. This new thing is defined by the Traditionalist as wild, unsound and left wing, and is looked on, at this point, with extreme distrust.

As more and more innovators reach the same conclusions, a style begins to be created. A recognizable movement is taking place, even though no two of its examples seem very much alike in the beginning. The movement begins to be associated in every one's mind with the upper middle class, i.e., with "rich" and "nice" people, even though queer. At this point the Traditionalist begins to feel an interest which he disguises in a supercritical attitude. To the Modernist, the intensity of the Traditionalist's

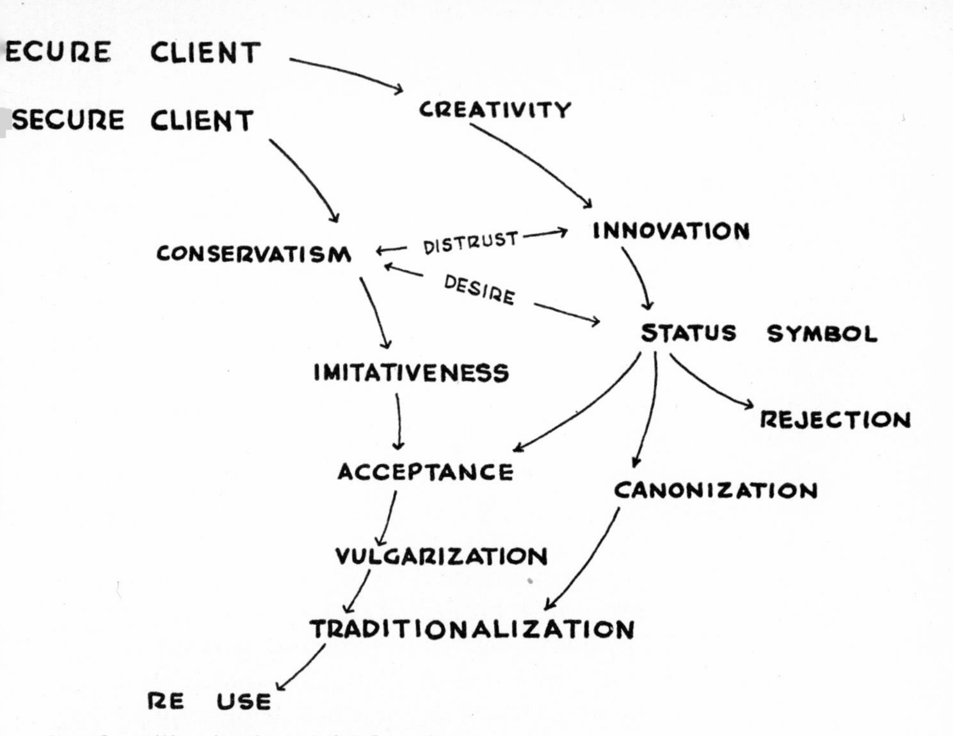

first hostility is almost frightening.

As the new style continues to grow, proliferate, and gain prestige, the Traditionalist slowly becomes reconciled to it. Its symbolism has become clear. At about the time when it has begun to run its course, new things having been invented, he begins to copy it. He does not use its principles. He imitates its outward forms, or uses some of its "features" indiscriminately. Today, for example, the picture window is everywhere. This vulgarization, plus functional obsolescence, kill the new style as far as its founders are concerned, and they move off in new directions. Its best examples are canonized. They become "our fine old homes" or in other words, traditional. They also become better understood. They are studied. Their principles get lost, but their rules become well known. The copies become more successful with the passage of time, rather than less so. These latter day imitations are compromised for the sake of plumbing, or some other symbol of Modernity. But they are obsolete in terms of livability. Thus the Modernist blames the public for Traditionalism, rather than the architect. He assumes that the architect, at least, knows what the score is. The Modern client, like the Modern architect, fails to sympathize with the Traditionalist's problems in security.

Aims

The traditional architects offer the average man a sensation which he holds nearly priceless. As a result they are well established, prosperous and very much in the majority. They design by far the largest block of upper middle class houses.

Modern architects on the other hand are relatively small in numbers, and less well established. Their most necessary sales argument is that belongingness (and therefore security) does not pertain to Traditional style, but to an harmonious personal relationship with the social and technical character of our times. This is a hopelessly abstruse notion, totally unconvincing to those who have not arrived at it through their own inner means. The dedicated Modern client accepts the relationship between creativity and better living with social and psychic security. But even these are not entirely indifferent to the effect of the style of their house on the social judgments directed at them by their neighbors. The frequency of occurrence of psychic security as a motive among them is ample proof of this. Because it is the norm to be "traditional," those who deviate often find their security in the concept of belonging to an elite avant guard. Thus the tendency among Modernists is towards stylistic perfectionism, while the Traditionalists take life with a far more easy-going philosophy.

The shopping client may ask for "traditional front, modern behind," trying to have his cake and eat it too, or he may attack his security problem with the greatest sophistication. But it is always there. It is for this reason that both camps lay claim to traditionalism. One of the most radical modern architects claims his houses are in the "American Tradition" because they have fire places in the living room. Others make the point more subtly. Marcel Breuer is quoted in the New Yorker as follows:

> "Mr. Breuer hopes his house will show how different modern architecture is from the stark-white concrete cubes that most people think of when the term is used. 'Modern architects don't like severity in a house,' he said. 'Perhaps we did once, but we don't any more. Little by little, we've learned how to use the

Eliot Porter.

old natural materials—stone, unpainted wood—in fresh ways. We've learned to make houses that grow gently out of the land and will weather and become more beautiful with age."

The various claims to traditionalism made by architects of every stylistic persuasion are aimed, of course, at weaning away converts from the opposing camp. In order to validate them, a most bewildering variety of definitions is used. The Traditionalist-Modernist arguments get bogged down in the resulting confusion. Obviously, the situation will remain beclouded until all architects use the word in the same way—the way it is defined by the other arts, sciences and professions.

Tradition is defined by Webster's as "the oral transmission of information, beliefs, customs, etc. from ancestors to posterity without written memorials; also a belief, practice, etc. so transmitted." Traditional architecture is, by extension, that which is designed according to rules, ways of doing, cultural biases, attitudes towards materials, functions, climate, etc. etc. which are learned by sons of fathers—by apprentices of masters. Time, Place and Process are of the essence. The oral method of transmission precludes historical gaps, unless bridged by mediumistic interchange with the "other world." Geographical gaps are equally impossible. Measured drawings, history books, photographs and the like are no substitute for the hot breath of one's master.

Traditional architecture in this country was most typical of rural areas. It was usually produced by farmers, or master builders, or by architects steeped in a traditional culture. It was rooted in clearly understood and simple rules, in a limited and consistent palette of materials, and depended on a high degree of cultural homogeneity. The farm architecture of Bucks County, Pennsylvania, is a case in point, as is the farm and town architecture of New England. This method, because it is largely free of books and other "outside" influences, results in a highly stable, unified and conservative local style. Its development was slow and careful.

It is obvious that in this sense no present day architect can lay claim to traditionalism. He learns his trade in school, depends on a mass of documentation, draws his models from the world's stock, and practices in a style having little to do with his period. The primitive type of traditional builder is now all but nonexistent. The reasons for his disappearance need not be gone into in any detail. But a summary of a few causes would include the proliferation of materials, the nationalization of materials supply, excellent communications, immigration with its attendant period of low cultural homogeniety, in short, the industrial revolution with the concomitant shift from local to national to international source material. The Industrial Revolution not only killed off the traditional builders, it changed, as Riesman has shown, the very character of man. The rugged individualism of the last century replaced, as a guide to behaviour, the heavy outer discipline of the earlier traditional societies.

Though traditional ways of operating are dead, the legacies left us by our various primitive sub-cultures are still very much to be reckoned with. They are the most potent mementoes of our past, of our history. They are tremendously important to our sense of continuity, security and belongingness, as the numerous "Societies for the Preservation of . . ." indicate. They constitute our ideal image, against which all other environments, and most new individual structures are measured.

The proliferation of styles since 1800 can be seen as the wild search for a way to fill the vacuum created by the death of tradition. As the old ways of design became obsolete, new methods of operating had to be discovered. The history of architecture in our times is the history of this search. And it continues with unabated force today, for no generally accepted substitute has as yet been found. The contemporary architect is reacting essentially to the same pressures which have influenced every architect since 1800.

The fact that this search has created such a variety of styles implies that there are a large number of variables. And indeed there are. The traditional architect's adjustment was based on one relationship to Period, Place and Process. But within this framework there are nine factors. The possibilities, arranged for the primitive traditionalist, can be visualized as follows:

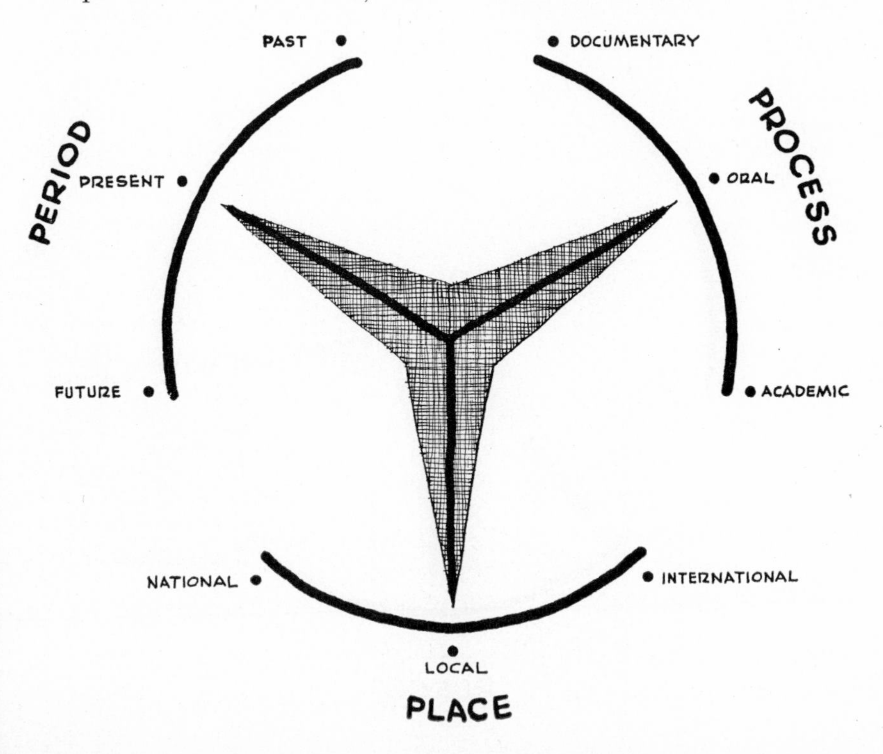

Science and history have made the oral process obsolete. The revivals, followed by our current Eclecticism, have very nearly invalidated the local place. Otherwise all the possibilities are fully open. The character of any given style is largely determined by which of the three factors in each category it identifies itself with. By the same token, marked similarities between styles which are, visually, poles apart, arise from the fact that they share two identical factors, and differ only on the third. For example, the current Eclectics and the International Stylists share the Academic process and the international place. Their only difference is that the Eclectic postulates period as the past, the International Stylist as the future. This two-thirds agreement gives them in fact more similarities than differences. This suggests that Place, Period and Process describe a value system within which the architect makes certain choices. Changes in style can be seen as the result of shifts within this field. This might be visualized as follows, where the perfect and untenable adjustment would resemble the primitive, but where the individual actually creates a distorted starfish shaped field, its form depending on the choices made.

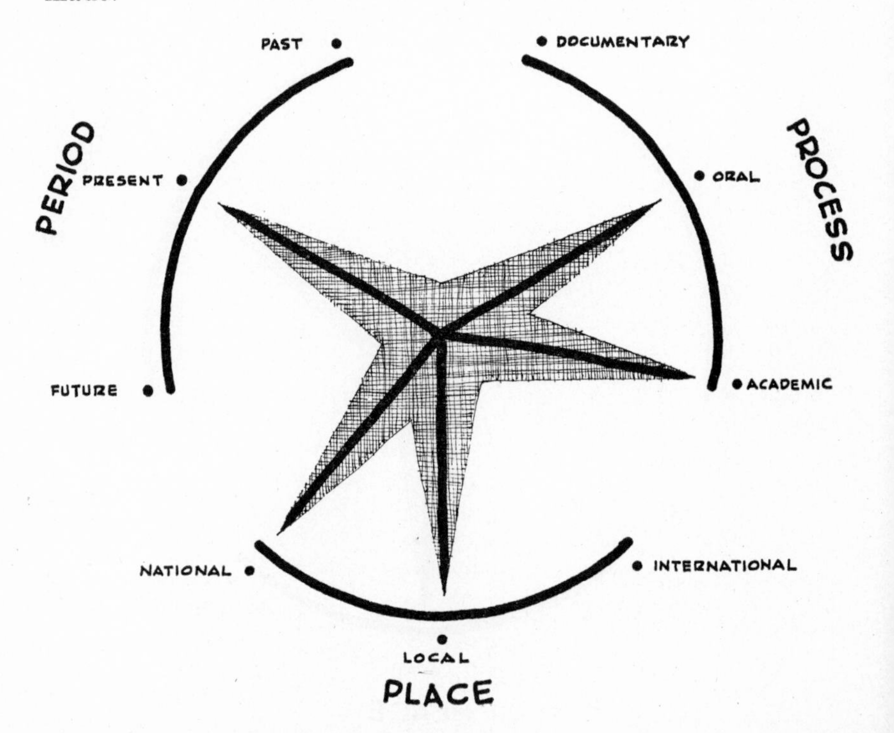

Aims

The architect, in choosing some point of adjustment in the period-place-process field can be thought of as selecting his aims. He wants to be cozy and homey, or grand and worldly, etc. But how is he to approach these ideals? Here it would seem necessary to lean heavily on Sullivan. His triad, Form, Function and Expression, are the most useful symbols yet discovered for the understanding of the architect's *technique*, as distinct from his goals. If Sullivan can be said to have been limited, considering the state of the art in his time, it surely was only in that he did not penetrate far enough behind his triad of symbols. He regarded the will to synthesize them as a *moral* force, leading to skill and technique. It seems more likely that once the architect has adopted a position in the goal system, he has only that control over form, function and expression which his native skill allows him. The main tenor of his work is already determined. Thus, for example, function within Traditionalism is difficult of achievement, while personal expression is denied the International Stylists. This relationship may be visualized as follows:

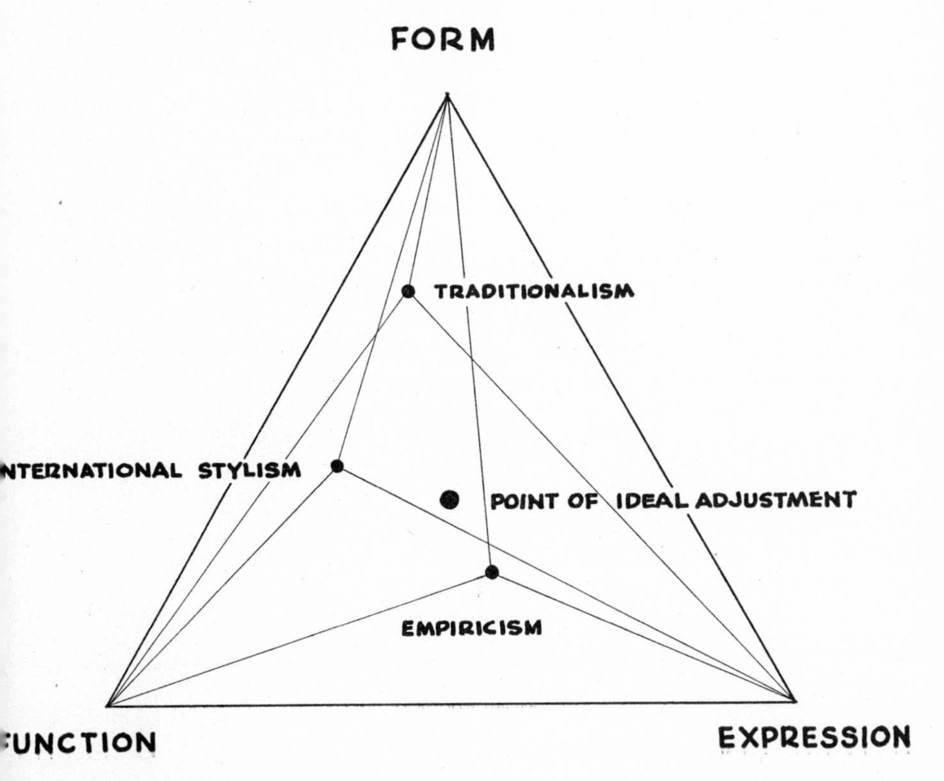

The cause and effect relationship between the architect's value system and his means is, however, highly complicated. As was mentioned earlier he is pulled, in the first instance, towards art, business and technique. The art aspect of his field is again subdivided, as are the other two. His business dealings must harmoniously combine his own interests with those of his client and his contractors. His technical skill must reach out towards materials, engineering and assembly. Thus the forces at work within, on, and around him are numerous and delicately interrelated. The nature of this complex adjustment goes far to explain the very great variety in appearance of the two principal styles, as against their very great similarities in most practical respects. For, while a difference in past-present-future orientation can materially alter the looks of things, no single, nor any combination of differences, can alter the final point of equilibrium to any great extent. Such is the check and balance nature of the forces at work that the more things are different, the more they are the same. This might be visualized as in the following figure. It is for this reason that the war between the Traditionalists and the International Stylists appears, most of the time, as a case of the pot calling the kettle black, rather than as a genuine divergence. But, as this war is the principal architectural phenomenon of our time, it seems worthwhile examining its background, its separate positions and the results of the conflict itself in some detail.

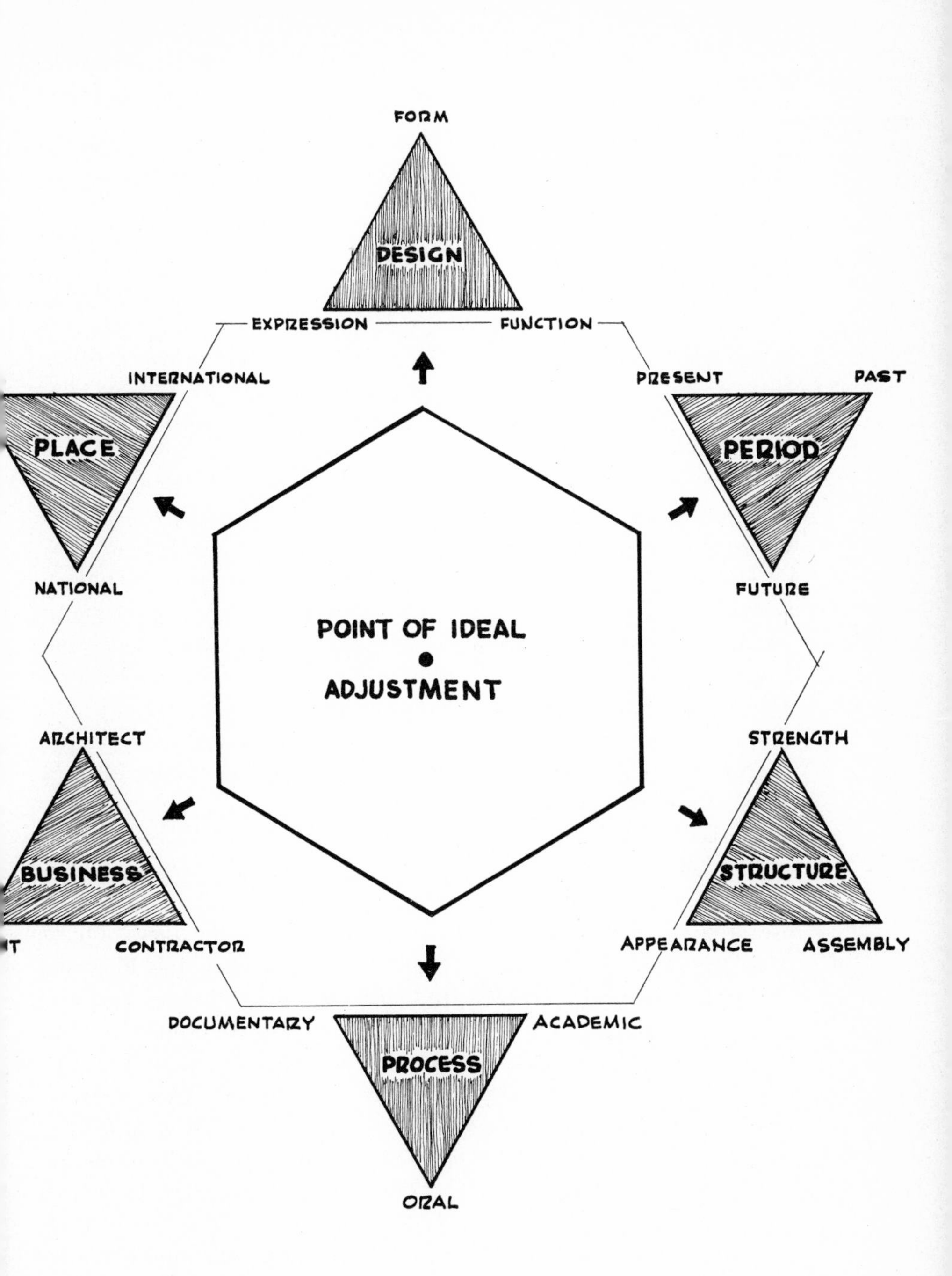
FORM
DESIGN
EXPRESSION
FUNCTION
INTERNATIONAL
PLACE
NATIONAL
PRESENT
PAST
PERIOD
FUTURE
POINT OF IDEAL
ADJUSTMENT
ARCHITECT
BUSINESS
CONTRACTOR
STRENGTH
STRUCTURE
APPEARANCE
ASSEMBLY
DOCUMENTARY
ACADEMIC
PROCESS
ORAL

The Main Stream

"Continuity with the past is only a necessity, not a duty."
Justice Holmes.

The architect's interest in style, while for the most part identical with his client's, does differ in one respect. As a professional or as an artist, he wants his work to be in the main stream of architecture. His greatest satisfaction comes from knowing that he has advanced that stream—if only an iota. Streams involve constant movement from several sources to an outlet. For United States' architecture these sources were the primitive traditional styles. Movement was created by the need to fill the vacuum left by the disappearance of the social conditions which produced them. The outlet is as happy an adjustment to our current social situation as the traditional builders enjoyed with theirs. Architecture in the stream, just as medicine in the stream, is in constant change. Innovation and progress is the order of every day. Doctors, while they revere medical tradition, do not leaf through old medical books in order to find some nice antique operation to try on some nice unsuspecting patient. That sort of malpractice is reserved for architects.

The scarcity of antique operations is more complete, but hardly less significantly so, than the scarcity of truly traditional buildings in our average urban and suburban environment. The few that remain can only constitute a reminder of the past. Those that do exist often contain, if they have not been too liberally restored, fascinating truths. But they are, nevertheless, rarities. The Romantics actually created most of the buildings in our older cities and suburbs. The Romantic environment is the one with which the architect is principally concerned. And, because architecture is first and foremost the art of adjusting a new idea to an existing environment, the nature of that created by Romanticism is of the essence.

Romanticism is, far too frequently, lumped as a single, rather hair-brained phenomenon. But as John Coolidge has pointed out, it actually involved three stages.

Eliot Porter.

"In the first or decorative stage, details from the past are used to decorate buildings which in their essentials are still traditional. The mass is generally simple, and the delicate ornament is often executed in a contrasting material or color. A fine product of this way of thinking is St. Anne's church in Lowell. In the next, or archaeological, stage the total form of the building is conceived as the accurate duplication of some accepted model. The decorative elements are larger in scale and bolder in handling. Often these ranges of buttresses or pretentious porticoes seem to swallow up the whole building, as in the first railroad station in Lowell, for instance. Finally, the attempt to organize the whole structure according to canonical principles is given up. There had been an eclecticism among the historical styles that produced a great variety of building types. Now there is an eclecticism of motifs derived individually from the past. These compose a vocabulary. They are organized according to original principles, so that the multiplicity of historical forms constitutes but a single style. Detail is more disciplined, and is subordinated to hierarchical compositions of masses."

As is suggested here, no abrupt change from the primitive traditional adjustment was ever visible. The traditional ways of operating broke down slowly. The first phase of Romanticism was continuative, a matter of a new flavor applied to a basically primitive skeleton. This continuative phase was superceded by a revivalist surge. Whereas Traditionalism continued (or Revivalism begun) has long since expired, the worst aspects of Revivalism have continued to this day. But it is also true that the Greek Manner, typical of the second stage, produced a great period in American architecture. Henry-Russell Hitchcock, Jr. has described it as follows:

". . . in the late thirties the Greek Revival had become without any question the national style in architecture and building. For the last time in this country architects and carpenters, engineers and farmers of the East, the South and the West, all built in a single homogeneous way, as consistently, if less

Eliot Porter.

instinctively, as the colonies had done before the introduction of English pattern books in the early eighteenth century and the gradual establishment of the Late Baroque hierarchy of design."

The Greek Revival, as was the case with Continuativism, was, at its best, concerned with the present as well as with Greece. True, at its worst it produced arbitrary and tactless revivalist buildings. But many of our most wonderful houses stem from this period.

The first two stages of Romanticism were, at their best, fully in the main stream. No arbitrary theory was allowed to intervene between place and period. The builder was in more or less constant contact with Europe, accepted the use of handbooks, yet he stuck firmly to traditional ways of building. Where the location, during the process of expansion, did not become obsolete, the whole history of the place is expressed in its architecture. But the thread of local custom, attitude, materials and techniques remains in evidence. Despite varieties in style, or more accurately flavor, a great unity results. Brattle Street in Cambridge, Massachusetts, is such an environment, in that it contains examples of every style used in New England, unified by a common local attitude. This is the method of variation within a continuity, and has produced the most successful environments we know.

The continuative method always depended on handbooks and outside influences of other sorts. As the Industrial Revolution continued, it came to rely more and more on statics and dynamics, functional thinking, measured drawings, in short on the whole paraphernalia of reference now so well developed. At the same time, it lost contact with the traditional rules. This process in effect gave the architect an increasing personal freedom. Theory replaced dogma. A need for a conscience vis a vis environment developed. The new freedom, released by the end of the heavy discipline of tradition, required curbing. In a purely technical way this freedom was used by the continuative architects to increase glass areas, flatten roof pitches, and rationalize house plans, a trend which has continued to the present. Thus Brattle Street, in Cambridge, Massachusetts, for example, exhibits most of the phenomenon we think of as uniquely modern, limited only by the techniques of the time. Their success in that environment lies in the fact that they have been absorbed, rather than flaunted. The huge windows and flat roofs of the Hastings' House, the open plan of H. H. Richardson's contribution have to be looked for, so modestly and skillfully have they been used.

The culmination of this movement was that "single style" mentioned by Coolidge, the High Victorian. This was perhaps the first American architecture in the sense in which the word is used today. It was thoroughly professional, as distinct from the provincial building which preceded it. But at this point, when the slide rule, the architectural school, and the trip to Europe took over, tradition was of course totally dead. Thus on Brattle Street the high Victorian mansions are somewhat obtrusive in spite of their great merit. The best of them show a distinct element of compromise with place. H. H. Richardson's Stoughton House, or his W. H. Potter House in St. Louis, for example, express a National rather than a local ethos. But their period was still their present.

This sequence within Romanticism, continuing through Richardson, Sullivan, Wright, Wurster et al is the main stream of U. S. architecture. It is, typically: a) of the present, b) of the locality or national, and c) its academicism is tempered by local structural usage. Those manners of building, on the other hand, which are placed in the past, or in the future, or in the international scene, cannot be continuative by their very nature and

House in Massachusetts. Photograph by William Wilson Wurster.

orientation. They are thus outside the main stream of United States architecture.

The security inherent in the main stream takes on different colors according to whether it is for the architect or for the client. The architect wants to achieve an adjustment within the style cosmos which will release the greatest possible amount of his creative energy. He is standing on a knife edge, between past and future. His creative moments are of infinitesimally short duration. He himself is primarily a bundle of legacies from the past, and intuitions about the future. In order for his work to contain any lasting esthetic validity, it must bridge the gap between the two. If he is not constantly reacting to the real situation of his moment (created in the past) and if he is not constantly attempting to alter this situation towards his desires for the future, his creativeness is bound to be stymied.

The client's interests are those of the consumer. If his house does not belong to the present, if it does not bridge past and future, it will both miss architecture altogether and be obsolete before it is finished. Its form, its functional, and its expressive qualities, i.e. those aspects of architecture which are *used*, will, like all worn out tools, offer precious little security. It is for such reasons that the architect's best clients are innovators. Their drive to symbolize the creative elements in their own lives is, in large part, the energy which keeps the main stream moving. Architecture, which has no "life" in the human sense, nevertheless does have a life of its own—the life of ideas. In the U. S., this life is expressed in the writings of Whitman, Emerson, Thoreau, Greenough, Sullivan et al, and continues in that of Mumford. The most satisfactory architecture is created by the impact of the one on the other; of the client's immediate life on architecture's old, sequential, life of ideas.

The life of the main stream was seriously threatened by the Eclectic movement, which grew out of, and followed, Romanticism. But it was never in danger of drying up. Sullivan existed in the vortex of Eclecticism, and Modernism is directly attributable to it. But Eclecticism is still in full flower and bids fair to continue to burgeon for some lengthy period of time. Because of its age and importance, it seems worth while examining in some great detail. The subject is an unpleasant one, however, not only because of the horrible work the Eclectic practitioner nearly always produces, but because of the degenerative effects this sort of adjustment has had on the profession as a whole. Hitchcock has noted of its beginnings that:

> "Although the most serious and earliest opposition (to the Greek Manner) arose from the proponents of the Gothic, there was no drawn battle in which the Greeks were routed and the country delivered over to the Goths. The country was never delivered over to the Goths any more than was England, where the Gothic Revival was much more successful. But it was, as a matter of fact, delivered over to architectural advisors who were barbarians in the literal sense, in that they spoke all manner of strange tongues and spoke them very ill."

Style is conceived of, by the currently practicing Eclectic architect, as a commodity. Its source is the book and the measured drawing. The choice of style is based on arbitrary rules. Thus government buildings are classic and universities Gothic. For the rampant Eclectic there is, however, no restriction on the style of houses. But, as will be shown later, Eclecticism and Traditionalism have merged in practice, so that it is now necessary to do houses in revivals of native styles. There is, given enough building types, no restriction on the number of styles the individual practitioners may use. Nor is physical distance between the place of origin of the style and the place it is to be used is considered important. Thus Cape Cod invades Texas, while Ranch Houses invade Cape Cod.

Distance in period between the architect's own time and that of the style selected is likewise ignored. This attitude towards style is essentially *anti*-traditional. The notion that styles from other times and places are better than those from one's own time and place is an invidious one. Anti-traditionalism makes it logical for the Eclectic to introduce the most bizzare structures into the most unified environments. He is irresponsible towards environment, with the result that those in which he works lose their unity. Eclecticism produces chaos. Anyone who has seen the

DESIGNING THE EXTERIO

ANY BASIC PLAN ALLOWS A WIDE CHOICE OF EXTERIO

FROM THE SMALL FOUR ROOM PLAN SHOWN BELOW WE HAVE DEVELOPED THESE EIGHT DIFFERENT EXTERIOR DESIGNS FOR A STORY AND A HALF HOUSE. THIS SAME PLAN CAN ALSO BE USED FOR A ONE STORY OR A TWO STORY HOUSE AND A GREAT MANY OTHER EXTERIOR DESIGNS ARE POSSIBLE. GARAGE, PORCH AND CHIMNEY ARE SHOWN IN DIFFERENT LOCATIONS

Reprinted by permission from "The House for You to Build, Buy, or Rent," by Catherine and Harold R. Sleeper, John Wiley and Sons, Inc. Copy. 1948.

horrible brownstone Romanesque libraries in the squares of the traditional New England towns must wonder at the extreme esthetic insensibility of the era which could accept such a dichotomy.

This "method or practice of selecting what seems best from various systems" (Webster's definition) is the antithesis of the artist's approach. It is design by accretion. Thus the artist was sure to revolt from Eclecticism. Furthermore its destructive effect on environment was bound to be noticed sooner or later. And the science of history, with its emphasis on accuracy of view, was also bound to have its effect. In such circumstances Revivalism inevitably seems to offer a way out. The notion that to steep oneself in the architecture of a certain period, to understand thoroughly its frame of reference, will enable one to recreate it is tempting, but highly naive.

Design can be defined as the art of synthesizing form and function at a certain point in time. To place this act in time is highly important, for the synthesis is a temporary one. Architecture as an art is so durable as to seem eternal. Architecture as optimum shelter is short lived. Time gradually separates form from function. Man's sense of beauty, while it drifts, does not change; whereas his sense of appropriate function is constantly changing. As we lose sight of and forget earlier functional requirements, our view of architecture becomes more and more purely esthetic. And the further back in time we go, the more difficult it is to see a building as the synthesis of form and function which it originally was. By default, that ability becomes the province of the scholar. Leonardo da Vinci, for example, in his Codice Atlantico manuscript described the living functions of his time as follows:

> "The large room for the master and that for the family should have the kitchen between them and in both the food may be served through wide and low windows, or by tables that turn on swivels.
>
> "The wife should have her own apartment and hall (sala) apart from that of the family, so that she may set her serving-maids to eat at another table in the same hall. She should have

> two other apartments as well as her own, one for the serving-maids, the other for the wet nurses, and ample space for their utensils."

Today we could not guess without some preliminary study that the Italian Sixteenth century house was used thus. It is small wonder then that in our ignorance of its true function, ancient architecture appears in the guise of a slow and beautiful evolution of form, as art for art's sake.

It is out of this distorted view of the past that the fallacy of architecture as historic form arises. As soon as ancient architecture is seen separated from its functions, it immediately seems logical to go on using its forms, in that they are still beautiful. Because these forms were part and parcel of the functions of their day, they must be altered to fit the new requirements, or our new requirements must be abandoned in favor of the old forms. To attempt either is, as Sullivan pointed out, technically unsound. The numerous and horrible revivals of our own and of the Romantic periods are indications of the accuracy of his analysis.

The forms clothing function are, of course, made up of structure, and are thus inextricably bound up with techniques. One of the constants in architecture is that the techniques used are always more or less contemporaneous. The way a building is put together is usually typical of its period, even though what it expresses may not be, and even though its functional provisions may be behind or ahead of its time. Thus the architect who is using forms which are disconnected from the techniques of his time is faced with two alternatives. First he may alter the forms in favor of his techniques. Bulfinch was content, as were all the continuative architects, to dress up his work *a la mode*. The Italian Renaissance architects and the Greek Revival builders modified their source material in favor of their then current techniques. The second alternative is to retain the pure form—the original model—intact, and to construct it as best one can. This is the method of the Eclectic and of the average Revivalist. The effects produced vary from an ingenious adaptation of techniques to form, to a clothing of pure structure in pure form. The divorce of form from structure has the effect of releasing form. As there is no structural necessity to force it into a new shape, it must be given a shape arbitrarily. Thus the designer picks out some example and slavishly copies it, or he goes completely wild. He has no immediate, or functional, guide to use.

A lack of concordance between form and structure is a falsification, an architectural lie. The type of mind which will accept such a lie, and, consistently operate on it, will of course accept other lies. Thus the Eclectic building is almost sure to contain not only structural dishonesties, but functional and spatial dishonesties as well. This tolerance of dishonesty has become characteristic of architects. Underlit rooms behind oversize porticos, chimneys with horizontal runs, and the like, are familiar features of American building. Thus the chaotic environments created by the Eclectics usually carry strong overtones of artificiality, while the primitive and continuative traditional environments exhibit opposite qualities. They are honest, directed, and by contrast, grimly real.

The best known and most successful Eclectic Revivalist is certainly H. H. Richardson. He carried Revivalism as far as opportunity and talent could take it. He remained, however, a true despoiler of his environment. The phenomenon for which he stands can be seen as a result of the wild exuberance, the rugged individualism, the newly rich extravagance typical of the whole era in which it flowered. The continuative phase, followed by the Greek Revival, followed by the magnificent High Victorian Style had used up every vestige of traditional discipline. There seemed to be no further native worlds to conquer, and at the same time there was infinite money, materials, and opportunity. Eclecticism was tied down neither by dire necessity, nor by a place in a sequence of ideas. One can thus think of it, now, as a sort of zero point, between the various current adjustments to style, and those of the Romantics. Because it constitutes our most immediate past, and also of course because it still exists, it necessarily has a powerful effect on all current adjustments to style. Our present cosmos of styles are all, in one way or another, attempts to avoid its failings. Is it too soon to tell how well they have succeeded?

The Style Cosmos

"I say to you that unless we keep the stream of the past with living significance for the present, we not only have no past, but we have no present."

Justice Frankfurter

Eclecticism and Revivalism are, in terms of the individual's adjustment, very far apart. The former is little more than business. The latter is little less than art-for-art's-sake. Nevertheless, they have, in our time, merged. Just as heat flows naturally from the warmer to the cooler body—the tendency is for everything to become the same temperature—so ideas flow from the more doctrinal hot heads to the less doctrinal cool heads. Thus Revivalist purism, flowing naturally towards Eclectic pot-pourriism, has created a new mixture—Traditionalism. Traditionalism's character is also due, in part, to its reformist nature. Eclecticism amounted to a kind of orgiastic revel. Released from the pressures of the continuative tradition, the Eclectics celebrated in the fashion of their time, in an exuberant, expansionist, undisciplined, and unprincipled way. They were neither willing nor ready to accept the responsibilities their new found freedom demanded. Traditionalism was the first attempt to check the ravages of Eclecticism, to fill the gap left by the death of traditional ways of assuring conformity and unity. It is, in a very real and useful sense, the dawn of a new-found conscience vis a vis environment. Its fundamental proposition might be cartooned as follows:

> The Eclectic period produced environmental chaos because it used foreign styles.
>
> Therefore, we will select native styles and use them exclusively.
>
> Native styles are our tradition. Therefore we will be in tradition.

The Traditionalist postulates the proper period of style as post-Pilgrim and pre-Victorian, and its proper place as the United States. In the time sense it is identical with Eclecticism, the difference being only one of degree, and the same can be said of its place orientation. The gap between the Traditionalist and his models is now some one hundred years in extent; a century marked by the tremendous changes in our culture, economy and technology. It constitutes a moat between the practitioner and his idealized models. He is effectively isolated from his sources. This leads quite inevitably to a nostalgic orientation, and results in a derogatory attitude towards contemporaneousness—or conservatism. In adopting this position, the Traditionalist cuts himself off from the principal well of creative energy, the present. Expression is denied him.

For example, an important characteristic of building, as expression, is that it must open for us some new perception of the nature of our time. This feeling is completely absent from traditional work. What we miss is the sense of an intuitive reorganization of our current position. This need not be at all complex. Many an architect's rendering appears in the press over the ridiculous caption "Artist's conception of the Future." And, in its more subtle forms, this desire for prophecy is still news to those who seek it. Ortega y Gasset expresses this beautifully, and incidentally ties art, science, and expression together in a particularly significant way when he says

> ". . . it is in art and pure science, precisely because they are the freest activities and least dependent on social conditions, that the first signs of any changes of collective sensibility become noticeable. A fundamental revision of man's attitude towards life is apt to find its first expression in artistic creation and scientific theory. The fine texture of both these matters renders them susceptible to the slightest breeze of the spiritual trade-winds. As in the country, opening the window of a morning, we examine the smoke rising from the chimney-stacks in order to determine the wind that will rule the day, thus we can, with a similar meteorologic purpose, study the art and science of the young generation."

It will be argued later that the Internationalists do little better on this score. Their substitution of a crude futurism for the

Farm house in New Hampshire.

nostalgia of the Traditionalist gets us no closer to changes in our collective sensibility.

The Traditionalists' sources, the dead American styles, are of course now incapable of growth. Nor can the Traditionalist himself change them very greatly, lest they become unrecognizable. They must remain forever static. The Traditionalist, therefore, defines tradition as fixed, dead, unchanging and unalterable. This is the essence of the conservative approach. Thus while the Traditionalist falls into the previously mentioned fallacy of architecture as historic form, he manages to do it in a far less blatant way than the Eclectic. Conservatives, particularly of the more nostalgic variety, are usually remarkable for their good manners, if not for their good sense. The Traditionalists are no exception. By the same token, they lack the spark, the daring, and the dynamic qualities typical of the Eclectic and of the International Stylist, though they avoid the former's nouveau riche, and the latter's revolutionary manners. They have settled in the center of the socio-esthetic spectrum. As seen from the left they are reactionary. As seen from the right, however, they seem to assure the quality of belongingness. Reactionary or not, the Traditionalists have, in their ability to suggest security, a fast selling and almost universally wanted commodity. No left wing movement will ever have a solid effect on style, and thus on environment, until it too puts the average man in touch with his place.

Traditionalism is essentially a flaccid reform movement within Romanticism. The International Style is a violent revolt from all that Romanticism means. Typical of revolutions, it is highly dynamic and dogmatic. Its fundamental proposition can be cartooned as follows:

> The failure of the previous styles is due to their neglect of the present
>
> Therefore we will reintroduce contemporaneousness.
>
> Our times are characterized by science and technology.
>
> Therefore we will design for biological and physiological man (science) in a way in tune with current techniques (the machine).
>
> As biological man is universal, and as the machine *should* be common to all cultures, our theory will necessarily be universal in applicability.

This proposition, naive though it is, has had the effect of freeing architects from the bondage of "Ruskin Type" thought. The energy it has released is due to its opening up of science and technology as legitimate stimulae. Its failure lies in the narrow-

Huson Jackson.

ness of its definition of man, and in the inaccuracy of its application of technology to building. Both faults are outgrowths of the self conscious, rather than intuitive, definition of the present. While the machine is perhaps symbolic of our time, it has very little place indeed in the building industry—a craft operation par excellence. Thus the smooth stucco surfaces typical of the earliest International Style, "as if rolled out of a machine," and the current attempts to achieve the same effect in wood in this country, are at best prognostications, and at worst distortions of fact. The same obscurantist effect is produced by the basic proposition as it relates to man. Such slogans as "the house is a machine for living," and the over-emphasis on biology and physiology, tend to obscure the fact that houses are environmental in nature, and that man's spirit and intelligence are as important to his total adjustment as his body. The distinction here is similar to the one made in medicine between the organic and psychosomatic approach to disease. The Internationalist position does not allow man a soul.

The peculiar character of the International Style is directly traceable to these two distortions. To design a hand-made building as if it were to be made by a machine is futuristic. The robot-like concept of man is also typically futuristic. Thus while contemporaneousness is the desired goal, errors in definition have caused the movement to miss the present. In this sense it is a new phenomenon in the history of architecture. It is a prognostication of things to come. The future is used to guide the present. A natural result is that the past seems of no relevance to either.

Style is yet again placed out of the immediate present and is considered placeless, as it was by the Eclectics. As in Eclecticism, the result is essentially anti-traditional and lacking in responsibility towards environment as such. But Internationalism is closer to Traditionalism than to Eclecticism. It is selective, dedicated, exhibits conscience, if not towards environment then in other ways, and is largely guided by theory.

Any theory designed for world-wide use must be extremely clear, well documented, and dogmatic. It must also carry a reformist emotional charge. It need not, however, be practical in the pragmatic sense. International Stylism is no exception. Its bible is the complete work of Le Corbusier; its Golden Age was the Bauhaus at Weimar, its collegium Romanum is the C.I.A.M., its rules were codified in "The International Style—Architecture since 1922" (Henry-Russell Hitchcock, Jr., and Philip Johnson). Its connection with science is reflected in Sigfried Giedion's "Time, Space and Architecture" (Courtesy of Mr. Einstein), while its idealization of the machine is reflected in his "Mechanization Takes Command."

Its slogans, such as that of Le Corbusier's just quoted, or Sullivan's famous "form follows function," will not bear examination. Indeed in the latter case, it seems quite clear that Sullivan meant not at all what the Internationalists have made him mean. In his essay on Function and Form, he makes his position extremely clear. His student says:

> "What you want me to understand and hang onto is that just as every form contains its function, and exists by virtue of it, so every function finds or is engaged in finding its form."

Later in the same essay he goes on to describe how this idea develops. His student says:

> "Then I infer that I can go on and consider my detail as of itself a mass, if I will, and proceed with the regular and systematic subdivision of function with form, as before, and I will always have a similarity, an organic quality—if I can guess what you mean—descending from the mass down to the minutest subdivision of detail. That's interesting, isn't it? The subdivisions and details will descend from the mass like children, grandchildren, and great grandchildren, and yet, they will be, all, of the same family." . . . "Yes, yes, very good so far as you go. But I wish to warn you that a man might follow the program you have laid down, to the very last detail of details, and yet have, if that were his make-up, a very dry, a very pedantic, a very prosaic result. He might produce a completely logical result, so-called, and yet an utterly repellent one—a cold, vacuous negation of living architecture—a veritable pessimism."

Obviously Sullivan considers the business of relating, properly, form and function a matter of *professional technique*, not an end in itself, and he makes this abundantly clear. Later on his student asks:

> "Well then, tell me now . . . what characterizes a real architect?" "First of all a poetic imagination; second, a broad sympathy, humane character, common sense, and a thoroughly disciplined mind; third, a perfected technique; and finally, an abundant and gracious gift of expression." "Then you don't value logic?" "It has its excellent uses."

The idea here is that the bare synthesis of form and function is not enough. It must be accomplished with an ulterior, clearly defined, artistic motive in mind. The person using a building is happiest when his emotions and intellect are excited. Expressiveness is one of the *functions* of architecture. It is worth noting that for many people this requirement outweighs their practical demands. One of Mr. Wright's clients is quoted as saying:

The Style Cosmos

> "I know the roof has leaked, and that the skylights leak, but I would rather live in this house than any other house in the world."

There are several facets of expression in architecture, each one of which helps produce this kind of response. One of them is of particular interest here in that it is absent in virtually all current building. It is that quality imparted to his work by the architect himself. Herbert Read says that art is the expression of the uniqueness of a personality and he goes on to say:

> "Since the Renaissance the personality of the architect is stamped on every building of any artistic value, until we come to the functional architecture of our own time."

This distrust of self on the part of the architect, this tendency to lean on standardized and accepted forms, has had the effect of making the International Style dated and cliché-ridden before its time.

The Traditionalists' failure to produce architecture, and the Internationalists' failure to respect environment was bound to cause yet another search for a new point of adjustment. The London "Architectural Review" has dubbed this last movement "The New Empiricism," i.e. "the effort to humanise the aesthetic expression of functionalism." Empiricism is an attempt to return, at least in part, to continuative traditionalism—to something approaching the first phase of Romanticism. But it owes most of its character to the International Style movement. On the one hand it is very similar in many respects. On the other, it is influenced as much by opposition to some of the Internationalist precepts as by a strong new direction of its own. Thus it largely eschews science, theory and dogma, and depends instead on experiment and experience. The very word "Empiricism" carries overtones of quackery. And the Empiricists, in that they are apt to be common sensical, anti-rule, anti-style, anti-dogmatic, careless of techniques,—all qualities opposite to those of the Traditionalists and Internationalists—perhaps deserve this invidious overtone.

Carl Koch and Robert Woods Kennedy.

These qualities result in an easy going and rounded atmosphere. Empiricist work is humanly robust. The reverse is often true in terms of structure. The Empiricist style is fragile and temporary, particularly in contrast to the over-development of form typical of the previous adjustments. It necessarily lacks the extreme clarity, the sharp and easily understood outlines typical of architecture based on dogmatic theory. It enjoys neither the models, the measured drawings, and details of the Revivalists, nor the sure knowledge of what is right, typical of the Internationalists. It is rooted in the present, i.e., in the person of the practitioner, in his feelings, intuitions, and observations. It thus tends to become regional in character, rather than to internationalize itself, and to breed anonymity rather than the high visibility and notoriety more typical of the brilliant Internationalist architects. It tends to create loosely organized schools rather than to attract ardent disciples. The greater freedom the method allows its practitioners results in a far more varied, less obviously "modern," often less brilliantly organized and proportioned type of work, with much greater emphasis on personal expression, emotion, play, and the like. The Bay Region style is an example in point.

The Empiricist adjustment to the period factor in style is accurately between past and future, and its adjustment to place is equally complete. It takes a responsive view of environment, and its understanding of and respect for tradition is profound. Thus in terms of the criteria here utilized as a guide to the comparison of the various present day adjustments, it is the most complete and well founded movement since the death of tradition. The factors within Empiricism which cause it to fall short of complete success are, perhaps, not fundamental, but rather matters of degree. The Empiricist proposition can be cartooned as follows:

> The failure of the previous adjustment was due to their emphasis on techniques, documentation, rules, and dogma, at the expense of human feelings and intuition.
>
> We will therefore avoid rules, form, permanence, and theory, in favor of warmth, humanity, and flexibility.

This proposition tends to be reactive, i.e., it is against the previous adjustments. By the same token, it is not thoroughly based in its own positive and inclusive philosophy. Thus while the Empiricist adjustment to Period, Place, and Process is complete, its adjustment of Form, Function, and Expression is heavily weighted towards Expression, and tends to avoid Form.

This de-emphasis of techniques, of form, and of the sort of simple rule on which the average person can hang his hat is, perhaps, essentially unbalanced. It is bound to result in yet another search for a new point of adjustment. The Empiricist thinks of the Internationalist as "The man with the iron whim" and there is more than a little truth in this epithet. On the other hand, the need for iron, for an easily understood skeleton, is, depending on how one looks at it, a human strength or failing which cannot be too long denied.

Thus one might predict that "Directivism" or a new resolution of Style, Environment, Tradition, and of Form, Function and Expression in an esthetically directed manner, will sooner or later supersede Empiricism. It can be argued that this sort of adjustment comes perilously close to completing the circle. It may very well be that the introduction of a ramrod into the Empiricist's jacket will, sooner or later, cause the whole somewhat "neo-traditionalist" movement to go the way of its progenitors.

Pietro Belluschi.

The various points of adjustment indicated by these descriptions represent the situation typical at the centers of spectra. In actuality of course, architects adjust at points closer or farther from the center, and also between spectra. In order to appreciate their real relationships, one must organize each spectrum on the perimeter of a circle, as are the keys in music, where C natural is center, though it is actually on the perimeter, and where G flat and F sharp, compounded, seem to occupy a point between right and left. This, for the current U. S. scene, can be visualized as follows:

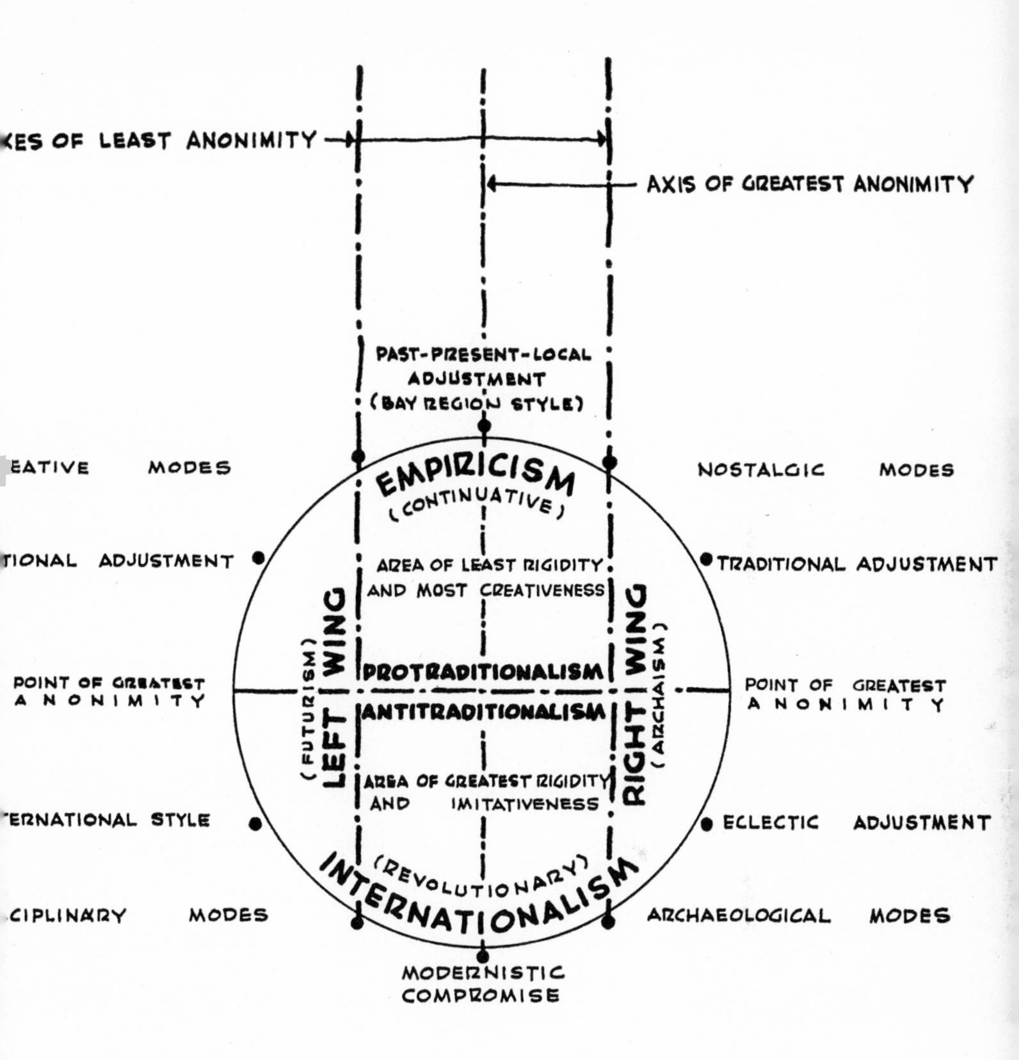

The fact that these various points of adjustment involve not only real personalities, famous and anonymous, but myths, shibboleths, slogans, recriminations and *rapprochements* need not be argued. On the other hand, it might be useful as preparation for what is to follow, to remind the reader of those signs and portents which allow one to recognize an Empiricist or a Traditionalist or an International Stylist wherever he be met. For this purpose, the following table, "*The Art of Freezing Music,*" is offered. Such is the richness of the source material, that it can only be considered as a preliminary report rather than as a definitive statement.

	ITEM	*THE INTERNATIONALISTS*
CULTURE	The greeting	"The left is right!"
	The times	Industrial revolution
	The motto	"No one can stop me!"
	The comic	Superman
	The word	"Pilotis" (Fr. = Lally Column)
	The master	Le Corbusier
	The author	Giedion (Mechanization takes . . .)
	The value	Science
MANKIND	His nature	Bio-physiological
	Children	Animals-in-transition
	Youth	Clear headed
	The aged	Masters
	The sexes are	The same
	Wives are	Architects
	Their place is	In the office
	Clients are	To be reformed
	Contractors are	To be shown
	Draftsmen are	Technicians
	Consultants	Bio-physio-micro-climatologists
NATURE	The earth	Free the house from . . . ! etc.
	The weather	Enjoyed from within
	Water	Microclimatological determinant
	Stones	"People who live in glass houses . . ." etc.
	Trees	Cactus
	Plants	Rubber plant
	The outdoors	"Bring the outdoors in!"
ARCHI-TECTONICS	Architecture	Clean
	Art is	"Time-space in tension"
	Modernism is	Functional nudism
	Form	"Follows function"
	Design is	Research
	Architects are	Design specialists

Freezing Music

THE EMPIRICISTS	*THE TRADITIONALISTS*
"The right is wrong!"	"Wright is left!"
"The Middle Ages were better."	"The Greeks had a word for it."
"The importance of being earnest."	"It can't be done."
L'il Abner	Orphan Annie
"Integration"	"Architectonic"
Wright	Violet le Duc
Sullivan (Kindergarten Chats)	Ruskin (Seven Lamps)
Romance	Conservatism
Aestho-somatic	Business-like
Artists in miniature	To be seen but not . . . etc.
Vital!	Inexperienced
Moribund	Experienced
Mated	Different
Soul mates	"The ball and chain"
Handy	In the home
To be educated!	To be expected
To be helped	To be told
Budding souls	Drafting machines
Native Characters	Bulldozer operators
Root the house in . . . ! etc.	Moved by Bulldozers
Experienced within	In the morning newspaper
Poems in running brooks . . . etc.	Comes in around flashings
"Sermons in stones . . . " etc.	"Remember the three little pigs"
Roof tree	Firewood
Ledge	Entourage (Fr. = Spinach)
"Build the outdoors in!"	"Throw the outdoors out"
Organic	"Frozen music"
"My work"	In museums
Psychic nudism	Bathrooms
Grows like Topsy	Precedes function
"The Search"	Lost and Found Dept.
Synthesists	"Jacks of all trades"

	ITEM	*THE INTERNATIONALISTS*
THE HOUSE	Definition	"A machine for living"
	Home life is	Contemporaneous
	Programs are	Analyzed
	House type	Bi-nucleated
	View point	"From above, what with the airplane and all."
	The plan is	Open!
	Appearance is	Cold
	Prototype	Chicken coop
	Perceptions	"Artist's conception of the future"
TECHNIQUES	Roof type	Butterfly
	Roof Appearance	Floating planes
	Skylights are	Plastic domes
	Walls are	Glass
	Partitions are	Rightist deviations
	Foundations are	Archaic feet of clay
	Materials—type	Synthetic
	Materials—texture	Slick
	Materials—excuse	Link with the machine
	Materials—use	In tension!
	Glass bricks	"Can only be used as a wall!"
INTERIORS	Kitchens	Laboratories
	Fireplaces are	"Sops to sentiment"
	Mantlepieces are	"Opportunities to experiment"
	Bathrooms are	Compartmented
	Bedrooms are	Sleeping cells
	Living rooms are	"All-purpose rooms"
	Reactions	"I can't stand being behind all that fixed glass"
	Pictures	"You can't have pictures in a . . ." etc.
	Reactions	"You can't have a mess in a . . ." etc.

Freezing Music *(cont'd)*

THE EMPIRICISTS	*THE TRADITIONALISTS*
Shelter	A good investment
Aculturative!	Gracious living
Experienced!	Filed
Organically Integrated!	Bi-symmetrical
From inside out!	From front center
Free!	Closed
Flimsy	Clumsy
Grass shack	Mausoleum
"They say nudists live there!"	"Built like a brick . . .!" etc.
Pitch	Dormer
Enveloping forms	"A nice bright color"
Poetic!	"Sure to leak"
"Determine chiarascuoro effects"	Between windows
Space modulators	Preservers of morals
Roots in the Soil	To put foundation planting in front of
Natural!	Proven
Fuzzy	Crispy-crunchy
Link with nature!	"The architect's palette."
Without finish!	In compression!
"Vulgar!"	"Make a nice modernistic bathroom."
Farm	Stock
"The fire"	Centered
Primitive	Georgian
Rejuvenative!	Tiled
Love nests!	Upstairs
"Home!"	"Where you entertain"
"I can't stand all these glass doors"	"I can't stand not being able to see out"
Picturesque!	Picture windows
"You can't rearrange the furniture in a . . ." etc.	"There's no place to put anything in a . . ." etc.

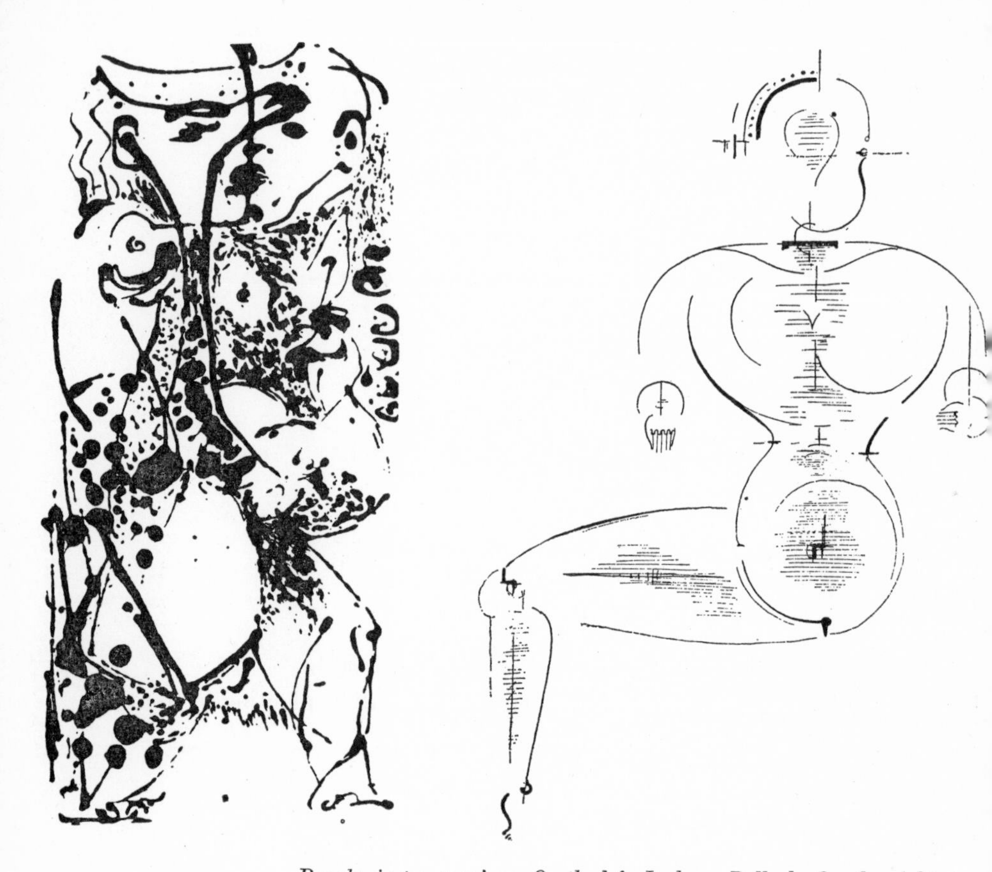

People, in two versions. On the left Jackson Pollock. On the right Oskar Schlemmer. The latter is from "Bauhaus Weimar 1918–25".

Whether dogmatic people tend to become Internationalists, or whether Internationalism tends to make people dogmatic need not concern us here. Most probably the person with a weakness for art tends towards Empiricism, and his weakness is encouraged because of that tendency. The person who values conservatism naturally drifts towards Traditionalism, and in so doing becomes yet more conservative. In any case, his stand is directly reflected in his architecture. The expressive message of a building is largely determined by the attitudes on which its style is bred. The relationship of fundamental proposition to mood can best be expressed as follows:

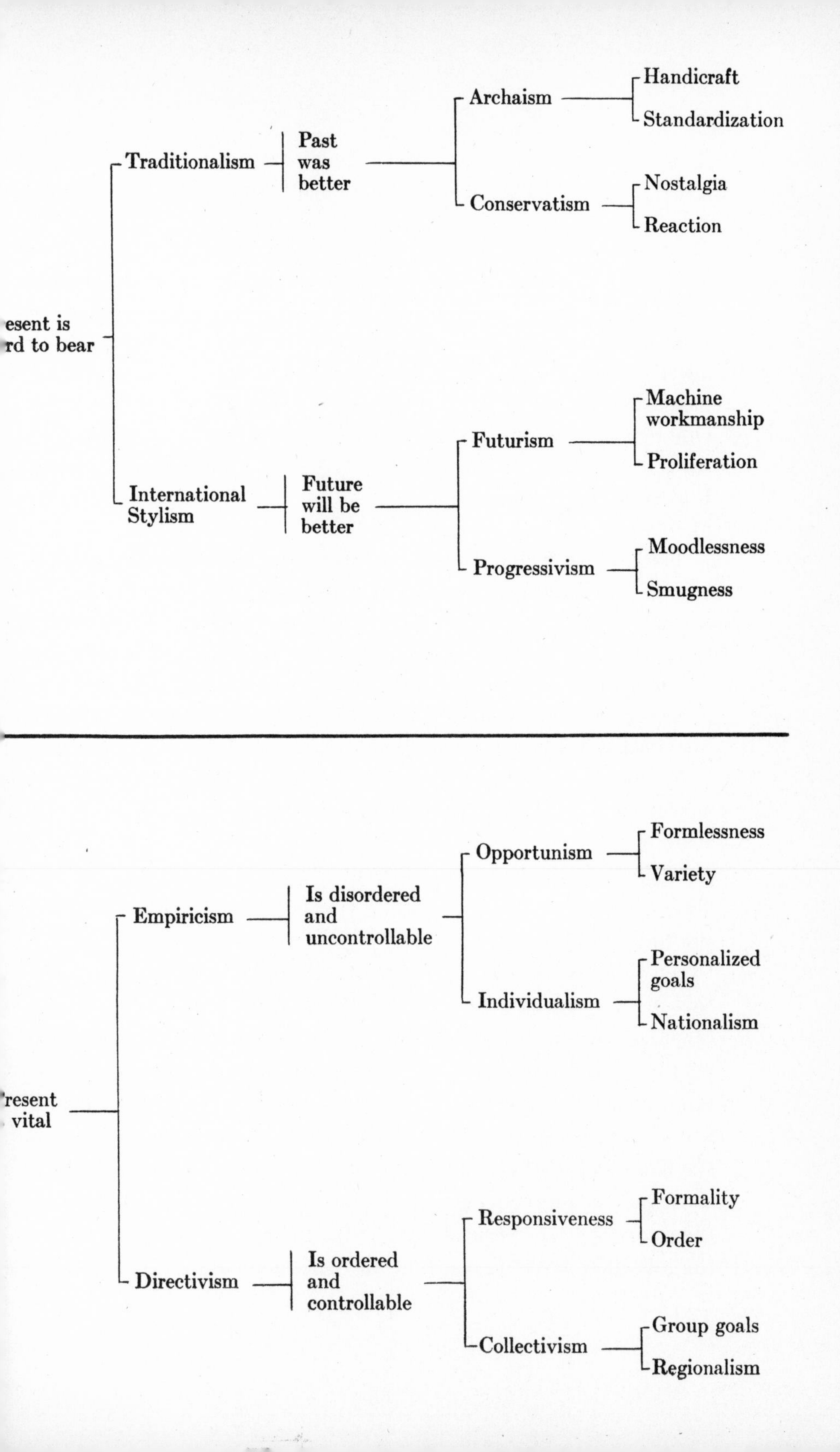

esent is
rd to bear
Traditionalism
Past
was
better
Archaism
Handicraft
Standardization
Conservatism
Nostalgia
Reaction
International
Stylism
Future
will be
better
Futurism
Machine
workmanship
Proliferation
Progressivism
Moodlessness
Smugness
'resent
vital
Empiricism
Is disordered
and
uncontrollable
Opportunism
Formlessness
Variety
Individualism
Personalized
goals
Nationalism
Directivism
Is ordered
and
controllable
Responsiveness
Formality
Order
Collectivism
Group goals
Regionalism

The degree of personal freedom an architect is able to exercise within the larger discipline of his style, is a function of the degree of his identification with it. The architect who is fully identified is apt to follow the rules, go down the slot, as it were, and to turn out a type of work recognized as in the central position of his chosen adjustment. The architect who fails to identify totally is apt to develop a personal mode within the style, if he is skillful, based on his refusal to follow certain, but not all, of the rules. One reason such refusals occur is that the modal force of the style prevents certain of the possible types of appeal to the senses. For example, International Stylism prevents a warm dark cave-like expression.

The architect comfortably ensconced in the central position is largely inhibited from personal expression. His work is apt to contain only the fundamental characteristics of the style in which he works. And as style is essentially the concensus of a group, it is impersonal or even inhuman. The architect who refuses to be pinned down by the rules is most free to express himself. Bernard Maybeck's work is a case in point.

The personal manner of the average architect can thus be seen as the sum of 1) those elements he has chosen to accept out of the style he uses, minus 2) those rules he refuses to accept and use, plus 3) the characteristic elements from other sources he has chosen to fill the place of the rejected rules. This involves considerable shuffling. He must at all times maintain harmony between those rules he is retaining, and those he is substituting, and this involves cutting and trying. Where the old rules are totally rejected, as was the case with J. J. P. Oud, a new style of course results. Where they are in a constant process of minor shuffling, the sequencial type of career results, as in the work of Frank Lloyd Wright. The more able the architect to deal, shuffle, and stack the rules, the greater his opportunity for personal expression, and the more apt he is to locate himself and remain between the spectra of two basic stylistic adjustments. Or, in other words, the less classifiable his work at any one moment.

Modernist's Conception of how a Traditionalist Would Design an Airplane. From the Architectural Forum, August 1940.

The Fight

From the public's point of view Internationalism, Empiricism, and all the little "isms" clustering around them are one phenomenon—Modern, or as the case may be, "Modernistic." The split across both profession and public separates on the one hand Eclectic, Revivalist, and Traditionalist; and on the other Internationalist, Empiricist, and Modernistic. Thus both the sincere Modernist, and the sincere Traditionalist are constantly finding themselves in bed with people whom they regard as very unsavory characters. To call an Empiricist a "modernistic architect," is more insulting than to call his mother a bitch. The Traditionalist-Modernist fight—because its issues are so disparate and confused—usually appears more as an *opera bouf* than as a drawn battle. Its farcical nature is further reinforced by the fact that the most serious proponents, the ultra-conservative Traditionalist faction versus the ultra-dogmatic International Stylists, are, in every technically significant respect, more alike than unlike. Their only real divergence is in appearance.

Again with the criteria here used as a guide to style, the two warring camps compare somewhat as follows:

	TRADITIONALISM	INTERNATIONALISM
PERIOD	Past	Future
	(Neither achieves the present)	
PLACE	National	International
	(Neither regards the local place)	
PROCESS	Academic (archaistic)	Academic (dogmatic)
FORM	Historic Rules	New Rules
	(Neither allows personal freedom)	
FUNCTION	Fully Compromised	Partially Compromised
	(Neither frees function of aesthetic rules)	
EXPRESSION	Absent	Absent

Because of the very great similarities between them, it will be useful to be able to refer to Traditionalism and Internationalism together. The qualities they share in common are: a dependence on theory, i.e., on "a more or less plausible . . . general principle offered to explain a phenomena" (Webster) in this case anent style; and a dedicated and unquestioning attitude towards their total adjustment. Both of these qualities involve the *selection*, out of a welter of possibilities, of certain tenets, for the purpose of simplifying and anchoring their work and professional behavior patterns. Thus *Selectivism* would appear to be an appropriate word to signify both.

In order to appreciate the intra-Selectivist fight, and its consequences, it seems necessary, first of all, to define the meaning of style. The word style means a characteristic and distinctive mode of construction. But the real impact of style, to the person seeing architecture, is largely influenced by the nature of the environment by which an individual building is surrounded. A satisfactory environment is like a forest. The total forest is a complex affair, dependent for its character on every aspect of climate, on cross fertilization, on death, decay, and on cycles of new growth. All its aspects are interrelated. The typical forest tree is warped and twisted by its relationship to its neighbors. Roots interconnect, branches touch, the sun is let in haphazardly. One seldom finds a specimen tree in such an environment. The well-rounded tree comes from open fields, or a more symmetrical environment. Houses come in forests. To all intents and purposes they are never isolated. The person viewing them brings with him, in his cultural baggage, a series of invisible houses with which they are compared. And, in any case, they are usually cheek by jowl. The house which is one with its environment might be described as of its time; and as warped and modified by its neighbors, its position, its climate and its style. This sort of compromise with environment was typical of the continuative tradition. One has only to compare the Greek Revival architecture of New England and the South East to appreciate the sea change the original concept went through in becoming adapted to its new environment.

The selectivists agree in their definition of the forest as an orderly arrangement of specimen trees, rather than as the tangled, and interconnected network of warped and anonymous units. They reserve the right to pick one tree out of the center, develop, feed, prune and generally manicure it, and still claim that it is of the forest. This sort of approach is highly artificial, and as a result those environments created by Selectivists are characteristically stage sets. Their artificiality is the result of the dogmatic insistence on one style, or type of tree, impossible in a real forest.

To pick out a single style and develop it for its own sake, regardless of environment, or period, or place, is to postulate tradition as a series of disconnected specimens. History is used as a grab bag full of tricks to be dipped into at will, or as a forest full of dying trees, which in order to be used must be operated on and generally fixed up. This presents a most unpleasant picture. The next logical step is to dislike the whole forest. On the Internationalist side one symptom of this is the prevalent dislike and disregard for history. Another, typical of Selectivism, is the derogation of the Romantic era; that is, of the very styles with which the architect must deal, because they form so large a part of his environment. The fact that much Romantic work was lively and utterly charming does not sway the overall dislike.

One result of these attitudes is the current emphasis on stylistic consistency. Having postulated each style as distinct and separate, as essentially disconnected from both environment and all other styles, it becomes necessary to demonstrate this with greater and greater insistence. On the Traditionalist side the period piece, the exact reproduction, and the archeologically correct become the highest goals. On the Internationalist side the greatest fidelity to the rules takes the place of archeology. The most touted Internationalists do not hesitate to follow them far beyond the limits of good sense, such is their ardor, such is the degree of their dedication. Sagging cantilevers, propped up porches, and all glass houses are the physical signs of their race with dogma. Livability is similarly affected. The grouping of incompatible functions for the sake of stylish space effects, the cult of the open plan, hit the individual where he really lives.

The reliance on dogma seems, typically, to be accompanied by tendencies towards nostalgia, alternating with strong moods of revolt from discipline. The nostalgic moods are directed towards the past, when things were wonderful and warm and easy, or towards the future when things will be clear cut and neat and simple. The reactive moods are directed against the tyranny of current techniques and socio-economic demands. The Traditionalists scuttle around after old summers, hand adzed, genuine antiques, while the Internationalists scuttle through Sweets Catalogues for the summer of the future. This is currently believed to be the bar joist.

However the International Style's preoccupation with technology, pseudo though it sometimes is, has by and large been beneficial. It has recreated a desire for sensible thinking on both planning for function, and on siting. These reforms were so vitally necessary and are so close to the heart of architecture that Internationalism, in spite of its unpopularity, has achieved some startling success.

This must be explained by the history of our architectural times. The architectural schools were largely created after the death of tradition, in the Eclectic and Revivalist heydays. And,

Gothic Cottage, Minnesota.

even though the universities themselves continued to build in the Eclectic manner, those in charge of the schools plus a few critics fully realized its untenable nature. The first movement to offer reform and progress was Internationalism. As a result it was adapted precipitously, and unquestionably wisely, even though the powerful majority within the profession were, and in fact still are, in the Eclectic phase, and even though they were, and still are, doing most of the work. The Internationalists at the time they achieved their initial success were very few in number, usually in more or less financially difficult positions, generally disliked by the public, and starving for work.

At about the same time the commercial architectural press reached the same conclusions the universities had come to, and changed over to an almost exclusive fare of modern work. During World War II the dream magazines also "switched to modern," following their own peculiar rules, and the curious phenomenon of schools and mass media on the International Style side, with the practice of architecture on the Traditionalist side, has resulted. It is for this reason that Modern is so often thought of as sure to sweep the country—later if not sooner.

However, because Selectivism is to all intents and purposes, a single phenomenon, a switch to modern will have no basic effect on American fine architecture. Like the earlier attempt to switch from the Greek Manner to Gothic, it will probably never actually take place. And in any case this conflict of style is essentially a symbol of the split personality of the architect in our society. Modern will no more solve the problem than has Traditional. The establishment of a contemporary style rivaling American Colonial, or the Greek Manner, or High Victorianism, can only come about through a resolution of some of the social pressures on architecture and architects.

These conflicts—there are several of them—are first formalized for the architect when he starts school. He is brought up according to the Traditional myths. But at school he is suddenly plunged into the rule system of the Internationalists, often brilliantly expounded. He is thus faced with a contradiction between what he knows in his bones, and what he is being taught. This primary conflict would probably be resolved more often were it not for two commonly accepted dichotomies, which further confuse the situation. One of these is: "Artists are impractical people with their heads in the clouds"—versus—"Engineers are practical people with their heads well screwed on." Another is "Art is feminine and is learned at mother's knee"—versus—"Structure is masculine and is learned with dad," or his extension—school. These time-honored notions are used to justify a view of architecture as either all engineering, or all art; of architectural schools as properly technical, or properly artistic; and of architects as impractical dreamers, or as sound business-technical types.

As against this we have the definition of architecture (in Webster's) as the: "Art or science of building especially for the purpose of civil life." The learned lexicographers who wrote this definition were unable to decide whether architecture is in fact an art or science, which was both thoughtful and accurate of them. With equal thoughtfulness they also say that this art or science of building is especially for civil life, in other words, for man at his most courteous and urbane. Implicit in this definition is the idea that architecture is not concerned with minima. Architecture is shelter transformed by man's instinct for workmanship. It is building into which has been poured more than the minimum of thought and labor required for its primary purpose. It is concerned with optima in the biologist's sense—with "the most favorable conditions as to temperature, light, moisture, food, etc., for the growth and reproduction of an organism." And it is also concerned with optima in a cultural sense. It must be expressive of its author, of its time and place, and it must be beautiful. The first of these requirements is usually miscalled function. The second is, equally inappropriately, called form. This is to confuse form, (bricks and mortar), with expression, an appeal to the sympathetic affections. Form and function are actually parts of the same idea. And this idea is, in its turn, inextricably involved with expression.

The two Selectivist adjustments are powerfully affected by the art versus technique myths. In the confusion the unitary architectural reality gets lost sight of. Such myths are seldom expressed (at least in polite society) as they were above. They occur euphemistically. For example, there are thought to be two proper stages in a designer's life. The first is a period of wild exuberance and experimentation, which is confined to school. This is followed by a life-long conservative, or scientific, approach, based on the "realities"; the realities being defined as detailing and money on the one hand, and as structure and function on the other. This is further rationalized by the postulation of an apparent impossibility, to wit, that creative design is parthenogenic in process, while architecture is either imitative (archeological) or "rational" (scientific). This is consistent with the school-is-play—work-is-grim notion, and its general acceptance no doubt results from their close correspondence. It allows the equation of creative design, particularly if it is also obviously deviant, with such invidious qualities as adolescent, arty, feminine, school boy, unsound, and against the rules. To define the creative process as entirely divorced from reality makes it unnecessary to examine reality, i.e., the nature of environment, of society, and of the creative process itself. The patent impossibility of parthenogenic birth allows the person who believes it to define the whole business of creation as a mystery; as "beyond human ken." The Traditionalists use this device to excuse their plagiaristic method of design, while the Internationalists use it to excuse their break with past and present. Both positions reflect the wish to avoid charges of artiness and radicalism. The Traditionalist is by and large exclusively concerned with techniques and advertises the fact that he gets his art out of books. The reverse is true of the International Stylist and so he must achieve his protective coloration in other ways. The hope that Internationalism might allow opportunity for creative work has attracted those most dedicated to the idea. But the fierce insistence on the rules, in the name of science and in the interests of social cohesion within the discipline, war against creativeness. As a result the Internationalist is apt to be on the one hand rationalistic and hard boiled and on the other passionately devoted to and defensive about his adjustment. "There are some things," he says in effect, "which cannot be questioned." This gives the Internationalist a rather clear-cut, sharp, and contained view of his world, in contrast with the fuzzy view more typical of the Empiricist, or with the pedestrianism typical of the Traditionalist.

The Fight

For those who take the intra-Selectivist stands seriously, rather than as different sides of the same coin, there inevitably occurs the possibility of a compromise. Thus there is a good deal of current architecture based on the "Something old, something new, something borrowed and something blue" formula. Such houses use old materials, new methods of assembly, borrow forms from the International style, and use on their walls that "international blue" made famous by Le Corbusier.

The degree of sense contained in some old saws is a constant source of amazement, and this formula is no exception. Many of the houses produced with the receipt are quite pretty. They are far warmer than the strict architecture produced by the conformists. The key to their success lies in their flexibility and suppleness, both very human qualities. The canny bridegroom however is more concerned with the soul, skeleton, and flesh beneath the bridal gown than with the gown itself. He is to live with the former, while he will never see the latter again. The wedding dress architectural compromise, stripped bare, rarely exhibits a pretty shape, let alone the well-proportioned skeleton which is necessary to beauty in age. To be taken in by a wedding dress is short-range thinking. The trouble is that it is also great fun while it lasts.

The classic definition of architecture given above, even as expanded by Sullivan's triad, is not enough, in an immediately practical or usable sense, to be of much help to the architect. Nor would further definitions be of any greater use. Architecture is the most pragmatic of arts. There seems no point in attempting what would be sure to be a fruitless word search for some better, more complete, more humane, more scientific, more expressive kind of architecture than the Selectivists have offered us; or to attempt to add to, modify, whittle down, and piece out the Empiricists' definition. Whether from the client's or the architect's point of view, a *way towards* architecture rather than a *goal* is the essential need. In order to achieve goals such as style, every other relevant consideration must be compromised. Style, in the best sense, is achieved automatically, even involuntarily, when design is broadly and accurately approached.

It is all too easy, particularly while in the grip of the inequalities and uncertainties of practice, to think of design as involving a program, and T-square, triangle, scale, pencil and paper, with an eraser handy for when things get rough. Actually all these tools are used for is to create symbols of the true intention, an idea. The three-dimensional and textural nature of architecture is such that good draftsmanship may, and does with certain kinds of individuals, play an important role in design. With others it hardly features at all. Thus while in no way derogating fine draftsmanship as an aid, the real truth of the matter is that few if any important decisions are made at a drafting board. Every essential characteristic of every job is determined far in advance of the pencil and paper stage.

Because definitions, goals, and draftsmanship are at best only aids, and can easily become dead ends, there remain the questions —where does creative design take place and what determines its nature? The design problem is so complex that it cannot be worked out rationally and consciously. Engineered architecture usually falls short even of functional adequacy. On the other hand, it cannot be left to a vague, inaccurate, "intuitive" process. Thus, in order to simplify the final act of synthesis, the architect must develop attitudes towards (or ideas about) various sub relationships such as house-view, house-ground, house-neighborhood, and house-climate. These ideas amount to a series of flexible subassemblies. He knows ahead of time how he will treat views, the ground, the north-west wind and thus he simplifies the process of final assembly. They are theses on which he is continuously at work. If he changes, they change. If he becomes set in his ways they become rigid. If he evolves slowly, they evolve. The character an architect imparts to his work is largely dependent on them.

The Selectivists on the dim side, and the Empiricists on the bright side, both point to the importance of developing these fundamental attitudes within the context of a local place. They cannot be generalized. There is no such thing as universally, internationally, nationally, or even regionally applicable attitudes, let alone rules. The very thought is repulsive to the creative person. Freeing rather than confining attitudes can only be adequately and accurately developed within the limited framework of a specific situation. That in itself is a huge order. From the creative architect's point of view, to drag in archeology or futurism, or other places, or academic rules, only vastly complicates his problem. Such additions are aids to the non-creative because they substitute for the knot of real issues some simple and clear-cut guide or source, and in this way the more complex problem can be avoided.

Each sub-relationship includes technical, esthetic, social, and psychological elements more or less unique to the locality. For example, house-ground relationships in California may involve earthquakes and wind; in the Middle West they may involve lack of foliage; and in New England, the Lilliputian scale of a geologically and culturally old and worn down region are the ruling conditions. Such clusters of connected factors are the real element with which the architect deals—they are all his joys. Every place contains the elements of its own salvation, and it is his peculiar task to discover and use them.

Obviously a listing of all the locally rooted determinants of architecture would be an endless and fruitless task. Some few of them can be so approached: for example, *House Beautiful's* and the A. I. A.'s guides to the U. S. climates. But the less technical variety are too subtle of ready characterization, and in any case are usually intuitively grasped and used by the individual architect and client. There remain certain other design determinants of more or less national scope. For example, the nails, boards, plumbing fixtures, and the like, which go to make up structure are largely distributed nationally. The suburbanization of the upper middle class is a more or less nationwide phenomenon. Certain quasi-technical problems having to do with the nature of existing buildings are met by almost every architect, wherever he practices. And, finally, an appeal to our esthetic sensibilities is recognized and responded to wherever we encounter it. This does not mean that a fine building, like a lovely lady, will look equally well in any State of the Union. Buildings are forever still, whereas we carry our sensibilities with us, and modify them according to the situation at hand. Thus the concluding chapters are addressed to these more or less nationally shared sub-attitudes which, when assembled at the drafting board, result in the design's tone, texture, and meaning.

CHAPTER IX

Environment

Creativeness versus Environment

DESIGN STARTS WITH THE ADJUSTMENT of a new idea to an old location. One cannot adjust to chaos. Unity of environment is therefore extremely important. Secondarily, this adjusted structure, once it is introduced, in its turn affects its location. This new environment, as changed by the architect, will affect every person who uses it, whether they like it or not, and whether they intend to be affected or not. Thus the architect must accept a socio-esthetic responsibility as one of the honors and pleasures of his profession.

The exercise of a conscience in any realm is sure to create a conflict within the individual. It opposes the moral good against the natural pleasure. Architecture is no exception. One of the most perplexing problems of our time is that of creativeness versus environment, of new versus old. There is no rule, no system, which can be used to resolve these opposing forces. Every job involves its own unique problems. As a start, the architect must, for each new building, analyze the ambient pressures in the existing environment. It is this process which, in part, takes the place of the defunct traditional rules. Such analysis, as it becomes increasingly necessary, has altered the proportion of time the architect must spend on the various phases of his work. Environmental understanding has become as much an aspect of the program as the client's stated needs and must consume a greater and greater amount of time. It is the fashion to dichotomize between program and design, i.e., to term programming "research" and design "creative." This is an exceedingly inaccurate notion. Programming and design are simply two stages in a single creative process. Programming is not research. Research is an exploration into new and unknown areas. Programming is the development and digestion of the specifications for design, and is concerned with known and understood facts.

The program is particularly subject to creative genius. The special quality of the greatest contemporary designers is their consuming interest in their environment, and the dim view they take of style as such. Every site has an existence of its own. The discovery of its atmosphere, and the development of a point of view as to how its essences should be used is one of the architect's most significant jobs.

Such is the diversity of the U. S. scene that our present native environments come in too many varieties to be adequately catalogued. On the other hand, the various styles tend to create unique situations, and these might be classified as follows:

1. Invisible—In an architect's mind.
2. Undetermined—Large virgin sites.
3. Traditional—Unified and dead.
4. Continuative—Varied and dynamic.
5. Eclectic—Stylistically chaotic.
6. Selective {Internationalist / Traditionalist} Artificially unified.

The first of these, the invisible environment, is a curious and delicate phenomenon. The compositor of a Traditional invisible environment picks out of his city or region or nation only those buildings conforming to his ideal, and relates them internally. He denies the existence of all but the chosen style. Thus out of the

50,000 buildings in his city, he chooses the five remaining authentic English Colonial farm houses, and claims that they constitute his environment and "tradition." He ignores the other 49,995 structures. He is, unhappily, blind as a bat. The architect who, on the other hand, builds Spanish Colonial because Cortez spent a night, it is rumored, in the vicinity, is seeing things. In fairness to some Traditionalists it must be said that models for their plagiarism do exist. Furthermore, in recently resurrected areas, such as certain towns in New England and counties in Pennsylvania, the architect actually does work in a thoroughly homogeneous environment and, for reasons of conscience and social pressure, must cut his cloth accordingly. But of course in this latter case, the environment *is* visible—not imaginary.

In the case of the Internationalists, only a few factories and bridges were available for use in composing the invisible environment. Models had to be sought in other structures. The early Internationalist books were seldom without a picture of an airplane or a ship. Analogy was used, as in Dr. Sigfried Giedion's comparison of a balloon frame, a Windsor chair and house by Mr. Richard Neutra. Photographs of familiar objects from new angles, as in the work of Mr. Moholy Nagy helped to create the impression of a "new order"; and there are many other such devices. There *are* good uses for an invisible environment. The Internationalist's is, certainly, good in the sense that it is aimed at creative ends. The Traditionalist's is good in that it tends to preserve the unity of environment. But the fundamental purpose of the device, i.e., to create a precedent, seems often to have resulted in great harm. When the invisible environment becomes a more potent factor than the real, the latter is usually destroyed. One can hardly blame the architect for creating in the image of his ideal. But when an old and distinguished place begins to appear as a hated obstruction in the way of that ideal, as in the case of the Eclectic, Revivalist, and Internationalist movements, chaos is usually the result. The lesson here is that in architecture compromise achieves the more lasting results. The real genius is in the nature and extent of this compromise. On the one hand the environment must be furthered. On the other the individual building must not fail. This is the environmental problem.

Fig. 221. "Architecture."

The illusion of spatial interpenetration is secured by superimposing two photographic negatives. The next generation will perhaps really see buildings like this, when glass architecture develops.

Photo: Jan Kamman, Schiedam

Last illustration from "The New Vision" by L. Moholy-Nagy.

The Ideal Neighborhood

It has been argued, above, that the style of an individual building, like the form of an individual forest tree, must be affected by the form and purport of its neighbor's style. Ideally the introduction of a new building into an existing neighborhood should further the growth of that neighborhood, not only in terms of capital increase, but also in terms of stylistic increase. A total change implies rejection and hatred of what has gone before. No change implies moribundity and decay.

But the question of style, though it is important, does not seem to be fundamental. Variety in style does not necessarily imply a lack of homogeneity. There must therefore be other forces operating which, in proper combination, cancel out the centrifugal effects of stylistic variety. The most exciting neighborhoods are those in which a succession of styles are represented, but where some underlying unity of concept makes them appear as the varied interests of a single and continuing culture. The architect himself is the agent of this culture, and carries on his conscience all of its desires, both self-destructive and self-perpetuating.

Faced with a virgin site he is apt to see himself in a Tarzan role. Such a role is just apt enough, and just ridiculous enough, to be exceedingly difficult to play well. In its spell, the architect tends to think of a site as unifluenced by its town, county, region, state, country, and continent. It therefore seems logical to be as abstract, dogmatic, "free," "wild," as he pleases. This view has its uses but, like that of parthenogenesis, it does not conform with the facts as we know them. The proper circumstances surrounding the marriage of architecture and a virgin site are very much akin to those which surround the marriage of a virgin female. Her socio-economic status and temperament largely predetermine the qualities of the man who will marry her. But this predetermination, far from spoiling the occasion, adds greatly to its pleasures. It makes it appropriate in a more general and social sense. The same distinctions operate in the relationship between sites and their architects. Every site is seen in the context of its region and the traditions of that region, just as every woman is seen in the context of her class. And while these two elements like

Top, Saul Steinberg.
Right, Eliot Porter.

the air we breathe and live in may not be consciously and continuously felt, still we reference all our esthetic impressions to them.

There is something of the satyr in the creative person, and this quality is never stronger in architects than when they face a virgin site. The urge is to rape it and go about one's business. But the raped site, the environment created for the temporary and selfish pleasure of one individual and of one point of view, in-

evitably reflects the inherent ugliness of a unilateral attitude. Architecture, simply because one cannot escape it, is a social art. It is for this reason that so many of the Internationalist's and Traditionalist's developments carry such smugly exclusive overtones. They reflect the monotony of a single, essentially antisocial point of view, hammered home over and over again.

In the absence of style, building must be approached from the standpoint of man's fundamental relationship to nature. This, as Eckbo notes, is by no means a constant.

> "In the relation of man to nature it is man who is responsible for decisions as to the growth or decline in the quality of the landscape. His values are constantly expanding in terms of imagination and creative synthesis. Those of nature, as expressed in man's outlook on the landscape, are shifting, shrinking, becoming more rational, more sensitized, precisely because the forces of wild nature remain approximately the same, while the forces extracted by man from wild nature expand and develop at a constantly accelerating rate."

As a partner he can not afford to be either subservient or masterful. To change every contour of a site is not only to strip it of every precious root, tree, and flower. It is to make an enemy of it. When sites are so violated, their injured subsurface drainage patterns break out in the form of leaking basements, and their mangled top soil departs with wind and water. The "touch not a hair of yon grey head" motto is often more successful. But in its negation of man's impact, it is equally unbalanced. The skillfully blended contour road; the straight double row of trees, the geometric or free patterning of areas, emphasize the connection between the site's natural patterns and the human uses imposed. This sort of contrast is one source of esthetic pleasure. Another, depending on synthesis rather than contrast, is the realization than the finite site is related to the ethos of its region's landscape. New England, for example is sad, worn down, ingrowing, old, small scale, and luxuriant. The site which does not, in its developed state, reflect its region's qualities and contradictions is but half used. Because the materials involved in this marvelous art of siting are so rich, beautiful, and varied, it is the most exciting and rewarding of the architect's jobs.

The ethos in question here is like the atmosphere of a marriage. It is invisible, over and above the two parties concerned, yet inseparable from them. The good designer regards site and building in the same light. He sees them, deals with them, dreams of them as one and the same entity. No rule, no plan type, no style, no external pressure of any sort can make him separate them in his mind. Faced with a site and his client's program, it is impossible for him to remember that he has ever heard of a "salt box," of a "bi-nuclear" plan, or of any other such cliché. And this characteristic reflects itself in as unimportant a matter as his drafting technique, for he cannot draw a house plan except on a site plan, nor can he draw a site plan without the whole house plan.

This leads to a view of the ideal environment as one in which the additions to, and changes in nature required by man's living functions seem to be half natural, half artificial, both in terms of expression and material. The ideal upper middle class neighborhood can be defined, by extension, as one in which every house is individually motivated, at one with its site, expressive of its owner's life, and of its region's ethos.

There are numerous social, economic, and selfish factors which conspire against the quick realization of such an ideal. The architect, face to face with a neighborhood to design, is in a particularly difficult position. If he designs all the houses himself he is bound to create a boring uniformity. He knows that if several architects of similar persuasion build the houses, the results will be far happier; that the terrible monotony of slight variation will be avoided. But such unselfish interest in environment goes against the grain, and he mitigates the fact that he is creating a monument to himself with the hope that his message and his skill will transcend the infirmity. And indeed there are enough cases where this has happened to enable him to postulate this hope as possible of achievement, if not probable.

Economic factors may increase the pressure for uniformity. One or a few house plans may save money, but no matter how carefully each is set down on its site, no matter how consistently (or inconsistently) they are rotated, they are still fundamentally all the same, and still fundamentally divorced from their location. Variations in doorways, porches switched from side to side, different colored roofs, different sidings, only increase the monotony. It is impossible to fake the ideal. The aficionado of architecture, offered the same house from various angles, like the child offered beet greens, reacts with "I say it's spinach and I say to hell with it."

The sort of neighborhood which has here been termed ideal exists, in greater or less chronological depth, in most urban communities. The Brattle Street area in Cambridge, Massachusetts, will serve as an example even though it is, perhaps, the premiere street of its kind. It contains examples of American Colonial still flavored by medievalism, of American Colonial flavored by the Greek Revival, of Greek Revival, of Romanticism, of High Victorianism, of Traditionalism and of the International Style. It is a concrete example of the dynamics of change. Such monumental streets as Chestnut in Salem make better pictures. But for those who are interested in the main stream of architecture, they are far less exciting.

Brattle Street points up a fundamental truth. Our tradition has not consisted of one style, or of one type of house. Rather it has been a slow evolution of approach to social and technical problems on which was superimposed a succession of flavors. Every so often these flavors coalesced into a style. The moments in which abstract order triumphed were usually destructive. When they were not, what had gone before was implicit in each new step.

The dynamic environments allow, or more correctly *demand,* that contemporary taste be represented. They are stimulating to work in, because they challenge the architect to understand his moment in history. The problem is one of continuity and variation, the most interesting he is called upon to solve. Such areas, furthermore, actually leave the architect as free as it is possible for him to be. Virgin sites make far more stringent demands on his socio-esthetic conscience. The pressures in this case are general and all pervasive, while in the specific and limited environment they are finite, and easily translatable into form and materials.

Problems in Geriatrics

The two environments considered above involve new construction. Both offer the architect great stylistic latitude. Another type of problem, far more restrictive, is where the homogeneity of the existing environment is total and physical, rather than of ideas in chronological depth. Such places are characterized by great unity of style, materials, feeling; very small variations from one or more typical models; and, in our time, by the fact that the socio-economic conditions which produced them no longer exist.

In their urban guise they often came about as the result of a large scale speculative venture. Louisberg Square (Bulfinch) in Boston is a case in point. In small towns they are most often the result of a development compressed in time, as the old main street of Wickford, Rhode Island. A Greek Revival example is the main street in Nantucket. Certain Pennsylvania coal towns have unclassifiable but wonderfully unified main streets, sometimes arcaded. In their rural guise they may have taken several generations to develop and may exhibit some of the shifts typical of living traditions. The rural architecture of Bucks County, Pennsylvania is an example. Where such environments have died and stayed dead, because of the economic death of the whole locality, the architect is seldom called upon to intervene.

But, because of their esthetic harmony and our increased physical mobility, such areas seldom stay buried long. Thus, in localities which continue to prosper the architect is usually called in first to bury them, and then to disinter them. Louisberg Square is in the process of shift from a street of beautiful and magnificent mansions to a rooming house, small apartment district. The architect is here functioning in his undertaking capacity. Those areas which at the time of their death are abandoned, and these are more typical of rural districts, usually go through a slow and natural process of decay and deterioration. They become slums. Where their charm is great and their distance from economically prosperous localities is small, they are disinterred. Urban examples are Georgetown in Washington, D. C., and Beacon Hill in Boston. A rural example is Bucks County, Pennsylvania; and New England contains dozens of rural islands thus resurrected. Any archi-

Samuel Chamberlain: Rockport, Massachusetts.

tect who practices within designing distance of such areas cannot consider himself as a specialist in architectural obstetrics. He must be something of a geriatrician as well.

The problems involved in dealing with stylistically static environments are basically two—of budget, and of esthetic adjustment. The corpse-like fragility typical of the individual units, a function of age and of the neglect they experience during their period of abandonment, makes their cost almost impossible to estimate in advance. The slightest alteration may open up a Pandora's Box of hidden troubles. As the architect is blamed for such situations, it is in his interest to leave the delicate balance intact. Where he is forced to make extensive changes his only defense is a clear understanding with his client that the cost may outstrip that of new construction. But, because of the fact that existing space is usually cheaper than new, the possibility the client will bank on is that he will save money, somehow. *Mr. Blandings Builds His Dream House* is a monument to this situation.

Such is the acceptance of the two Selectivist points of view that it is the exceptional client who, faced with an old building, does not exhibit one or the other of the attitudes typical of its two branches. The practice and theory of renovation enjoyed by Europeans is non-existent in this country, and too professional in nature to have been picked up by travelers. Thus on the one hand old buildings are "restored" as exactly as possible within the limitations of budget, architect, and client. On the other the old building is gutted to the extent needed to indicate clearly the modernity of its client and architect. A typical change of this sort involves ripping off all the trim, adding one picture window, and painting what is left dead white. Such alterations can only be seen as mutilation, not therapy. "Look, Ma," they cry, "I'm Modern."

The operations which can justly and decently be performed on old and distinguished houses seem to fall into three categories.

1. The building is considered adequate functionally, or impossible to correct, and only repairs, maintenance and replacements need be undertaken. Color and finish are the principal visible factors to be considered. Such buildings should by and large be

left intact. They can best be given extra snap by the judicious use of the currently most fashionable color scheme.

2. The building, in addition to the repairs, maintenance, and replacements typical of the first category, needs certain minor interior alterations in order to bring it up to date mechanically and functionally. This almost inevitably involves a new kitchen and better electric wiring, usually means increases or changes in the bath rooms, and often includes changes in circulation patterns and the suppression of numerous doors. Such jobs rarely offer any excuse for a change of style. The introduction of picture windows and the like, or the kind of archeological tizzy which insists on the new sash being identical in all respects with the old, both smack of the extremist. One has only to examine the Victorianization of the early colonial houses, or more currently, the Internationalization of some of the great Victorian houses to be convinced that growing old gracefully consists of learning one's own strengths and weaknesses, and in compensating for the latter as silently and inconspicuously as possible. Such jobs should really be regarded as piecing out operations. A little platinum may be added to a rotten bone, but it is modestly covered by the old flesh. Some new fangled plastic may be used to fill in a tooth, but it is given a tint appropriate to its mellowing companions.

3. The third category involves those alterations typical of the first two plus additions or drastic changes to certain parts of the house. And in this case, the architect who does not use the opportunity to express himself fully, guided only by the colors, texture, proportion, massing, etc. of the older parts which are to remain, is losing one of the most stimulating and productive possibilities open to him. The opportunity to contrast closely, and to move freely from new to old and back, is a unique and marvelous one. Anyone who has visited the old Chateau on the Loire River, or any building which consists of wings in a succession of styles in the mode of the time in which they were built, must realize the delights of such mixtures. To go from an authentic seventeenth century dining room to an authentic twentieth century living room is not only to understand and enjoy each far more fully—it is to know a sense of continuity, and of timelessness.

Eliot Porter.

Finally, there is the problem of the new building in a physically homogeneous environment, and this is the same, in every important respect, as the problem of adding to an old building. In the one case a specific structure as well as an environment must be understood and adapted to. In the other the specific is absent, but the general environmental pressure remains equally in force.

Stage Sets

The most difficult environments are those characterized by a total lack of uniformity of style, together with an absence of expression of local cultural and climatic factors. These are typical of cities built up under the aegis of Eclecticism. Fine architecture in its guise of *abstract order*, depends both externally and internally on governed relationships. It is antithetic to the chaotic environment. The finest building, seen thus, appears as the wildest and most virulent personal whim, or as the Victorians had it, "folly." Even the most touted chaotic environment cannot but appear as a succession of follies. Copley Square in Boston, for example, can be seen in terms of its whole as dominated by McKim Mead and White's folly (The Public Library), closely seconded by H. H. Richardson's folly (Trinity Church) while the lesser architects who completed it were simply not brilliant enough to make such colossally compelling mistakes.

The contemporary architect faced with such an environment can only join the ranks. There is no other alternative. Since to modify or compromise will do no good, he might just as well behave in as contemporaneous a manner as possible. This is of course, looking at the problem in terms of environment. In terms of the individual building, Richardson's church is, perhaps, a great structure. Furthermore, in its own time it undoubtedly was lent verisimilitude by its participation in that invisible Romanesque environment its architect created for his contemporaries. Similar advantages, in the same situation, are available to all of the various kinds of contemporary architects.

But the contemporary architect is less free than were his Romantic forebears. Due to the current Selectivist philosophies it is now considered bad taste to mix styles. The Selectivists themselves go so far as to derogate even the monumental continuative-dynamic environments because they are not pure. Thus up to date New Englanders restrict themselves to "Exclusive New England Type Ranch House." This restrictiveness spreads like a disease through the whole social structure of the community. The people concerned are not only restricted to one type and style of house, but to one kind of neighbor, to one income group, to one

Robert Woods Kennedy.

race, to one occupational category, and so on to ever greater exclusiveness. Such social and architectural artificiality resembles nothing so much as the theater. The exclusive development looks like a stage set, and often operates like a poor play, where the characters are obviously projections of one rather limited author, and are further restricted by the demands of a tedious plot. Fine architecture does not thrive in such environments. Its strict reality makes it appear grim, its orderliness is by contrast stiff, its expressiveness seems naked. Those who have not experienced such unfortunate juxtapositions have only to imagine a Palladian villa, or an Aalto country house, or the Fairbanks house for that matter, set down in the local neighborhood of "Fine modern colonial homes" (fully restricted). In this case to operate creatively within such an environment is not to join a company of fools but to make fools of one's company. And this is of course the gravest social defect, the surest way to lose friends and alienate people known to man.

The mechanisms which operate to make architecture always expressive of certain facets of its time are inescapable. The fundamental philosophical connection between the Traditionalist point of view and that series of race, esthetic, and social prejudices usually embodied in deed restrictions is a case in point. International Style neighborhoods seldom exhibit social exclusiveness based on race. Smugness is the worst fault they can be accused of. On the other hand it is the exceptional Traditionalist site which does not carry with it either explicit injunctions, or a well understood conspiracy against Jews, Negroes, Mexicans, Indians, Portuguese, Finns, Italians, Poles, "modern" design, all but a favored income group, all but a favored house type (Salt Box, Ranch House, Cape Cod,) all but a favored architectural element (pitch roofs, fences,) and so on. Such are the interdictions which maintain the "unity," of the average traditional surburban environment. This depressing subject might seem to be a far cry from the gentle, rewarding, and productive art of siting. But, as every architect knows, forces such as these, unleashing themselves with the venemous thrust of a cobra, kill off an appreciable number of jobs, and spoil the human or esthetic pleasure still others might have enjoyed.

A conservationist attitude towards environment is essentially that which accepts the social good as a drag on selfish desires. Artists no less than the general public are subject to the notion that they, personally, are exempt from such a drag. The reason artists give is that social factors inhibit "self expression," by which they mean personal symbolism. This, as has been argued earlier, usually cannot appear except as superimposed on a foundation. Social expression comes before symbolism. Expression and symbolism are essentially ways of transmitting a message. In the case of expression this message is clearly readable, and easily translatable into verbal symbols. In the case of symbolism the message is intuitively grasped. But, to those so minded, it, also, can be exposed to the clear light of reason. There are other and equally important facets of art however, which seem to be entirely abstract. The ability to operate in the abstract realm is a function of the artist's relationship with his environment. Herbert Read has noted that:

> "Artists are to a considerable degree automata—that is to say, they unwittingly transmit in their works a sense of scale, proportion, symmetry, balance and other abstract qualities which they have acquired through their purely visual and therefore physical response to their natural environment."

Sensitivity towards environment is, in the fine architect's case, of extra importance in that he is actually using it, rather than representing an abstract from it. This makes his relationship with any given environment highly complex. Aside from such questions as what it is, and what he wants it to be, there are such others as how far can he reasonably force it in his direction, and how far will his means carry him in such an enterprise. But of course as his aim is to give his work that same abstract order a sense of which can only be extracted from environment itself, the closer he is connected with it, the more he is able to draw from it. Few modern architects have failed to experience, as they first looked down from an airplane window, the sense of being ushered into a fabulously beautiful new world, oddly tempered by the sense of being, at last, at home. The feeling is: "Here is the kind of order I always knew was there, but could never quite put my finger on."

An invisible environment, precisely because it is synthetic, cannot but impair the artist's relationship with his natural one. Thus the Selectivists, lacking the stimulus which comes of accepting the world as it is, must depend on stylistic abstraction for order, rather than on the sense of relatedness with environment which we know as proportion, free form, texture, etc. It is these abstract qualities which make us feel at home in architecture, which connect the new experience with all that we have known before. Thus there is only one system of good proportion. And there is no such thing as new proportion. Relationships rediscovered may seem new, but they are as old as nature. The element which, it will be argued later, imparts newness, or more accurately freshness to a style, is its position in a sequence of ideas.

On architecture. It is the ideal itself; everything in it is idealized by men. The straight line itself is of his invention, for it exists nowhere in nature. The lion seeks his cavern; the wolf and the wild boar take shelter in the depth of the forests; a few animals make homes for themselves, but they are guided by instinct alone; they do not know what it is to modify or embellish them. Man, in his habitations, imitates the cavern and the aerial dome of the forests; in the periods when the arts are carried to perfection, architecture produces masterpieces: in all periods, the taste of the moment, and new departures in practice introduce changes which testify to the freedom of taste.

Directly, architecture takes nothing from nature, as sculpture or painting does; in this it approaches music, unless one affirm that, as music recalls certain sounds of the world, architecture imitates the lair or the cavern, or the forest; but that is not direct imitation, in the sense understood when speaking of the two arts which copy the precise forms offered by nature.—Delacroix

CHAPTER X

Site

Cave versus Bower

To COUNTERACT THE DRAG ON CREATIVENESS exerted by a conservationist attitude towards environment, an equally strong pull towards the future must also be in force. Where one or the other force is absent, a reactionary or radical art is the result. The social phenomenon which, today, constitutes this positive, anti-reactionary force is the de-urbanization of the upper middle class. A combination of increasing physical mobility and the failure of our urban environmental planning has transferred the ideal locus of the building class from the city to the suburbs, and now, increasingly, into the country or "bed room town." Quite obviously this alters the nature of demands made on the house. Safety from urban riff raff is no longer important. The advent of the mechanical trades makes climate less important. The existence of glass and natural beauty makes transparency more important. Lower densities make privacy less important. These and numerous other technical and cultural factors are causing our concept of house to shift from one basic image, that of the cave, to the other, that of the nomadic tent.

Cave, a natural form, and tent, an artificial form, are not strictly comparable. It might be that the natural equivalent of the tent is the bower, and that the "primitive" choice is CAVE or BOWER. Bosquets, dingles, arbours, leafy bowers, aeries, and pergolas, have always been the favorite outdoor pleasure places, while caves, grottos, dens, lairs, holes etc. are enjoyed for their safety and cozyness. The old expression "bowers of bliss" synonymous with the Elysian Fields, Arcadia, etc. expresses the root feeling.

There is a direct connection between these two forms and the client's motivations. Security, for example, implies both immediate and secondary ends, and these are opposed by opposite qualities: good versus bad, health versus illness, safety versus exposure.

Again on a fundamental plane, we see the good and bad forces in our environment as attacking from various directions. From above come the elements, hail, rain, dust, the wrath of God and the like. From below come rats, mice, germs, dampness, etc., and of course the Devil lives there. Our enemies come in sideways. But by the same token sun and air and the stars and the benign emanations of heaven come from above. The food we eat, the water we drink and the rest we enjoy are products of the ground. And our friends come in sideways. Thus while the cave protects us from above, it exposes us to below. And there arises the other fundamentally expressive structure, the tent, which is all air, sun, mobility and danger, as opposed to the darkness, dampness, permanence, and safety of the other. Much modern architecture is an attempt at an ideal compromise between the two. Frank Lloyd Wright's Taliesen West, with its "cave" living room and canvas roofed music room provides both, in their pure and unadulterated forms.

Frank Lloyd Wright: Taliesen West.

This radical tent image, this more or less unrealized direction in which the culture and technology of our time tends to direct us, is squarely opposed to the conservationist idea. Most traditional clients want caves. The modernists want tents, while a very few want both. Of these some ask for the impossible—tent and cave in one—while others consciously recognize that both must be developed along their own lines. The average contemporaneously minded architect and client split the difference. The solid protective cave-like roof, over the delicate translucent tent-like walls of the modern house, sometimes further compromised by skylights, comes very close to an ideal junction of the two. Buckminster Fuller's dymaxion structures will, when they are finally developed, vastly expand the possibilities in this realm. As the nature of the bower is further explored, and as our techniques allow us greater and greater freedom to play with form, this radical image will unquestionably become more overtly visible in fine architecture.

But how "radical" is the bower image? E. Baldwin Smith in "The Dome, A Study in the History of Ideas" finds that "The memory of a god's hut in his sacred grove was too old and common in the ancient world to be attributed to any one source." He explains its probable background as follows:

"A. The domical shape must be distinguished from domical resulting because the dome, both as idea and as method of roofing, originated in pliable materials upon a primitive shelter and was later preserved, renovated, and translated into more permanent materials, largely for symbolic and traditional reasons.

1. At the primitive level the most prevalent and usually the earliest type of constructed shelter, whether a tent, pit house, earth lodge, or thatched cabin, was more or less circular in plan and covered by necessity with a curved roof. Therefore in many parts of the ancient world the domical shape became habitually associated in men's memories with a central type of structure which was venerated as a tribal and ancestral shelter, a cosmic symbol, a house of appearances and a ritualistic abode."

Thoreau, marvelously sensitive to architecture, must have built his house in the woods in unconscious imitation of the gods. And, as it became more sophisticated, it also became, for him, less divine. He remarks on the change as follows:

> "When I began to have a fire at evening, before I plastered my house, the chimney carried smoke particularly well, because of the numerous chinks between the boards. Yet I passed some cheerful evenings in that cool and airy apartment, surrounded by the rough brown boards full of knots, and rafters with the bark on high overhead. My house never pleased my eye so much after it was plastered, though I was obliged to confess that it was more comfortable. Should not every apartment in which man dwells be lofty enough to create some obscurity overhead, when flickering shadows may play at evening about the rafters?"

Thoreau, even had he been less eccentric, would have been limited by the techniques of his time. Ours are so far superior that we can enjoy all of those sensations he liked, and still be comfortable. There are increasingly fewer excuses for limiting our use of form. But, and this the history of architecture amply attests, new uses must be firmly tied to the reality of our demands on form. The first of these is that it symbolize some generally desirable social goal. The second is that it stimulate us at our most primitive and archaic level. Frank Lloyd Wright's success is due to his ability to manipulate form on these two levels.

In the case of the bower, the social, economic, and technical factors which make the idea desirable seem fairly clear. Its fundamental symbolic impact has not yet, however, been very largely explored. Obviously, the enclosed spaces in bowers are, in the case of the bosquet, roughly semi-spherical, and in the case of the dingle more or less that of the barrel vault or Cathedral. But while the plan shape is tremendously telling—while the pentagon, the octagon, and the circle are the most satisfactory living spaces —it is perhaps less important than the structure of the walls at eye level, and the quality of light overhead. Thus the tree trunk motive is experimented with over and over again, as surface texture, fenestration, decoration and structure. As contrast between solid and open it was used quite consciously and rigidly by Mr. Wright in the Richard Lloyd Jones House in Tulsa (1929). The author's Stokes House, essentially a bower, uses the tree form to support the roof, and to let in light, as well as for the view of sky, tree tops, and sea gulls it affords.

Our fundamental sympathy with the combination of form, light, and texture characteristic of the bower undoubtedly accounts for the tremendous appeal of the frame house, after it is studded, and before it is closed in. No house, architects are wont to say, ever looks better than at this moment. Its delicate studs, orderly against the sky, represent perhaps a kind of pluperfect forest, an unachievable Elysian Grove. Unfortunately this extreme structure can only be achieved by the painter. Piranesi's caves, Rousseau's delightful house made of the branches of trees are full realizations of the fundamental human desire. On the other hand, who knows but that with the expansion of techniques, such structures as Rousseau's may yet be achieved by the architect.

The appropriateness of round and poly-sided forms to nature, and the appropriateness of their inside volumes to people, leads one to a new view of the cube and the rectangle in the landscape. Silos, round towers, granaries, the octagonal barns and houses of New England etc. are always more sympathetic than their equivalents in rectangular guise. The tall round tower is nearly always at home, the tall rectangular house nearly never. The geometrical rectangular form stresses the contrast between society and nature. The circular form stresses the oneness of man and nature. For example Edward Hopper's heavy, vertical, and rectangular Victorian houses seen over a railroad track are essentially critical comments on an ugly aspect of our culture. Houses such as the Petite Trianon are affirmations of the power and glory which may be obtained through socio-political means. The rectangular volume is necessarily reminiscent of social mechanisms. But when it is capped by the sloping planes of a pitch roof, and when rather than one volume, the effect is as of many, interconnected and inter-penetrating, then a sort of compromise is reached between nature and society. The broken volumes reduce the scale to that of one family, the smallest social unit. The single volume increases scale to that of the "power in the community."

Rousseau: "Carnival Evening."

Charles Sheeler.

Surface Modeling and Links

Our image of house as cave or tent profoundly affects its relationship to topography. The cave house must suggest rootedness. The tent's airy disconnection from an infinite level plain, such as the endless "lower astral planes" in Salvador Dali's pictures, is the other extreme. Quite aside from this cave–hill, tent–plain relationship, the ground plane operates on our sensibilities in numerous other ways. Every house architect must be struck by the emphasis clients place on floors, particularly the women. This is based largely on utilitarian grounds. But it is also true that the appearance, texture and modeling of floors has an effect on one's sense of luxury all out of proportion to their relative area. Soft floors (carpets, rubber tile) bespeak luxury more forcefully than any other single factor. Fine woods, in herringbone and basketweave patterns, carry an air of polished elegance no other surface can so well suggest. This preoccupation with the horizontal surface does not end in the house. Fine lawns, the peculiar qualities of certain ground covers, granite, bluestone, and limestone walks, all are intensely admired.

One looks towards the ground far more often than one looks up, and perhaps even more often than out horizontally. Once a beautiful floor or ground cover is established as such in one's mind, one sees it frequently. Because one also feels it, it affects one's whole physical tone. Hard floors jar from the heels up. Soft floors cushion against shock. The rich, wicked, temptress in the average detective story always has a rug in her boudoir into which the shamus' strong feet sink knee deep. When this point is reached one knows that the luxury will get him, at least for the nonce.

Our room's relationship with the ground, felt most strongly in moments of relaxation, is that while we push down on it—our weight responding to gravity—it pushes up against us, bearing us up, with an exactly balanced pressure. Our true distance from it, or more accurately, from the largest horizontal area in our ken, is never really lost sight of by our consciousness. The sensation of height above ground, be it a few feet or a number of stories, remains more or less continuously in operation. This feeling at its extremes causes dizziness—or the exhilaration steeplejacks and riggers experience. Finally, the ground in its various symbolic aspects, as "mother earth," or as "the last resting place," exerts yet another kind of power over our emotions.

Here are several emotional strings which need only be plucked by the design of the house in order to vibrate sympathetically. One device for setting them in motion is the concept of its floor and ground as *one modeled surface*—modeled for esthetic as well as functional reasons—or as a modeled surface with suspended planes (upper floors) related to it. Such a surface, because it is part indoors–part out, part natural, part artificial must achieve unity by rational and artistic means. Its continuity, its modeling, the contrasts it offers, must be expressed, heightened, and given that significance proper to the materials and functions involved.

Due to the peculiar limitations and demands of house work, the whole surface dealt with is seldom seen in one piece, and thus its full impact is never concentrated as one emotional reaction. In other types of work however, this does occur. Norman Bel Geddes' sets for Dante's Inferno is an interesting example of the unitary surface carried to an extreme. The author's project for a Festival Theatre in Newport, Rhode Island uses the full impact of the device in architecture. In a theoretical way, the floating planes typical of some non-objective painting illustrate the sharp impact which can be achieved by but a few planes in space.

The most interesting problem to be met in the attempt to achieve a unitary surface is at the walls of the house, i.e., between indoors and out, and more particularly, at those points where one can circulate between the two. Due to structural, to climatic, and often to topographic obstacles as well, a smooth transition is usually impossible. In-between elements—links—must be employed. The most successful of these is undoubtedly the Japanese porch. Our common devices; porches, the sou' westers, porticos, etc., when properly conceived as links, are delightful and charming elements of our architecture. The most brilliant example of the link is, perhaps, to be found in Bernard Maybeck's Christian Science Church in Berkeley, California. The disengaged columns reach out, both on the ground and into the air, allowing ground and air in turn to reach in to the actual wall of the building. The result is, almost literally, facadelessness. At the other extreme, i.e., in the most restrained possible manner, the wide granite stoops, sunk in the grass, of the early New England farm houses exercise a fascination apparently out of all proportion to their dry simplicity. And in these same houses the bare granite foundation showing not more than six inches in height, the absence of foundation planting, and the smooth lawn running right up to the wall, again exercise a charm apparently incommensurate with the means.

It is the fashion to stress the desirability of the least possible change in grade between indoors and out. More than one riser is thought to break the continuity. There is unquestionably a great deal of truth in this. On the other hand the Japanese porch, and the common Greek revival side porch indicate that several risers are no obstacle to physical ease or esthetic unity *provided the house reaches out* onto the land and into the air, with the corresponding counter penetration. This effect, as has been con-

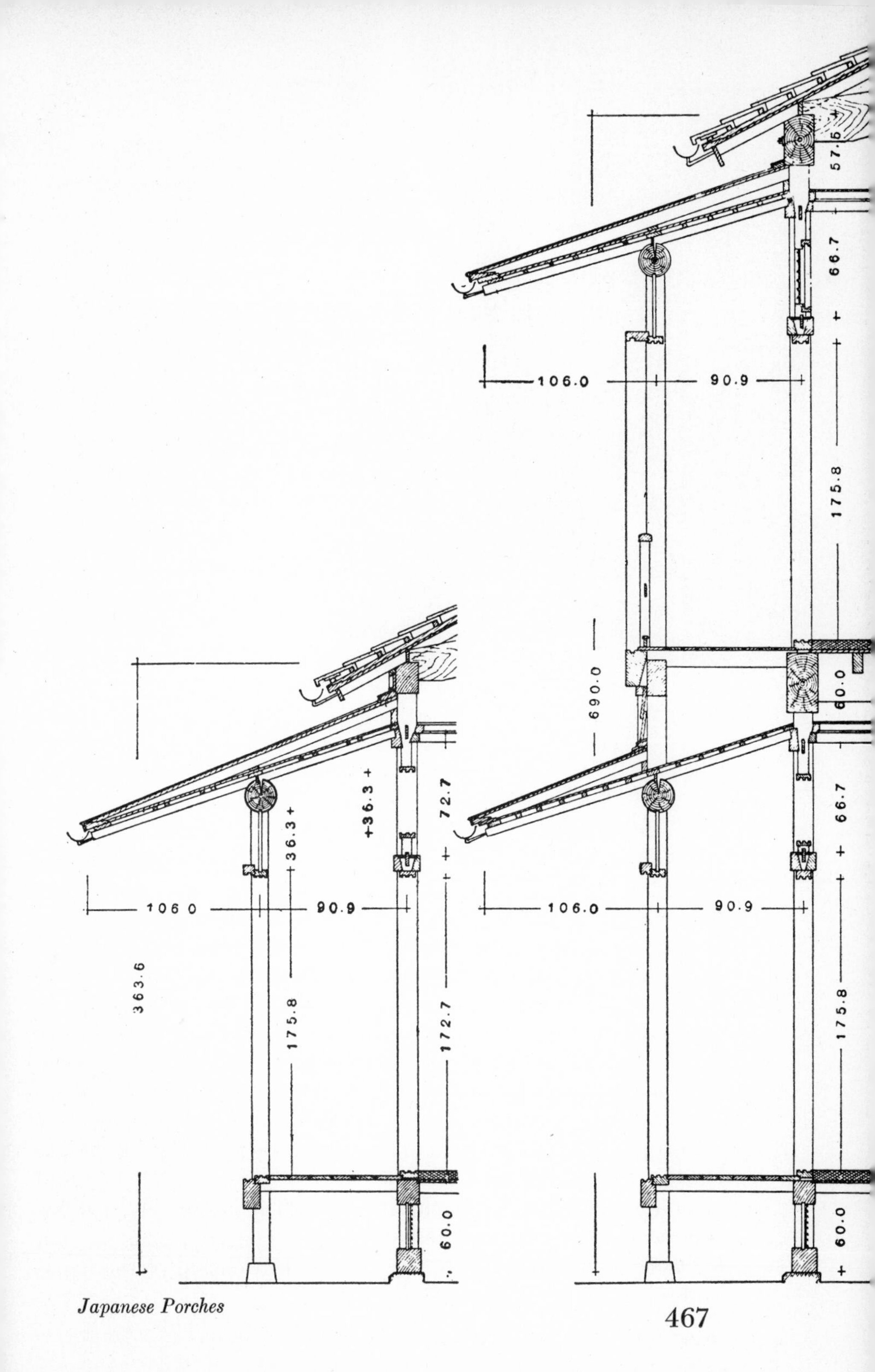

Japanese Porches

From "The Gardens of China" by Osvald Siren. (Copy. 1949, The Ronald Press Company.)

clusively proved by the International stylists, cannot be achieved by means of glass areas alone, no matter how large. Because glass is transparent it fools no one that it is porous, or open, or in fact anything more than a hard, latently dangerous, and impenetrable physical barrier. Thus while it may be made to play its part in the creation of the link, it can only be a part among others. Porches, or terraces, or overhangs, or spurs, or disengaged columns must cloak it, if the fullest linkage is to be achieved.

The transitional elements between house and ground are of course most potent in their effect as one walks or climbs over them. They are, in every sense of the word, experienced. To classify them is nearly impossible, and would be perhaps quite useless in any case, due to the variety of means and to the element of opportunism which enters so largely into their successful design. On the other hand, the average architect uses a very small and standardized palette of such devices, and it is obvious that his choices and rejections are based on larger considerations, i.e., on his basic assumptions as to the proper relationship of the house as a whole to its landscape as a whole.

Surface Modeling and Links

There seem to be four broad attitudes towards this problem. There is the theory that the house must blend in with its landscape, cling to the ground, and appear in every sense as if it had grown there. This is the "organic" theory, and is brilliantly achieved, for example, in Frank Lloyd Wright's personal houses. The organic school worships nature, though is not above tampering with it, and seeks always to *use* it to the fullest extent. Then there is the theory that the house is a man made jewel, placed on the ground. But, rather than being of the ground its mechanical and artificial contrast with nature is stressed. This man versus nature attitude is seen most clearly perhaps in the work of Ludwig Mies Van der Rohe, his Rezor house being an example. In this mode, nature's continuity is broken at the house walls. But both transparency and/or the mirroring characteristic of the glass has several effects. Nature is sometimes continued *through* the house, and at others is reflected, multiplied, and abstracted. It is subjected to a kind of transfiguration. The result can be extremely beautiful. This manner is "unnatural" in the sense that it is sophisticated and arbitrary. In its extreme development not so much as a canopy over the front door is allowed.

A third manner attempts to leave nature exactly in its natural state, without in any way adjusting it, and to create a house as far separated from the ground as possible. This, one feels, is Le Corbusier's own proprietary mode, and the Savoy house is perhaps its premiere example. In the U. S. A. there have been many projects and trials based on the theory, but no body of work, as in Europe and South America.

These three theories of siting might be characterized as the *with*, the *on*, and the *off* the ground manners. One must distinguish a fourth general approach, typical of the majority of houses, where the house is on the ground but not "organically" connected, and where links are used, occasionally to an extent reminiscent of the *with* or *off* the ground manners. Its first recommendation is certainly that it lacks that frigidity typical of art in which a theory is interposed between the artist and his medium. It is sympathetic.

The lack of an easily formulated theory puts the architect very much on his own, and makes him much more dependent on

Le Corbusier and Pierre Jeanneret: Top, the villa Savoye—off the ground. Middle, house at Mathes—on the ground. Bottom, week-end house in the suburbs of Paris —in the ground.

the mass relationship of ground and house, on skillful modelling of the ground plane, and on consistency. As he is free of theory he must choose and discard with the greatest discrimination, lest his house present a rude surprise every time one turns a corner. For the architect working in this mode, the study of the mass relationship of house and ground—because of the technique of locating a house by means of a topographic survey—is not too difficult a problem. Actually however, the house is seen not only in relation to the ground, but also in relation to the apparent volume of the surrounding foliage. Because these combined volumes do not show clearly on a survey, the architect must take special pains if he is to visualize the true conditions at a given site.

The principal determinants of links, house–ground relationships, and modeling are of course the functions which are to take place indoors as well as out. The magic with which a house can invest indoor-outdoor living is, like all architectural expression, the result of a complex receipt. Functional adequacy is only one ingredient. The sense that nature is being used, not only as environment but as a weather modifier for shade, to increase humidity, or to decrease noise, is another. One must also be able to touch nature, not only in the physical sense, but in the sense that the whole scene in which one lives has been subjected to human impact. Nature so modified is touchable in the more fundamental and abstract sense—it is related to man within as well as without.

Our current version of indoor–outdoor living would seem to leave a great deal to be desired. In neighborhoods of International Style houses, at dusk and in the evening, great glass areas allow every casual passer by a full view of the family's doings. For the peripatetic architect, the sociologist, and the person who simply likes to snoop (if these are not all the same character) this intimate view of the upper middle class is full of fascination. In the city the brilliantly lit pantomime through glass is such that it is not unknown for the neighbors to have binoculars about, so that no faintest change in facial expression need go unappreciated. It can be argued that as long as the occupants of glass houses go unaware of their exposure, no great harm can result. On the other hand those aficionados of architecture who value privacy can only decide that the Puritans did it better.

The currently stylish and untramelled use of large glass areas is questionable on other grounds. First glass, because it is, willy nilly, an impervious wall does not, in phsychological terms, connect the indoors and the out. For some people it actually has quite the reverse effect, i.e. it engenders claustrophobia, a desire to break the glass, and to get out. Secondly, in the most practical terms it does not allow of easy movement back and forth, and is therefore rather tantalizing. It seems to promise a freedom which it fails to provide. Our real needs are for ease of movement back and forth; for the arrangement of fixed glass areas so that they do not create a wall (the glass wall being a snare and a delusion); for the location of large glass areas in such a way that they are not

Richard Neutra.

overlooked, and finally for an arrangement which gives the family the feeling that its activities are not the cynosure of all eyes.

These general requirements point up one of the cardinal principles for the siting of houses on difficult terrain. The manifold activities which take place outdoors involve one common denominator—fairly level ground. The house does not. It is as easy, and twice as stimulating, to locate buildings on precipitous topography as on the level. Thus the best, most level, most beautiful parts of sites should seldom be built upon. Once they are covered by a bulky building their original charm is gone. They should be saved, in all their pristine beauty, for outdoor living. The poorer spots, which can only be improved by being covered, are best used for the house itself.

Views

"For now we see through a glass, darkly; but then face to face: now I know in part; but then shall I know even as also I am known."

Corinthians, Chapter 13, 12

The average client is content to leave manipulation of the ground plane, of volume relationships, and of links exclusively to the architect. But he considers views his own personal property. The architect must go at the problem of their proper use with the greatest circumspection. Certainly the uses of views are very real. They must have a beneficial effect on our eyes in that they make us change focus from near to far objects. They are restful, because they occasionally divert our attention. They are splendid excuses for the quietness necessary to self-communion. They are a sort of crystal ball in this sense. Looking at a view is not sloth. It is the enjoyment of an active esthetic experience. To be caught staring at a blank wall is probably to be accused of laziness, introspection or worse: to be caught looking at a view is not too great a shame. Views, like a fire, also serve as points of focus for social groups. And finally they are par excellence the best means of creating surprise, or wonder, and thus a sense of liveliness and richness of experience.

In principle, perhaps, one should never see the same view from more than one place, unless the second viewpoint offers some contrast to, or some new aspect not enjoyed by the first. To see a view from the outside, from the front walk or driveway, and then to be faced with the same view from the living room windows is to lose all sense of variety and surprise. A particularly good view should thus be hidden except from one well worked out vantage point.

The natural tendency, difficult to resist, is to be greedy about the locus of the first vantage point. The most comprehensive view, for most sites, is from the hightest point. But it is not necessarily the best. And even if it is the best it need not inevitably be seen from within the house, particularly if there are other good views available. The restraint which saves a view for lonely or sociable visits, as an excuse for a stroll, or for privacy, has much to recommend it. The compulsive, greedy, and self important overtones of houses placed on the highest point, fixedly staring from every window at the best view, are very real and unpleasant.

Short views, particularly in contrast with long ones, have a peculiar fascination of their own. It is possible to create a pleasant outlook in seven feet, though it must, of course, be quite artificial and in every sense a non-objective picture. A small enclosed garden in contrast with a large exposed view, a seascape for example, offers an ideal inversion of space. The principal difficulty in the handling of small outdoor spaces comes about through our tendency to exaggerate the size of indoor space, and to minimize that of outdoor space. Our sense of proper size increases vastly as we move from indoors to out, and thus the space relationships of small artificially created views must be, as it were, over-size.

Most views can be broken down, as does a painter his picture, into a series of receding planes, and not infrequently these planes seem to have ground traces along some definite compass direction. They may be parallel, or not. The parallelism, or non-parallelism, of the frame of the opening through which a view is seen to that view's first plane, has the utmost esthetic significance. Thus for example an opening parallel with a river creates a movemented and centrifugal picture, which must necessarily be cut off arbitrarily, and thus questionably, at each side. An opening at an appreciable angle on the other hand, may create a focused and centripetal effect; and thus a more satisfying picture.

Most views and gardens contain invisible, but none the less very significant axes, which if ignored or unduly emphasized can prove visually harassing. Again the temptation is to place the picture window on and perpendicular to one of these lines, rather than off and at an angle with it. One needs to be *related* to such axes, not transfixed by them. One source of our pleasure in views is the sense of physical relatedness, unconsciously perceived, which the proper arrangement of these planes and axes creates.

The manner in which the picture plane, the usual view point, and the elements of the view itself are related is deep in the realm of artistry. But certainly the size of the angles employed is significant. Angles, the traces of which are intuitively felt, usually appear less great than they are, and so must be magnified if one is to feel the full effect of their angularity. This is even more true of axes. As they are not overtly visible, they tend to be "wavey" rather than fixed. Thus, for example, the addition of fifteen degrees to a right angle usually will be felt, but not consciously realized, unless the onlooker searches for the reasons for his "expanded" feeling.

By the same token, the view arranged to be seen perpendicularly through glass is unpleasant. It is picture like, compulsively demanding, and is thus apt to be rejected. It is easy to forget that glass is transparent from nearly every practically approachable angle. The sense of increased space one feels when looking through glass at an angle, the sense of space "around the corner" can be played upon much more fully when the glass itself is in an angular pattern. In such cases one has the feeling that one has, somehow, actually seen around a corner, and the sensation is delightful.

When a view has a climax, that is such a feature as a tall peak, or a slot between two islands, again the temptation is to center this in the opening, as seen perpendicular to it or from the average viewpoint, and this arrangement must be avoided like the plague. Again it compels rather than leads the eye. In views as in pictures, the center of interest loses all punch when in the center of the frame.

In addition to the need to relate the viewer and the view, the architect must battle the tendency of views, like pictures, to become invisible. He is helped here by the views themselves, which unlike pictures, change on a daily and seasonal cycle. On the other hand they cannot be rotated as pictures can, to bring them back from invisibility. The quickest way to kill a view is to place a picture window parallel with the traces of its planes, on the axis of the center of interest, through which one looks at right angles. This is the ideally boring condition. Views are perhaps most visible in the morning when one is at work, in the kitchen for example, and in the evening, at tea or cocktails. They are also wonderful when they are tucked away, when one sees them in passage, from a hall or staircase or bath room window. And, whatever the locus from which they are seen, they must always be treated as part of one's own space, for they are not pictures.

Determinants

"The health and prosperity of a person were considered to depend on the location and planning of the dwelling-house chiefly in reference to "direction." With due consideration given to the various necessary elements for making the house pleasant and hygienic, the following rules have come to be regarded as the standard to be followed: an ideal site for a house should have a stream on the left (east) and a long road on the right (west), a pond in front (south) and hills at the back (north). According to the ancient Chinese astrologers and physiographers, the stream represents "green dragon," the road "white tiger," the pond "Shujaku" (a sort of phoenix), and the hills "genbu" (delineated in art by a turtle entwined with a snake), the four symbols representing the Buddhist deities safeguarding the four directions. The principle involved is the same as that which governs the growth of all living things in the universe. It is the principle of the positive and negative, of male and female, or of sunshine and shadow, in which one mingles harmoniously with the other."—Harada

The three sections just above contain examples of attitudes towards the various relationships involved in houses; house–ground for example. While individual architects may differ with the detailed judgments expressed, there is not too much room for argument, once the fundamentals are thought out. The pressures exerted on us by our culture, class, and environment tend to make for uniformity in house planning. People and sites exert the contrary effect. When they are fully understood and used they lead to fresh regroupings of all the factors involved, and thus to variety. One is dealing in clusters of sub-relationships; house–climate; house–man; house–activities; and house–topography, to mention only a few. No one problem must be allowed to usurp the whole show. Each must be allowed to exert its own pressure.

A knowledge of climate is a tool, it is not science; of itself it leads nowhere, and cannot be a single determinant of design. A knowledge of structure is a tool; it is not engineering; of itself it leads nowhere; and cannot be a single determinant of design. For

Mies Van Der Rohe, project for a mountain house.

the culturally and emotionally broad person tools and techniques can never be satisfactory ends in themselves. Their only real interest is as means to humanist ends, and then only as one or the other is more appropriate to the peculiar end in view. For example, the International Stylists' emphasis on climate as a controlling factor in planning, or the speculative builder's complete disregard of it, both result in an almost identical esthetic brutality. In the former case, the attitude reaches its nadir in the "Solar" house. Here all rooms of any importance face due south; all have all glass walls; all face the same view; typically all the bed rooms are exactly the same size and shape; all have exactly the same light conditions; and all, more likely than not, lack cross ventilation. The housewife is condemned to tend such a jail of the spirit for the sake of a few lengths of pipe, a few gallons of oil, made necessary again for technical reasons, by an over-indulgence in glass area. One can only marvel at the involutions of the purely technical mind. The solar house happens to be a peculiarly "technical" example. But the technocratic approach is found everywhere.

Views, topography, planting and the like are also used as single determinants, and while they produce, in terms of exterior appearance, less rigidity than the "solar" plan, in the reality of twenty-four hours a day, three hundred and sixty-five days a year, they are equally muscle bound.

The stiffness which accepts a single determinant is very similar to that lack of suppleness which is the bane of musicians. One object of instrumental practice is muscular relaxation. The architect must attack his site with that same relaxed self confidence with which the good musician attacks his instrument. Sites are neither sacred nor profane. They were made to be tweeked, thumbed, and manhandled. The siteless problems handed out in architectural schools are the poorest imaginable preparation for practice. Such clichés as "Respect the site!" stress an idealization of the status quo, rather than a workmanlike will to use it. The problem is one of synthesis of numerous physical, natural, and human factors. To allow any one set of criteria to steal the show inevitably unbalances it. William Wilson Wurster, when a student asked him, "What is the best orientation?", replied that there seem to be four good directions, to wit, north, south, east and west, and that he invariably used all of them. Similarly, a view of house and site as one indivisible whole, of the entire area as one field of operation, is of the essence. Its importance cannot be overemphasized. It comes as close to a commandment as any statement which can be made on the technique of planning.

Every square inch of the outdoors, as well as the indoors, is subservient to a specific *use*, including decorative and fallow uses. Lawns, woodlots, back yards, contain essences of their own, and it is as important to the whole that these be expressed and furthered in planning, as it is that the essence "living room" be expressed. Trees, for example, contain messages of their own, which are nearly always available, but which are invisible most of the time. These essences are made visible, and incidentally lent added significance, when they are related to other elements in such a way that the total scene relates to the total human being. Trees also exert important effects on noise levels and microclimate. The goal in siting is thus a balanced use of, for example, the evaporative effect of foliage, of sunlight, or solar radiation, of the

Pietro Belluschi.

acoustic shielding effect of banks, etc., while at the same time subordinating each such factor to the whole concept.

This leads to a view of a potential house as a lump of ductile clay—the client's program—first put down, quite arbitrarily, in the middle of the site, without prior shaping of any kind. Its form begins to merge when the pressures exerted by its surroundings are allowed to operate freely upon it. The object of a relaxed design technique is to allow ambient forces to exert their full energy, unmitigated by extraneous or personal redirection. These forces might be summarized as follows:

1. The ethos of the country, region, state, and locality.
2. The character of the neighborhood.
3. The characteristic combinations of sun, cloudiness, air temperature, wind, precipitation, and humidity, which results in climate.
4. The character and behaviour of ambient noise sources.

5. The size, location, use, character, shading effect, style, etc. of the surrounding structures.
6. The character, material, and protective effects of the topography, and flora.
7. Access and egress, of people, vehicles and utilities.
8. Laws, covenants, and restrictions.
9. Outlook and privacy.
10. The effects of the new structure on the status quo.

Siting would hardly be worthy of the adjective "problem" were it not that many of these elements and uses are in constant or cyclical flux. How simple it would be, for example, if houses were designed for the cocktail hour on a cool sunny afternoon in September, all other hours, climates and functions being of no relevance. But this kind of architecture is reserved to Worlds Fairs, and its limitations become apparent to those who happen to arrive at such shows on a drizzly day. The dwelling house must mirror all the seasons, the weeks, and the days.

In the course of a day the house mood shifts from cold dawn, to breakfast, to housework, to lunch, to the afternoon's doings, to the husband's return, to tea or cocktails, to sunset, to dinner, to an evening reading, to a midnight snack, to the blue insomniac's dawn again, all punctuated by the growth of the children, and by the occasional difficulties and tragedies which beset everyone. Tired Monday mornings, gay Saturday nights, homey Sunday afternoons, the middle week, washday, the day the waste paper is collected—all contain their essences. The house itself affects and responds to these occasions. It shrinks in winter and swells in summer. In wet climates the great symbol of the onset of school and the winter's work is the shrinking of the doors, so that they no longer bind in their frames. The deciduous trees which have been providing shade, absorbing sound and evaporating water, lose their leaves, their acoustic effect and their shading effect, to let in the winter sun. The front and back walks, deep in snow, become infinitely longer and wider. Architecture is not for the ages—it is for the moment.

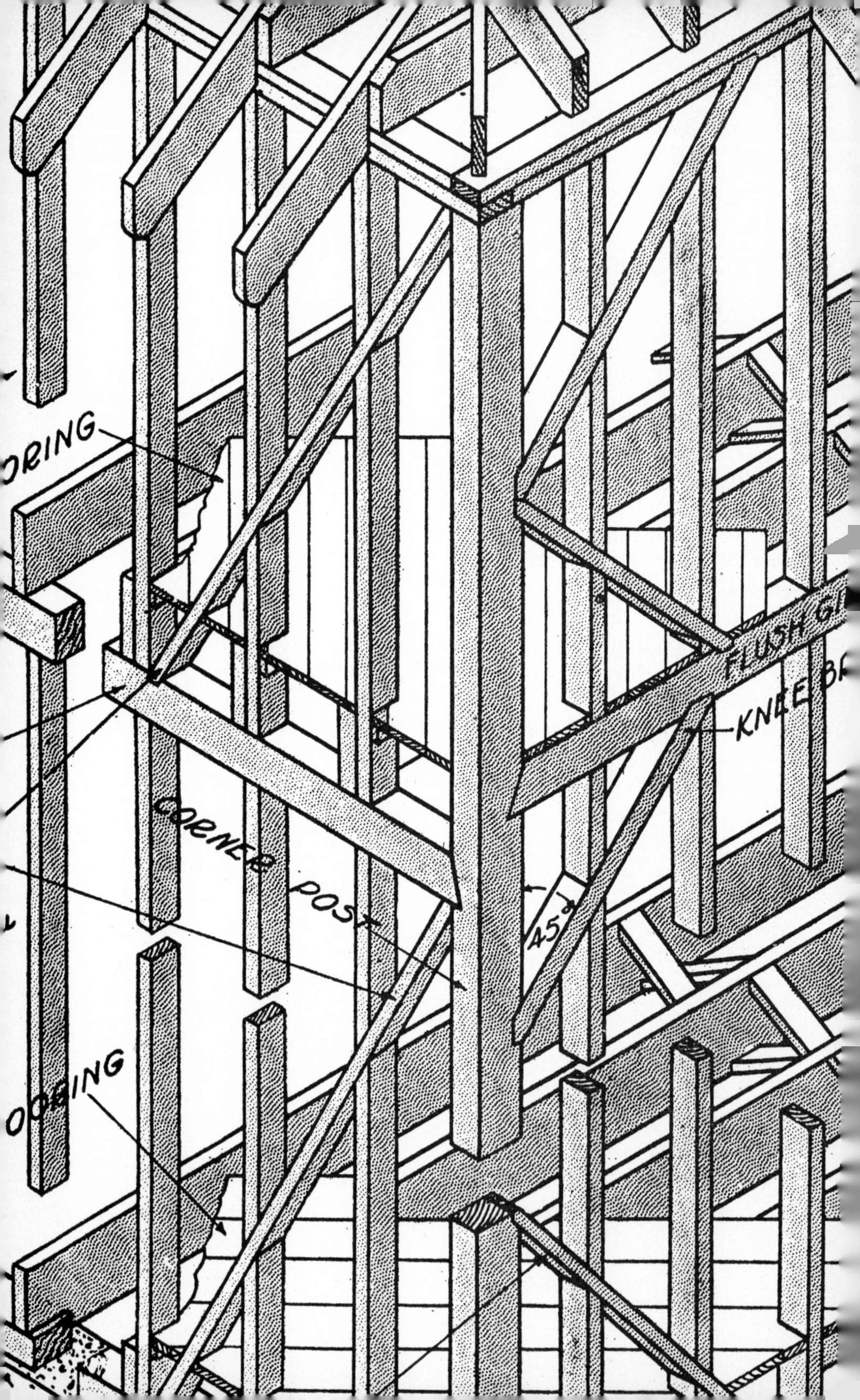

ORING
FLUSH GI
KNEE BR
CORNER POST
45°
OORING

CHAPTER XI
Structure

Here is my theory of structure: a scientific arrangement of spaces and forms to functions and sites; an emphasis of features proportioned to their graduated importance in function.—Sullivan

The Status Quo

THERE SEEM TO BE AS MANY APPROACHES TO STRUCTURE as there are to site and to style. The Internationalists tend towards contemporaneousness in technique. But they either warp structure for the sake of form, or warp function for the sake of structure. The nationally oriented direct themselves towards the processes of our time and place, on a scale less hopelessly broad than that of the Internationalists, and less narrowly confined than that of the Empiricists. This national scale is thoroughly appropriate to the subject. The handbooks of our time are for national use. Our schools are for national use. Our materials are distributed on a national basis. The scope of the structural field is the forty-eight states. This accounts for the fact that those architects who tend towards a United States place orientation, i.e., the right wing International stylists and the Traditionalists, produce on the one hand the most interesting, and on the other the "soundest" structure. It also accounts for the fact that the Empiricist adjustment, because it is local in place orientation, avoids the extremes of pure International Stylism, but fails to achieve its polish. Just as the architect's adjustment to period, place, and process profoundly affects his style, so it affects his sense of structure.

Braced frame.

The building industry, insofar as it is guided by architects at all, is most influenced by Traditionalist attitudes. The most obvious result of this influence is the large number of deceptively treated materials; the asbestos shingles made to look like wood, the "antique" brick, the copper cornice in imitation of wood, the tar paper brick, the "antiqued " title, the concrete "stone," the steel beam boxed in wood, and a thousand other bits of camouflage, "treatment" and falsification, a veritable Alice in Wonderland world in which things are never quite what they seem. Nor does make believe stop at materials. We have stone and wood pediments hung on intricate steel frames, brick chimneys poking up through the exact center of "Cape Cod" roofs by means of long steel supported horizontal runs, and soil pipes, suitably boxed, "expressed" as summers. The basic Traditionalist position, stressing as it does the form, rather than the content of the past, leads inevitably to the acceptance of make believe.

The low creativity and high ingenuity typical of the Traditionalist fits exactly with the stock Georgian mantelpiece, the stock Ionic column and the stock Colonial stair rail. The house is collected together, as style, as structure, and as equipment. Each part is chosen from a list or storehouse. Design tends to become accretion. The absence of a guiding idea inherent to the individual job is essential to the whole Traditionalist position, and is most marked in terms of structure. The light wood frame is of course the ideal medium, in that it needs no idea, demands no architectural expression, and incidentally can be made to hide a host of little lies, exigencies, and errors.

On the other hand, the Traditionalist structure is, in a purely practical guise, the most successful yet devised. It is relatively foolproof, relatively leakless, and not so permanent as to bar changes and improvements. Its lack of abstract integrity does not prevent it from functioning extremely well as a tool. Thus one of the most strenuously fostered myths is to the effect that structure requires tremendous skill, and that this skill is the exclusive property of the sound and conservative Traditionalist architect. The myth does contain a little truth. As is the case with the British, muddling through works in practice, though it fails to provide anyone with any very great satisfaction in the meantime.

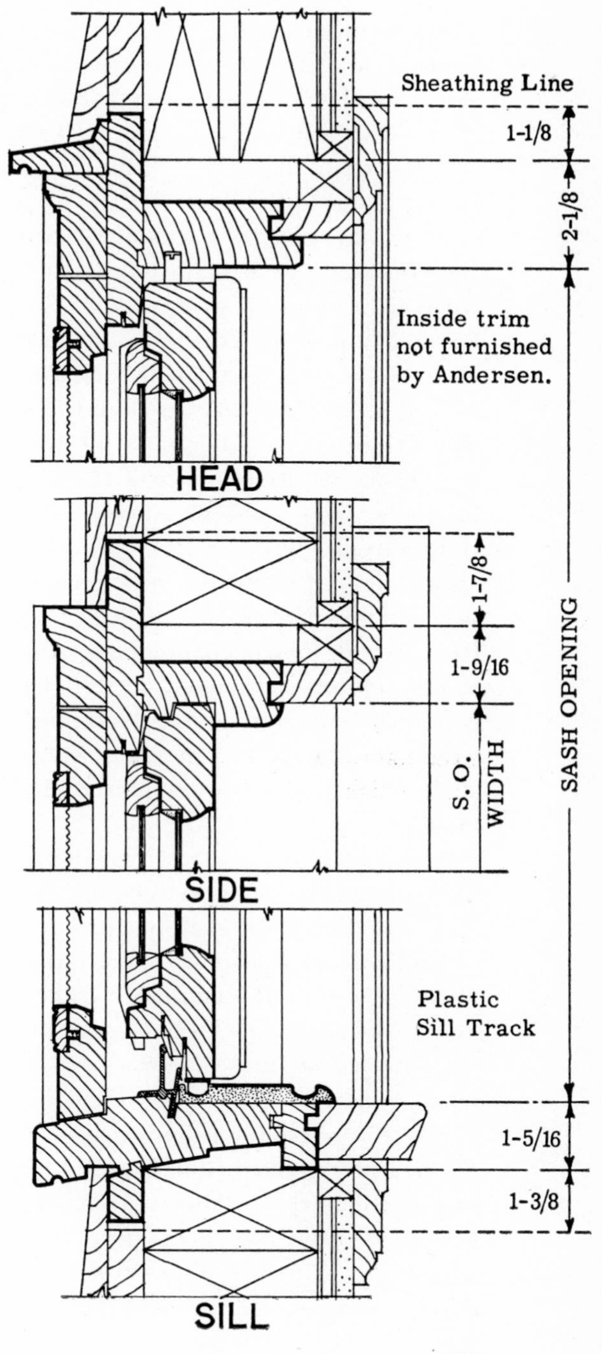

...e Anderson Corporation; ...iding window. The plastic ...l track has a "natural wood ...ish." The manufacturer ...so offers numerous details ...ich show how the stock sash ...ay be adapted to various ...ll and other conditions.

Those in the central position of the International Style have done nothing to affect, one way or the other, the Traditionalist structure. Its use of the wood frame is identical. It substitutes a slick finish for the "antique." But this is no real change. The centerists inherited the Traditionalist approach, and have simply made the best of it.

The right and left wings of the Internationalist movement, on the contrary, have made very real forays into the relationship between style and structure. The left wing has exhibited two types of approach. The first is typified by the forcing of structural elements and forms to their furthest limits, and by the introduction of bizarre methods of support. Very great cantilevers which, when the materials begin to fatigue, sag miserably, are typical, as is every device which will accentuate a feeling of airiness and lightness. This approach involves a consuming desire to hang things from above. Wires and rods abound, and though these same hanging elements must inevitably be supported by compression members sooner or later, in the meantime they allow "effects" which soon become clichés. The great majority of such work is more akin to exhibitionism than to workmanship. Shaky staircases, often without handrails; slippery glass bridges, open gratings over habitable rooms, sagging roofs, binding doors, and the once slick finish stained and blotched to dun color are its advertisments.

The defense of such extravagancies as research is also most disheartening. There is a tremendous need for an exploration of structure. But real research, a painstaking, long drawn out, largely theoretical exploration into an unknown area is entirely foreign to architecture. Buckminister Fuller's Dymaxion structures are examples of research. What goes under the name research among the Internationalists is at best experiment, and at worst, a stubborn denial of reality. Why must those gifted with a heaven-sent ability to design ape the scientists?

The other phenomenon typical of left wing International Style, and particularly of the more disciplinary and abstract modes within it, appears conservative in contrast with the somewhat adolescent exuberance described above. Here structure rather than function is conceived of as guiding the form of the building.

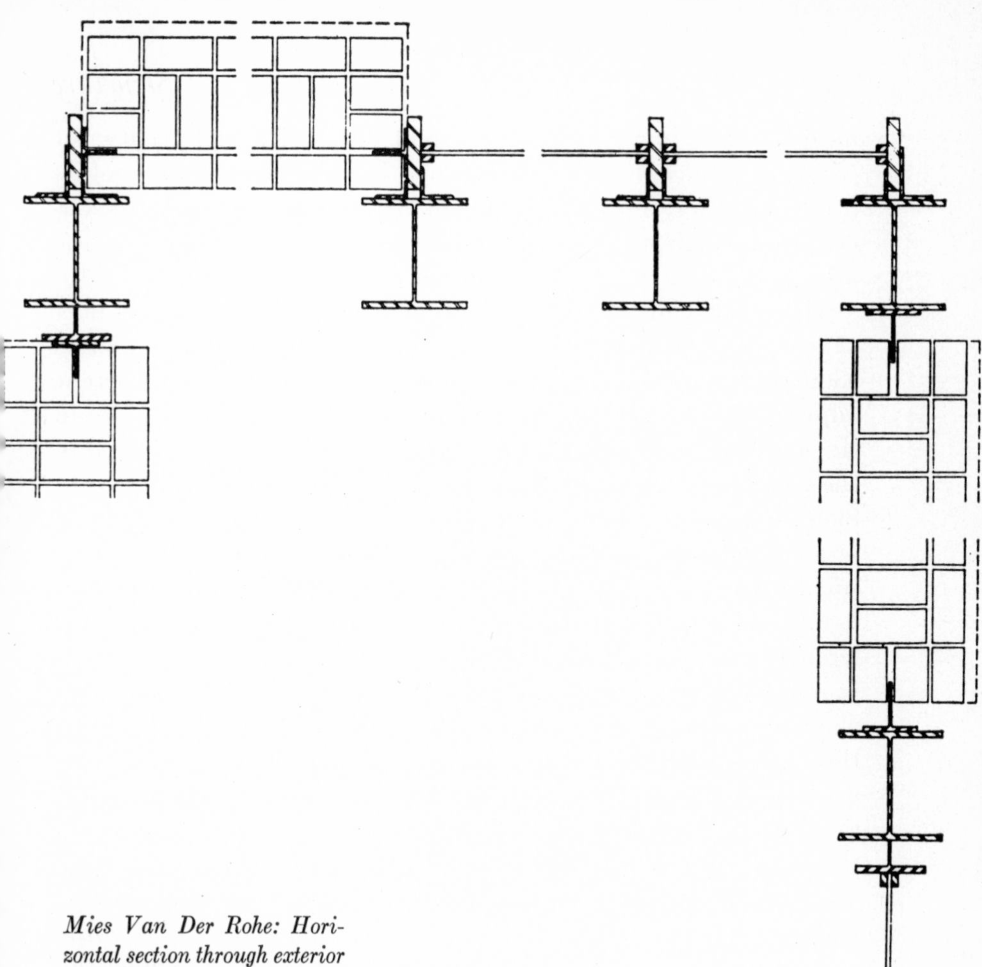

Mies Van Der Rohe: Horizontal section through exterior wall, Library and Administration building, Illinois Institute of Technology.

The activities to be housed are dispersed freely within the predetermined structure in order not in any way to disrupt or distort it. The Traditionalist distinction between structure and finish is done away with. The structural members are exposed and are, at the same time, the finished members, the trim, draft stops, weather strips, and expansion joints. The Traditionalist solves the various problems involved in assemblies by a proliferation of parts, each with a specific purpose. The Disciplinary Internationalist solves them, as far as is possible, with one material and one member. At its best, this approach achieves great distinction and clarity. At its worst it tends to place the form of building ahead of one of its prime purposes, that of keeping out the weather. It results in condensation, high radiant loss, inflexibility, high cost, and in the distortion of every function in favor of structure.

The right wing of the International movement, i.e., that part of it oriented towards the assimilation of the techniques of this country and period, has in contrast to all of the other current adjustments, made very real, tangible, and progressive strides in the use of structure. For example one of the problems involved in the wood frame is its inadaptability to large glass areas. The common method of solving the problem is to introduce a deep wood or steel lintel, flanked on either side of the opening by the usual small plate or girt. This not only lacks clarity and order. Because it introduces different depths of horizontal wood, it leads to differential shrinkage. Richard Neutra's various solutions of this problem are of the greatest interest. His development of a post-window-post-window exterior wall, with a lintel of uniform depth throughout the house, is an excellent solution of the problem. His work is full of other equally interesting solutions. The International Regionalists of the Southeast have also made attacks on structure, through the use of a modified type of mill construction. While the techniques used are a far cry from the original wood skeleton, the effects produced are directly comparable. The truths exposed, the fascination of being let in on the secret of how the house supports itself, are tremendously rewarding. One of the hopes which can be held for the future of American architecture is that the attitude towards structure of such architects as Neutra will permeate the whole of the profession.

On the other hand there is a very real danger in the technical approach. Its limitation is that it tends, very easily, to appear to solve all problems regardless of their nature. Thus it leads to a sort of inhuman aridity which, translated into architecture, is no less unattractive than it is in people. Structure by itself is no more important than any other of the numerous phenomena which go to make up architecture.

The Empiricist position, oriented as it is towards the local, the native, and the anti-theoretical, has added little to the exploration of structure per se. On the other hand the nature of the Empiricist's adjustment forces him towards very real efforts to decrease the cost of building. He is typically content to work with the cheapest materials, to omit as many layers as possible, particularly those in the category of finish, and to use the cheapest structural forms. This skimping of structure has led to the "grass shack" epithet so often levelled at him.

The pressures which force the architect in this direction are terrifically real. Because the client never seems to present a budget commensurate with his demands for space, the effort is always towards as many square feet as possible, considerations of structure and finish being secondary. This is in a sense a negative philosophy, i.e., "If I can't have everything, at least I'll get as much space as I can." If the Empiricist's position were purely this, they could not have achieved their very great success. Rather than leave the proposition in this simple negative form, they have developed an outlook which derrogates finish, slickness, "soundness," "abstract structure," and permanence, as too luxurious, as overindulgent, and as tending towards premature obsolescence. They extol the qualities of low cost, simplicity, hominess, flexibility, and of real rather than esthetic lightness, as unostentatious and genuine. "Because," they say in effect, "structure long outlasts functional adequacy, let us build for the short functional term." The shorter this term is conceived to be, the greater the emphasis on flexibility. A drive towards utter flexibility easily becomes compulsive. A structure which allows the greatest freedom to add, change, and remodel, and which may be used in varying ways without change in plan, while theoretically splendid, easily slips over into farce.

The wood frame, as it currently exists, is extremely well adapted to this philosophy. The Empiricists therefore see no very great need for a foray into abstract structure. In spite of the humanity of this position, elegance and order *are* two of the elements of fine architecture. And these qualities depend, in the first instance, on a noble skeleton. The portrait painter is as concerned with the skeleton of his subject as he is with the flesh it supports and which he represents. Bony structure is the first determinant of physical beauty.

The Empiricist notion that transcience of structure will obviate functional adolescence would seem to be highly questionable. The same desperate economic necessity which forces a choice between quality and space also tends to force structure to remain in use indefinitely, regardless of functional or physical obsolescence. The older the structure, the greater the number of square feet may be obtained per unit of cost. This does not in the least invalidate the Empiricist position. On the other hand the use of the economic argument to excuse a lack of essential clarity in structure hardly seems justifiable. Low cost and clarity, order and transcience, are by no means incompatible qualities. Thus it would seem to be inevitable that the phase to succeed Empiricism will bend its energies towards a further rationalization of structure, based on the right wing Internationalists' brilliant beginnings, while at the same time attempting to avoid the pitfall of a purely technical approach.

These various attitudes towards structure can be boiled down, for the sake of convenience, as follows: First, structure may be looked on as a purely and limitedly technical matter. It is seen as something to be worked out for such ends as the avoidance of leaks, dry rot, and excessive infiltration, and as divorced from style or expression. The individuals who adopt this view are apt to be walking Sweet's Files. They know the name, weight, length, strength, composition, gauge, and coating of every nail. They are unconcerned with visual or philosophic order. They see only the parts, missing the whole altogether. The second common view of structure tends to stress the total assembly as the field of action. Here each structural system is conceived of as subject to laws of its own, which must be carried through to their ultimate, if bitter, ends. A third view neither confirms nor denies the first two, but manipulates structure as simply another element of the whole building's expressive message. This is perhaps best stated by Ruskin, when he remarks:

> ". . . that building will generally be the noblest which to an intelligent eye discovers the great secrets of its structure, as an animal form does, *although from a careless observer they may be concealed.*" (Italics mine)

The Structural Problem

Because the average American house is framed in wood, we must look to the wood frame for the great secrets of its construction. The fact that it has developed as the Braced, Balloon, and Western varieties seems of little importance. The three types are only regional variations on an identical theme. What is this theme? From where did it come, and why did it develop in its present directions? Obviously there are several points of attack; cultural, technical, environmental, and functional, each of which could be counted upon to reach one aspect of the problem. However, for the practicing architect, who must manipulate the wood frame daily, there is only one promising direction of approach. This is towards an understanding of the ideas behind the wood frame and its development. The great secrets to which Ruskin refers are ideas. E. Baldwin Smith, for the case of the dome, expresses this as follows:

> "Once the long history of pagan and Christian domical ideas begins to take shape, it becomes evident how necessary it is for the history of architecture to be freed from the purely racial, environmental and utilitarian theories regarding the origin of the dome."

This is true of racial, technical, environmental, and functional theories as unique explanations for any structural form. The architect who views structure as unconfined technically, as subject to manipulation for the sake of the *idea* involved, rather than for the sake of either "truth" or leaks, enjoys the greatest freedom of expression. This is not to say that leaks should be welcomed, or truth avoided. They are simply secondary goals, eminently achievable on a far lower level of skill than that of idea.

The original American or English Colonial wood frame was in essence a wood skeleton, to all intents and purposes similar to the steel skeleton and to the human skeleton. In one of its original forms it contained no studs. Because the size of the members used was very great, and because exterior walls and interior partitions

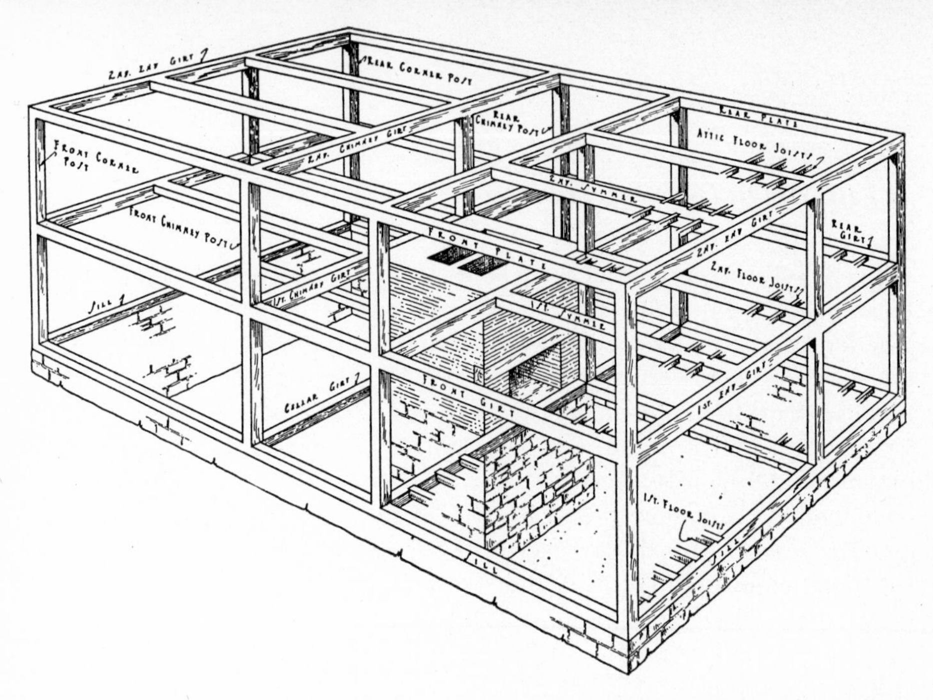

Kelly: Wood skeleton.

were often one board thick, the skeleton perforce showed. This type of structure is deeply satisfying. The reasons usually given for its success, i.e., "big beams" or "old beams" or "hand adzed beams" etc. are significant. Here is a tree, from the earlier and sacred grove in which its god lived, and on which the house stands, living a new kind of life. And, because of the way it is used, its divine attributes continue to remain available to the indweller. There are also secondary benefits. The method presents the onlooker with a fact; i.e., "This is what it takes to hold this building up." It tells a story, by means of the size, jointing, and design of the frame, of the technology of the time, and of the way in which the loads of the particular structure are handled. This story engenders in us that most desirable of all sensations, an intuition to the effect that there is an underlying concordance between man and nature.

From a technical point of view the wood skeleton presents a large three dimensional module. This type of structure is, in every aspect of its use, an exceedingly difficult thing with which to deal. Technically, esthetically, in terms of plan, etc., it presents problem after problem. But whatever its difficulties the large three dimensional structural module shows a higher correlation with fine

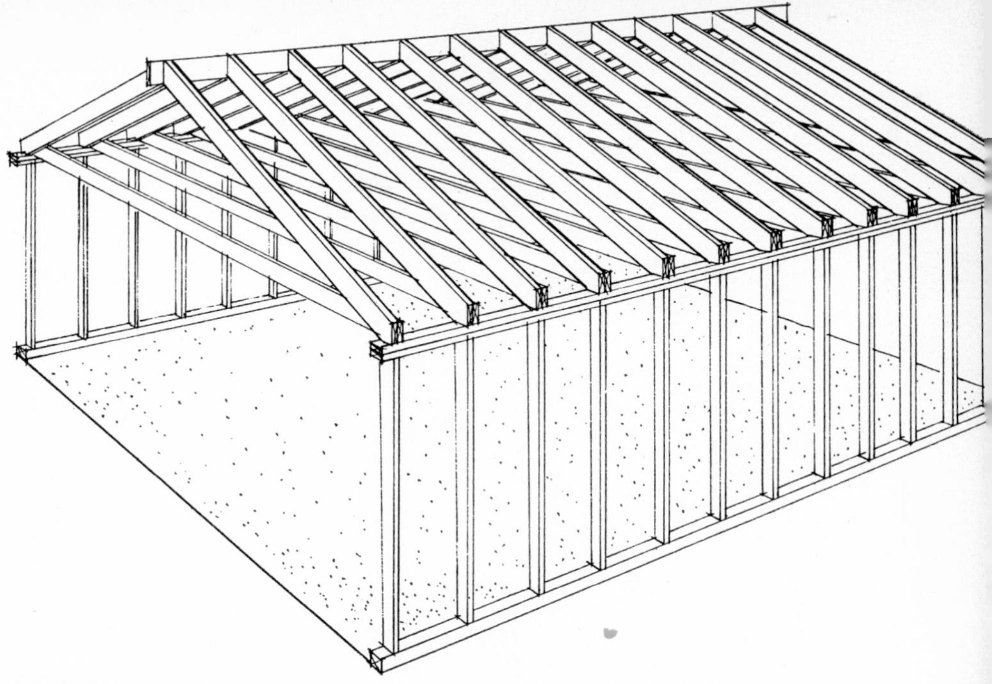

Wood frame.

architecture than any other single non-human factor. The vault, the Japanese house frame, the classic portico, the atrium, the barn frame, the colonnade are all deeply satisfying because they are whole, orderly, and expressive.

The wood frame developed from a module bigger than a man in all directions to our sixteen inch spacing in only two directions. The third dimension was in effect lost—the heroic scale abandoned. This distinctive character of the contemporary wood frame has inevitably affected our stylistic and functional adjustments. The wood skeleton is complete within itself; but can be logically multiplied in six directions. The wood frame is unstable in several ways, it lacks rigidity in its joints, it can be pieced out in two directions indefinitely in that it is a one way span, etc. Thus, in essence, it involves a space rectangular in cross section, of unlimited length, a sort of hollow tube. Large openings are only really appropriate at the ends (provided the structure can be braced elsewhere). The wood skeleton, on the other hand, can be left open anywhere.

The technical reasons for the shift from the skeleton are obvious and need not concern us here. The shift brought with it some potent benefits. The greatest of these is flexibility. The wood frame

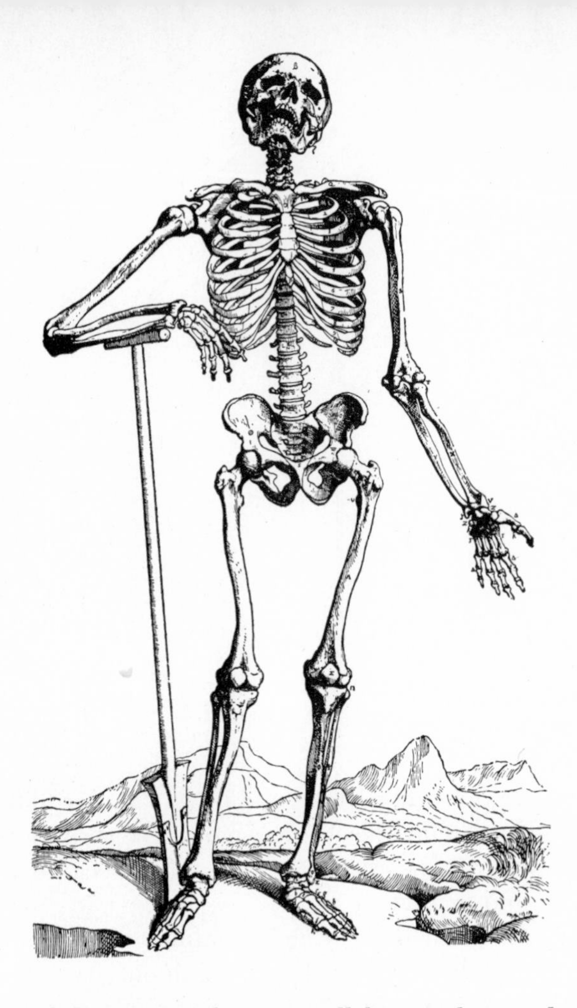

can be used for any style, not well but at least adequately. Its small module allows infinite fudging, exceptions, second thoughts, patching, and remodeling. Secondly, it has proved extraordinarily adaptable to the mechanical trades. It adsorbs pipes and wires with the greatest of ease, and duct work can be adapted to it with the slightest outlay of ingenuity. It is as nearly a foolproof system as could be devised. Like burlesque it is essentially a vulgar medium, but one which holds attractions for all types. The wood skeleton by contrast is difficult, cranky, inflexible, and will not absorb the mechanical trades easily. Its one asset is its nobility.

The inherent flexibility of the light frame has had several questionable effects. It has released architects from the necessity of really thinking out structure, and of integrating form and structure. It is the lazy man's dream. More seriously, it has released the building industry in general and the mechanical trades in

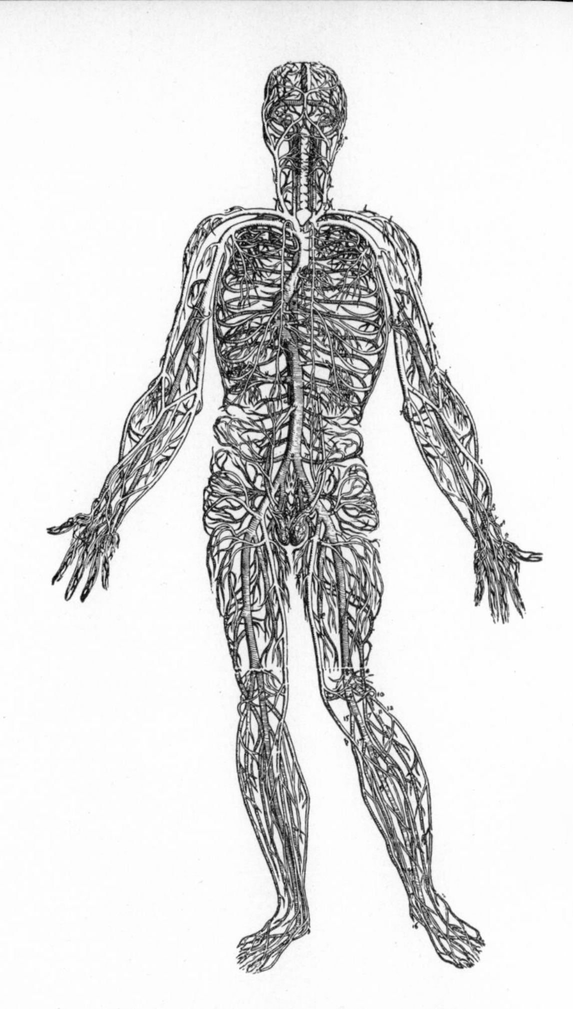

These, and the illustrations on the following four pages, are from the works of Andreas Vesalius.

particular from the necessity of integrating plumbing and heating and wiring with structure. They are now considered as entrails, slightly drippy, embarrassing to hear, and available for repair only by means of an expensive operation. To show pipes and wires goes beyond the indecent exposure of exhibitionism—it is as shocking as the exposed entrails of the victim of an accident. The plumbing, wiring, and heating systems do contain truths, and fascinating truths to those so minded, i.e., to surgeons and engineers. But we choose to hide them and, as far as is possible, to deny their existence. The contemporary architect strives to express the truths of structure, and at the same time to suppress the truths of the mechanical equipment. The large module, and the network of pipes, wires, and ducts war with each other. To bring about a state of amicable compromise is the principal structural problem of our time.

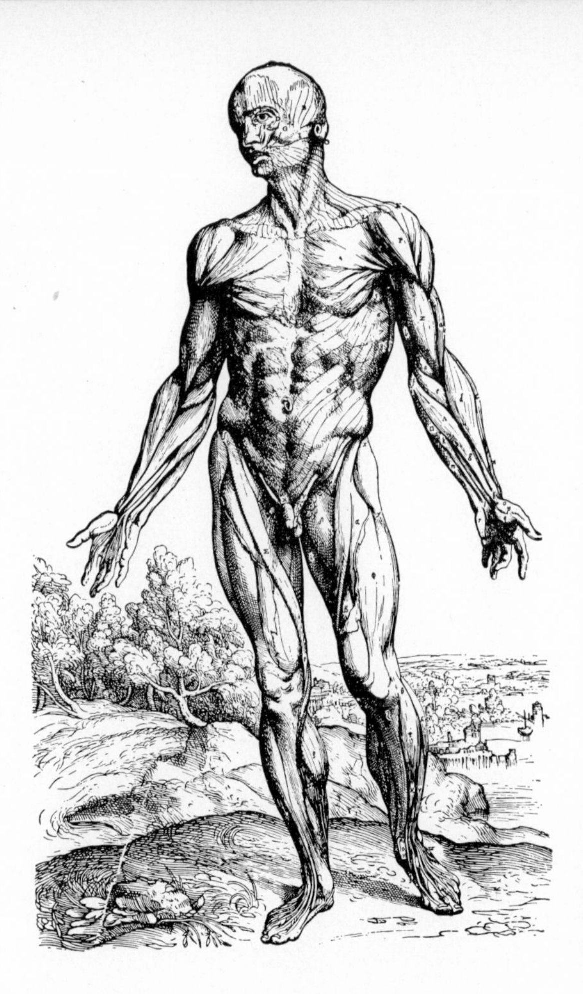

"Man is the measure of all things"—

Protagoras of Abdera

The parallels between our skeleton and the structural skeleton; between the plumbing system and our system of consuming, digesting, and excreting; between the heating system and our own necessity to release heat; between the electrical system and our nervous system; between the tensile and compressive forces in structure and our combined use of muscles and bones; between the finishing materials and our skin, are all so close as to influence largely our reactions to building. This concordance between the human being and his house sets up certain limits beyond which the architect cannot go without violating our sense of relatedness —of just proportion. Regardless of the strengths of the materials

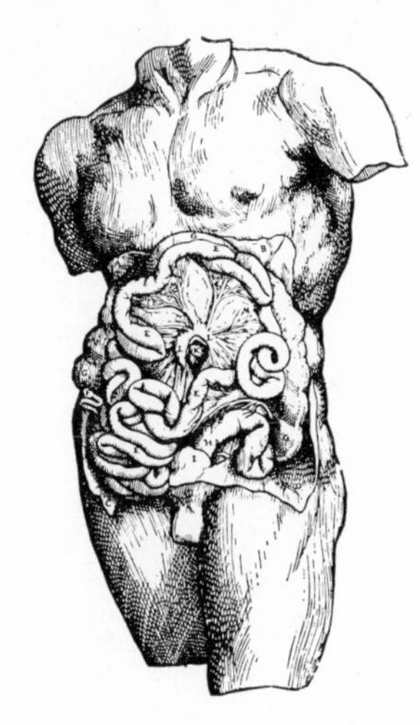

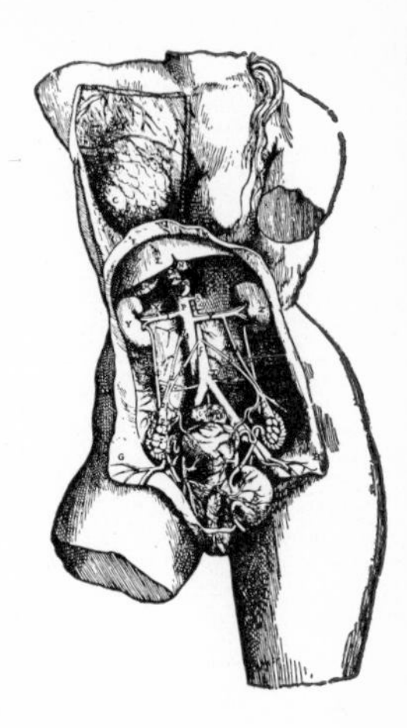

he has available and of the capacities of the mechanical systems he can envisage, they must still be believable in man's own terms. Thus we can encompass the calculating machine as "the mechanical brain" while the atomic bomb or the hurricane are beyond our limits.

Structure for example, is subject to expansion and contraction even as we expand and contract in height on a daily and life cycle. No element of structure is without this movement, and it must be allowed to take place without causing damage. Structure, like people, is also subject to fatigue. Its extreme fibers get tired and allow of unyouthful sags, like an old man's pot belly. Cantilevers, like arms held out too long, will droop downwards. The decrepitude of human old age is exactly paralleled in houses. They also tend to change color and dry up in the sun, but to remain more or less the same in the shade, a factor which totally invalidates

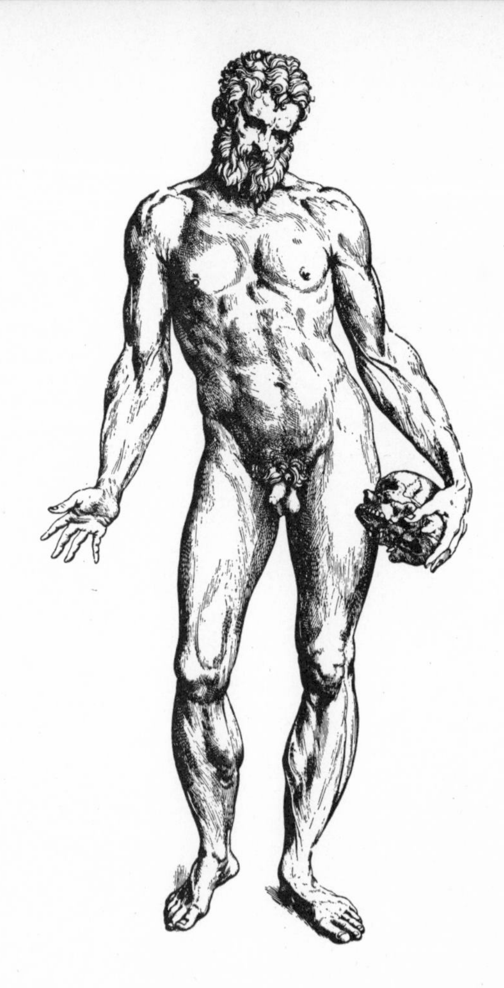

a great many of the stylish continuous indoor-outdoor features typical of today. The fact that houses smell, that walls must breathe if they are not to rot, that houses drip and leak, just as we do, also influences us. A dripping ceiling, like a dripping nose, is first of all a human weakness. The house also creates heat. Here the tremendous interest in panel heating is significant. The house, like the body, is warm to the touch—heated by an invisible internal process. The panel is a direct translation into structure of the large area, low temperature, radiant loss, and concealed means principles of our own body warmth.

There appear to be certain exceptions to this principle. For example Le Corbusier's bold placing—to American eyes—of a very old fashioned radiator in front of a wall of glass is, at first sight, thrilling honesty. Here, he says, is what heats this room, and in so doing, expresses the essential essence *radiator*. As an esthetic

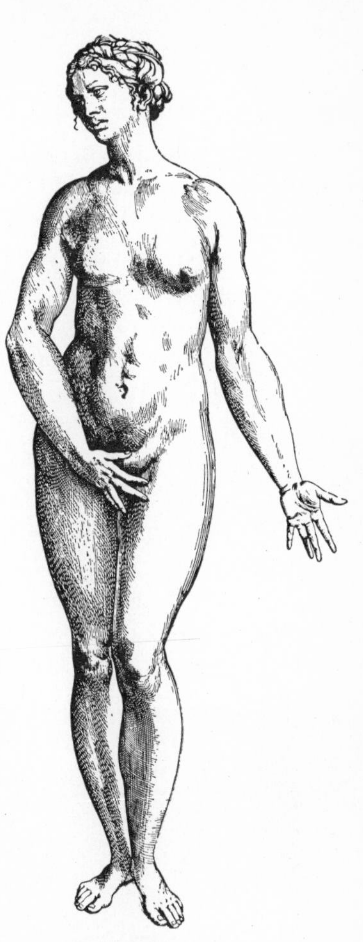

experience this is certainly well worth while. As a life pattern it seems extreme, akin to the boring bathroom talk of children, or to the tiresome emphasis on sex talk of some adults. Leaving aside for the moment the valid and exhilarating esthetic purpose in such an arrangement of a radiator, its human message is exhibitionistic. Prudism is no more attractive. The typical American radiator uneasily concealed behind an obtrusive box dotted with a rash of holes expresses, in essence, nothing but shame in this "indecent" function of heating. It is small wonder that the radiant panel enjoyed such instant and enthusiastic acceptance.

Such attitudes apply, of course, to all of the mechanical systems of the house. Heating is perhaps the most obvious because our standards for it are very high, and because it is so integral a part of the structure. But the same principles apply to the others. For example, the average client asks for "concealed cove lighting" as well as for radiant heat, and for the same fundamental reason —it is concealed. The fact that it sheds a ghastly light is less important than the way that light is apparently produced.

The obvious analogy between interior and exterior finish, and our skin's color and texture has a profound affect on our sense of the period to which a building belongs. In youth our skin is bright, smooth, fat, and satiny. In age it is dark, wrinkled, tough and rough. It is no accident that the Internationalists, who tend towards a youthful outlook, prefer the former sort of finishing materials. Such architects as H. H. Richardson, who looked far backwards for inspiration, preferred dark and highly textured surfaces. Such buildings as his Ames Gate Lodge, where the surface texture is on a mammoth scale, suggest the peculiar strengths, and the noble decrepitude of old age. The flush, sanded, much jointed finishes of the Internationalists suggest the beauty, uncertainty, and inexperience of youth.

While the mechanical systems and the finish of houses are tremendously important to the whole expressive content of structure, the arrangement of the skeleton is the fundamental basis on which expressivity is built. Man is most expressive, physically, in the dance, and here it is the arrangement he gives his bones which impart the message, rather than his facial expression. In any given period, in any given culture, there is usually the most startling concordance between expression in building and in dancing. The Balinese house and the Legong; the classical ballet and the Romantic house; the modern dance and modern architecture; all are cut from the same cloth. Martha Graham has much to teach the modern architect, both positively and negatively, for what she does in essence is to explore those peculiar attitudes of the human body most expressive of the ethos of our time.

Over and above its part in expression, structure also plays an explanatory role. The human curiosity to know what makes things tick must be satisfied. Theoretical explanations satisfy the few. The average person gains most insight when he receives an explanation in terms of himself. The classic architects explained the loading of structure not only in their use of the fundamental elements, but also by means of symbols. Thus not only the columns and arch supporting a wall above, but the flat pediment, side trim, and sill of the Classic window express a body, supported on the pelvic arch, in turn supported on two legs, which in their turn are on the sill, symbol of the ground.

Quite obviously, as our knowledge of the structure of invisible things increases, our capacity to build with apparently invisible means increases. But in order to understand such structures the onlooker must be as familiar with what makes them possible as he is with his own capacities. Thus an architecture based wholly on science and theory can never be a popular one. The non-theoretically minded, the children, and all those who live in concrete terms, i.e., most everyone, will not enjoy it. The skeleton of the house must always be proportioned to man's, its entrails and nervous system must be partially hidden as are man's. Its exterior envelope must be related to man's. And, most of all, its moods must be variegated.

Barbara Morgan: Martha Graham in "Deep Song."

ANNO DOMINI
BENEDICTVS XIV
PON · MAX
GLYPHIS TABVLIS IVSSV CLEMENTIS XIII PONT MAX
POSITIS SIGNIS ET ANA

CHAPTER XII

Expression

get but gloom and simplicity, and all good things will follow in their place and time;

—Ruskin

The Appeal to the Intellect

Our tendency to experience architecture in terms of anthropomorphic analogy explains two curious and typically architectural problems. First, structure, the physical material to which we immediately react, is significant only as form. It is only as form that we can relate it to ourselves. This is why the technocratic approach to architecture is always so disappointing. Structure for structure's sake leaves us cold because it is entirely foreign to the way in which we react to architecture. The form in which the structural elements are arranged can, however, explain and rationalize the forces at work (an intellectual task) without appealing to our emotions. On the other hand our emotions cannot be touched unless the explanation we require is implicitly or explicitly in evidence. Thus the end result of anthropomorphic analogy is that the way to expression in architecture is through the intellect, rather than direct to the emotions, as is sometimes possible in the other arts.

An appeal to the intellect must fundamentally be made by the intellect; i.e., through the reasoning or conceptualizing process. We regard the fundamental schemes of buildings in terms such as these:

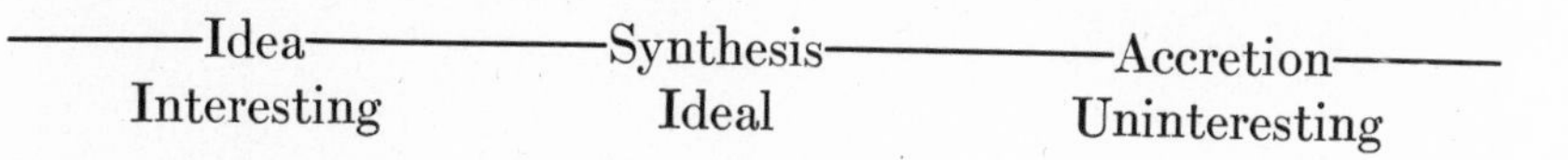

Paul Letarouilly: Trevi Fountain, fragment.

This should be visualized as a spectrum, with pure idea at one end, for example the bi-nuclear house plan, and no idea at the other, i.e., confusion and total lack of abstract concordance. The ideal point is where the idea has been applied; where it has lost its doctrinaire and dogmatic aspects in favor of a mutiple set of adjustments to its physical and social environment. It cannot be absent, yet it cannot be obtrusive. Our first attempt is always to *feel* a building. We cannot do this if an idea gets between it and us. Neither can we feel if inconsistency or lack of explanation arouses our intellect before our emotions get a chance to operate. Thus idea, while it is secondary to the onlooker, is primary to the architect. He has it, so to speak, in reserve—as a necessary condition to feeling.

The application of a fundamental idea to structure, or in Sullivan's terms ". . . the regular and systematic subdivision of function and form . ." can be seen as proliferation as well as subdivision. In any case it faces the architect with the need to relate numbers of elements. It is a problem in rhythm. This relating process is generally performed, in the first instance, by means of either symmetry or balance, the distinction being similar to that between rhymed or free verse. Our time is marked by the arguments between conservative and progressive architects, poets, musicians, painters, and sculptors, over the respective merits of explicit versus implicit balance, to the accompaniment of the banshee-like wails of the public. Every sign of our time points to the superiority of asymmetry, dissonance, balance, implicit rhythm rather than explicit, as the most appropriate tools for the

expression of its ethos. The symmetry vs. asymmetry argument is an argument about tools, not about fundamentals. Both tools are, for different purposes, handy. Symmetry is not bad, or out, or unusable. It is simply less appropriate to most of our present tasks of expression than is balance.

The manner in which a central idea is applied involves numbers, and this brings up a very fundamental relationship. The one, the single thing, is unique. Its oneness is an essential aspect of its expression, whatever it is. One church tower or one roof carries with it certain special qualities simply because it is alone. Two things are quite different in feeling, they are a pair, a couple, a duet, etc. They are, in the first instance counted—one, two—and related without rhythm. Two church towers as in Chartres Cathedral, are simply compared, and their twoness, the lack of rhythm involved, is again an essential aspect of their expressive force. Two elements, unless exactly similar in apparent weight, will *not* balance, and tend either to oppose each other or to operate in concert.

When the number three is reached, rhythm or balance becomes possible. From three on up, the tendency to count is less and less in evidence, and the tendency of the onlooker to accept what he sees at its face value is increased. A whole, as a triad or more, is the most usual subdivision of form and function, while a pair, because it is dichotomistic, is less often tried and is still less often successful. These qualities apply to details as well as to massing. Two windows in a wall tend to look like eyes, while three are simply "a number" of windows, and their abstract qualities can be enjoyed, because one is unhampered by the specific number and its connotations.

Too many subdivisions, at the other extreme, suggest chaos. Sheer numbers become worrisome, because one wonders whether one can count up that high, or understand so complex a thing at all. One's inherent laziness takes command, and a large number of things are rejected, simply because it is too much like work to understand. For example, too many kinds of windows remind one of a window manufacturer's display, and thus seem vulgar. This point is reached, in houses, when more than six or seven types of openings are used. Because the multiplicity of functional and technical requirements often demand a real multiplicity of means, the

Barbara Morgan: Martha Graham in "American Provincials."

Canaletto: Cà Torre di Malghera, fragment. The building seems to exemplify nearly every element of magic—contrasts of several kinds, play with numbers (in the building elements, three chimneys) vertical versus inclined versus horizontal planes, masculine and feminine symbolism, etc.

architect must usually create what amounts to an artificial simplicity. There are several ways to do this. A group of minor and dissimilar elements may be grouped so that they appear as one whole, with minor and unimportant subdivisions within the whole. Or these same elements may be given a family resemblance by means of creating them of identical parts. Or they may be given a family resemblance and a relation to a whole, or sub-division of the whole, by means of equality of ratios. While, in terms of real numbers, the upper limit is very flexible, it is very small in terms of apparent numbers. The architect, in applying his central idea, must make the onlooker feel that he is dealing with one, or from three to six elements only, except in very special circumstances. Proportion and rhythm are tools with which to relate and explain large numbers of elements.

The appeal to the intellect is an exercise in persuasion. Thus the onlooker must not be allowed to question one's conclusions. The attempt is to make him explore them with you, not apart from you. The minute he begins to question the intellectual framework of architecture, he loses his sense of identification with it, and becomes a more or less hostile critic. Once the central idea is established, its *proliferation* in detail must be absolutely consistent. If it is not, the onlooker, feeling along with the scheme up to that point, suddenly asks "Why". He begins either to question the whole thing, or to improve it mentally. He is no longer operating on a plane of pure pleasure. Exceptions and inadvertencies must be rigorously suppressed. The ability to scotch inconsistency, or at least to conceal it so skillfully that it is not discerned, is the keystone of good technique.

The Appeal to the Emotions

The intellect deals in rationality, order, idea, and especially values simplicity, i.e. the reduction of things to a least common denominator. The affections on the other hand deal in a very wide band of mercurial emotions, and variety is the principal value. A fundamental demand on the architect is that he achieve a suitable variety of mood with a limited variety of means. In potpourriism, where a large number of "features" are used, the mood is apt to be uniform throughout—the mood of the curiosity shop. The means overwhelm the ends. At another extreme, the work of Ludwig Mies van der Rohe gains its uniform but very strong mood because of the spartan simplicity of means. Here is strength and discipline and morality, a kind of teetotalism, which is extremely telling and impressive, but of limited appeal. The middle ground, the atmosphere made for gaiety and Saturday night baths, gloom and morning hangovers, is harder to achieve, for here the most variety exists, and the fight to limit one's emotional way of life to one's intellectual means is most difficult. The strength and weaknesses of the work of Frank Lloyd Wright arise from his ever firm position in the center of the middle way.

The difficulty with middle ways is that they are confusing. Nothing is sharp and clear and neat. This situation is obnoxious to the intellect, and pleasing to the anti-intellect. In appealing to the emotions one is dealing, essentially, with a welter. But the art of architecture exists only on a foundation of practical goals. Order is of the essence. The painter can deal with pure welter. The architect cannot. He must abstract from it certain of the affections which make it up, and pursue these rather single mindedly. The architect offers the onlooker a token or two of the whole. The tokens suggest to the onlooker the complex from which he intuitively knows they were abstracted, and he immediately and automatically fills in the others, putting the whole thing back in its proper confusion. This is the "work" involved in the appreciation of architecture. As it is slightly more onerous than that demanded by painting, for example, the aficionados of architecture are fewer than those of painting.

The Appeal to the Emotions

Obviously, the more suddenly the onlooker recognizes the architect's token, the quicker will he fill in the whole welter, and the more enjoyment he will extract from the building. It would seem logical, at least in the case of clients, that the most obvious tokens would be those most directly connected with their motives for building. This is the peculiar complex with which they are most intimately concerned, and by which they are most ready to be moved. For example, the motive "better living" which results in the act of building, must involve, at various removes, such ends as:

Utility (Health, Cleanliness, Salubrity)
Safety (Refuge, Escape)
Use (Action)
Success (Prosperity)

A motive such as "self aggrandizement" which in its very nature cannot be approached directly, could be considered as involving the opposite contingent ends; i.e. inutility, a pitfall, disuse, and mediocrity. As has been argued earlier, contrasting motives actually do result in such contrasting results.

Utility, safety, use, and success are expressed in architecture through appeals to the personal and sympathetic affections. The house should be cheerful, tasteful, hopeful, should invoke wonder, and suggest friendliness. Responses such as these are caused by direct analogy. Cheerful people have "sunny dispositions" and a cheerful house is a sunny one. Hopeful people are willing to try something new, they are flexible, and so is a hopeful house. All of these affections have opposites and in-between states. They are very much dependent on discrimination and comparison. They are expressed in architecture by quantities of things in comparison to the quantities of the same sort of things in other houses. The amount of glass, the size and appointments of the front entrance, the refinement of detail suggest greater or less cheerfulness, friendliness, and tact. One is dealing primarily with functional facilities. Friendliness is shown a guest by foreseeing his needs for a place to park his car, for shelter, a place to wipe his feet, and to hang his coat. All of these functional facilities can be arranged with taste, or fashionably, which is again a comparative matter. It is not difficult to discover the principles of the ruling taste at any one moment. The slick magazines are monthly instruction sheets in its rules.

The appeal to the sympathetic and personal affections is the foundation of architectural expression, but that is all. No one could *love* his house on this basis alone. He could only feel affectionate towards it. The analogies which arouse our deeper feelings are connected with the deeper layers of our consciousness. They are

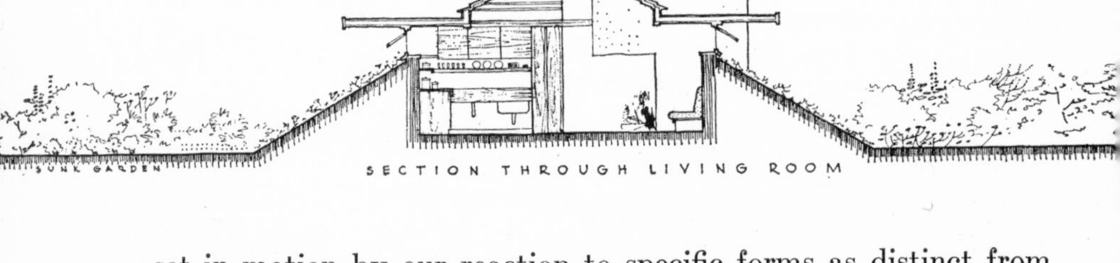

set in motion by our reaction to specific forms as distinct from the whole fabric *house* previously considered. For example the form, or expression, cave suggests not only shelter and dampness, but also cowering. The form, or expression, tent suggests not only danger and dryness but courage—the readiness to fight off danger oneself. It is no accident that wedding breakfasts are so often set up in tents. They are not only beautiful and airy and exciting; they subtly compliment the bridegroom. The architect who is after a feeling of safety must know what forms suggest it, and why. It is all too easy inadvertently to suggest the opposite quality. Also, the client's definition of that state can vary tremendously. The conservative's safety is suggested by the cave, where he can retire, barricaded. The innovator's safety is suggested by the tent, where he can get out fast and give himself room to swing. We are dealing here of course with archetypes which now infrequently appear in their pure guise. They are often suggested, however, by means of a complex and sophisticated process. The glass wall is a token of tent. The enveloping roof is a token of cave.

The analogies we make between the parts of buildings, and the

Frank Lloyd Wright: Sections through a Berm and through a conventional house.

parts of our own body, are perhaps even more moving than those of a total nature. The relationship is not only more intimate, it is better, more profoundly understood. Holes, for example, are significant because we consume breath, excrete, hear, see, and copulate by means of them, and the moral judgments involved add further significance to an already tremendously potent form. The pure use of a hole is typified by the Chinese moon gate; by the slot; or by the floor window often used by Frank Lloyd Wright, which offers an essentially "secret" view of water or of the ground.

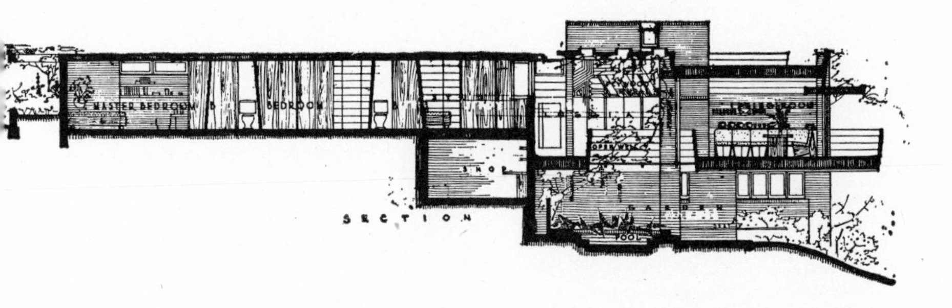

Front doors are holes into, that is vaginal symbols, while picture windows are holes out of, that is eyes. The plastic dome as a skylight is not only very close indeed to an eye, it is an eye directed at heaven, and therefore not only particularly moving, but actually poetic. The conventional window is a hole, and thus loses all significance when it is expressed as anything else. Small holes are, naturally, the most intriguing of all. The average architect will have difficulty in remembering a client who has not either worried, or joked excessively, about the knot holes in the lumber going into his house.

Holes in the ground suggest death, burial, fertility, the devil, and the hope that one might thus communicate with the Chinese. Excavations, foundations, wells, graves, and pits invariably excite our interest, as every sidewalk superintendent attests. Pools carry the overtones both of the hole and of water, or of life and death at once. The hole in the floor, surrounded by seats, with a fireplace, is a sort of grave for the living, and is therefore seldom successful. And the cave is of course a hole, as well as the delight of children —primitive, womb-like, hidden—tremendously engaging.

Top, Vermont Barn. Below, Paul Rand: Advertising Design. One obvious interpretation is: In summer man (the sun) looks (glasses) at woman (free form) on the ocean (shell) beach (dotts). But the shell is also, of course, a symbol of woman, and thus an amusing double meaning is created.

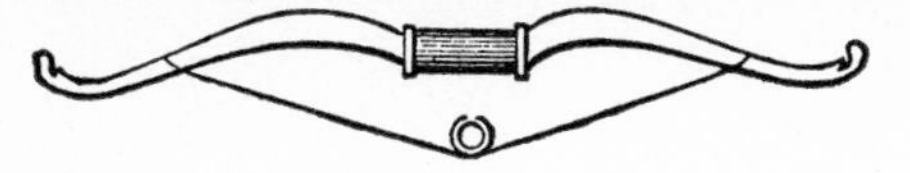

The Appeal to the Emotions

The fascination of holes undoubtedly arises from the similarity with the female genitals. In the case of a window for example the connection, while it is there, is very remote. In order to utilize the full emotional charge of the analogy, symbols of the female are used. The sign of Venus, the hour glass, the bow and arrow, cherubim, the moon, lace, locks, and most fundamental of all, shells, are the symbols of women. These symbols are translated into structure as lunettes, balusters, arches, barrel vaults, and round holes of all kinds. In the Renaissance in particular they appeared constantly not only in terms of architecture, but in themselves, as the appropriate decoration of the feminine structural forms. In our time the most marked feminine analogy is with the free form, a direct translation of femininity into materials. The drawing of such forms must relate to the female body—the reason that architects must take life class in school. In the typical Italian Renaissance building these symbols appeared as tokens of the emotional welter the architect wished to engage. The house structure as a whole, particularly the urban house, remained however, fundamentally masculine. In our time the analogy is often drawn between the whole house and the whole feminine concept. For example the following house by John Yeon is fundamentally feminine in its ground relationship. This comes about, perhaps, because of our tendency to view both the house and the earth as feminine. The expression "mother earth", the tendency of artists and photographers to draw analogies between the peculiar profile of the feminine body and hills or dunes and their valleys, are examples. Mounds hark back to breasts and buttocks, and are typically reminiscent of women. Burial mounds, the pyramids, the Mansard roof, and those bosomish thatched roofs typical of European peasant architecture are examples. Domes, the surface modeling of gardens, the fascination of sloped sites all tie back to the mound with its concomitant hollow. Where holes symbolize the actions of taking in and rejecting, mounds symbolize permanent enclosure. The one represents sociality, the other refuge. The dome, our skull, the enclosure of our intellect, is thus particularly the form of schools, observatories, and of the tombs of the great, and is most potent when it is open at the top, when it has an eye fixed on heaven and the divine effulgence.

Opposite, Paul Letarouilly: Tomb of Hieronymo Basso. Above, John Yeon.

Analogies with our arms and legs are even more important a device for the understanding of architecture. Columns are legs, or trees. Beams are arms, or branches, or cantilevers. Our whole body can become a column, as a Caryatid or as Atlas. We understand rhythm in terms of arms and legs in motion. The peculiar delight of such analogies are due also to the fact that they tie nature and man together by means of architecture. For example the window tracery of the Venetian Gothic houses is reminiscent not only of arms and legs in rhythmic pattern, but of trees and flowers. Our ability to pinch, grip, enclose with our arms or legs —*to fit*—as sexually or in a hand clasp, is very often reflected in architecture. It is at once one of the most attractive qualities, and the one most easy to abuse. The difficulty involved is that to grip is an action, while architecture is static, and should be expressed as such. Thus the "pistol grip" facade, typical of the beginning student, is apt to excite our fingers rather than our affections, and the airplane wing motive, indeed all forms reminis-

Lubov Rondenko and George Skibine in "Seventh Symphony." Opposite, Rudolf Freund: Birds and Eels. Leonardo da Vinci: Cannon.

cent of movement, worry us because of the obvious improbability involved. But where such actions are statically expressed, they are, because of their connotations of love, very pleasant. Thus atriums enclose us in the crooked arms of the building, and the structure which fits the ground gives one the impression that it is at one with mother earth.

While we understand the dynamics of structure in terms of our pendula, the column, the sphere, and the flat lintel are too close to masculine genital and body forms to be seen as anything but masculine symbols. Again, the Italian Renaissance made abundant use of masculine symbolism. And, as is the case with feminine symbols, two kinds of devices are used. There is the direct analogy, as between the obelisk and the erect phallus. And there are the secondary symbols of men; tools (particularly drills and reamers), keys, prayer towers, birds (particularly the Phoenix), snakes and eels, the Mars symbol, pens and pencils, and most apt of all, the gun. Such symbols appear during the Renaissance as the decoration on purely masculine structures. The close analogy between them and towers, chimneys, silos, columns, airplanes, and radio antenna are obvious. Much of the language of architecture and particularly of plumbing relates directly to those images, as couples, male and female connections, nipples, etc.

Masculine symbolism in architecture does not seem to have changed as often or as radically as the feminine. In our time such objects as the Trylon and Perisphere of the New York Worlds Fair 1949 are all too obvious. The essential masculinity of our rectilinear and triangulated structure, in contrast with vaulted and domical constructions, tends to standardize buildings as masculine. This would seem to be an apparent contradiction, in view of the essentially feminine nature of the house. But actually houses have always been combinations of masculine and feminine elements. The typical house is conceived of as a womb in spatial terms, but it is supported by masculine strength and pierced by the masculine symbol, the chimney or tent pole. Ideally perhaps, every element should combine the symbols of both men and women. The more the two are intertwined, the richer the emotional experience. The aim is the expression of unity, or love, rather than of a dichotomy, or opposition.

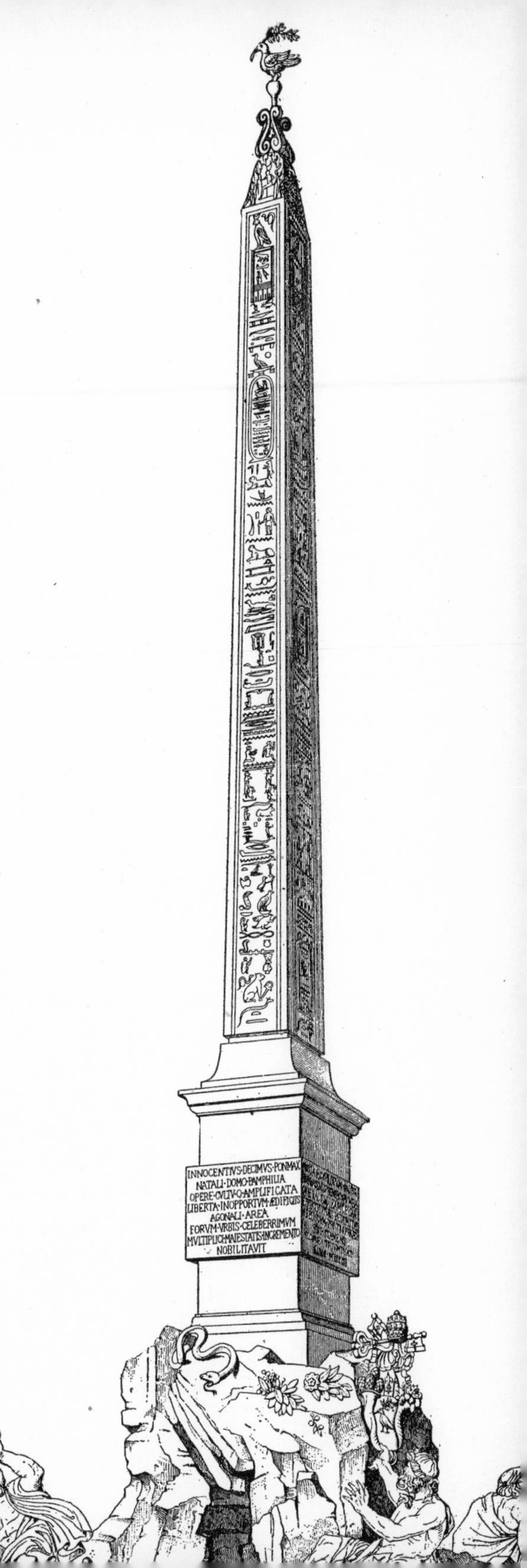

Paul Letarouilly: Obelisque in the Place Navona, Rome.

Techniques

The intertwining of opposites should, nevertheless, never be so complete that the story inherent to the juxtaposition is lost. Where one is dealing with a single form, the analogy with the human body must be close. Thus for example, the obelisk proclaims man's eternal potency, even in death; and the chimney his living heat in the death of winter. A story is told. A man or nature is dead, but man lives. One is dealing essentially in contrasting closely related elements, and the manipulation of contrasts of all sorts is one of the foundations of good technique. As in music, where a loud bang followed or preceded by a rest galvanizes one's attention, so in architecture the tent beside the cave as in Taliesen West, the tower beside the nave as in the cathedral, trigger one's emotions.

The contrasts with which the architect deals are too numerous to detail here. But they can be suggested by such examples as wall and hole, shade and light, solid and transparency, low and high, darkness and brilliance. Such oppositions are the tokens of more fundamental truths, they represent hollow against mound, tent against cave, night versus day, life versus death. Where the forms used to create such contrasts are in themselves essentially anthropomorphic, a greater power results.

The house contains numerous such contrasts, willy nilly, and a host of others are possible. The window versus the solid wall, i.e., the opposition of transparency and solid, is such a contrast; the porch versus the plain wall, in its creation of shade and shelter, is another; and the vertical element versus the horizontal is yet another. Contrast, creating as it does brilliance, increased luminosity, and radiance, comes very close to our definition of beauty. It is no accident that the automobile, vulgar as it is in essential design, nevertheless draws every American's attention. Its deep shiny paint versus its shallow bright chrome makes it nearly irresistible. We speak of young girls as "radiantly" beautiful. Heaven is "radiant," and blondes are beautiful because they are "fair." In order to appreciate fairness and radiance there must be darkness and gloom. If everything were fair; if, as in the far north, there were no night for months on end; the value of light would

Paul Letarouilly: The artist has sensitively placed the figures under their appropriate architectural symbols.

be very slight indeed. The glass wall is most brilliant and beautiful when it is juxtaposed with gloom; the roof is most sheltering when it encloses outside as well as interior space; the chimney is most massive when it is free in air; and stairs are at their most spidery when most open, because they are support versus nothingness. The clear expression of the essential weight and purpose of form results in contrast and brilliance.

Scale is another fundamental tool with which to evoke emotion. It has been argued earlier that scale and proportion are essentially methods of relating physical structure to environment. They are symbols of certain kinds of abstract order. The word scale has gathered so many other uses that it has become professional jargon. What does it mean? The closest official interpretation is perhaps: "*Scale* III. 4. Relative or proportionate size or extent; degree, proportion 1607" (The Shorter Oxford English Dictionary, 1933). This definition does cover one meaning of the word as we use it. We say one part of a building is "out of scale" with another, meaning it is in poor proportion. But we also say whole buildings are out of scale. Out of scale with what? In this case we must define the word as *the relationship in size between a building or its parts, and man*. Our judgment as to what this relationship should be is not a constant. It changes from century to century. The Victorian house or the Italian sixteenth century house are in one relationship to man. The Cape Cod Cottage and the contemporary house are in quite another. In terms of absolute size both are quite appropriate. In terms of our feeling for scale at any one moment in history one or the other may seem inappropriate. Scale as relatedness to environment is a constant. Scale as relatedness to man is mercurial.

We are now in a small scaled era. There are several reasons for this. The democratic and communist idealogies may be one. Both tend towards the equalization of people. The high cost of building, the lack of servants, the introduction of heating, mechanical ventilation, and cooling, the transfer of some of the need for conspicuous consumption from the house to the automobile, from space to equipment, may be others. In terms of pure feeling, very large scale excellently expresses the ability to consume, and other kinds of social importance. But it also minimizes the individual's stature.

Biago Rossetti (1495).

The insides of human beings have seldom been studied with more passionate interest than in our time. It would seem likely that our sense of the importance of our own stream of consciousness has never been greater. High ceilings and great arches suggest regimentation and public authority. Next to such forms the individual feels dwarfed. He is personally attacked and demeaned by large scale architecture. He prefers a scale in which he feels big. The fact that he may still be regimented, controlled by the State, that social relationships are as complicated as they ever were, has no bearing on this reaction. The emphasis is on the individual, not on society.

The kind of architecture most antipathetic to our current domestic temper is undoubtedly the classic and its revivals. The qualities we find most sympathetic are length and lowness, cozyness, intimacy, informality. The vernacular house may revive the English Colonial style, but it eschews the original, bare, firm, and formal character. Explicit rhythm, order, and symmetry suggest the discipline imposed by society. Implicit balance, broken rhythm, abstract relationships express the tension and flux of the human psyche. We may understand the values Haydn, Delacroix, the brothers Adam, and Byron expressed. But we react as do Stravinsky, Picasso, Wright, and Eliot. We are concerned with inner, and thus necessarily with abstract order.

The first requisite of house architecture today is that it should make people feel physically and emotionally important. This does not imply that houses should be small. Rather their elements, clearances, and divisions should be closely related to people's physical dimensions. So should the volumes of the individual structural elements. It is not solely economy which makes the pipe an appropriate substitution for the Doric Order, the drip for the Entablature. Human beings gain importance in direct proportion as such elements are reduced in mass. The pipe column may have less surface area than man himself, the Doric Order must have infinitely more. The pipe column is delicately and accurately adjusted to the superimposed loads. The Doric Order symbolizes rather than expresses its loading. The ancients symbolized statics. We symbolize dynamics. We wish to understand our own inner stresses. Thus the characteristics of our contemporary architecture are the broken plane, the cantilever, the absence of details, extreme thinness and delicacy of structure, transparency and translucency. We are fascinated by the inner workings of our buildings.

The word *proportion*, like *scale* and *tradition* is also nearly meaningless. It has, like scale, taken on a series of extra connotations, so many that the architect must give it a bonus every payday. Its use discriminatively, as good proportion or bad proportion, is quite incomprehensible by itself. It is a pure "taste" judgment. Hambidge, Umbdenstock, and others have worked out geometrical systems for the analysis and even the creation of façades. Palladio, Scammozzi, and others suggested the use of various formulae for the proportioning of the interiors of rooms; while Le Corbusier uses the Golden Rule for the proportioning of both the profiles and subdivisions of façades, and has gone so far as to market a ruler for this use. This work has proved rather conclusively that the façades of the most monumental architecture of the past, particularly the Greek temples and the Gothic cathedrals, can be reduced to formulae with a good deal of ease. It is difficult to see that it proves anything else, in that a great deal of very poor and vulgar architecture is similarly proportioned, and in that a tram is absolutely unusable as a primary creative tool These various systems, furthermore, are most convincing when applied to façades, least when applied to volumes and spaces. Contemporary house architecture is characterized by its complex three dimensional nature.

The great monuments of the past, and the work of the symmetrists, have conspired to make the monumental, numerical, and impersonal proportion the standard. But it should be remembered that this sort of proportioning is most successful in its applications to temples, churches, and tombs—i.e., to monuments. Houses are not monumental in the strict sense of the word. They are highly personal temples to human frailty, rather than to divine strength. Numerical proportion is that most appropriate to the religious affections. These have no place in house architecture today.

No *system* of proportion is appropriate to the house, and no house can be designed to a system unless its whole scheme is warped and twisted to that end. There are no Venuses among housewives, no Zeuses among husbands. These are idealized projections, a perfect standard which it is not only impossible but positively undesirable to attain. The equality of ratios and the floor grid are valuable and useful techniques with which to create apparent simplicity. But the relation of parts must be subservient to a variety of more or less base emotions—in other words to life, itself.

Good proportion in house architecture is that relation which serves to emphasize the magnificent ungainliness of passionate emotion, and is therefore essentially unbalanced. Rather than the just proportion, ordered, geometrical, and impersonal, we desire the stressed proportion, a little warped perhaps, but all the more lovable for that very reason. Good house proportion (or bad classical proportion) goes back to that characteristic disbalance in living people's proportions which gives them expressive meaning. The fat person is famously cheerful and a good dancer. The fat doorway is also cheerful, and has its graces and strengths. As Lachaise knew the truths of his enormous, graceful, strong, and heavy model, so the house architect must know the tricks of strong rather than ideal proportion. He must be a Lachaise and a Lehmbruck, rather than a Praxiteles.

The architect setting about to titillate, dazzle, and bewilder

Pietro Belluschi.

Mosque, Djerba, Tunisia.

his client through the techniques of expression is acting in his capacity as medicine man, or magician, or sorcerer. And in architecture as in these other professions, the absolute secrecy of the trick is of the essence. As in the appeal to the intellect, one cannot afford to be asked questions, so in the appeal to the affections, one cannot give away the catalyst. The minute a dome brings the image breast to one's conscious mind, it becomes an object of ridicule. The minute a tower brings the image phallus to mind, it becomes shocking. The roof too obviously fortified against wrath from the heavens is a symbol of weakness, not strength—timidity, not refuge. And by the same token the creation of too startling a contrast becomes a joke rather than wit, a Mutt and Jeff, or Jack Spratt and his wife type of contrast, designed for laughs. Critics, and other artists will of course discover the secrets of a form's expressivity, but the average man pays his money, sees the show, leaves no wiser than he came, and is glad of it. He went to be bewildered and mystified and to enjoy himself. The magician who ended his performance by explaining all his tricks would not succeed for long. In architecture, the architect who leaves us mystified, who excites us with an invisible technique, is the most rewarding. To allow one's slip to show, be it silk, steel, or Freudian is, because it spoils the show, the unforgivable, unprofessional, inartistic sin.

Self Expression

In the beginning of this book the general question of expression, Louis Sullivan's "sweet and abundant gift," was posed as its leit motif. It would seem that each new aspect of architecture which has been touched upon had something to do with the theme—something, but never very much. The upper middle class house expresses the general living standard of its sponsoring group. It reflects the strengths, problems, uncertainties etc., of the individuals of which it is composed. It reflects the structure of the social unit, the family, which it is designed to house. It reflects its owners' reactions to each of the various living activities, this over and above a social digestive process they have already gone through. These functions are put together in a certain way—according to a style—which itself reflects a larger scale gestatory process, in that it deals not only with our culture's present and past, but with its hopes for the future. Structure, now a nationalized phenomenon, and environment, an historical one, also add elements to the individual building's expressiveness. These are all social modes of expression, as formal as a judge's robe. This social story which architecture tells is given communicability through appeals of various sorts, to the intellect, to the sympathetic affections, and to our latent ability to invest forms with the excitement inherent in those of analagous nature found in our own bodies. So far no single factor here suggests that the artist himself is anything more than Herbert Read's "automaton." Does he ever truly express himself?

Every architect feels, at one time or another, that he, personally, has nothing to say. He realizes that he is working in a style created by others. Its historical background and a large part of its contemporary manifestation have nothing to do with him. His clients seem to determine in large part the specific story told by each building, through the mechanisms outlined above. True, the very fact that he has reached a certain point of adjustment between all the factors involved can give him a position in a small and select coterie. But he may feel, still, that his own strivings had the least to do with this adjustment—that it was reached largely through accident, opportunism, the storms and calms of fate, sun spots, or what have you. Where, he asks, is himself? And search his mind as he may, he will seldom get an answer to this question—in spite of the fact that he may be doing the most creative, original, and personal work.

The creative process has been postulated earlier as starting with the collection of all of the objective criteria a given design must meet, together with a constant examination of certain non-specific problems or sub-assemblies. Orderliness here is important. It is the first stage of digestion. This orderly collection of facts and attitudes is more or less automatically fed to the unconscious, which in turn more or less automatically suggests a solution and feeds it back to the conscious mind, or to fingers in possession of the requisite tools, skill, and experience. One element in experience is the ability to tune in on the unconscious' wave length. It would seem likely that the true personal element of expression is added by the unconscious while it is performing the synthesizing process, during the so-called "inspiration time" all architects seem to require. This is borne out by an interesting observation of Dr. Otto Fenichel's:

> "The artist who has withdrawn from reality into his fantasies, which represent derivatives of his Oedipus wishes and about which he feels guilty, finds his way back to the objective world by presenting it with his work. The acceptance of this work means for him that the public shares his guilt, and this relieves him of his guilt feelings. . . . There is a decisive difference in the kind of success needed by the pseudo artist and the real artist. The pseudo artist needs to be accepted as a person, requiring applause at any cost. He adapts himself to his audience to make sure of getting applause. The artist needs to have a specific fantasy of his accepted; he wants applause for his work, not for himself. He adapts the public to himself. This sharing of guilt through art is anticipated by the "common daydreams" of children who feel relieved of their guilt feelings if their comrades participate in their fantasies.
>
> "A powerful force for group formation is the attainment of relief in the identical way and through the same initiatory act. The admirers of an artist feel themselves in a community."

The "guilt" of which Dr. Fenichel speaks is not, of course, consciously realized. It must be translated into artistic terms, before it can be recognized. Among International Stylists the idea of "tension" is, perhaps, such an expression. The goal of a "stretched' or "taut" characteristic applied to space and form in combination is one projection of the more fundamental drive. Another is the frequent use of forms which pierce the main structure, indoor-outdoor elements for example. Among Empiricists the idea of "organic" growth is such a translation. Indeed, at the moment, the strange insistence on this concept, in every possible and impossible context, suggests that the word is a sort of signal flag, to warn the cognoscenti that more is going on than meets the eye. The Traditionalists would seem to have no ability to use the forces here being considered. The modal drive of their adjustment is more or less exclusively directed at social security, and inhibits or even precludes the exercise of artistry.

These fundamental wells of emotion are, variously, archaic or primitive or infantile. Some are continuations of forces which must go back to the creation of man. Others are lent significance by the peculiar mores of our society. As such they are anti-social. The expression of anti-social images is of course met with alarm, particularly when their true message is first understood. The distrust, dislike, fear, and ridicule with which new art forms are met is due to this perception of a new and therefore more telling expression of emotions generally considered evil.

Though this is true of all of the arts, fine architecture labors under a peculiar difficulty because of its largely social symbolism. To create a building expressive of the power and majesty of a great society, at a great moment in its history, and at the same time to overlay that message with primitive Oedipal symbolism, is, in a sense, to give with one hand and take away with the other. But obviously, no single type of contrast could be more exciting. The story is one of man at his most urbane and of man at his most savage.

The more overt the self-expressive overlay becomes, the "wilder" the architect is conceived to be. But this wildness can, on the one hand, be unconscious and embarrassing, or on the other so subtly and skillfully knit into the whole fabric of the design that the fear with which it is met is largely counteracted by the respect it arouses. Thus Boston University's two breast-like domes are ridiculous, while Bruce Goff's umbrella house, in section below engages one's complete attention and commands one's respect. In the one case a "shameful" analogy is blurted out. In the other a fundamental truth is arrestingly and subtly expressed. Thus the element of trade secrecy enters in. Or put in another way, those

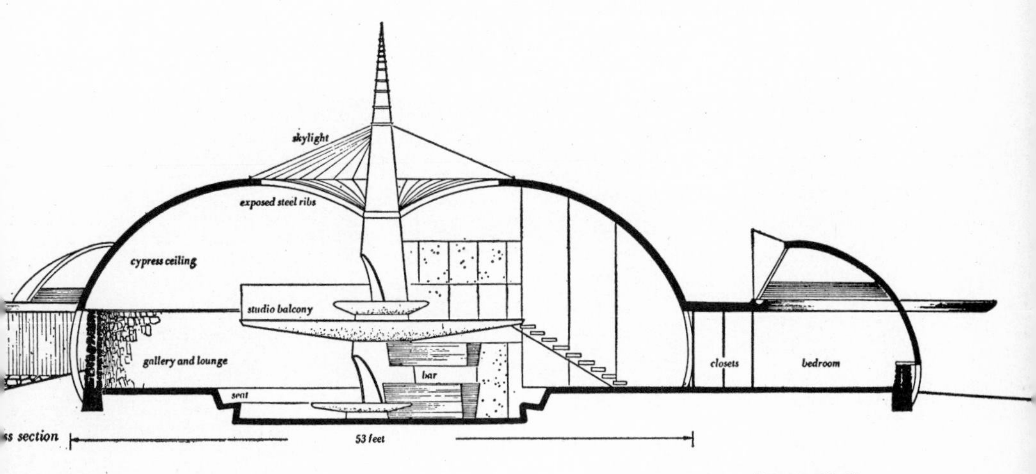

Bruce Goff.

appeals made by the artist's unconscious to the unconscious of others must remain beneath the surface of our minds. *Overt* self-expression is to be avoided like the plague. It can only cause embarrassment. The *real* self expression, given propitious circumstances by the artist's adjustment to his craft, takes care of itself. The distinction here is analagous with that between radio waves and direct sound waves. The architect bent on self expression broadcasts a message the nuances of which are lost in distortion and interferences. The architect who broadcasts direct loses in range, but nevertheless assures clear reception of what he wishes to express.

The "primitive" nature of the relationships suggested in art accounts for the fascination that primitive art and society have for all artists. The artist bent on real self expression is bent on discovering and projecting emotions and relationships which are far in the rear not only of his conscious mind, but of himself as a civilized member of society. It is small wonder that in the constant search for forms expressive of his drives he returns, over and over again, to those of primitive societies for inspiration. This is most visible in the work of painters: Picasso for example has at various times gone through "African" and "Classic" periods; Gauguin escaped physically to a more primitive society; Covarrubias became an expert on Bali, while numerous artists have looked to the

House, Mandan Indians of North Dakota.

farm or the peasant, that is to the less advanced sections of their culture, for stimulus. The social nature of architecture makes such direct connections more difficult and less obvious. Nevertheless they exist. The fascination of Japanese architecture, the retreat of at least two contemporary architects to Japan, the occasional production of a really "primitive" structure by such men as Alvar Aalto, the interest that such structures as Liberian palaver huts never fail to arouse, the "nature" houses which are becoming increasingly popular, where exposed ledge and growing trees form, ostentatiously, part of the interior—all of these are evidences of the same urge toward the primitive, typical of painters, somewhat watered down by the external discipline of architecture. The recollection of more primitive forms or techniques occurs in architecture as it does in painting. On the west coast there have been several houses influenced by the Japanese, notably Gardner Dailey's house. The "natural" house carried to greater or lesser extremes is now to be seen everywhere. Whether consciously or not, the latest variety of pilotis reminds one inevitably of Lacustrine and South Pacific buildings, and some of the "umbrella" forms hark back to African prototypes. The wonderful American Indian structures, still more or less unknown, are sure sooner or later to engage every architects' attention.

The value of the primitive as a stimulant of creative imagination need hardly be belabored. It has been bruited about at least since Viollet-le-Duc's time if not long before. The lesson such prototypes contain has, in the last analysis, little to do with self expression, however. The fundamental reason for their fascination is probably their simplicity, or in the case of the Japanese, their apparent simplicity, a quality which allows the anthropomorphic association to operate faster and more effectively. Even the simplest equations such as chimney-phallus cannot be grasped when, for example, the flue, conceived of solely as an object of service, is made to appear non-existent. Thus the artist, seeking constantly for a greater and greater "primitive" simplicity of form, in order to express more clearly through that form's fundamental meanings his own story, is in constant conflict with the tendency toward more and more complex, civilized, and polite (i.e. dishonest) expression, structure, and functions typical of complex social adjustments. There is no more interesting continued story in the world's movie house than this constant search for primitive sophistication, for a resolution of the old Adam and the latest thing in group consciousness. The fundamental incompatability of these two idealized goals, just as in the space-money, the tradition-modernity, the environment-conscience conflicts, and all the others mentioned above, makes it impossible for a final, or right, or permanently satisfactory solution ever to be reached. By the same token the elusive nature of the relationship searched for, together with our fundamental belief in its rightness, leads us on and on with unflagging attention and unabated pleasure. The architect's liking for his "art or science", increasing as it does with his age, is surely due to the fact that he works on a perpetual frontier. There are always new worlds to conquer ahead of him, fresher, more meaningful, more simple. He can never be satisfied with his own production. And so it comes about that architecture is the oldest, most complex, most enthralling attempt to be simple known to man.

Photo Dr. Jiro Harada.

References

1 Louis Sullivan: KINDERGARTEN CHATS, George Wittenborn, Inc., New York 1947.

2 HOUSING ACT OF 1949. p. 1. HR, 4009

3 *Ibid.* p. 26

4 *Ibid.* pp. 3 and 4

8 W. Lloyd Warner and Paul S. Lunt: THE SOCIAL LIFE OF A MODERN COMMUNITY, Yale University Press 1941. p. 107

10 *Ibid.* p. 108

10 *Ibid.* p. 142

11 *Ibid.* p. 155

13 *Ibid.* p. 189

16 Irving Rosow: MODERN ARCHITECTURE AND SOCIAL CHANGE, Detroit, Michigan 1948. (Unpublished thesis. Wayne University)

23 Anton Tchekov: "My Life—A Story of a Provincial" from PLAYS AND STORIES, Everyman's Library, H. M. Dent & Sons, Ltd., London 1937. p. 203

33 Lewis Mumford: THE CULTURE OF CITIES, Harcourt, Brace and Company, New York 1938. p. 433

36 F. Stuart Chapin: CONTEMPORARY AMERICAN INSTITUTIONS, Harper and Brothers, New York 1935. p. 96

36 Lewis Mumford: THE CULTURE OF CITIES, Harcourt, Brace and Company, New York 1938. p. 114

38 Thorstein Veblen: THE THEORY OF THE LEISURE CLASS, Viking Press, New York 1943. p. 59 (First published in 1899)

38 *Ibid.* p. 66

40 Bernard de Voto: "The Easy Chair," "Ninety Day Venus," HARPER'S MAGAZINE, September 1950. p. 93

41 Ernest Hemingway: ACROSS THE RIVER AND INTO THE TREES, Charles Scribner's Sons, New York 1950. pp. 178–179

41 Thorstein Veblen: THE THEORY OF THE LEISURE CLASS, Viking Press, New York 1943. p. 60 (First published in 1899)

45 Arnold Gesell, M.D., and Frances Ilg, M.D.: THE CHILD FROM FIVE TO TEN, Harper and Brothers, New York 1946. p. 38

46 Thorstein Veblen: THE THEORY OF THE LEISURE CLASS, Viking Press, New York 1943. p. 81 (First published in 1899)

48 Lynn White, Jr.: EDUCATING OUR DAUGHTERS, Harper and Brothers, New York 1950. pp. 68–69

50 American Public Health Association Committee on the Hygiene of Housing: PLANNING THE HOME FOR OCCUPANCY, Public Administration Service, Chicago 1950. p. 40

61 Lewis Mumford: CULTURE OF CITIES, Harcourt, Brace and Company, New York 1938. p. 432

63 Charlotte M. Fleming: ADOLESCENCE, International Universities Press, Inc., New York 1949. p. 17

64 *Ibid.* p. 157

65 Henry David Thoreau: WALDEN, Penguin Books Inc., New York 1942. p. 13 (First published in 1854)

67 Edward K. Strong, Jr.: CHANGE OF INTERESTS WITH AGE, Stanford University Press 1931. p. 22

69 Henry Green: LOVING, Viking Press, New York 1949. p. 6

75 Ruth S. Cavan: THE FAMILY,

Thomas Y. Crowell Company, New York 1946. pp. 24–25

76 F. Stuart Chapin: CONTEMPORARY AMERICAN INSTITUTIONS, Harper and Brothers, New York 1935. p. 91

77 Irving Rosow: MODERN ARCHITECTURE AND SOCIAL CHANGE, Detroit, Michigan 1948. p. 192 (Unpublished thesis, Wayne University)

77 F. Stuart Chapin: CONTEMPORARY AMERICAN INSTITUTIONS, Harper and Brothers, New York 1935. pp. 98–99

80 Thomas Mann: "Disorder and Early Sorrow" from CHILDREN AND FOOLS, Alfred A. Knopf, New York 1928. pp. 105–106

83 Lewis Mumford: THE CULTURE OF CITIES, Harcourt, Brace and Company, New York 1938. p. 432

86 Dr. Benjamin Spock: THE COMMON SENSE BOOK OF BABY AND CHILD CARE, Duell, Sloan and Pearce, New York 1946. p. 199

99 W. Lloyd Warner and Paul S. Lunt: THE SOCIAL LIFE OF A MODERN COMMUNITY, Yale University Press 1941. p. 105

106 Lewis Mumford: THE CULTURE OF CITIES, Harcourt, Brace and Company, New York 1938. p. 465

106 W. E. Woodward: THE WAY OUR PEOPLE LIVED, E. P. Dutton & Co., New York 1944. p. 40

113 Garrett Eckbo: LANDSCAPE FOR LIVING, Duell, Sloan and Pearce, New York 1950. p. 135

127 Dorothy J. Field: THE HUMAN HOUSE, Houghton Mifflin Company, Boston 1939. pp. 16–17

128 TALIESIN, Frank Lloyd Wright, Editor, The Taliesin Fellowship sole contributor and factor. pp. 16–17

134 Vern O. Knudsen and Cyril M. Harris: ACOUSTICAL DESIGNING IN ARCHITECTURE, John Wiley and Sons 1950. p. 1

138 National Bureau of Standards: SAFETY FOR THE HOUSEHOLD, Circular 463, January 12, 1947, United States Government Printing Office. p. 1

140 Earnest A. Hooton: A SURVEY IN SEATING, Heywood-Wakefield Company, Gardner, Massachusetts 1945. p. 30

141 *Ibid.* p. 6

141 Charles George Ramsey and Harold Reeve Sleeper: ARCHITECTURAL GRAPHIC STANDARDS, John Wiley and Sons, New York 1932.

141 Francis de N. Schroeder: ANATOMY FOR INTERIOR DESIGNERS, Whitney Publications, Inc. 1932.

144 Louis H. Sullivan: KINDERGARTEN CHATS, George Wittenborn, Inc., New York 1947.

144 HOW TO BUILD A SAFE HOUSE, Good Housekeeping Building Forum Booklet No. 4, New York 1948. p. 5

145 American Public Health Association Committee on the Hygiene of Housing: PLANNING THE HOME FOR OCCUPANCY, Public Administration Service, Chicago 1950. p. vi

145 HOW TO BUILD A SAFE HOUSE, Good Housekeeping Building Forum Booklet No. 4, New York 1948. p. 11

150 Vern O. Knudsen and Cyril M. Harris: ACOUSTICAL DESIGNING IN ARCHITECTURE, John Wiley and Sons, New York 1950. p. 54

152 Hale J. Sabine: LESS NOISE,

BETTER HEARING, Celotex Corporation, Chicago 1941. p. 24

154 *Ibid.* p. 80

157 Henry David Thoreau: WALDEN, Penguin Books Inc., New York 1942. p. 46 (First published in 1854)

157 T. S. Eliot: THE COCKTAIL PARTY, Harcourt, Brace and Company, copyright 1950 by T. S. Eliot. Reprinted by permission of Harcourt, Brace and Company.

158 Speech by Winston Churchill in House of Commons, October 28, 1944, MAXIMS AND REFLECTIONS, Houghton Mifflin, Boston 1949. p. 34

178 Vern O. Knudsen and Cyril M. Harris: ACOUSTICAL DESIGNING IN ARCHITECTURE, John Wiley and Sons, New York 1950. p. 367

192 Dorothy J. Field: THE HUMAN HOUSE, Houghton Mifflin Company, Boston 1939. p. 81

196 Henry David Thoreau: WALDEN, Penguin Books Inc., New York 1942. pp. 122–123 (First published in 1854)

206 American Public Health Association Committee on the Hygiene of Housing: PLANNING THE HOME FOR OCCUPANCY, Public Administration Service, Chicago 1950. p. 41

210 Oregon State Agricultural Experiment Station Bulletin No. 348, June 1937.

211 University of Illinois Bulletin, Cic. C5.3. Small Homes Council, Urbana, Illinois. p. 5

229 Vern O. Knudsen and Cyril M. Harris: ACOUSTICAL DESIGNING IN ARCHITECTURE, John Wiley and Sons, New York 1950. p. 367

236 *Ibid.* p. 368

244 MINIMUM PROPERTY REQUIREMENTS FOR PROPERTIES OF ONE OR TWO LIVING UNITS LOCATED IN THE STATE OF MASSACHUSETTS, Federal Housing Administration (1204B Privacy). p. 27

246 Sigfried Giedion: MECHANIZATION TAKES COMMAND, Oxford University Press, New York 1948. p. 628

256 Vern O. Knudsen and Cyril M. Harris: ACOUSTICAL DESIGNING IN ARCHITECTURE, John Wiley and Sons, New York 1950. p. 367

259 Milton Blum and Beatrice Candee: FAMILY BEHAVIOR, ATTITUDES AND POSSESSIONS, Pierce Foundation 1944. p. 50

263 Francis de N. Schroeder: ANATOMY FOR INTERIOR DESIGNERS, Whitney Publications 1948. p. 39

267 Vern O. Knudsen and Cyril M. Harris: ACOUSTICAL DESIGNING IN ARCHITECTURE, John Wiley and Sons, New York 1950. p. 212

272 Arnold Gesell, M.D., and Frances Ilg, M.D.: INFANT AND CHILD IN THE CULTURE OF TODAY, Harper and Brothers, New York 1943. p. 303

273 Dr. Benjamin Spock: THE COMMON SENSE BOOK OF BABY AND CHILD CARE, Duell, Sloan and Pearce, New York 1946. p. 249

273 Arnold Gesell, M.D., and Frances Ilg, M.D.: INFANT AND CHILD IN THE CULTURE OF TODAY, Harper and Brothers, New York 1943. p. 230

275 Lewis Mumford: THE CULTURE OF CITIES, Harcourt, Brace and Company, New York 1938. p. 431

275 *Ibid.* p. 432

284 Dorothy J. Field: THE HUMAN

HOUSE, Houghton Mifflin Company, Boston 1939. p. 101
292 Henry David Thoreau: WALDEN, Penguin Books, Inc., New York 1942. p. 39 (First published in 1854)
294 Irving Rosow: THE ARCHITECT AND PROFESSIONAL STRAINS. pp. 11–12 (Unpublished manuscript)
296 Edward K. Strong, Jr.: CHANGE OF INTEREST WITH AGE, Stanford University Press 1931 p. 125
307 James T. Fisher, M.D., and Lowell S. Hawley: A FEW BUTTONS MISSING, J. B. Lippincott Company, Philadelphia 1951. pp. 191–192
307 W. H. Auden: "In an Age Like Ours, the Artist Works in a State of Siege," NEW YORK TIMES SUNDAY BOOK REVIEW, February 4, 1951. p. 3
308 Wayne Andrews, NEW YORK SUNDAY TIMES MAGAZINE
312 Henry David Thoreau: WALDEN, Penguin Books, Inc., New York 1942. (First Published in 1854)
312 Irving Rosow: "Home Ownership Motives," AMERICAN SOCIOLOGICAL REVIEW, Vol. XII, No. 6, December 1948. p. 754
314 *Ibid.* pp. 752–753
315 Irving Rosow: MODERN ARCHITECTURE AND SOCIAL CHANGE, Detroit, Michigan 1948. p. 138 (Unpublished thesis, Wayne University)
321 Aline B. Louchheim: "Blueprint of a Working Architect," NEW YORK SUNDAY TIMES MAGAZINE, September 10, 1950. p.25
322 Carl Binger, M.D.: THE DOCTOR'S JOB, W. W. Norton, New York 1945. p. 50
323 Ibid. p. 37
333 David Riesman with Ruel Denney and Nathan Glazer: THE LONELY CROWD, Yale University Press, New Haven 1950. p. 364
335 W. Lloyd Warner and Paul S. Lunt: THE SOCIAL LIFE OF A MODERN COMMUNITY, Yale University Press 1941. Table 35, p. 390
340 Irving Rosow: MODERN ARCHITECTURE AND SOCIAL CHANGE, Detroit, Michigan 1948. p. 160 (Unpublished thesis, Wayne University)
348 Henry David Thoreau: WALDEN, Penguin Books Inc., New York 1942. p. 30 (First published in 1854)
360 Aline B. Louchheim: "Blueprint of a Working Architect," NEW YORK SUNDAY TIMES MAGAZINE, September 10, 1950. p. 38
364 Irving Rosow: MODERN ARCHITECTURE AND SOCIAL CHANGE, Detroit, Michigan 1948. p. 181 (Unpublished thesis, Wayne University)
367 *Ibid.* p. 182
371 Garrett Eckbo: LANDSCAPE FOR LIVING, Duell, Sloan and Pearce, New York 1950. p. 38
374 Carl Binger, M.D.: THE DOCTOR'S JOB, W. W. Norton, New York 1945. p. 38
382 Otto Fenichel, M.D.: THE PSYCHOANALYTICAL THEORY OF NEUROSIS, W. W. Norton, New York 1945. p. 48
382 *Ibid.* p. 51
388 David Riesman with Ruel Denny and Nathan Glazer: THE LONELY CROWD, Yale University Press, New Haven 1950.
396 John Coolidge: MILLAND MANSION, Columbia University Press, New York 1942. p. 60
396 Henry-Russell Hitchcock, Jr.: THE ARCHITECTURE OF H. H. RICHARDSON AND HIS TIMES, The Museum of

Modern Art, New York 1936. pp. 4–5

400 *Ibid.* p. 6

403 Leonardo da Vinci: NOTEBOOKS, arranged by Edward MacGurdy, Reynal and Hitchcock, New York 1939. p. 1036

406 Honorable Felix Frankfurter: "History in Brick, Stone, and Mortar," JOURNAL OF THE A. I. A., February 1951. p. 69

407 José Orgeta y Gasset: THE DEHUMANIZATION OF ART AND NOTES ON A NOVEL. Princeton University Press, Princeton, New Jersey 1948. p. 42

411 Henry-Russell Hitchcock, Jr., and Philip Johnson: THE INTERNATIONAL STYLE—ARCHITECTURE SINCE 1922, W. W. Norton, New York 1932.

411 Sigfried Giedion: TIME, SPACE AND ARCHITECTURE, Harvard University Press, Cambridge, Massachusetts 1941. p.

411 Sigfried Giedion: MECHANIZATION TAKES COMMAND, Oxford University Press, New York 1948.

411 Louis Sullivan: KINDERGARTEN CHATS, George Wittenborn, Inc., New York 1947. p. 46

412 *Ibid.* pp. 47–48

412 *Ibid.* p. 48

412 Mrs. Gregor Affleck: PROGRESSIVE ARCHITECTURE, October 1946. p. 70

413 Herbert Read: THE GRASS ROOTS OF ART, George Wittenborn, Inc., New York 1947. p. 15

413 ARCHITECTURAL REVIEW, June 1947, Vol. CI, No. 606. p. 199

440 F. R. S. Yorke: THE MODERN HOUSE, The Architectural Press, London 1934.

440 Sigfried Giedion: TIME, SPACE AND ARCHITECTURE, Harvard University Press, Cambridge, Massachusetts 1941. pp. 270–271

444 Garrett Eckbo: LANDSCAPE FOR LIVING, Duell, Sloan and Pearce, New York 1950. p. 38

449 Eric Hodgins: MR. BLANDINGS BUILDS HIS DREAM HOUSE, Simon and Schuster, New York 1946.

455 Herbert Read: THE GRASS ROOTS OF ART, George Wittenborn, Inc., New York 1947. p. 11

456 THE JOURNAL OF EUGENE DELACROIX, Covici, Fried, Inc., New York 1937. p. 276

460 E. Baldwin Smith: THE DOME, A STUDY OF THE HISTORY OF IDEAS, Princeton University Press, Princeton, New Jersey 1950. p. 65

460 *Ibid.* p. 6

461 Henry David Thoreau: WALDEN, Penguin Books Inc., New York 1942. p. 205 (First published in 1854)

477 Jiro Harada: THE LESSON OF JAPANESE ARCHITECTURE, edited by C. G. Holme, The Studio Publications, Inc., New York 1936. p. 47

483 Louis Sullivan: KINDERGARTEN CHATS, George Wittenborn, Inc., New York 1947.

490 John Ruskin: THE SEVEN LAMPS OF ARCHITECTURE, George Allen-Kent, England 1889. p. 35

491 E. Baldwin Smith: THE DOME, A STUDY OF THE HISTORY OF IDEAS, Princeton University Press, Princeton, New Jersey 1950. p. 93

503 John Ruskin: THE SEVEN LAMPS OF ARCHITECTURE, George Allen-Kent, England 1889. p. 100

529 Otto Fenichel, M.D.: THE PSYCHOANALYTICAL THEORY OF NEUROSIS, W. W. Norton, New York 1945. pp. 498–499

Sources of Illustrations

3 Courtesy of the Museum of Modern Art, New York.

5 PLANNING YOUR HOME FOR BETTER LIVING, by C. W. Dunham and M. D. Thalberg; Whittlesey House, N. Y. Copyright 1945 by McGraw Hill Books Co., Inc.

15 From THE MAGAZINE OF BUILDING, October, 1951, page 164. Courtesy of Time, Inc.

22, 47, 219 From THE ART OF LIVING by Saul Steinberg, Harper & Bros., New York. Courtesy of the artist.

29, 31 Photos Fred R. Dappich.

33 From MODERN DRAWINGS, edited by Monroe Wheeler; The Museum of Modern Art, New York, 1944. Courtesy of the Museum.

34 From DESSINS, by Jean Cocteau; Librairie Stock, Paris, 1925. Courtesy of the publishers.

35 From LANGUAGE OF VISION by Gyorgy Kepes; Paul Theobald, 1944.

39 From PICASSO, FORTY YEARS OF HIS ART, edited by Alfred H. Barr, Jr., in collaboration with The Art Institute of Chicago; The Museum of Modern Art, New York, 1939. Courtesy of the Museum.

44 By permission of the Chicago Sun Times Syndicate. This strip appeared Monday, October 2, 1950.

50, 517 By permission of the Instituto Geografico de Agostini, Novara. Raccolta Reale Di Windsor.

52, 59, 84, 85, 86, 87 Courtesy of Dr. Benjamin Spock, and of Duell, Sloan and Pearce, Inc. New York.

55 Reproduced from an unpublished original drawing. Courtesy of the artist.

62 THE EVOLVING HOUSE, A HISTORY OF THE HOME, by Albert Farwell Bemis and John Burchard, 2nd; published by The Technology Press of the Massachusetts Institute of Technology.

65 From ART WITHOUT EPOCH, edited by Ludwig Goldscheider; Oxford University Press, New York, 1937. The original is in Ny-Carlsberg Glyptothek, Copenhagen.

73 Courtesy of the artist and of THE ARCHITECTURAL RECORD, November, 1950, p. 15.

74 From CARICATURES, No. 31, September 15, 1932; Arts et Metiers Graphiques, Paris.

90 Courtesy of the architect.

91 Photo Dearborn-Massar.

93 Courtesy of The British Museum, Department of Prints and Drawings, London.

95 Courtesy of the Fogg Art Museum, Harvard University.

97 Courtesy of the architect.

101 Photos© Ezra Stoller.

103 Photo Hedrich Blessing Studio.

104 The Library of Congress.

114 House for Mr. and Mrs. Robert Wilson, on the Deschutes River, Oregon. Courtesy of the architect.

115 HOUSE AND GARDEN Nov., 1946.

119 Same source as page 62.

123 The Ladies Home Journal Small House Competition, 1938.

125 MAIREA (Gullechsen House). Plan reproduced from the ARCHITECTURAL FORUM, June, 1940.

129 Courtesy of Mr. Frank Lloyd Wright.

136, 237, 277 The John Hay House, Brewster, Mass. Plan reproduced from PROGRESSIVE ARCHITECTURE, April 1949. Photos P. A. Dearborn.

139 From ACCIDENT FACTS, 1949

140 edition, National Safety Council.

151 Knudsen and Harris, ACOUSTICAL DESIGNING IN ARCHITECTURE, Copyright 1950 John Wiley and Sons. The bottom figure is after plate 3:1 of LESS NOISE, BETTER HEARING by Hale J. Sabine.

153 Courtesy of the Acoustical Materials Association, and of the Celotex Corporation.

154 From LESS NOISE, BETTER HEARING, by Hale J. Sabine, Copyright 1941–1950 by the Celotex Corporation, Chicago.

156, 175, 502, 514, 519, 521 From EDIFICES DE ROME MODERNE, John Tiranti and Co., London.

159, 191, 239 Turner House, Modesto, California. Photo Roger Sturtevant, Courtesy of the Architects.

163, 243, 373, 534 From THE LESSON OF JAPANESE ARCHITECTURE, Dr. Jiro Harada, The Studio Publications Inc., New York.

165 van Eckhardt-Preiss Associates.

167 Courtesy of Mr. Eliot Porter.

176 Cincinnati Museum, Courtesy of the artist.

177 Photo Fred R. Dappich.

186 THE ARCHITECTURAL HERITAGE OF NEWPORT, RHODE ISLAND 1640–1915, Antoinette F. Downing and Vincent J. Scully, Jr. The Harvard University Press, 1952. Plan originally appeared in ARTISTIC COUNTRY SEATS.

187 Courtesy of the architect.

191 See page 159.

195 Menefie House. Photo © Ezra Stoller. Courtesy of the architect.

196 ANATOMY FOR INTERIOR DESIGNERS. Copyright 1948, Whitney Publications, Inc. Courtesy of the publishers.

198 Photo Damora.

220 Photo © Ezra Stoller.

222 Courtesy of Duncan Kennedy.

223 Courtesy of the Edison Institute, Dearborn, Michigan.

230, 231 Photo Roger Sturtevant.

233 Courtesy: Encyclopedia Britannica Films Inc.

241 Courtesy of the artist.

245 Courtesy of the architect and of the Museum of Modern Art, New York.

246 "Morning at Nozawa Hot Springs"

257, 258 OEUVRE COMPLETE DE 1910–1929. Editions Dr. H. Girsbercer, Zurich, 1937. Courtesy of the architect.

266 SVENSKT TENN Stockholm. Drawing originally appeared in FORM. Courtesy of the architect.

269 Photo Julius Shulman. Courtesy of the architect.

271 Photo © Ezra Stoller.

274 Courtesy of the artist.

281 From THE MANSIONS OF ENGLAND IN THE OLDEN TIME. The Studio, London, 1905.

302 Courtesy of Lavare Newspaper Features.

307 Reproduced from PICASSO, FORTY YEARS OF HIS ART by Alfred H. Barr, Jr. The Museum of Modern Art, Copyright 1939. By permission.

316 From the Boston Globe. By permission of John F. Dille Company.

333 Copyright 1948, Whitney Publications, Inc.

338 Photo P. A. Dearborn.

341 Photo Werner Bischof, Courtesy of Magnum Photos Inc.

342, 343 Courtesy of Carl Koch, Architect, and Associates.

351 Photo Robert Damora.

352, 353 Courtesy of Mr. William Wilson Wurster.

387, 395, 397 Courtesy of Mr. Eliot Porter.

399 Photo courtesy of Mr. William Wilson Wurster.

408 Photo by the Author.

410 Courtesy of the architect.

414 Photo © Ezra Stoller.

416 Photo © Ezra Stoller, Courtesy of the architect.

422 The Pollock drawing is reproduced by permission of the artist. The Schlemmer drawing is reproduced by permission of the Museum of Modern Art, New York.

425 THE MAGAZINE OF BUILDING.

429 Photo Wayne Andrews.

436 Photo by the author.

439 Courtesy of Mrs. Sibyl Moholy-Nagy.

442 Courtesy of the artist.

443 Courtesy of the photographer.

448 Photo Samuel Chamberlain.

451 Courtesy of the photographer.

453 Photo George M. Cushing, Jr.

458, 459 Photos © Ezra Stoller.

463 Courtesy of Mr. Louis E. Stern. Photo Peter A. Juley and Son.

464 Coll. Whitney Museum of American Art. Courtesy of the artist.

467 Reproduced from Das Japanische Wohnhaus—Tetsuro Yoshida Verlag Ernst Wasmuth—Berlin—1935.

468 Courtesy of Mr. Osvald Siren.

470, 471 Courtesy of Mr. Le Corbusier.

473 Courtesy of the architect. Photo Julius Shulman.

478 Courtesy of the architect. Photo Hedrich-Blessing Studio.

480 Courtesy of the architect. Photo Dearborn-Massar.

482 Courtesy of the National Lumber Manufacturers Association.

485 Courtesy of the Anderson Corporation.

487, 504 MIES VAN DER ROHE by Philip Johnson. The Museum of Modern Art, New York. 1947. Courtesy of the Museum.

492 THE EARLY DOMESTIC ARCHITECTURE OF CONNECTICUT, John Frederick Kelly, Yale University Press, 1927.

494, 495, 496, 497, 498, 499 ANDREAE VESALII BRUXELLENSIS ICONES ANATOMICAE, Library of the University of Munich and the New York Academy of Medicine (History of Medicine Series, No. 3), 1934.

500, 504 From MARTHA GRAHAM by Barbara Morgan. Duell, Sloan and Pierce, 1941. Courtesy of Mrs. Morgan.

506, 507 Courtesy of the Print Room of the New York Public Library.

510, 511 THE ARCHITECTURAL FORUM.

512 Photo by the author. Mr. Rand's design is from LANGUAGE OF VISION by Gyorgy Kepes Paul Theobald, 1944.

515 Photo Roger Sturtevant.

516 BALLET by Maurice Seymour. Pellegrini and Cudahy, 1947.

517 The Freund drawings originally appeared in "Life." They are reproduced here courtesy of Nettie King Associates.

523 From ARCHITETTURA DEI POLAZZI DELL'ITALIA SETTENTRIONALE E DELLA TOSCANA. Cosce Editrice d'Arte Bestetti e Tumminelli, Milano—Roma.

526 Courtesy of the Architect. Photo © Ezra Stoller.

527 Photo courtesy of Mr. G. E. Kidder-Smith.

531 Courtesy of the Magazine of Building.

532 Courtesy of the Peabody Museum, Harvard University. Photo George M. Cushing, Jr.

Index

Aalto, Alvar p. 55, 126, 453, 533
Adam Brothers 524
Accidents 57, 91, 138–40, 144–5, 160, 162–3, 229, 250, 266, 272
Acorn stove 198
Acoustics 102, 134–5, 178, 180–3, 189, 230, 236, 266, 269, 480–1 (see also, Noise)
Activities 27, 32, 37, 46, 95, 97, 105–13, 117–18, 121–2, 124, 127, 130–3, 135, 155, 157–291, 380, 476, 487, 528
Administering 109, 111–12, 133, 184, 188
Air conditioning 146, 268
Air movement 148, 154, 190, 194, 268, 291
American Public Health Assn. 50
Architectural Review 413
Architect, the 1, 2, 4, 6, 7, 10, 12, 14, 16, 18, 19, 23–26, 27, 30, 32, 35, 43, 77, 80, 108, 130, 135, 137–8, 158, 173, 178–9, 193, 200, 210, 260, 282, 291, 293–376, 377, 379–94, 398, 400, 412–3, 416, 418, 424, 435, 437–8, 440–2, 445–7, 449, 455, 460, 462, 464, 468–9, 472, 474, 476–7, 529–31, 533–4
Architecture 1, 6, 7, 8, 11, 25, 27–33, 102, 106, 115, 130, 134, 137, 142, 160, 166, 173, 200–2, 207, 299–300, 305–11, 312, 335, 340, 349, 371, 374–5, 386–9, 396–400, 403, 405, 409–13, 418, 422, 426, 430–5, 437, 439, 444, 452–4, 456, 458, 460–1, 466, 481, 483, 486, 488, 491, 503, 507–8, 516, 518, 524–5, 527–8, 530, 532, 534
American Home 335
American Institute of Architects 294, 329, 359, 379, 435
Anderson Corporation 485
Andrews, Wayne 309
Art 1, 6, 23, 26, 30, 138, 183–4, 202, 272, 305–8, 341, 350, 392, 403–4, 407, 413, 418, 431–2, 455–6, 462, 466, 469, 475, 503, 508, 529–33
Arts and Decoration 335
Auden, W. H. 307–8
Automobiles (see Garages)
Babies (see Children)
Bachelors 7, 94
Bath rooms 12, 50–4, 67, 85, 87, 91–2, 96, 98, 106, 109–10, 112, 122–4, 127, 130–2, 141, 144, 170, 240–58, 273, 276, 289, 346, 352, 354, 420, 450, 476, 495–6 (see also Excreting)
Bath tubs 53, 58, 96, 110, 241–4, 248–51, 275
Bauhaus 411, 422
Bed rooms 81, 90, 96–9, 106, 111–2, 122–5, 127, 130, 133, 168, 170–1, 179, 183, 189, 209, 229, 233, 236, 243–4, 259–77, 346, 420, 478
Babies' 50–1; Children's 1–5, 52, 83–4, 87–8; School Children's 57–60; Teen Agers' 62–4; Grandparents' 90–1
Behavior patterns (see Living)
Bel Geddes, Norman 466
Belluschi, Pietro 90, 114, 195, 416, 526
Bennati, Gisela, house 341
Berm house 510
Berman, Eugene 33
Better Homes and Gardens 335
Binger, Dr. Carl 322–3, 374–5
Blum, Milton and Candee 259
Bodies 32, 137–45, 146–8, 149
Boston Public Library 452
Boston University 531
Botticelli, Alessandro 40
Bower, the (or Tent) 457–62, 464, 510, 520
Breuer, Marcel 386
Bulfinch, Charles 381, 404, 447
Budget (see Costs)
Buffers 116, 133–6, 150–2, 154
Building 10, 18–19, 32, 48, 295, 308–9, 319, 323, 325, 330, 356, 360–7, 410, 484, 494, 496 (see also Structure)
Builders 2, 4, 7, 8, 360–7, 388 (see also Speculative Builders)
Bungalow 5
Byron, George G. 524
Caeser, Julius 1
California Growth Study 61
Canaletto, Antonio 506
Cape Cod (see Styles)
Cavan, Ruth S. 75
Cave, the 1, 457–62, 464, 510–11, 520
Centro, L. R., house 9
Chamberlain, Samuel 448
Chapin, F. Stuart 76–7
Chartres Cathedral 505

Child care 20–1, 35, 37–40, 50–1, 52–5, 56–60, 71–2, 75, 81, 83–8, 91–2, 109–12, 118, 121, 125, 127–8, 131–3, 141, 203, 206–7, 233, 234–5, 246, 278, 311
Children 7, 20–1, 27, 35, 37–42, 43, 45–6, 77–9, 83–8, 93, 100, 102, 108, 120, 122, 124, 139, 147, 152, 158, 166–70, 178–9, 180, 183, 188, 192–3, 200, 202, 207, 229, 232, 237–8, 257–8, 259, 265, 267, 269, 271–3, 278–80, 282–4, 418, 481, 501, 511
Babies 50–1; One-to-Five 52–5, 272–3; School Age 56–60; Teen Age 61–4, 122
Christian Science Church, Berkeley, Cal. 466
Churchill, Winston 158
C. I. A. M. 411
Circulation 96, 110–11, 116, 135, 144, 155, 170–1, 173–9, 186, 195, 199, 204, 207–8, 215, 227–8, 236, 246, 260, 348, 450
Classes 2, 4, 6, 7, 8, 10–14, 18–21, 32, 35, 99, 116, 137, 140–2, 149, 162, 166, 191, 203, 238–9, 278, 284, 296, 308–9, 313, 315–17, 327, 334–5, 338–9, 348, 362, 365, 381, 384, 386, 435, 445, 472, 528
Middle 4, 6; Upper-middle 11–14, 16, 19, 21, 27, 37; Lower-middle 13, 14, 19, 21, 99; Upper 8, 17, 99; Upper-upper 8, 10, 11, 12, 18, 20, 41, 99; Lower-upper 10, 11, 18, 20; Working 4; Upper working 14; Lower working 14
Cleaning 37, 71, 87, 110–21, 167, 187, 194, 205, 208, 229–30, 238, 250, 253–5, 278–9, 282, 289, 388 (see also Housekeeping)
Clients 7, 8, 12, 16–17, 18–22, 26, 27, 30, 32, 35–6, 65, 75, 92, 108, 130, 138, 178–9, 193, 199, 200, 210, 260, 264, 291, 293–376, 400, 418, 435, 445, 457, 460, 464, 474, 480, 489, 509–10, 527–8
Climate 28, 76, 138, 146–9, 165–6, 265, 427, 434–5, 457, 466, 477–81
Closets 92, 99, 101, 117, 212, 132–3, 135, 139, 168–9, 174, 283, 291, 354
Cocteau, Jean 34
Codice Atlantico 403
Colonial (see Styles)
Comfort, 28, 146–8, 149, 155, 158, 179
Communication 49, 78–9, 81–2, 87, 92, 94, 100–3, 105, 107, 116–8, 120, 122, 124, 190, 196–7, 200, 237, 282, 311, 528
Compound, Africa 62
Conflict 89, 92–4, 127–8, 279
Congress, Act of 2, 4
Contemporary architecture (see Modernism; Styles; etc.)
Contracts 12, 319, 329–31, 356, 359
Contractors 319, 331, 360–7, 418
Construction (see Building)
Conversation (see Communication)
Cooking 35, 71–2, 82, 109, 111–12, 118, 120–1, 127, 133, 143, 183, 188, 203–32, 278, 280, 282, 287 (See also Kitchens)
Coolidge, John 394
Corridors (see Halls)
Costs 4, 12–14, 25, 27, 46, 72, 76, 84, 115, 162, 173, 187, 194, 203, 238, 308–11, 315, 318–20, 325–31, 338, 342, 354–7, 358–9, 360, 362–3, 367, 372, 449, 488–90, 522, 534
Covarrubias. Miguel 49, 240, 532
Creating 109, 111–12, 124, 132
Creativity 7, 8, 11, 14, 17, 32, 37, 42, 297, 301–2, 342, 386, 400, 431, 435, 437–40, 444, 457, 529, 533
Cruikshank, George 74
Culture 7, 13, 25, 61, 78–80, 84, 87, 94, 96, 102, 122, 131, 230, 239, 246, 248, 277, 371, 388, 407, 419, 450, 491, 528, 533
Dailey, Gardner 533
Dali, Salvador 464
Da Vinci, Leonardo 50, 403, 517
Dean, Robert 333
Decibels 152–4, 267 (see also Noise)
Decorators 334, 370
Delacroix, Eugene 456, 524
Delano, Jack 104
Della Quercia 75
De Noailles, La Comtesse 33
Design 4, 6, 18–19, 26, 30, 32–3, 36, 46, 131, 140, 145, 149, 158, 160, 192–3, 295, 298–9, 305–6, 310, 312, 319, 325, 330–1, 336, 347, 348–50, 358–9 365–6, 369, 402–3, 418, 432–5, 437–8, 465, 480, 484 (see also Architecture)

Index

De Voto, Bernard 40
Diffraction (see Buffers)
Dimensions 4 (see also Size; Scale; etc.)
Dining rooms 86, 99, 185, 203–5, 233–9 (see also Eating)
Doing nothing 109–10, 182, 190
Doors 11, 13, 96, 98, 113, 131–2, 135, 140–3, 145, 150, 154–5, 158–61, 165–7, 170–2, 173, 176, 179, 186, 194–5, 208–9, 229, 236, 257–8, 260, 265–6, 346, 450, 469, 511, 526 (see also Entering)
Dressing 52–3, 67, 83, 92, 97–8, 109–10, 112, 122–3, 132, 242–4, 246, 257, 260, 266
Drinking 40, 82, 98, 108–9, 111–12, 118, 121, 180, 188–90, 200, 204–6, 226, 233, 234–5, 236, 251, 282, 481
Dunn, Alan 73
Dunn & Farnsworth 151
Dwelling units 1–4, 7, 14
Dymaxion structures 460, 486
Eating 27, 50–1, 52–4, 57, 71–2, 81–2, 85–7, 92, 96, 98–9, 101, 109, 111–12, 121, 127, 133, 185, 200, 203–7, 228, 233–9, 280, 288, 347, 481 (see also Dining rooms)
Eckbo, Garrett 371–2, 444
Eclecticism (see Styles)
Economics 7, 12, 13, 14, 41, 76, 145, 162, 186, 338, 445 (see also Classes; Costs; Income; etc.)
Einstein, Prof. Albert 411
Eliot, T. S. 157, 524
Emerson, Ralph Waldo 400
Emotions 27–8, 42, 76, 155, 157, 176, 275, 314, 504, 508–19, 520, 522, 524, 526, 530, 532
Empiricism (see Styles)
Encyclopedia Britannica Films, Inc. 233
English (see Styles)
Entertaining 20–1, 47, 64, 67–8, 91–2, 96, 98–9, 109, 111–12, 118–22, 184, 188, 190, 234–5, 236–8, 316
Entrance (or Entering) 47, 87, 92, 99, 109, 111–12, 117–18, 130–3, 157–72, 186, 200–1, 207, 239, 280, 354, 509
Environment 3, 24–5, 32, 139, 145, 155, 158, 333, 410, 416, 426–8, 436–55, 457–8, 491, 504, 528, 534
Equipment (see Storage; etc.)
Esthetics 13, 14, 16, 18, 19, 25–6, 32, 173, 178, 277, 282, 300, 305, 348, 353, 374, 400, 403, 413, 435, 447, 449, 454, 465, 474–5, 489, 492, 498–9
Excreting 27, 50–1, 52–4, 97, 109–10, 112, 124, 131–2, 155, 240–58, 264–5, 273, 496 (see also Bathrooms; Toilets)
Expression 2, 12, 27–8, 32, 48, 324, 384, 391, 415–6, 431, 454, 501, 503–34
Fairbanks house 453
Family, the 3–4, 7, 16, 17, 20–1, 27, 32, 38, 41–2, 46, 56, 58, 60, 64, 66, 68, 75–103, 105, 107–9, 117–25, 127, 131, 166, 168–70, 188–9, 203, 207, 227, 233, 234–5, 238–9, 258, 284, 314–15, 381–2, 403, 528
Fathers 7, 43, 45–6, 54, 56, 60, 75, 78, 80, 83–8, 100, 109, 127, 170, 238, 279
Federal (see Styles)
Federal Housing Administration 6, 244, 329
Fees 14, 18–19, 325, 329, 359
Fenichel, Dr. Otto 381–2, 529–30
Festival Theatre, Newport, R. I. 466
Field, Dorothy J. 123, 127, 192, 285
Fireplaces 182–3, 192–8, 232, 277, 354, 386, 420, 511
Fisher, Dr. James T. 307
Floor plans 3, 5, 9, 15, 62, 90, 114, 115, 119, 123, 125, 126, 129, 136, 164, 186, 187, 245, 343–4, 349, 352, 402 (see also Room arrangements; Space; Plan; Zones; etc.)
Floors 12, 89, 155, 167–8, 178, 182–3, 229, 236, 243, 250, 255–6, 464–5
Flowers, E. B. 344
Form 32, 391, 415–16, 418, 431, 433, 462, 483, 494, 503–5, 527, 530, 532–3
Fox, Dorothea 59, 84–7
Frame 363, 488–9, 491–3
Frank, Josef 366
Frankfurter, Justice Felix 406
Franklin stove 198
Freund, Rudolf 517
Fuller, Buckminster 460, 486
Function 8, 27–8, 32, 98, 131, 137, 173, 187, 191, 200, 203, 279-80, 282, 321, 324, 334, 383, 391, 403–4, 411–13, 415–16, 418, 428, 431–2, 465, 481, 483, 486, 489–90, 491, 493, 504–5, 519, 528
Furniture 8, 12, 37, 42, 50–1, 58, 70, 82,

84–5, 91, 102, 130–2, 140, 145, 152, 168, 172, 173–4, 180–5, 188–92, 195–9, 202, 208, 238–9, 260, 268–70, 273, 279–80, 282–3, 285, 290, 339, 348, 352, 370
Garages 117, 127–8, 132, 135, 161–5, 170, 172, 209, 228, 290
Gardens 11–12, 13, 33, 83, 110, 113, 117, 119, 121, 128, 180, 184, 190, 197, 276, 285, 364, 371–2, 468, 475
Gauguin, Paul 532
Georgian (see Styles)
Gesell and Ilg 45, 53, 57, 60, 272–3
Giedion, Sigfried 246, 411, 418, 440
Goals 4, 8, 16, 17, 32, 299, 307, 313–14, 316, 378, 380, 382–3, 391, 461, 534
Goff, Bruce 531
Good Housekeeping Building Forum 144–5
Gothic (see Styles)
Government Sponsorship 2–4, 6, 7, 26
Graham, Martha 500, 504
Grandparents 7, 65–8, 75, 89–91, 100, 108, 114, 124–5, 130, 133, 145–233 265, 418
Greek Revival (see Styles)
Green, Henry 69
Greenough, Horatio 400
Grubert, Carl 44
Guest, Edgar 381
Guests 68, 72, 98–9, 109, 113–14, 120, 122, 124, 158–61, 166–8, 171, 179, 184, 186, 191, 227, 234–5, 238–9, 252, 279, 346, 509 (see also Entertaining)
Haddon Hall 336
Halls (and corridors) 51, 116–7, 130–1, 152, 154, 165–8, 170, 173–6, 178, 183, 203, 228, 290, 476
Hambidge, Jay 525
Harada, Dr. Jiro 163, 243, 373, 477, 534
Harris, Harwell Hamilton 15, 29, 31, 177
Haydn, Franz Joseph 524
Hayward Wakefield 140
Heating 12, 27, 133, 135, 138, 146, 149, 172, 194, 243, 294, 251, 352, 494, 498–9, 522
Hemenway, Roscoe D. 9
Hemingway, Ernest 41
Hillmer and Callister 165
Hitchcock, Henry-Russell, Jr. 396, 401, 411
Hobbies 110, 180, 185, 202, 206
Holmes, Justice Oliver Wendell 394
Home builders (see Builders)
Homes 1–2, 4, 6, 7, 381 (see also Houses)
Hooton, Earnest A. 140
Hopper, Edward 462
House Beautiful 335, 435
Housekeeping (and housework) 20–21, 35, 37–42, 43, 71, 80, 81, 92, 109, 203, 209–10, 278–91, 311, 316, 481
Houses—definition 1, 7, 510 (see also Architecture; Dwelling Units; Homes; Housing; Styles; Floor Plans; etc.)
Housewives 35–42, 48, 71, 75, 78, 80, 81–2, 83–8, 109, 210, 220, 127–8, 132, 139, 142, 158, 167–9, 179, 185, 192, 203, 208, 210, 227–8, 232, 238, 260, 278–9, 282, 284, 315, 403, 418, 526
Housing—Definition 1, 7
Private 1–4, 6–8, 14
Public 1–4, 6, 14
Husbands 38, 43–9, 81–2, 120, 132–3, 168–9, 232, 260, 315, 526
Ií, Lord, house 163
Illinois Central Station 144
Illinois Institute of Technology Library 487
Income 2–3, 7, 8, 13, 46, 71, 76, 127, 138, 203, 260, 284, 296–8, 300–1, 305, 308, 314–17, 355, 452 (see also Classes)
Ingres, J. A. D. 95
Innovation 16, 18–19, 27–8, 130, 377–85, 400, 510 (see also Modernism)
Intellect 8, 503–7, 508, 527
Interior designers (see Decorators)
Internationalism (see Styles)
Jackson, Huson 410
Japanese (see Styles)
Jeanneret, Pierre (see Le Corbusier)
Johnson, Philip 411
Jones, Richard Lloyd, house 462
Juhre, William 316
Kelly, John Frederick 482
Kennedy, Robert Woods 101, 115, 123, 125, 136, 164, 198, 236, 271, 277, 338, 350, 414, 453, 462, 466
Kepes, Gyorgy 35
Kepes, Juliet 35, 54–55
Kinsey, Dr. Alfred C. 61
Kitchens 46, 51–2, 60, 62, 70, 72, 81–2, 83, 85–8, 91–2, 96, 101, 113, 121, 125,

127–8, 131, 133, 141, 143–4, 165, 170, 179, 183, 186, 189, 203–32, 234–5, 236, 279–80, 282, 346, 352, 354, 403, 420, 450, 476
Knudsen and Harris 134, 150–1, 178, 229, 236, 255, 267
Koch, Carl 101, 115, 220, 271, 414
Lachaise, Gaston 526
Landscaping (see Gardens; Outdoor Areas)
Laundry 42, 45, 86–7, 98, 109–10, 112–13, 120–1, 123, 154, 203, 206, 240, 278, 282–3
Lavatories 12, 84–5, 96, 142, 240, 242, 244, 248, 252–7, 288
Le Corbusier, 96–7, 257, 258, 372, 411, 418, 433, 469, 470–1, 498, 525
Left-handedness 143–4, 161, 215
Lehmbruck, Wilhelm 526
Leisure 17, 38, 47, 278, 334 (see also Doing nothing)
Le Notre, André 372
Letarouilly, Paul 156, 502, 514, 519, 521
Life 341
Lighting 27, 102, 155, 160, 179–82, 184–5, 188–9, 194, 200–1, 229, 237–8, 248, 254, 256, 259–60, 265, 268, 273, 277, 499
Link, the 464, 466, 468, 472
Livability 4, 6, 25, 105–156, 232, 291, 428, 509
Living patterns 2, 7, 16, 27–8, 32, 50, 65, 71, 77, 80, 89, 99, 105–6, 130, 132, 165, 180–202, 203, 236, 238, 270, 279, 316, 333–4, 336, 383–4, (see also Activities; Room arrangements; Children; Fathers; Grandparents; Housewives; Servants; Cooking; Eating; Entering; Sleeping; etc.)
Living rooms 12, 47, 82, 83, 85, 90, 96, 99, 100, 101, 103, 119, 127, 130, 133, 144, 166, 170–1, 176, 179, 180–202, 204, 234–5, 244, 275, 279–80, 334, 346, 364, 386, 420, 458, 479
Locustrine house 119, 533
Louchheim, Aline 321, 360
Lovemaking 33, 37, 42, 61, 81, 97, 109–10, 112, 122, 124, 246, 264–6, 270,275–7
Luckman, Charles 295
Magazines 18–19, 40–1, 277, 312, 334–41, 430, 510
Maintenance 38, 43, 49, 109–10, 112, 119, 122, 124, 132, 145, 158, 162, 206, 278
Mandan Indian house 532
Mann, Thomas 80, 88
Materials 4, 12, 48, 150, 232, 250, 254, 282–3, 310–11, 342, 360, 383, 387–8, 392, 420, 435, 464–5, 483–4, 489, 496, 500
Mathes house 470–1
Maurois, André 40
Maybeck, Bernard 424, 466
McBride, Clifford 302
McCullough, Helen 211
McGuire, Carson 296
McKim, Mead & White 452
Michelangelo 156
Middle class (see Classes)
Mies van der Rohe, Ludwig 469, 478, 487, 508
Milne, A. A. 55
Modernism 10, 11, 12, 13, 14, 16–21, 77, 299–304, 306–7, 312–13, 319–21, 346, 365, 367, 377, 379–87, 389, 400, 415, 418, 425, 430, 454, 460, 501, 525, 534 (see also Styles)
Moholy-Nagy, L. 439–40
Morgan, Barbara 500, 504
Mothers 7, 36, 56, 82, 83–8
Mumford, Lewis 33, 36, 43, 61, 83, 106, 275, 299, 400
Music 40, 58, 110, 118, 180–1, 188, 198, 200, 276, 282, 456, 458, 479, 520
Nash, Joseph 281
National Bureau of Standards 138
National Safety Council 161, 165, 250, 253, 265
Nature 24, 146, 346, 445, 469, 472, 516
Needs 8, 17, 24, 27, 30, 77, 80, 83–4, 106, 137, 146
of Babies 50–1, 84–7
of Children One-to-Five 52–6, 87–8
of School children 56–60
of Housewives 35–42, 81–2
of Husbands 43–9, 81–2
of Grandparents 65–8, 89–91
of Servants 69–73, 91–2
Neighborhood 3, 158, 298, 318, 434, 441–6, 472, 480
Nelson, Paul 245
Neutra, Richard 3, 187, 269, 440, 473, 488

New Yorker, The 386
Noise 58–9, 64, 94, 97, 100, 113, 115, 117–8, 120, 122, 124, 133–4, 149–55, 178, 181, 186, 188, 200, 204, 229, 236–7, 255–6, 266–7, 280, 479–80 (see also Acoustics; Buffers)
Open plan 96, 115, 280
Ortega y Gasset, José 407
Oud, J. J. P. 424
Outdoor areas 50–1, 57, 59, 110, 112–3, 119–20, 123, 132–3, 145, 160–1, 180, 184, 189–91, 198, 207, 228, 234–5, 283, 346, 364, 418, 465–6, 468–9, 470–3, 475, 477, 479, 481, 498
Palladio, Andrea 453, 525
Parents (see Fathers; Housewives; Family)
Parking 161–5, 209, 509
Patterns of behavior (see Living patterns)
Payne, Oliver L. 308
Perspectives 353–4
Photography, architectural 337–40
Picasso, Pablo 39, 307, 524, 532
Piranesi, Giovanni B. 462
Plan 27, 60, 79–80, 82–3, 105, 280, 319, 348, 351 (see also Floor plans; Zones; Room arrangements; etc.)
Play areas and play rooms 50, 52, 57, 59, 83, 85–8, 90, 109, 111–2, 127, 133, 180, 189, 193, 279
Plumbing (see Bath rooms, etc.)
Pollock, Jackson 422
Porch 99, 113, 117, 119, 159–60, 170, 190, 228, 446–8, 520
Porter, Eliot 167, 387, 395, 397, 443, 451
Potter, W. H., house 399
Practicality 14, 22–6, 30, 48, 173, 319, 365
Praxiteles 526
Price, George 361
Privacy 28, 37, 46, 58, 60, 64, 68, 71–2, 82, 83, 88, 89, 91–2, 93, 95–9, 100–1, 105–6 109–10, 112–3, 116, 118–22, 124, 127, 131, 133, 149, 178, 185, 189, 200, 227–8, 239, 246, 248–9, 266, 269, 271, 273, 276, 280, 311, 457, 475, 481
Private housing (see Housing)
Process 333–75
Programming 130–1, 333–47, 348, 352, 358, 369, 438, 445
Protagoras of Abdera 496
Proust, Marcel 40, 67
Public housing (see Housing)
Publications (see Magazines)
Radiant panels 498–9, 500
Radiators 498–9
Radios 57–8, 60, 95, 102, 110–1, 118, 149–50, 152–4, 181, 188, 198, 270
Ramsey & Sleeper 141
Ranch house (see Styles)
Rand, Paul 512
Ranges 210–11, 215, 218–24, 232
Read, Herbert 32, 413
Recreation 60, 67–8, 76, 88–9, 91, 109, 111–12, 133, 182–5, 188, 200–2, 455
Relations (see Architects; Clients; etc.)
Remodeling 10–11, 18–19, 320, 449–50
Renaissance (see Styles)
Rental 2–4
Repton, Humphrey 372
Revivalism (see Styles)
Rezor house 469
Richardson, H. H. 372, 398, 399, 405, 452, 500
Riesman, David 333, 388
Romanesque (see Styles)
Romanticism (see Styles)
Rondenko, Lubov 516
Room arrangement 8, 23, 27, 50, 72, 79–80, 82, 83–8, 89–92, 99, 106, 111, 116, 282, 342, 354 (see also Dining room; Eating; Space arrangements; Zones; etc.)
Rosow, Irving 16–17, 76–7, 294, 312, 314–15, 340, 364, 367, 380
Rossetti, Biago 523
Rousseau, H. 462–3
Ruskin, John 32, 409, 419, 490, 491, 503
Sabine, Hale J. 153
Safety 27, 52, 68, 86, 138–40, 143–5, 166, 176, 178, 229, 259, 509–10 (see also Accidents)
St. Ann's Church, Lowell 396
Saint-Saens, Camille 40
Savoy house 469, 470–1
Scale 165, 173, 210, 280
Scamozzi, Vincenzo 525
Schindler, R. M. 341
Schlemmer, Oskar 422
School (see Children)

Schroeder, Francis de N. 141, 160, 262–3, 333
Security 13, 306, 377–85, 386, 389, 400, 457
Selectivism (see Styles)
Servants 7, 20–1, 37–8, 69–73, 75, 78, 89, 91–2, 99, 108, 120–1, 124–5, 127–8, 130–3, 162, 171, 178, 203, 210, 233, 234–5, 278–9, 403, 522
Serving 173, 233, 203–8, 210-1, 220, 224, 226–7, 233
Sex (see Lovemaking)
Sheeler, Charles 176, 464
Shelter 6, 27, 37, 106, 137, 158–9
Shiro 247
Sick care 56, 88, 91, 109–12, 121–2, 144, 233, 234–5, 252–3, 258
Signorelli, Luca 93
Siren, Osvald 468
Site 28, 30, 32, 135, 342, 348, 352, 428, 438, 441–2, 444–6, 454, 457–82, 483
Size 4, 80, 99, 140–3, 158, 161–3, 166, 174, 176, 179, 181, 191, 210–11, 224, 249, 254–5, 259–60, 262–4, 363–4, 493, 522, 524
Skeleton 491–6, 501
Sketches (preliminary) 320, 330–1, 342, 344, 348, 359, 369
Skibine, George 516
Sleeper, Catherine & Harold R. 402
Sleeping 27, 50–1, 52–3, 54, 57, 106, 109–10, 112, 124, 128, 132, 147, 154, 200, 242, 246, 259–77 (see also Bed rooms)
Smells (see Ventilation)
Smith, E. Baldwin 460, 491
Social relationships 1, 2, 4, 7, 10–14, 17, 20–1, 25, 28, 32, 39–40, 43, 57, 61, 65, 70, 76, 82, 87–8, 94, 102, 105, 109–10, 117–22, 137, 155, 298, 313, 316, 332, 345, 375, 382, 454, 524, 528, 530, 522
Social Security 71
Socio-economic status (see Classes; Income; etc.)
Solar house 478
Sound 149–55 (see also Acoustics; Buffers; Noise)
"Southside" (house) 186
Space arrangement 8, 16, 58–9, 72, 82, 83–4, 92, 96, 117–18, 121, 124, 130–3, 134–5, 155, 167–72, 174, 181–6, 188, 191, 196, 198–201, 203–5, 207–8, 211, 246, 260, 279–80, 282, 354, 357, 358, 360, 428, 461–2, 475–6, 483, 490, 522, 530, 534
Specifications 12, 319, 363, 365
Speculative builders 6, 14, 19, 310, 326
Spock, Dr. Benjamin 59, 84–7, 273
Stairs 52, 55, 141–5, 154, 160, 174, 176, 178–9, 200, 290, 476, 486, 522
Steffens, Lincoln 6
Steinberg, Saul 22, 47, 219, 241, 274, 442
Stokes house 462
Storage 57–60, 86–7, 92, 102, 111, 117, 121, 122–3, 127, 132–3, 135, 155, 163, 168–72, 180–6, 188–90, 194, 204–21, 224–9, 238, 242, 246, 251–3, 256, 260–4, 270–3, 279, 282–91, 404
Stoves (see Ranges)
Stoughton house 399
Stravinsky, Igor 524
Strong, Edward K. 67–8, 296–7
Structure 30, 32, 105–6, 131, 134–5, 154–5, 305, 324, 404–5, 431–2, 435, 477, 482–501, 503–4, 518, 524, 528, 530, 533 (see also Building; Construction; etc.)
Styles in architecture 12–13, 17, 23–4, 32, 105, 302, 314, 336, 341–2, 359, 362, 377–435, 438, 441, 444, 447, 462, 466, 494, 528
  Cape Cod 13, 454, 484, 522
  Colonial 13, 28, 159, 359, 381, 430, 440, 450, 453, 454, 491, 522
  Directivism 416, 423
  Eclecticism 14, 16–17, 102, 371, 390, 396, 400–1, 403–6, 409, 411, 425, 428, 430, 438, 452
  Empiricism 413–17, 419, 421–3, 425, 432–4, 446, 483, 488–90, 520
  English 13
  Federal 10
  Georgian 10, 381, 484
  Gothic 401, 429–30, 516, 525
  Greek revival 28, 396–7, 401, 404, 427, 430, 446–7, 466, 525
  International 28, 280, 359, 381–3, 390–2, 407, 409–11, 413–15, 417–18, 420, 422–6, 428, 430, 432–3, 438, 440, 444, 446, 450, 454, 468, 472, 478, 483, 486–8, 490, 500, 530

Japanese 163, 242–3, 247, 373, 466, 533–4
Ranch house 14, 401, 452, 454
Renaissance 404, 413, 513, 516, 518, 522
Revivalism 404–6, 414, 425, 428
Romanesque 372, 403, 452
Romanticism 394–6, 399, 404–5, 426–8, 446, 452, 501
Selectivism 426–31, 433, 438, 449, 452, 455
Victorian 280, 398, 446, 450, 452, 462, 522
(See also Modernism; Traditionalism)
Studios 128, 132, 136, 152–3, 345–7
Studying 109–110, 121, 124–5, 127, 132–3, 180, 184, 188
Sullivan, Louis 1, 32, 144, 299, 391, 399, 400, 404, 411–12, 419, 433, 483, 504, 528
Supervision 359, 360–7, 400, 460–1, 465, 501, 511–18, 521, 527, 530–1, 533
Surface 280, 464–73, 500
Sweets catalog 428, 490
Symbolism 4, 6, 12, 27, 38–9, 42, 46–8, 158–9, 174, 191–2, 193, 200, 222, 239, 283, 313, 324, 327, 380–5, 454
Taliesin 103, 458–9, 520
Tchekov, Anton 23
Techniques 4, 24, 26, 28, 30, 32, 97, 135, 305–6, 310–11, 383–4, 392, 404, 411, 415, 428, 432, 461, 478, 483, 488, 490, 491–2, 503, 520–7, 533
Teen agers 61–4, 88, 122, 133, 205
Telephones 95, 118, 152–3, 168, 178, 185, 208–9, 236, 251, 270
Television 58, 181, 188
Tent, the (see Bower)
Terraces 119, 180, 190, 236, 346, 364
Thoreau, Henry David 65, 157, 196, 305, 312, 348, 400, 461
Thurber, James 43, 298
Tisserant, Cardinal 49
Toilets 87, 92, 98–9, 110, 121, 123–4, 132, 141, 178, 186, 240, 242, 244, 255–7 (see also Bath rooms)
Traditionalism 10, 13, 14, 17, 299–300, 306, 321, 377, 379–92, 394–8, 401–9, 411, 413, 416–7, 419, 421–3, 425–6, 428, 430, 432, 438, 440, 444, 446, 454, 460, 483–4, 486–7, 525, 530, 534 (see also Styles)
Traffic 145 (see also Circulation; Zones; etc.)
Trinity Church, Boston 452
Trylon & Perisphere 518
Tubs (see Bath Tubs)
Tunisian mosque 527
Umbdenstock, Gustave 525
Unconscious, the 30 (see also Symbolism)
U. S. Public Housing Act 2–4
University of Illinois 215
University of Oregon 210
Upper class (see Classes)
Utilities 128, 133, 168, 203
Veblen, Thorstein 16, 38, 41, 46
Ventilation 118, 120, 135, 182, 188–9, 194, 218, 243, 250, 256, 268–9, 352, 478, 522
Venus 40
Victorian (see Styles)
View 173, 181–2, 197, 275, 346–7, 474–6, 478–81, 511 (see also Windows)
Vignola, Giaconio B. da 372
Viollet-le-Duc, Eugene F. 419, 533
Vogue 40
Walls 63, 149, 152, 154, 181, 199, 236, 267–8, 290–1, 520, 522
Warmth (see Heating)
Warner, W. Lloyd 8, 10–11, 13, 99, 296
Warner & Lunt 18–22, 335
Wash rooms (see Bath rooms; Lavatories)
White, Lynn, Jr. 48
White, Stanford 308
Whiting, John W. M. 78
Whitman, Walt 400
Whitney, Payne 308
Wilson, Charles, house 90
Windows 119, 135, 141–2, 146, 152, 154, 174, 179, 182, 194, 197, 182, 194, 197, 229, 236, 248–51, 254, 466–9, 346–7
Wives (see Housewives)
Working class (see Classes)
Working drawings 331, 344, 358–9, 360
Wright, Frank Lloyd 103, 128, 299, 372, 399, 412, 419, 424, 458–9, 461–2, 469, 508, 510–11, 524
Wurster, Bernardi & Emmons 159, 191, 231, 239, 352, 399, 479
Yagi house 373
Yeon, John 513, 514
Yungar Compound, Africa 62
Zones 42, 79, 84, 111, 114–29, 130–5, 178, 279, 283, 342, 348 (see also Eating; etc.